The Wetland Bird Su1 Wildfowl and Wadc_

Mark Collier, Alex Banks, Graham Austin, Trevor Girling, Richard Hearn and Andy Musgrove

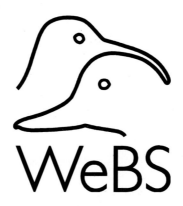

WeBS

Published by

British Trust for Ornithology, Wildfowl & Wetlands Trust, Royal Society for the Protection of Birds and Joint Nature Conservation Committee

November 2005

ISBN 1-904870-50-3
ISSN 1353–7792

This publication should be cited as:
Collier, M.P., Banks, A.N., Austin, G.E., Girling, T., Hearn, R.D. & Musgrove, A.J. 2005. *The Wetland Bird Survey 2003/04: Wildfowl and Wader Counts.* BTO/WWT/RSPB/JNCC, Thetford.

Published by: BTO/WWT/RSPB/JNCC

Cover: Little Egret by Andrew Mackay. See www.ajm-wildlife-art.co.uk for more of Andrew's art.

Photographs: Dawn Balmer, Mark Collier, Paul Collier, Al Downie, Tommy Holden and Mike Weston.

Produced by the British Trust for Ornithology.

Printed by Crowes Complete Print, 50 Hurricane Way, Norwich, NR6 6JB.

Typeset in Times New Roman and Arial fonts.

Available from: BTO, The Nunnery, Thetford, Norfolk IP24 2PU, UK, and Natural History Book Service, 2-3 Wills Road, Totnes, Devon TQ9 5XN, UK.

This report is provided free to all WeBS counters and those who participate in the other national waterbird surveys, none of whom receive financial reward for their invaluable work. Further feedback is provided to counters through the annual WeBS Newsletter. For further information please contact the WeBS Office at the BTO.

ACKNOWLEDGEMENTS

This book represents the twenty-third report of the Wetland Bird Survey and comprises information from WeBS and complementary national and local surveys, *e.g.* goose censuses. It is entirely dependent on the many thousands of dedicated volunteer ornithologists who supply the data and to whom we are extremely grateful. The Local Organisers who coordinate these counts deserve special thanks for their contribution.

We are also grateful to the following people for providing technical assistance, supplementary information and additional data, and comments on draft texts:

Helen Baker, Stella Baylis, Niall Burton, Dave Butterfield, Peter Cranswick, Olivia Crowe, Emma Davis, Simon Gillings, Martin Heubeck, Steve Holloway, Baz Hughes, Rowena Langston, Ilya Maclean, John Marchant, Heidi Mellan, Margaret Morris, Malcolm Ogilvie, Mark Rehfisch, David Stroud, Chris Waltho and Jenny Worden. Many amateur observers also provide reports of their studies; these are acknowledged within the text.

Grateful thanks to all and apologies to anyone who has inadvertently been missed.

Any maps partially based on Ordnance Survey products have been produced under the following license agreement. © Crown copyright. All rights reserved. JNCC. License Number 100017955.2005.

The WETLAND BIRD SURVEY

Organised and funded by

British Trust for Ornithology
The Nunnery, Thetford, Norfolk IP24 2PU
www.bto.org

Wildfowl & Wetlands Trust
Slimbridge, Gloucestershire GL2 7BT
www.wwt.org.uk

Royal Society for the Protection of Birds
The Lodge, Sandy, Bedfordshire SG19 2DL
www.rspb.org.uk

Joint Nature Conservation Committee
Monkstone House, City Road, Peterborough
PE1 1JY
www.jncc.org.uk

CONTACTS

WeBS National Coordinator: Andy Musgrove
WeBS Core Counts: Mark Collier
WeBS Low Tide Counts: Alex Banks
WeBS Counter Coordinator: Steve Holloway

General queries: webs@bto.org

WeBS Office
British Trust for Ornithology
The Nunnery
Thetford
Norfolk IP24 2PU
UK
Tel: 01842 750050
Fax: 01842 750030
E-mail: firstname.surname@bto.org
or webs@bto.org
www.bto.org/survey/webs

NATIONAL GOOSE CENSUSES

Organised and funded by the Wildfowl & Wetlands Trust and the Joint Nature Conservation Committee.
Contact: Richard Hearn
E-mail: Richard.Hearn@wwt.org.uk

Wildfowl & Wetlands Trust
Slimbridge
Glos GL2 7BT
UK
Tel: 01453 891185
Fax: 01453 981901

www.wwt.org.uk/research/monitoring

OTHER NATIONAL WATERBIRD SURVEYS

Details of and contacts for many of the other waterbird surveys used in this report, and of forthcoming surveys, can be obtained via the web sites of the four WeBS partner organisations.

CONTENTS

Summary

The Wetland Bird Survey and Wildfowl and Wader Counts

The Wetland Bird Survey (WeBS) is a joint scheme of the British Trust for Ornithology (BTO), the Wildfowl & Wetlands Trust (WWT), Royal Society for the Protection of Birds (RSPB) and Joint Nature Conservation Committee (JNCC) to monitor non-breeding waterbirds in the UK. The principal aims of the scheme are to identify population sizes, to determine trends in numbers and distribution, and to identify important sites for waterbirds. WeBS Core Counts are made annually at around 2,000 wetland sites of all habitats; estuaries and large still waters predominate. Monthly coordinated counts are made mostly by volunteers, principally from September to March, with fewer observations during summer months. Data from other sources, *e.g.* roost counts of grey geese, are included in this report where relevant.

This report presents total numbers counted for all species in the most recent year in Great Britain and Northern Ireland. Annual indices are provided for the more numerous species, as are monthly indices showing relative abundance during the winter.

Species accounts provide yearly maxima for all sites supporting internationally and nationally important numbers. Sites with changed status are highlighted and significant counts are discussed. Counts are placed in an international context where possible, and relevant research is summarised. Waterbird totals are provided for all sites meeting criteria for international importance and species occurring in internationally important numbers on each are identified.

WeBS Low Tide Counts are made on selected estuaries to determine the distribution of birds during low tide and to identify important feeding areas that may not be recognised during Core Counts, which are made mostly at high tide. A summary of results for these estuaries, and distribution maps for selected species, are provided.

Waterbird totals recorded by the Irish Wetland Bird Survey, a similar scheme operating in the Republic of Ireland, are also included.

The 2003/04 year

This report summarises counts during 2003/04 and previous years (since 1960 for wildfowl, 1969 for waders and the early 1980s or 1990s for other species). During 2003/04, WeBS counters covered 3,400 count sectors at around 2,000 count sites, during the crucial 'winter' period of September to March. At least 1,500 were counted in any one of these months and almost 1,200 were covered continually throughout this period. This represents a fantastic effort all around and a huge thank you must go to all those involved.

Whilst numbers of Black-throated and Great Northern Diver were similar to those in the previous year, Red-throated Diver totals were somewhat lower than of late, although very large numbers were recorded flying past the Suffolk coast. Little and Great Crested Grebe totals remained high, continuing the general trend seen since their inclusion in WeBS in 1985/86 and 1982/83 respectively. In contrast, counts of Red-necked Grebe were at their lowest ever and the Black-necked Grebe maximum was almost half that of the previous year. Numbers of Cormorant, Grey Heron and Little Egret all continued to rise; each reached their highest totals to date and although this increase was small in the two former species, Little Egret rose substantially.

There were mixed fortunes among swans with little change for Mute and Bewick's Swans, whereas Whooper Swans increased in Britain but declined in Northern Ireland. Fewer European and Greenland White-fronted Geese were recorded than during 2002/03. In contrast, counts of Pink-footed Geese remained high and totals of Greylag, Canada and Barnacle Geese did not differ greatly from the previous year. The recent decline in Dark-bellied Brent Goose numbers continued and resulted in the lowest total for over twenty years. Encouraging, however, was an indication of higher breeding success during 2003. Light-bellied Brent Geese of both the Svalbard and East Canadian High Arctic populations experienced similar increases, largely attributable to high counts at Lindisfarne and Strangford Lough respectively; the latter achieved its highest ever total during October 2003.

Totals of many duck species were similar to those recorded in recent years. Gadwall numbers continued their long-term increase and reached record levels. Teal numbers showed a distinct upturn, as did Shelduck in Northern Ireland, whilst Mallard numbers dropped slightly yet again. Pochard, Tufted Duck, Scaup and Goldeneye all remained at low levels in Northern Ireland, due largely to numbers at Loughs Neagh & Beg. However, Scaup numbers in Britain were relatively high. Eider increased in Northern Ireland. The Ruddy Duck control program led to a reduction in the index and the lowest counted total for eight years. Coot numbers declined again, being at a low ebb particularly in Northern Ireland.

Avocet numbers were up on the previous year, to a level just below the exceptionally high peak in 2001/02. This total included the highest ever site total from Breydon Water and Berney Marshes. Counts of Oystercatcher and Ringed Plover were slightly below those of the previous year, although they hardly differed from their respective five-year means. The downward trend of Grey Plover continued and counts were at their lowest level for about 15 years. More encouragingly, Golden Plover and Lapwing totals both rose although the occurrence of large numbers of these two species on non-wetland habitats that are not covered by WeBS means that trends need to be treated with caution. Knot numbers remained similar to 2002/03 and the British index for Sanderling fell to its lowest level for over half a decade. Although the British Turnstone index has been in steady decline since the high point in 1987/88, a small increase has been recorded in Northern Ireland over the past two winters. Dunlin, Bar-tailed Godwit, Curlew and Redshank counts were similar to recent winters. The increase in Black-tailed Godwit numbers that has been recorded over the past two decades continued, with 2003/04 indices reaching their highest ever levels in both Britain and Northern Ireland.

Declines were noted in most of the main gull species with Black-headed, Common, Lesser Black-backed and Herring Gull all well below average. Great Black-backed Gull numbers, however, were greater than expected, as were those for Common Tern. With the recording of gulls and terns being optional the largest influence on the counts of these groups remains the amount of coverage.

Introduction

The UK is of outstanding international importance for waterbirds. Lying on some of the major flyways for Arctic-nesting species, large numbers of waterbirds are attracted, especially during winter, by the relatively mild climate and extensive areas of wetland, notably estuaries. The UK thus has both moral and legal obligations to conserve both these waterbirds and the wetlands upon which they depend.

As a signatory to a number of international conservation conventions, and as a member of the EU, the UK is bound by international law. In particular, the 'Ramsar' Convention on Wetlands of International Importance especially as Waterfowl Habitat, the EC Birds Directive and the EU Habitats and Species Directive, between them, require the UK to identify important examples of wetland and other habitats and sites important for birds and designate them for protection. Implicit in these obligations is the need for regular monitoring to identify and monitor such sites. These instruments also lay particular significance on the need to conserve migratory populations, and consequently most of the waterbird populations in the UK.

The UK has ratified the Agreement on the Conservation of African-Eurasian Migratory Waterbirds (AEWA) of the 'Bonn' Convention on the Conservation of Migratory Species of Wild Animals. AEWA entered into force in 1999. It is a specific Agreement requiring nations to take coordinated measures to conserve migratory waterbirds given their particular vulnerability due to their migration over long distances and their dependence on networks that are decreasing in extent and becoming degraded through non-sustainable human activities. Article three of the Agreement requires, among other things, that sites and habitats for migratory waterbirds are identified, protected and managed appropriately, that parties initiate or support research into the ecology of these species, and exchange information and results. Explicit in this Agreement is that adequate monitoring programmes are set in place to fulfil these objectives and the Action Plan to the Agreement specifically requires that nations endeavour to monitor waterbird populations.

AIMS AND OBJECTIVES OF WEBS

The Wetland Bird Survey (WeBS) aims to monitor all non-breeding waterbirds in the UK to provide the principal data on which the conservation of their populations and wetland habitats is based. To this end, WeBS has three main objectives:

- to assess the size of non-breeding waterbird populations in the UK;
- to assess trends in their numbers and distribution; and
- to assess the importance of individual sites for waterbirds.

These results also form the basis for informed decision-making by conservation bodies, planners and developers and contribute to the sustainable and wise use and management of wetlands and their dependent waterbirds. The data and the WeBS report also fulfil some of the objectives of the Conventions and Directives listed above. WeBS also provides UK data to Wetlands International to assist their function to coordinate and report upon waterbird monitoring at an international scale.

Structure and organisation of WeBS

WeBS is a partnership scheme of the British Trust for Ornithology (BTO), Wildfowl & Wetlands Trust (WWT), Royal Society for the Protection of Birds (RSPB) and the Joint Nature Conservation Committee (JNCC), the last on behalf of English Nature (EN), Scottish Natural Heritage (SNH) and the Countryside Council for Wales (CCW), and the Environment and Heritage Service in Northern Ireland (EHS).

WeBS continues the traditions of two, long-running count schemes which formed the mainstay of UK waterbird monitoring since 1947 (Cranswick et al. 1997). WeBS Core Counts are made at a wide variety of wetlands throughout the UK. Synchronised counts are conducted once per month, particularly from September to March, to fulfil all three main objectives. In addition, WeBS Low Tide Counts are undertaken on selected estuaries with the aim of identifying key areas used during the low tide period, principally by feeding birds; areas not otherwise noted for their importance by Core Counts which are normally conducted at high tide.

The success and growth of these count schemes accurately reflects the enthusiasm and dedication of the several thousands of volunteer ornithologists who participate. It is largely due to their efforts that waterbird monitoring in the UK is held in such international high regard.

Aim of this report

This report presents syntheses of data collected between April 2003 and March 2004, and in previous years, in line with the WeBS objectives. Data from other national and local waterbird monitoring schemes, notably annual goose censuses, are included where WeBS data alone are insufficient to fulfil this aim, so that the report provides a single, comprehensive source of information on waterbird status and distribution in the UK. All nationally and internationally important sites for which data exist are listed.

WEATHER IN 2003/04

This summary of UK weather is drawn from the Meteorological Office web site at www.metoffice.gov.uk. Figures in brackets following the month refer to the Core Count priority date for the month in question. European weather is summarised from information provided in the journal Weather. Arctic breeding conditions for birds that winter in the UK are summarised from information collated by Soloviev & Tomkovich at the web site www.arcticbirds.ru.

United Kingdom

April (20) began warm and sunny, although by the second week colder conditions, especially at night, were widespread. This brought frosts and a band of sleet and snow, which affected southern England on the 10th. Warmer conditions returned by the third week although by the end of the month a series of low-pressure systems brought heavy thundery showers and windy conditions to western and southern areas.

The first few days of **May** (18) remained unsettled and despite a brief period of warm sunny weather frequent rain and heavy showers returned, particularly in the south and east; while sunny periods led to thunder storms

in some other areas. By the middle of the month widespread frost and heavy bands of rain moved across the southwest. Towards the end of the month these conditions were replaced by dry, warm and sunny weather, and as temperatures rose fog affected southern areas while thundery showers prevailed over the midlands and northeast.

Unsettled conditions continued into the first week of **June** (15) until broken by a warmer spell in the second week. Thundery showers broke out in the southwest and widespread heavy thunderstorms lead to flooding in the northeast. Mist and coastal fog affected the southwest and South Wales during the 19th, following which a ridge of high pressure gave led to warmer conditions, until the month ended with thundery rain.

July (20) began dry with rising temperatures; a brief cold spell on the 11th soon gave way to hotter weather. Low pressure brought rain in the second half of the month. Cooler temperatures remained throughout the rest of the month with heavy thundery showers over much of the country.

The first couple of days of **August** (17) were breezy and wet, followed by high temperatures over the midlands and southern England, whilst northern and western areas experienced thunderstorms. Low pressure brought fresher winds on the 18th giving light rain and drizzle in many places. Cooler, cloudier conditions dominated the remainder of the month with rain in the last few days.

High pressure during the first few days of **September** (14) provided higher temperatures, although rain had returned by the 5th. The middle of the month was characterised by a period of dry, hot and sunny weather. The third week saw prolonged rain in north Wales and northern England, whilst the rest of the country basked in sunshine. Rain then spread across the country on the 22nd and the month ended rather unsettled with rain and showers affecting most parts.

October (12) began with strong westerly winds bringing changeable conditions and rain to the northwest. High pressure during the middle of the month meant sunny and dry conditions for most areas, which later became cold with north easterly Arctic winds. The third week was very unsettled and cold with laying snow in parts of Scotland, the Pennines and Dartmoor, and widespread frosts on most nights. Cold conditions continued with patchy mist and fog turning into heavy thundery rain by the end of the month.

Rain continued into the first few days of **November** (16) until light south easterly winds brought dry, mild, sunny conditions. Strong winds and heavy rain returned to most areas from the 9th. Changeable conditions continued with heavy rain leading to localised flooding in the southeast and widespread overnight frosts. The end of the month remained unsettled and wet with heavy rain across most areas.

December (14) began generally dry over the whole country with overnight fog and frost, followed by rain in the north. The third week saw cold northerly winds and heavy wintry showers. Most areas of high ground in the north and west, including Wales, experienced coverings of snow, as did eastern counties. High pressure then moved south raising temperatures before damp westerly winds and heavy rain, especially in Wales and the northwest, took hold. The month ended with heavy rain in the south, while clearer skies further north led to widespread frosts. Rain spread across the country, which turned to snow over high ground.

January (25) began cold and damp until high pressure brought hill and coastal fog to some places. The second week was very unsettled with gales and thundery showers. Snow lay between 5 cm and 15 cm deep in parts of the midlands and Wales. The end of the month saw an Arctic air stream, which brought more snow to northern areas, eastern coastal counties and the southeast.

Starting with low pressure to the north, **February** (22) began very mild, wet and windy, especially in Wales and Cumbria where snow melt and heavy rain caused severe local flooding. The second week was split with a cold snap. Snow on higher ground and overnight frosts were followed by drizzle and rain with some mist and fog. Damp weather continued although colder conditions returned to southern England. The end of the month turned colder still bringing overnight frosts and snowfall to Wales, northern England, the east coast and East Anglia. Further snow fell in southern England and there were persistent snow showers and widespread frosts over Scotland, Wales and northern England.

High pressure during the first week of **March** (21) brought sunny periods and overnight frosts. This was followed by fog and occasional rain and, despite sunny periods, winds turned easterly bringing snow in the east. Temperatures then rose bringing light winds and sunny days. These conditions were short lived as northerly winds brought severe gales to many areas. Eastern areas became warm with showers becoming heavy and thundery. The end of the month was dull and overcast with patchy mist and fog, some rain gave way to drier brighter conditions and warmer temperatures.

Table 1. The percentage of stillwater count units (lakes, reservoirs and gravel pits) in the UK with any ice and with 75% or more of their surface covered by ice during WeBS counts in winter 2003/04 (England divided by a line drawn roughly between the Humber and the Mersey Estuaries).

Region	Ice	S	O	N	D	J	F	M
Northern Ireland	>0%	0	0	0	0	0	0	0
	>74%	0	0	0	0	0	0	0
Scotland	>0%	0	0	<1	5	8	14	3
	>74%	0	0	<1	3	4	7	2
N England	>0%	0	0	<1	3	4	4	0
	>74%	0	0	0	<1	2	3	0
S England	>0%	0	0	<1	3	3	2	<1
	>74%	0	0	0	<1	<1	<1	0
Wales	>0%	0	0	0	0	0	0	0
	>74%	0	0	0	0	1	1	0

Northwest Europe

Autumn temperatures were above average across most of northwest Europe, but by December had fallen more in line with averages for the time of year. An unusually mild start to February was ended by a cold spell that lasted through into March.

Arctic Breeding Conditions

June 2003 started with low air temperatures across much of the Arctic, although a warm May was experienced in the Kola Peninsula. July was generally warm although early August brought heavy rains to the Taimyr Peninsula causing some mortality to late wader broods. Lemming numbers were high in the Kola Peninsula, although abundances in Norway and the Taimyr Peninsula were lower than expected. However, low predator numbers in parts of the Taimyr Peninsula helped the breeding success of birds. Sites in Greenland also recorded average breeding successes, specifically among the waders, this was despite a high predation rate and extremely low lemming abundance.

Waterbirds in the UK

SURVEY METHODS

The main source of data for this report is the WeBS scheme, providing regular monthly counts for most waterbird species at the majority of the UK's important wetlands. In order to fulfil the WeBS objectives, however, data from a number of additional schemes are included in this report. In particular, a number of species groups necessitate different counting methodologies in order to monitor numbers adequately, notably grey geese and seaducks, and the results of other national and local schemes for these species are routinely included.

The methods for these survey types are outlined below and more detail can be found in Gilbert *et al.* (1998). It should be noted that site definition is likely to vary between these surveys (see *Interpretation of Waterbird Counts*).

WeBS Core Counts

WeBS Core Counts are made using so-called 'look-see' methodology (Bibby *et al.* 2000), whereby the observer, familiar with the species involved, surveys the whole of a predefined area. Counts are made at all wetland habitats, including lakes, lochs/loughs, ponds, reservoirs, gravel pits, rivers, freshwater marshes, canals, sections of open coast and estuaries. Numbers of all waterbird species, as defined by Wetlands International (Rose & Scott 1997), are recorded. In the UK, this includes divers, grebes, cormorants, herons, Spoonbill, swans, geese, ducks, rails, cranes, waders and Kingfisher. Counts of gulls and terns are optional.

In line with the recommendations of Vinicombe *et al.* (1993), records of all species recorded by WeBS, including escapes, have been published to contribute to the proper assessment of naturalised populations and escaped birds. Following Holmes & Stroud (1995), non-native species which have become established are termed 'naturalised'. These species are categorised according to the process by which they became established: naturalised feral (domesticated species gone wild); naturalised introduction (introduced by man); naturalised re-establishment (species re-established in an area of former occurrence); or naturalised establishment (a species which occurs, but does not breed naturally, *e.g.* potentially Barnacle Goose in southern England). With the exception of vagrants, all other non-native species have been classed as 'escapes'. The native range is given in the species account for naturalised species, escapes and vagrants.

Most waterbirds are readily visible. Secretive species, such as snipes, are generally under-recorded. No allowance is made for these habits by the observer and only birds seen or heard are recorded. The species affected by such biases are well known and the problems of interpretation are highlighted individually in the Species Accounts. Most species and many subspecies are readily identifiable during the counts. Categories may be used, *e.g.* unidentified scoter species, where it is not possible to be confident of identification, *e.g.* under poor light conditions.

Species present in relatively small numbers or dispersed widely may be counted singly. The number of birds in large flocks is generally estimated by mentally dividing the birds into groups, which may vary from five to 1,000 depending on the size of the flock, and counting the number of groups. Notebooks and tally counters may be used to aid counts.

Counts are made once per month, ideally on predetermined 'priority dates'. This enables counts across the whole country to be synchronised, thus reducing the likelihood of birds being *double count*ed or missed. Such synchronisation is imperative at large sites, which are divided into sectors, each of which can be practically counted by a single person in a reasonable amount of time. Local Organisers ensure coordination in these cases due to the high possibility of local movements affecting count totals. The priority dates are pre-selected with a view to optimising tidal conditions for counters covering coastal sites at high tide on a Sunday (see *Coverage*). The dates used for individual sites may vary due to differences in the tidal regime around the country. Coordination within a site takes priority over national synchronisation.

Counts suspected to be gross underestimates of the true number of non-secretive species present are specifically noted, *e.g.* a large flock of roosting waders only partially counted before being flushed by a predator, or a distant flock of seaduck in heavy swell. These counts may then be treated differently when calculating site totals (see *Analysis*).

Data are input by a professional data input company. Data are keyed twice by different people and discrepancies identified by computer for correction. Any particularly unusual counts are checked by the National Organisers and are confirmed with the counters if necessary.

WeBS Low Tide Counts

This survey aims to assess numbers of waterbirds present during low tide on estuaries, primarily to assess the distribution of feeding birds at that time (see the section *Low Tide Counts* for a full explanation of methods).

This survey occasionally provides higher counts for individual sites than Core Counts, for example, where birds feed on one estuary but roost on another. These data are validated before being used for site assessment against 1% thresholds.

Supplementary daytime and roost counts

Supplementary counts are made at some sites where WeBS counts are known to under-represent the true value of the site. In particular, some species occur in much larger sites when using the site as a nighttime roost, *e.g.* geese, Goosander and gulls, that are not present during WeBS daytime counts. Some sites are also counted more frequently than once monthly by some observers.

Supplementary counts are collected by counters familiar with the site for WeBS survey, thus employing the same site definition and, for daytime counts, the same counting methods, and are submitted on standardised recording forms adapted from those used for WeBS Core Counts.

Goose roost censuses

Many 'grey' geese (*Anser* spp) spend daylight hours in agricultural landscapes, and are therefore missed during counts at wetlands by WeBS. These species are usually best counted as they fly to or from their roost sites at dawn or dusk since these are generally discrete wetlands and birds often follow traditional flight lines approaching or leaving the site.

Even in half-light, birds can generally be counted with relative ease against the sky, although they may not be specifically identifiable at mixed species roosts.

In order to produce population estimates, counts are synchronised nationally for particular species (see *National totals* below), though normally only one or two such counts are made each year. The priority count dates are determined according to the state of the moon, since large numbers of geese may remain on fields during moonlit nights. Additional counts are made by some observers, particularly during times of high turnover when large numbers may occur for just a few days.

In some areas, where roost sites are poorly known or difficult to access, counts of birds in fields are made during the daytime. As with WeBS Core Counts, the accuracy of the count is noted.

Additional counts

Additional, *ad hoc*, data are also sought for important sites not otherwise covered by regular monitoring, particularly open coast sections in Scotland, whilst the results of periodic, coordinated surveys - such as the non-estuarine coastal waterfowl survey (NEWS), International Greenland Barnacle Goose Census, International Whooper & Bewick's Swan Census - are included where the data collected are compatible with the presentation formats used in this report.

The accuracy of counts of waterbirds on the sea is particularly dependent on prevailing weather conditions at the time of or directly preceding the count. Birds are often distant from land, and wind or rain can cause considerable difficulty with identifying and counting birds. Wind not only causes telescope shake, but even a moderate swell at sites without high vantage points can hamper counts considerably. The need to count other waterbirds in 'terrestrial' habitats at the site often precludes the time required for an accurate assessment of seaducks. Many sites may be best covered using aerial surveys, though this technique has been little used in the UK historically. Consequently, the best counts of most divers, grebes and seaduck at open coast and many estuarine sites are made simply when conditions allow; only rarely will such conditions occur by chance during WeBS counts. Synchronisation between different sites may be difficult or impossible to achieve, and thus coordination of most counts to date has occurred at a regional or site level, *e.g.* within the Moray Firth and within North Cardigan Bay.

The extensive use of aerial survey methods in nearshore marine waters in recent years means that data are available for a number of sites. These surveys employ a 'distance sampling' methodology (see Buckland *et al.* 2001, 2004), whereby only a proportion of birds is counted, and the missed proportion estimated by statistical means. Most reports published to date from these surveys provide only the counted number, not the estimated true total, which often has relatively wide confidence intervals. Although known undercounts, these counts are used in this report, since most are nevertheless the largest to date for many sites.

Some data are provided directly by individuals (for example, reserve wardens), often undertaking counts for site survey purposes, but whose data are not formally published in a report.

A significant point is that these additional data are taken from published sources, from surveys with the specific aim of monitoring waterbirds, and where methods have been published - or where data have been collected by known individuals, usually undertaking site-based surveys, and are provided directly for use in *Wildfowl and Wader Counts*. Casual records and data from, *e.g.* county bird reports, where the methods and/or site boundaries used are not documented, are not included. Reports and data for important sites from surveys that the authors know to have taken place in recent years are actively sought for inclusion in this report, but it is likely that other sources of suitable data are overlooked. The inclusion of additional data for some species and sites does not, thus, indicate that the tables in the Species Accounts include all such suitable data.

Irish Wetland Bird Survey

The Irish Wetland Bird Survey (I-WeBS) monitors non-breeding waterbirds in the Republic of Ireland (Crowe 2005). I-WeBS was launched in 1994 as a joint partnership between BirdWatch Ireland, National Parks and Wildlife Service of Dúchas

- The Heritage Service of the Department of Environment and Local Government (Ireland) - and WWT, with additional funding and support from the Heritage Council and WWF UK (World Wide Fund for Nature). I-WeBS is complementary to and compatible with the UK scheme. The main methodological difference from UK-WeBS is that counts are made only between September and March, inclusive.

Productivity monitoring

Changes in numbers of waterbirds counted in the UK between years are likely to result from a number of factors, including coverage and weather, particularly for European and Russian breeding species which may winter further east or west within Europe according to the severity of the winter. Genuine changes in population size will, however, result from differences in recruitment and mortality between years.

For several species of swans and geese, young of the year can be readily identified in the field and a measure of productivity can be obtained by recording the number of young birds in sampled flocks, expressed as a percentage of the total number of birds aged. Experienced fieldworkers, by observing the behaviour of and relationship between individuals in a flock, can record brood sizes as the number of young birds associating with, usually, two adults.

ANALYSIS AND PRESENTATION

In fulfilment of the WeBS objectives, results are presented in a number of different sections. An outline of the analyses undertaken for each is given here; further details can be provided upon request. A number of limitations of the data or these analytical techniques necessitate caution when interpreting the results presented in this report (see *Interpretation of Waterbird Counts*).

Count accuracy and completeness

Counts at individual sites may be hampered by poor conditions, or parts of the site may not be covered. This may result in counts missing a significant proportion of one or more species. It is important to flag such counts since using them at face value would under-represent the importance of the site and give misleading results, *e.g.* when used for trend calculations and assessment of site importance.

Counts at sites - and at individual sectors of large sites that are counted using a series of sub-divisions (known as 'complex sites') - are flagged as 'OK' or 'Low' by the counter, where 'Low' indicates that the counter feels a significant proportion of the birds present at the time of the count may have been missed, *e.g.* because all of the site or sector was not visited, or because a large flock of birds flew before counts were complete. Such assessments may be provided for individual species, or for all species present.

Similarly, at complex sites, one or more sectors may be missed in a particular month, again rendering the total count for the site incomplete to a greater or lesser degree for one or more species.

For single sector sites, counts are assessed as incomplete based on the 'OK/Low' information provided by the counter. For complex sites, an algorithm is used to assess whether missed sectors and/or 'Low' counts in some sectors constitute an incomplete count at the site level. The mean count of each sector is calculated based on 'OK' counts from a window extending a month either side of the month of the count in question, and using earlier or subsequent years, such that within this window the 15 nearest counts are used to make the assessment. The total count for the site in any one month is considered incomplete if the sectors for which the count is missing or 'Low' in that month tend to hold, on the basis of their mean values, more than 25% of the sum of all sector means. The assessment is made on a species-by-species basis, recognising the fact that species distribution is not uniform across a site that and a missed sector may be particularly important for some species but not for others.

Completeness assessments are made for all WeBS Core Counts, and for most goose roost counts (which, as single-sector sites, are made on the basis of the 'OK/Low' assessment provided by the counter).

Because the completeness calculation for complex sites is based on a moving window of counts, and the use of different parts of the site by species may change, the addition of new data each year may result in counts flagged in previous *Wildfowl and Wader Counts* as complete now being considered incomplete, and *vice versa*.

Actual counts of birds obtained during aerial survey employing 'distance sampling' methods (see *Additional counts* above) are also flagged as incomplete.

Counts are not flagged as 'Low' if a large number of the birds present is routinely missed, *e.g.* because they are cryptic, secretive, or hide in reeds - such as Snipe, Teal and Water Rail. 'Low' indicates that a significant proportion of the birds that could reasonably be expected to be counted under normal conditions was considered to have been missed. Similarly, many counts of waterbirds on the sea may be undercounts. Indeed, if the distribution of a flock stretches beyond the limits of visibility, the counter - as with birds hidden in reeds - can never know with confidence whether the count included all birds present. Counts flagged as incomplete are treated differently in trend analysis and site importance assessments.

The WeBS Year

Different waterbird species occur in the UK at different times of year. Most occur in largest numbers during winter, some are residents with numbers boosted during winter, while others occur primarily as passage migrants or even just as summer visitors.

Although WeBS counts concentrate primarily on winter months, survey is made year-round. Accordingly, different 12-month periods are used to define a year to report upon different species, in particular, to define the 'annual' maximum and to identify the peak 'annual' count for assessing site importance.

For most species, the year is defined as July to June, inclusive. Thus, for species present in largest numbers during winter, counts during autumn passage and spring passage the following calendar year are logically associated with the intervening winter. For species present as summer visitors - notably terns, Garganey and Little Ringed Plover - the calendar year is used to derive national and site maxima. The different format used for column headings (*e.g.* 03/04 or 2003) in the 'header' and tables in each species account identify whether a 'winter' or calendar year has been used.

Note that national totals (reported in Tables 3 and 4) present data for the period April 2003 to March 2004, since this corresponds to the months for which counters have traditionally been asked to submit data *en masse*. This means that data for the most recent 'winter' year are incomplete, and may lead to apparent anomalies. For example, if the peak count at a site occurred in May, this will not be apparent until the following *Wildfowl and Wader Counts*, when data for April to June 2003 have been received, and the site maxima - and site importance - will then change. In reality, this will affect very few sites or species. Deadlines for the provision of data by counters have been revised to correct this apparent anomaly from 2004/05, although the requirement to use two different 12-month periods will always mean that published data for some species will be revised in subsequent reports or a six-month lag in reporting.

National totals and annual maxima

Total numbers of waterbirds recorded by WeBS and other schemes are presented (within Tables 3 and 4 and within individual species accounts). It is very important to appreciate that these national totals are not population estimates, as WeBS does not cover 100% of the population of any species. The totals are presented separately for Great Britain (including the Isle of Man but excluding the Channel Islands) and Northern Ireland in recognition of the different legislation that applies to each. Separate totals for England, Scotland, Wales, and the Channel Islands can be obtained from the BTO upon request. The count nearest the monthly priority date or, alternatively, the count coordinated with nearby sites if there is considered to be significant interchange, is chosen for use in this report if several accurate counts are available for the same month. A count from any date is used if it is the only one available.

Totals from different count methods are mostly not combined to produce national totals because the lack of synchronisation may result in errors, *e.g.* birds counted at roost by one method may be effectively *double count*ed during the WeBS count at a different site in that month. Total counts from several national goose surveys are, however, used instead of WeBS Core Counts where the census total provides a better estimate of the total numbers, as follows:

- Pink-footed and Icelandic Greylag Geese in October and November;

- Greenland White-fronted and Greenland Barnacle Geese in November and March;
- NW Scotland Greylag Geese in August and February;
- Canadian Light-bellied Brent Geese in October

Additionally, counts of Svalbard Barnacle Geese from North Cumbria and Dumfries & Galloway are replaced by Solway-wide dedicated counts and censuses between October and March. Finally, the maximum British totals for both Bewick's and Whooper Swan do include roost counts from the Ouse Washes in place of Core Counts at this site, given the particular concentration of these species feeding around and roosting at this site. Counts from other site or regional-based surveys, for example of seaducks, are not included in national totals.

Some of the goose populations are identified according to location (from research into movements of marked birds) and the different populations cannot be separated in the field by appearance alone. In such cases, a standard region of the UK is used each year to assign individual birds to particular populations and thus to derive national totals. For full details please contact BTO but broadly, the breakdown is as follows:

- NW Scotland Greylag Goose - Inner and Outer Hebrides plus Southwest Highland.
- Icelandic Greylag Goose - all other areas of Scotland plus Northumberland and North Cumbria.
- Naturalised Greylag Goose - other areas.
- Greenland Barnacle Goose - Scottish west coast plus Shetland and Orkney.
- Svalbard Barnacle Goose - other Scottish regions plus Northumberland and North Cumbria.
- Naturalised Barnacle Goose - other areas.
- Canadian Light-bellied Brent Goose - Northern Ireland, Wales, western and northern Scotland, Cornwall, Devon and Channel Islands.
- Svalbard Light-bellied Brent Goose - other areas.

(*Note that the separate populations overlap to some extent, and some birds are thus likely to be mis-assigned using these areas. This is particularly so in the case of Greylag Goose and future surveys are planned to help rectify this issue*).

Data from counts at all sites are used, irrespective of whether they are considered complete or not. Numbers presented in this report are not rounded. National and site totals calculated as the sum of counts from several sectors or sites may imply a false sense of accuracy if different methods for recording numbers have been used, *e.g.* 1,000 birds estimated on one sector and a count of seven individuals on another is presented as 1,007. It is safe to assume that any large count includes a proportion of estimated birds. Reproducing the submitted counts in this way is, however, deemed the most appropriate means of presentation and avoids the summation of 'rounding error'.

In the accounts of some scarcer species, including many escaped or introduced species, summed site maxima - calculated by summing the highest count at each site, irrespective of the month in which it occurred - have also been quoted. For some species, particularly more numerous ones, this is likely to result in *double count*ing where birds have moved between sites.

Annual indices

Because the same sites are not necessarily covered by WeBS on every month in every year, relative changes in waterbird numbers cannot be determined simply by comparing the total number of birds counted each year (Tables 3 and 4). This issue is addressed by using indexing techniques that have been developed to track relative changes in numbers from incomplete data.

In summary, for occasions when a particular site has not been visited, an expected count for each species is calculated (imputed) based on the pattern of counts across months, years and other sites. This effectively means that a complete set of counts are available for all years and all months for a sample of sites. Only sites that have a good overall level of coverage are used (at least 50% of possible visits undertaken) and the underlying assumption is that the pattern of change in numbers across these sites (the index) is representative of the pattern of change in numbers at the country level (see *Interpretation of Waterbird Counts* below). Annual index values are expressed relative to the most recent year, which takes an arbitrary value of 100.

The 'Underhill index' was specifically developed for waterbird populations (see Underhill 1989, Prŷs-Jones *et al.* 1994, Underhill & Prŷs-Jones 1994 and Kirby *et al.* 1995 for a full explanation of this indexing process and its application for WeBS data). This report uses Generalized Additive Models (GAMs; Hastie & Tibshirani 1990) to fit both index values and a smoothed trend to the WeBS count data (see Maclean *et al.* 2005 for a full explanation of this process and its application for WeBS data) whilst retaining elements from the Underhill method that allows the assessment of whether or not counts flagged as incomplete should be treated as missing data. The generated smoothed trends are less influenced by years of abnormally high or low numbers and sampling 'noise' than are the raw index values. This makes them especially useful when assessing changes through time (*e.g.* WeBS Alerts; Maclean *et al.* 2005). Months used for indexing are assigned in a species-specific manner following established recommendations (Underhill & Prys-Jones 1994 and Kirby *et al.* 1995).

Not all species are included in the indexing process. Gulls and terns are excluded because counting of these species is optional. Species that occur substantially on habitat not well monitored by WeBS (*e.g.* Moorhen, Snipe) are excluded as are species that occur at sites sporadically and/or in small numbers (*e.g.* Bean Goose, Smew).

The periods of years for which indices are calculated have been revised slightly in the light of recent analyses. Data for wildfowl continue to be presented for the period 1966/67 to the present. Data from 1974/75 onwards have been used for waders as a high proportion of counts before this winter were imputed. For species added later to the scheme, (*i.e.* Great Crested Grebe and Coot in 1982/83, Little Grebe in 1985/86, Cormorant in 1986/87 and gulls, terns, divers, rare grebes and other species from 1993/94), data from the first two years following their inclusion have been omitted from indices, as initial take-up by counters appears not to have been complete, resulting in apparent sharp increases in numbers during this time. For similar reasons the first two years of data have been excluded from Northern Ireland indices.

Index values, where calculated, are graphed within each account. The underlying trend, where calculated, is shown using a solid line. The actual index values used to produce the graphs in this report can be obtained on request from BTO.

Monthly indices

The abundance of different waterbird species varies during the winter due to a number of factors, most notably the timing of their movements along the flyway, whilst severe weather, particularly on the continent, may also affect numbers in the UK. However, due to differences in site coverage between months, such patterns cannot be reliably detected using count totals. Consequently, an index is calculated for each month to reflect changes in relative abundance during the season.

The imputing process used to derive missing data for generating annual trends also allows monthly indices to be calculated across the same suite of sites. This reveals patterns of seasonality for the species considered. These are presented as graphs in the species accounts, giving the value for the most recent winter and the average value and range over the five preceding winters. Monthly graphs are not presented for the goose species for which annual indices are based on censuses as data for these are available for a limited number of months only.

Broad differences in the monthly values between species reflect their status in the UK. Resident species, or those with large UK breeding populations, e.g. some grebes and Mallard, are present in large numbers early in the winter. Declines through the winter result in part from mortality of first year birds, but also birds returning to remote or small breeding sites that are not covered by WeBS. The majority of UK waterbirds either occur solely as winter visitors, or have small breeding populations that are swelled by winter immigrants, with peak abundance generally occurring in mid winter.

The vast majority of the wintering populations of many wader species are found on estuaries, and, since coverage of this habitat is relatively complete and more or less constant throughout winter, meaningful comparisons of total monthly counts can be made for many species.

Site importance

Criteria for assessing the international importance of wetlands have been agreed by the Contracting Parties to the Ramsar Convention on Wetlands of International Importance (Ramsar Convention Bureau 1988). Under criterion 6, a wetland is considered internationally important if it regularly supports 1% of the individuals in a population of one species or subspecies of waterbird, whilst any site regularly supporting 20,000 or more waterbirds qualifies under criterion 5. Similar criteria have been adopted for identification of SPAs under the EC Birds Directive in the UK legislation. A wetland in Britain is considered nationally important if it regularly holds 1% or more of the estimated British numbers of one species or subspecies of waterbird, and in Northern Ireland, important in an all-Ireland context if it holds 1% or more of the all-Ireland estimate. More detailed information about SPAs and Ramsar sites in the UK can be accessed via the JNCC website at http://www.jncc.gov.uk/page-4. There are currently 246 SPAs and 144 Ramsar sites in the UK.

Population estimates are revised once every three years, in keeping with internationally agreed timetables (Rose & Stroud 1994). International estimates used in this report follow recent revisions of international populations (Wetlands International 2002) and of estimates for Great Britain (Kershaw & Cranswick 2003, Rehfisch et al. 2003). The relevant 1% thresholds are given in Appendix 1. and are also listed at the start of each individual species account. (It should be noted that the estimates and thresholds for some species or populations which should be the same at an international and national level because all birds are found in Britain, e.g. for Pink-footed Goose, differ slightly because of the rounding conventions applied. In most Species Accounts, these differences have been rationalised and only one or other of the estimates used).

For some species (e.g. Lapwing and Golden Plover) no national thresholds are available and arbitrary levels have been used to compile the table of sites, the chosen level being given in the sub-heading of the table. Passage thresholds, applied to counts of some wader species in Great Britain, are also listed.

'National threshold' is used as a generic term to imply the 1% British threshold for sites in Great Britain, and the all-Ireland threshold for sites in Northern Ireland. Similarly, the term 'national importance' implies sites in Great Britain and in Northern Ireland that meet the respective thresholds.

Tables in the Species Accounts rank the principal sites for each species according to the mean of annual maxima for the last five years (the five-year peak mean), in line with recommendations of the Ramsar Convention, and identify those meeting national and international qualifying levels (see also *Interpretation of Waterbird Counts*). For each site, the maximum count in each of the five most recent years, the month of occurrence of the peak in the most recent year, and the five-year peak mean are given. Incomplete counts are bracketed.

In accounts for most wildfowl, divers, grebes, Cormorant, herons, gulls, terns and Kingfisher, annual maxima are derived from any month in the appropriate 12-month period (see *The WeBS Year*). Average maxima for sites listed in the wader accounts that are based on a 'winter' year are calculated using data from only the winter period, November to March. Data from other sources, often involving different methods, *e.g.* goose roost censuses, are used where these provide better, *i.e.* larger, counts for individual sites. The source of all counts, if not derived from WeBS Core Counts, is indicated using a superscripted number before the count (a list of sources is given at the beginning of the accounts).

In the first instance, five-year peak means are calculated using only complete counts; incomplete counts are not used if they depress the mean count. Incomplete counts are, however, included in the calculation of the mean if they raise the value of the mean. Where all annual maxima are incomplete, the five-year peak mean is the highest of these individual counts. Averages enclosed by brackets are based solely on incomplete counts.

Sites are selected for presentation using a strict interpretation of the 1% threshold (for convenience, sites in the Channel Islands and Isle of Man are identified using 1% thresholds for Great Britain and included under the Great Britain section of the tables). For some species with very small national populations, and consequently very low 1% thresholds, an arbitrary, higher level has been chosen for the inclusion of sites. Where no thresholds are given, *e.g.* for introduced species, and where no or very few sites in the UK reach the relevant national qualifying levels, an arbitrary threshold has been chosen to select a list of sites for this report. These adopted thresholds are given in the sub-headings of the table. A blank line has been inserted in the table to separate sites that qualify as nationally important from those with five-year peak mean counts of less than 50 birds.

All sites that held numbers exceeding the relevant national threshold (or adopted qualifying level) in the most recent year, but with five-year peak means below this value, are listed separately. This serves to highlight important sites worthy of continued close attention.

For a number of wader species, where different thresholds exist for passage periods, the peak count during this period and month of occurrence are also listed. This list includes all those sites with counts above the relevant threshold, even if already listed in the main part of the table by virtue of the five-year winter peak mean attaining the national threshold.

Where the importance of a site has changed since the previous *Wildfowl and Wader Counts* as a result of the data collected since then - *i.e.* it has become nationally or internationally important but was not following the previous year, or it has changed from international to national importance or *vice versa* – this is indicated in the table to the right of the five-year peak mean. Sites with elevated status have a black triangle pointing up (▲) to the right of the average, whilst those with lowered status are indicated using a triangle pointing down (▼). Sites for which the average fell below the threshold for national importance following 2002/03 are listed at the end of the table.

It should be noted that a site may appear to have been flagged erroneously as having elevated status if the most recent count was below the relevant threshold. However, a particularly low count six years previously will have depressed the mean in the previous report. The converse may be true for sites with lowered status and thus, in exceptional circumstances, a site may be listed in the relevant sections of the table as both no longer being of national importance yet also with a peak count in the most recent year exceeding the national threshold.

WeBS Alerts

WeBS Alerts have been developed to provide a standardised method of measuring and reporting on changes in wintering waterbird numbers at different temporal and spatial scales using WeBS data. General Additive Models (GAMs) are used to fit smoothed trends to annual population indices (changes in population size calculated using these smoothed values are less susceptible to the effects of short-term fluctuations in population size or to errors when sampling than are results produced using raw data plots). Alerts are triggered for populations that have undergone major declines, and are intended to help identify where research into causes of decline may be needed and inform conservation management.

Proportional changes in the smoothed index value of a population over short- (5-year), medium- (10-year) and long- (25-year) term time frames are categorised according to their magnitude and direction. Population declines of between 25% and 50% trigger Medium Alerts and declines of greater than 50% trigger High Alerts. Increases of 33% and 100% (values chosen to be those necessary to return a population to its former size following declines of 25% and 50% respectively) are also identified, albeit that these are rarely of conservation concern.

National Alerts are generated for species (or specific populations of a species) using data from across the WeBS site network, for Great Britain and the constituent countries of the UK (Maclean *et al.* 2005). Alerts status for Great Britain and Northern Ireland are given in the header information of the species accounts. These Alerts provide some context for understanding finer scale changes in numbers. Alerts are calculated only for native species for which WeBS annual indices are calculated. Alerts are not available for some species over long time periods because there were only relatively recently included in WeBS Core Counts. Full results from the latest Alerts report are available for download from http://www.bto.org/survey/webs/webs-alerts-index.htm.

Principal sites

In addition to the assessment of sites against 1% thresholds in Species Accounts, sites are identified for their importance in terms of overall waterbird numbers in the section *Principal Sites*. The peak count at each site is calculated by summing the individual species maxima during the season, irrespective of the month in which they occurred, or whether counts were complete or not. Data from all sources used for site assessment within the species accounts are used here, including wader numbers during passage periods. Non-native introduced or escaped species (*i.e.* those not in BOURC category A) are not included in these totals.

Counts made using methodologies that employ different site definitions to those used by WeBS (*e.g.* seaducks on the Moray Firth) are not incorporated into the calculations. Such sites are, however, listed at the end of the table.

INTERPRETATION OF WATERBIRD COUNTS

Caution is always necessary in the interpretation and application of waterbird counts given the limitations of these data. This is especially true of the summary form, which, by necessity, is used in this report. A primary aim here remains the rapid feedback of key results to the many participants in the WeBS scheme. More detailed information on how to make use of the data for research or site assessment purposes can be obtained from the British Trust for Ornithology (see *Contacts*).

Whilst the manner of presentation is consistent within this report, information collated by WeBS and other surveys can be held or used in a variety of ways. Data may also be summarised and analysed differently depending on the requirements of the user. Consequently, calculations used to interpret data and their presentation may vary between this and other publications, and indeed between organisations or individual users. The terminology used by different organisations may not always highlight these differences. This particularly applies to summary data. Such variations do not detract from the value of each different method, but offer greater choice to users according to the different questions being addressed. This should always be borne in mind when using data presented here.

For ease of reference, the caveats provided below are broadly categorised according to the presentation of results for each of the key objectives of WeBS. Several points, however, are general in nature and apply to a broad range of uses of the data.

National totals

The majority of count data are collected between September and March, when most species of waterbird are present in the UK in highest numbers. Data are collected during other months and have been presented where relevant. Caution is urged, however, regarding their interpretation both due to the relative sparsity of counts from this period and the different count effort for different sites. Data are presented for the months April to March inclusive, matching the period for which data are provided *en masse* by counters.

A number of systematic biases of WeBS or other count methodology must be borne in mind when considering the data. Coverage of estuarine habitats and large, standing waters by WeBS is good or excellent. Consequently, counted totals of those species which occur wholly or primarily on these habitats during winter will approach a census. Those species dispersed widely over rivers, non-estuarine coast or small inland waters are, however, likely to be considerably under-represented, as will secretive or cryptic species, such as snipes, or those which occur on non-wetlands, *e.g.* grassland plovers. Species which occur in large numbers during passage are also likely to be under-represented, not only because of poorer coverage at this time, but due to the high turnover of birds in a short period. Further, since counts of gulls and terns are optional, national totals are likely to be considerable underestimates of the number using the WeBS network of sites. Only for a handful of species, primarily geese, can count totals be considered as a census.

One instance of possible over-estimation may occur using of summed site maxima as a guide to the total number of scarcer species. For species with mobile flocks in an area well covered by WeBS, *e.g.* Snow Goose in southeast England, it is likely that a degree of double counting will occur, particularly if birds move between sites at different times of the year.

The publication of records of vagrants in this report does not imply acceptance by the British Birds Rarities Committee (*e.g.* Rogers and the Rarities Committee 2004).

Annual indices

For most species, the long-term trends in index values can be used to assess changes in overall wintering numbers with confidence. However, the comments above concerning the differential coverage of different habitats remain important. For some species, a substantial proportion of wintering birds occur away from those sites monitored by the WeBS Core Count scheme or use these sites at certain times of day that make them unlike to be encountered by WeBS counters. Consequently, this incomplete coverage needs to be borne in mind when interpreting the indices for some species. The proportion of some of these species being monitored by the WeBS Core Count scheme can be quantified and biases understood by comparison to other surveys. For example, from the Non-estuarine Coastal Waterbird Survey (NEWS) it is known that WeBS Core Counts monitor between one quarter and one half of wintering Ringed Plover, Purple Sandpiper, Sanderling and Turnstone and that the indices and trends reported will be biased towards changes occurring on estuaries. Similarly, trends reported for seaduck and grassland plovers will be biased towards changes occurring within estuaries although in these species the proportion of overall numbers monitored by WeBS Core counts is less well understood. In the case of winter swans, although the sites on which they occur are generally well monitored by WeBS Core counts they are mainly used as roost sites by the birds and therefore changes in the birds' daily routine with weather or local feeding opportunities may have considerable influence on whether they are present during the WeBS count and thus affect the reported indices and trends.

Indices and trends for Pink-footed Goose, Greenland White-fronted Goose, Icelandic Greylag Goose and Barnacle Goose can be considered to be especially representative of national patterns. The numbers of these species are not well monitored by monthly WeBS Core Counts but rather are preferentially monitored by the annual coordinated censuses that cover the majority of British wintering birds. Indices for strictly or principally estuarine species (*e.g.* Wigeon, Knot) can also be considered especially representative as over 90% of British estuaries, including all major sites, are counted each month between September and March. Similarly, species that occur principally on larger inland waterbodies (*e.g.* Pochard, Goldeneye) are well monitored by WeBS Core Counts although the proportion of the numbers not being monitored is largely unquantified. For these species the indices and trends reported can be considered representative of the national pattern. For more widespread species (Mallard, Tufted Duck, Curlew) a large proportion of birds occur at small inland sites and habitats not well monitored by WeBS Core Counts. The selection of such sites follows no formal sampling pattern and therefore it is unclear as to whether these wetlands are a representative sample of the country as a whole.

Because short-term fluctuations provide a less rigorous indication of population changes, care should be taken in their interpretation. The underlying trend, denoted by the smoothed line in the annual index graphs, will give a better overall impression of trends for species with marked inter-annual variation, although it should be noted that unusually high or low index values in the most recent year will have a disproportionate effect on the trend at that point.

Caution should be used in interpreting figures for species that only occur in small numbers. Thus, numbers tend to fluctuate more widely for many species in Northern Ireland, largely as a result of the smaller numbers of birds involved but also, being at the western most limit of their range, due to variable use being made of Ireland by wintering waterbirds.

It should be borne in mind that the imputed values, used in place of missing and incomplete counts, are calculated anew each year, as in the completeness calculation for 'complex sites' which may cause the same count to change from complete to incomplete or *vice versa* with the addition of a new year's data. Because the index formula uses data from all years, each new year's counts will slightly alter the site, month and year factors. In turn, the assessment of missing counts may differ slightly and, as a result, the index values produced each year are likely to differ from those published in the previous *Wildfowl and Wader Counts*. Additionally, data submitted too late for inclusion are subsequently added to the dataset. The indices published here represent an improvement on previous figures as the additional year's data allow calculation of the site, month and year factors with greater confidence.

Monthly indices

As for annual indices, the reduced numbers of both sites and birds in Northern Ireland result in a greater degree of fluctuation in numbers used in the analyses of data from the province.

Site definition

To compare count data from year to year requires that the individual sites - in terms of the area surveyed - remain the same. The boundary of many wetlands are readily defined by the extent of habitat (*e.g.* for reservoirs and gravel pits), but are less obvious for other sites (*e.g.* some large estuaries) and here count boundaries have often been defined over time by a number of factors to a greater or lesser degree, including the distribution of birds at the time of the count, known movements of birds from roost to feeding areas, the extent of habitat, and even ease of access.

Sites are defined for a variety of purposes, and the precise boundary of sites describing ostensibly the same wetland may differ accordingly. For example, the boundaries used to define a large lake may differ for its definition as a wetland (based on habitat), as a waterbird count area (some birds may use adjacent non-wetland habitat), and as a statutorily designated site for nature conservation (which may be constrained by the need to follow boundaries easily demarcated in planning and legal terms). It should be recognised that the boundary of a site for counting may even differ between different waterbird surveys, particularly where different methodologies are employed, *e.g.* the Forth Estuary comprises one large site for WeBS Core Counts, a slightly different area for Low Tide Counts, and two roost sites for Pink-footed Geese.

Data from different waterbird surveys have been used for assessment of site importance in this report if collected for ostensibly the same site, and are unlikely to cause significant discrepancies in the vast majority of cases (though see *Site importance*).

Particular caution is urged, however, in noting that, owing to possible boundary differences, totals given for WeBS or other sites in this report are not necessarily the same as totals for designated statutory sites (ASSIs/SSSIs, SPAs or Ramsar Sites) having the same or similar names.

It should also be borne in mind that whilst discrete wetlands may represent obvious sites for waterbirds, there is no strict definition of a site as an ecological unit for birds. Thus, some wetlands may provide all needs - feeding, loafing and roosting areas - for some species, but a 'site' for other species may comprise a variety of disparate areas, not all of which are counted for WeBS. Similarly, for some habitats, particularly linear areas such as rivers and rocky coasts, and marine areas, the definition of a site as used by waterbirds is not readily discerned without extensive survey or research that is usually beyond the scope of WeBS or other similar surveys. The definitions of such sites may thus evolve, and therefore change between *Wildfowl and Wader Counts*. Further, the number of birds recorded by WeBS at particular sites should not be taken to indicate the total number of birds in that local area.

In some cases, for example where feeding geese are recorded by daytime WeBS Core Counts over large sites, and again at discrete roosts within or adjacent to that same site, data are presented for both sites in the table of key sites given the very different nature or extent of the sites and often number of birds, even though the same birds will be counted at both. A similar approach is adopted for some seaducks; Common Scoter counts are provided for Liverpool Bay as a whole from aerial survey, and also from Core Counts for discrete WeBS sites that overlap part of the larger aerial site; and Eider counts from the wider Firth of Clyde area have been presented in addition to the numbers in the areas more generally recognised by WeBS. In these two cases, the 'supersite' is listed in upper case.

Site importance
Sites are selected for presentation in this report using a strict interpretation of the 1% threshold. It should be noted, however that where 1% of the national population is less than 50 birds, 50 is normally used as a

minimum qualifying threshold for the designation of sites of national importance. It should also be noted that the 'qualifying levels' used for introduced species are used purely as a guide for presentation of sites in this report and do not infer any conservation importance for the species or the sites concerned since protected sites would not be identified for these non-native birds.

It is necessary to bear in mind the distinction between sites that regularly hold wintering populations of national or international importance and those which may happen to exceed the appropriate qualifying levels only in occasional winters. This follows the Ramsar Convention, which states that key sites must be identified on the basis of demonstrated regular use (calculated as the mean winter maxima from the last five seasons for most species in this report), otherwise a large number of sites might qualify as a consequence of irregular visitation by one-off large numbers of waterbirds. However, the Convention also indicates that provisional assessments may be made on the basis of a minimum of three years' data. These rules of thumb are applied to SPAs and national assessments also. Sites with just one or two years' data are also included in the tables if the mean exceeds the relevant threshold for completeness but this does not, as such, imply qualification. This caveat applies also to sites that are counted in more than two years but, because one or more of the peak counts are incomplete, whose means surpass the 1% threshold based on counts from only one or two years.

Nevertheless, sites which irregularly support nationally or internationally important numbers may be extremely important at certain times, *e.g.* when the UK population is high, during the main migratory periods, or during cold weather, when they may act as refuges for birds away from traditionally used sites. For this reason also, the ranking of sites according to the total numbers of birds they support (particularly in *Principal Sites*) should not be taken as a rank order of the conservation importance of these sites, since certain sites, perhaps low down in terms of their total 'average' numbers, may nevertheless be of critical importance to certain species or populations at particular times.

Peak counts derived from a number of visits

to a particular site in a given season will reflect more accurately the relative importance of the site for the species than do single visits. It is important to bear this in mind since, despite considerable improvements in coverage, data for a few sites presented in this report derive from single counts in some years. Similarly, in assessing the importance of a site, peak counts from several winters should ideally be used, as the peak count made in any one year may be unreliable due to gaps in coverage and disturbance- or weather-induced effects. The short-term movement of birds between closely adjacent sites may lead to altered assessments of a site's apparent importance for a particular species. More frequent counts than the once-monthly WeBS visits are necessary to assess more accurately the rapid turnover of waterbird populations that occurs during migration or cold weather movements.

It should also be borne in mind that because a count is considered complete for WeBS, it does not imply that it fully represents the importance of the site. A site of importance for a wintering species may have been counted only in autumn or spring, and thus while a valid complete count is available for that year, it under-represents the importance of the site for that species. This problem is overcome to some extent by the selection of counts from a limited winter window for wader species, although this will also tend to underestimation of the mean if it excludes large counts at other times of year. A similar issue arises for counts derived from different survey methods. For example, many sites important as gull roosts are identified on the basis of evening roost counts. Valid and complete counts may have been made by WeBS Core Counts during daytime over the course of a particular winter but, if no roost counts were made, the mean will be depressed by the much lower Core Count in that year. Thus, when counts appear to fluctuate greatly between years at individual sites on the basis of data from different sources - particularly for geese and gulls in the absence of roost counts, and for seaducks in the absence of dedicated survey - the five-year means and apparent trends over time should be viewed with caution.

Caution is also urged regarding the use of Low Tide Count data in site assessment. Whilst this survey serves to highlight the importance of some estuaries for feeding birds

that, because they roost on other sites, are missed by Core Counts, the objectives of Low Tide Counts do not require strict synchronisation across the site and this may result in double counting of birds on some occasions. It should also be noted that count completeness assessments are not made for Low Tide Count totals at complex sites, and any undercounts from this scheme are not flagged in the tables, leading to under-estimation of the site's importance.

This list of potential sources of error in counting wetland birds, though not exhaustive, suggests that the net effect tends towards under- rather than over-estimation of numbers and provides justification for the use of maximum counts for the assessment of site importance or the size of a population. Factors causing under-estimation are normally constant at a given site in a given month, so that while under-estimates may occur, comparisons between sites and years remain valid.

It should be recognised that, in presenting sites supporting nationally or internationally important numbers of birds, this report provides just one means of identifying important sites and does not provide a definitive statement on the conservation value of individual sites for waterbirds, let alone other conservation interests. The national thresholds have been chosen to provide a reasonable amount of information in the context of this report only. Thus, for example, many sites of regional importance or those of importance because of the assemblage of species present are not included here. European Directives and conservation Conventions stress the need for a holistic approach to effect successful conservation, and lay great importance on maintaining the distribution and range of species, in addition to the conservation of networks of individual key sites.

For the above reasons of poor coverage, geographically or temporally, outlined above, it should be recognised that lists of sites supporting internationally and nationally important numbers of birds are limited by the availability of WeBS and other survey data. Whilst the counter network is likely to cover the vast majority of important sites, others may be missed and therefore will not be listed in the tables due to lack of appropriate data.

Some counts in this report differ from those presented previously. This results from the submission of late data and corrections, and in some cases, the use of different count seasons or changes to site structures. Additionally, some sites may have been omitted from tables previously due to oversight. It is likely that small changes will continue as definitions of sites are revised, in the light of new information from counters. Most changes are minor, but comment is made in the text where they are significant.

Note that sites listed under 'Sites no longer meeting table qualifying levels' represent those that would have been noted of national importance based on the preceding five-years (*i.e.* 1998/99 to 2002/03) but which, following the 2003/04 counts, no longer met the relevant threshold. It is not an exhaustive list of sites, which at any time in the past have been of national or all-Ireland importance.

COVERAGE

WeBS Core Counts
Coordinated, synchronous counts are advocated to prevent double counting or birds being missed. Consequently, priority dates are recommended nationally. Due to differences in tidal regimes around the country, counts at a few estuaries were made on other dates to match the most suitable conditions. Weather and counter availability also result in some counts being made on alternative dates.

Table 2. WeBS Core Count priority dates in 2003/04

20 April	12 October
18 May	16 November
15 June	14 December
20 July	25 January
17 August	22 February
14 September	21 March

Standard Core Counts were received from 2,015 sites of all habitats for the period April 2003 to March 2004, comprising 3,451 count units (the sub-divisions of large sites for which separate counts are provided).

WeBS and I-WeBS coverage in 2003/04 is shown by in Figure 1. Note that the map differs slightly to those in previous reports in that all count units are now plotted individually, rather than being grouped by 10 km squares. The location of each count unit is shown using only its central grid reference. The region and grid reference of all sites mentioned by name in this report are given in Table A2. in Appendix 2. Principal core sites are shown in Figure A1. in Appendix 2.

As ever, areas with few wetlands (*e.g.* inland Essex/Suffolk) or small human populations (*e.g.* much of Scotland) are apparent on the map as areas with little coverage. Northwest Scotland was typically poorly covered, although new surveys by the RAF Ornithological Society in 2004/05 will be reported upon next year. Northern Ireland remains relatively uncovered aware from the major sites and further volunteers from here, or indeed anywhere in the UK, are always welcome.

Goose censuses
In 2003/04, supplementary counts of Bean Geese were submitted by the Bean Goose Action Group (Slamannan Plateau) (Simpson & Maciver, 2004) and the RSPB (Middle Yare Marshes). National surveys of Pink-footed and Icelandic Greylag Geese were undertaken at roosts in October and November 2003 (Rowell & Hearn 2005). A census of the native Scottish Greylag Goose population on the Uists was made in August 2003 (R MacDonald *in litt.*). Censuses of Greenland White-fronted Geese were carried out in autumn 2003 and spring 2004 by Greenland White-fronted Study (Fox & Francis 2004). Greenland Barnacle Geese were counted regularly by SNH and others on Islay and other key locations (SNH data) whilst the Svalbard Barnacle Geese on the Solway were counted regularly by WWT staff and volunteers (Griffin & Mackley, 2004). Data were also provided by the All-Ireland Light-bellied Brent Goose census (K. Colhoun).

Seaduck surveys
Coastal counts of seaduck, divers and grebes were received from several sites. Aerial and/or shore-based counts from Orkney, the Hebrides, Aberdeen coast, Tay Estuary, St Andrews Bay were provided by JNCC (Dean *et al.* 2004). Continuing surveys of the Moray Firth were carried out between November 2003 and January 2004 (RSPB Scotland/Talisman Energy (UK) Ltd). Monthly aerial and/or land-based counts of Common Scoter in Carmarthen Bay were carried out between

November 2003 and March 2004 (Banks *et al.* 2005). Continuing counts of key sites around Shetland were provided by SOTEAG (Heubeck and Mellor 2005). Continuing survey of the Eiders of the wider Firth of Clyde area was carried out in September 2003 (Waltho 2004).

Figure 1. Position of all locations counted for standard WeBS and I-WeBS counts between April 2003 and March 2004.

TOTAL NUMBERS

The total numbers of waterbirds recorded by WeBS in 2003/04 are given in Tables 3 and 4 for Great Britain (including the Isle of Man, but excluding the Channel Islands) and Northern Ireland, respectively. Counts of waterbirds in the Republic of Ireland by I-WeBS are provided in Table 5.

Site coverage for gulls and terns is given separately since recording of these species was optional.

Introduced and escaped waterbirds

Many species of waterbird occur in the UK as a result of introductions, particularly through escapes from collections. Several have become established, such as Canada Goose and Ruddy Duck. The British Ornithologists' Union Records Committee recently established a category 'E' for 'species that have been recorded as introductions, transportees or escapes from captivity, and whose breeding populations (if any) are not thought to be self-sustaining' (BOURC 1999). WeBS records of these species are included in this report both for the sake of completeness and in order to assess their status and monitor any changes in numbers, a key requirement given the need, under the African-Eurasian Waterbird Agreement of the Bonn convention '. . . to prevent the unintentional release of such species . . .' and once introduced, the need '. . . to prevent these species from becoming a threat to indigenous species' (Holmes *et al.* 1998).

Numbers of established populations (*e.g.* Canada Goose and Ruddy Duck, which are placed in category 'C') are excluded from Figure 2 below since the large numbers involved would swamp numbers of other species. Additionally, species that occur in both categories A and E (*e.g.* Pink-footed Goose) are also excluded since separation of escaped from wild birds is not readily possible using WeBS methods. A total of 27 species were recorded in 2003/04 at 181 sites, both somewhat lower than the previous year. The summed site maxima of 452 birds was the lowest for several years. Over half the total was attributable to Black Swan, Bar-headed Goose and Muscovy Duck. Although this figure will undoubtedly include some duplication of individual birds recorded at more than one site and occasional records of pinioned birds, this figure probably provides a truer reflection of the numbers of introduced or escaped waterbirds frequenting WeBS sites than the peak monthly total of 160 birds in September 2003.

Figure 2. Number of species (white bars), number of sites at which birds were recorded (grey bars) and summed site maxima (black bars) for waterbirds in the BOURC's category E.

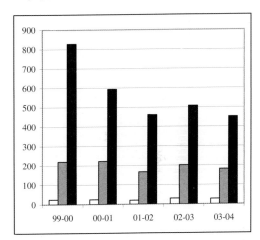

Table 3. Total numbers of waterbirds recorded by WeBS Core Counts in Great Britain in 2003/04

	Species	Apr	May	Jun	Jul	Aug
	Number of sites visited	*866*	*747*	*757*	*786*	*850*
RH	Red-throated Diver	194	40	23	37	45
BV	Black-throated Diver	21	10	4	2	3
ND	Great Northern Diver	104	16	5	3	2
UL	Unidentified diver	0	0	0	0	0
LG	Little Grebe	1124	802	807	1287	2929
GG	Great Crested Grebe	3449	2707	2979	4623	6397
RX	Red-necked Grebe	9	5	12	4	16
SZ	Slavonian Grebe	20	1	1	0	7
BN	Black-necked Grebe	28	19	22	36	28
CA	Cormorant	6286	5647	4831	7741	11344
SA	Shag	246	85	73	219	1125
XU	Unidentified Cormorant/Shag	0	0	0	3	15
BI	Bittern	12	7	3	2	3
ET	Little Egret	511	337	420	831	1586
HW	Great White Egret	0	0	0	0	1
H.	Grey Heron	1876	1583	2291	2160	2926
UR	Purple Heron	0	0	0	0	1
OR	White Stork	0	0	0	1	0
IB	Glossy Ibis	0	1	0	1	1
IS	Sacred Ibis	1	1	1	1	1
NB	Spoonbill	6	10	4	1	3
FL	Greater Flamingo	0	0	0	0	0
YV	Fulvous Whistling Duck	1	1	1	0	0
YU	Lesser Whistling Duck	1	0	0	0	0
MS	Mute Swan	7596	7777	9490	10680	12380
AS	Black Swan	13	14	16	22	23
BS	Bewick's Swan	0	1	0	0	0
WZ	Whistling Swan	1	2	1	1	1
WS	Whooper Swan	63	24	21	28	25
HN	Chinese Goose	9	7	5	5	2
BE	Bean Goose	0	0	0	0	0
XR	Tundra Bean Goose	0	0	0	0	0
PG	Pink-footed Goose	22488	72	33	11	15
WG	White-fronted Goose	1	0	0	0	0
EW	European White-fronted Goose	1	0	0	0	1
NW	Greenland White-fronted Goose	0	0	0	1	0
LC	Lesser White-fronted Goose	0	0	1	1	2
JI	Icelandic Greylag Goose	1095	831	2634	2900	2682
JH	NW Scotland Greylag Goose	334	193	366	774	5322
JE	Re-established Greylag Goose	5148	4907	10109	11894	15801
HD	Bar-headed Goose	7	7	4	4	18
SJ	Snow Goose	4	6	10	11	7
RJ	Ross's Goose	0	0	0	3	0
EM	Emperor Goose	5	10	0	1	15
CG	Canada Goose	12648	11696	27090	30059	39158
ZE	Canada Goose x Bar-headed Goose	0	0	0	0	0
ZI	Canada Goose x domesticated Greylag	0	0	0	0	0
NE	Hawaiian Goose	0	0	0	0	0
YE	Naturalised Barnacle Goose	318	211	166	356	392
YN	Nearctic Barnacle Goose	31	17	18	17	16
YS	Svalbard Barnacle Goose	9137	713	91	130	151
BG	Brent Goose	0	0	0	0	0
DB	Dark-bellied Brent Goose	13848	5902	24	38	30
QN	Nearctic Light-bellied Brent Goose	8	2	0	0	0
QS	Svalbard Light-bellied Brent Goose	5	0	0	2	1
BB	Black Brant	0	0	0	0	0
EB	Red-breasted Goose	4	1	5	2	3
ZL	Feral/hybrid Goose	318	286	294	299	302
UO	Unidentified goose	0	0	0	0	0
ZM	Hybrid goose	1	2	4	4	5

Table 3. continued

	Sep	Oct	Nov	Dec	Jan	Feb	Mar
sites	1445	1604	1640	1635	1727	1714	1640
RH	137	456	281	375	403	276	224
BV	7	57	45	38	37	42	66
ND	13	51	75	52	111	82	82
UL	0	0	0	0	2	0	0
LG	4879	5162	4333	3831	3846	3208	2430
GG	9268	9569	9131	9151	8894	7006	6626
RX	6	5	11	15	8	16	15
SZ	33	145	216	180	227	121	78
BN	35	35	40	39	34	29	33
CA	16921	18792	17909	16365	15498	13798	10793
SA	1045	2903	1235	2048	1068	563	749
XU	0	1	12	5	3	8	0
BI	2	7	12	19	36	21	9
ET	2777	2264	1502	1144	1204	1089	858
HW	1	1	1	0	0	0	0
H.	4496	4459	3613	3549	3666	3427	2575
UR	0	0	0	0	0	0	0
OR	1	1	1	2	0	1	3
IB	0	0	0	0	1	1	1
IS	1	1	1	1	1	1	1
NB	7	3	2	5	4	5	3
FL	0	0	0	0	1	0	1
YV	1	0	0	0	0	2	0
YU	0	0	0	0	0	0	0
MS	18356	20299	20068	20226	18820	17132	15266
AS	42	48	49	28	37	28	20
BS	9	29	3802	4732	6691	5646	516
WZ	1	1	0	0	0	0	0
WS	48	2676	6992	6510	7558	6411	5215
HN	9	11	9	8	11	8	8
BE	1	0	8	4	149	48	0
XR	0	0	1	0	0	0	0
PG	4079	254993	274594	80600	113198	47355	55663
WG	0	0	2	11	4	0	1
EW	1	11	44	655	2208	1581	222
NW	3	416	719	17449	391	595	16387
LC	1	2	1	0	0	0	0
JI	4131	37429	78070	16370	24341	23561	17991
JH	1141	326	641	528	1032	374	225
JE	24727	24564	27382	24342	22441	14207	10605
HD	44	8	8	12	4	7	10
SJ	15	49	20	22	34	23	29
RJ	3	3	0	3	2	0	0
EM	22	23	16	23	22	8	13
CG	51882	51825	49825	49171	48065	41287	28834
ZE	0	1	1	1	1	1	1
ZI	4	0	0	3	3	0	0
NE	0	0	1	0	1	0	0
YE	625	910	724	1011	641	433	368
YN	11	365	37272	384	232	114	45296
YS	278	20062	25418	25121	28318	18572	16625
BG	1	3	4	10	7	6	8
DB	556	11699	43988	55472	64366	62367	25719
QN	0	21	59	137	198	371	252
QS	487	2723	1218	3745	895	263	168
BB	0	0	0	1	1	0	0
EB	4	5	5	2	4	2	5
ZL	471	513	543	515	475	490	446
UO	1	1	12	12	6	2	1
ZM	4	3	1	4	4	6	1

Table 3. continued

	Species	Apr	May	Jun	Jul	Aug
EG	Egyptian Goose	114	117	281	313	298
QF	Upland Goose	1	0	1	0	1
UB	Paradise Shelduck	0	0	0	1	1
UE	Cape Shelduck	2	4	0	1	0
UD	Ruddy Shelduck	5	2	2	11	9
SU	Shelduck	23296	14869	19199	33259	20952
MY	Muscovy Duck	15	19	16	19	11
DC	Wood Duck	2	6	3	0	9
MN	Mandarin	124	65	94	182	200
WN	Wigeon	4490	224	199	330	987
AW	American Wigeon	1	0	0	0	0
HL	Chiloe Wigeon	0	0	0	1	0
GA	Gadwall	2898	1751	2713	2666	6498
QC	Cape Teal	0	0	0	0	0
T.	Teal	11710	560	876	1426	11018
TA	Green-winged Teal	1	0	1	0	0
KQ	Speckled Teal	0	2	0	0	0
MA	Mallard	28548	24370	37548	50499	75684
ZF	Feral/hybrid mallard type	209	200	234	359	181
ZB	Mallard x Pintail	0	0	0	0	0
QB	Chestnut Teal	0	0	0	0	0
PT	Pintail	271	36	12	12	35
PN	Bahama Pintail	0	1	0	0	0
YR	Red-billed Teal	0	0	0	0	0
GY	Garganey	25	15	21	4	19
TB	Blue-winged Teal	0	0	0	0	1
QA	Cinnamon Teal	0	0	0	0	0
SV	Shoveler	2848	450	421	459	2356
ZR	Hybrid Anas	1	0	0	0	1
IE	Ringed Teal	0	0	1	1	0
RQ	Red-crested Pochard	10	2	8	6	12
PO	Pochard	1267	710	873	2860	10613
NG	Ring-necked Duck	1	0	1	1	4
NZ	New Zealand Scaup	1	0	0	0	0
FD	Ferruginous Duck	1	0	0	0	4
TU	Tufted Duck	17239	7263	8398	22305	37668
SP	Scaup	388	11	6	13	30
AY	Lesser Scaup	0	0	0	0	0
ZD	Aythya hybrid	2	1	0	0	0
E.	Eider	15920	12484	13248	17140	20503
KE	King Eider	0	0	0	0	0
LN	Long-tailed Duck	358	6	0	0	0
CX	Common Scoter	3175	1827	327	1525	503
FS	Surf Scoter	2	0	0	0	0
VS	Velvet Scoter	427	257	18	19	104
GN	Goldeneye	1498	45	85	68	67
SY	Smew	6	0	1	0	0
RM	Red-breasted Merganser	1468	503	644	808	1210
GD	Goosander	274	300	243	396	975
RY	Ruddy Duck	1316	584	479	662	1502
OI	Argentine Bluebill	0	0	0	1	1
WQ	White-headed Duck	0	0	0	0	0
UM	Unidentified duck	0	0	0	0	50
WA	Water Rail	135	53	46	55	71
AK	Spotted Crake	0	0	0	0	0
CE	Corncrake	0	0	0	0	1
MH	Moorhen	5400	3516	3059	4389	7326
CO	Coot	19013	14165	17935	38271	61118
AO	American Coot	0	0	0	0	0
KF	Kingfisher	98	66	108	146	215
	TOTAL WILDFOWL	**229532**	**128437**	**168960**	**252403**	**358843**

Table 3. continued

	Sep	Oct	Nov	Dec	Jan	Feb	Mar
EG	211	232	122	137	132	109	130
QF	1	1	1	1	1	0	1
UB	1	1	1	1	1	1	1
UE	1	1	0	0	1	0	0
UD	6	2	5	8	2	6	2
SU	41381	52660	41278	50653	56339	50398	40441
MY	17	32	34	28	48	32	42
DC	5	2	1	0	2	5	6
MN	302	475	525	551	504	280	212
WN	42685	174221	276468	371948	447675	289281	135228
AW	1	1	0	4	5	3	0
HL	1	0	0	1	0	0	0
GA	10529	12422	14325	16527	15680	12710	6676
QC	0	0	0	0	0	0	1
T.	60760	121932	125155	156821	174438	95876	43658
TA	0	1	3	6	2	3	2
KQ	0	0	0	0	0	0	0
MA	119752	140510	136812	142045	131499	94156	57055
ZF	441	782	695	964	666	485	581
ZB	0	0	0	0	0	0	1
QB	2	0	0	0	1	0	0
PT	4487	11167	21189	22651	27418	20614	2854
PN	0	0	0	0	10	1	1
YR	0	0	0	0	2	0	0
GY	42	21	1	0	0	0	12
TB	0	0	0	0	0	0	0
QA	0	0	0	0	1	0	0
SV	7878	9202	9390	9621	9730	9761	7755
ZR	2	2	2	1	0	0	0
IE	3	1	0	1	0	1	1
RQ	48	150	143	164	100	115	90
PO	9441	13479	22646	29017	30675	24173	7084
NG	5	1	3	1	2	2	1
NZ	0	1	0	1	0	0	0
FD	2	1	1	2	2	2	2
TU	50135	47946	57149	56883	53801	46590	38030
SP	263	2224	1840	4714	2780	2871	971
AY	0	0	0	0	0	1	1
ZD	0	0	0	1	1	2	2
E.	23390	19726	17932	16589	15084	13189	13809
KE	0	0	0	1	0	0	0
LN	1	290	474	3015	1903	2703	701
CX	1280	7764	3895	7638	8198	11425	2232
FS	0	1	0	4	1	4	2
VS	557	768	688	566	1322	2332	898
GN	175	1306	6796	10878	13087	12968	9187
SY	1	2	24	199	258	185	30
RM	1458	2196	2661	2890	3458	2857	2972
GD	656	861	1928	2840	3216	2535	1330
RY	2358	3144	3359	3262	3580	2818	2237
OI	0	0	0	0	0	0	0
WQ	1	2	0	0	0	0	0
UM	2	2	76	2	2	2	2
WA	172	254	420	383	396	274	278
AK	0	1	0	0	0	0	0
CE	0	0	0	0	0	0	0
MH	13038	14728	14435	13037	13277	12231	10341
CO	90126	99419	106969	98823	88924	64991	45702
AO	0	0	0	0	1	1	0
KF	482	480	413	345	272	206	190
	628686	**1211345**	**1420919**	**1338845**	**1466529**	**1041108**	**631730**

Table 3. continued

	Species	Apr	May	Jun	Jul	Aug
	Number of sites visited	*826*	*736*	*754*	*784*	*850*
OC	Oystercatcher	50798	37849	27513	57124	153085
IT	Black-winged Stilt	1	0	1	1	1
AV	Avocet	1751	1078	1344	1733	2057
TN	Stone-curlew	0	0	1	0	0
LP	Little Ringed Plover	295	215	193	188	67
RP	Ringed Plover	3555	11852	1493	2070	15513
DO	Dotterel	1	15	0	0	0
ID	American Golden Plover	0	0	0	0	0
GP	Golden Plover	4535	97	61	8517	18349
GV	Grey Plover	33347	24400	3873	5378	23967
L.	Lapwing	6587	3938	10859	35729	48385
KN	Knot	97851	11863	11531	15212	102787
SS	Sanderling	13469	17262	1007	3150	14763
LX	Little Stint	5	6	4	4	13
BP	Baird's Sandpiper	0	0	0	0	0
PP	Pectoral Sandpiper	0	0	0	2	1
CV	Curlew Sandpiper	1	8	4	24	41
PS	Purple Sandpiper	571	66	0	3	15
DN	Dunlin	88492	57776	5087	63489	104019
OA	Broad-billed Sandpiper	0	0	0	0	0
BQ	Buff-breasted Sandpiper	0	0	0	0	0
RU	Ruff	339	28	29	399	859
JS	Jack Snipe	19	0	0	0	2
SN	Snipe	964	162	99	181	1024
WK	Woodcock	3	1	0	2	0
BW	Black-tailed Godwit	12690	2242	2217	9541	22218
BA	Bar-tailed Godwit	7544	1248	1037	5647	32664
WM	Whimbrel	784	685	53	713	528
CU	Curlew	22741	4329	7839	40648	67309
DR	Spotted Redshank	80	8	40	143	172
RK	Redshank	30671	3427	3206	26148	58538
GK	Greenshank	219	72	44	799	1799
LY	Lesser Yellowlegs	0	1	0	0	0
GE	Green Sandpiper	107	4	30	317	463
OD	Wood Sandpiper	0	6	2	18	18
CS	Common Sandpiper	215	235	173	945	944
TT	Turnstone	5863	1503	556	1209	6456
NK	Red-necked Phalarope	0	0	0	0	0
PL	Grey Phalarope	0	0	0	0	0
	TOTAL WADERS	**383498**	**180376**	**78296**	**279334**	**676057**

Table 3. continued

	Sep	Oct	Nov	Dec	Jan	Feb	Mar
sites	*1446*	*1605*	*1641*	*1636*	*1728*	*1715*	*1641*
OC	209022	248815	209836	209894	233678	211458	106327
IT	1	1	0	1	0	1	1
AV	2066	4192	3307	5921	4600	4621	2802
TN	0	0	0	0	0	0	0
LP	16	2	0	0	0	0	72
RP	12329	10337	7125	8167	7986	6395	3038
DO	1	0	0	0	0	0	0
ID	0	0	1	0	0	0	0
GP	24625	67282	150576	165731	169007	55581	24016
GV	26623	30600	24878	26719	34678	29584	28322
L.	76246	108952	259290	373202	343267	147722	21449
KN	125087	180599	238567	215309	199750	186124	111228
SS	9039	7603	7644	6314	6531	6419	5536
LX	78	7	7	1	8	7	6
BP	1	0	0	0	0	0	0
PP	16	4	0	0	0	0	0
CV	150	18	1	0	0	0	0
PS	91	249	599	852	1667	1011	864
DN	76404	124317	270312	319302	367792	306647	82172
OA	0	1	0	0	0	0	0
BQ	0	1	0	0	0	0	0
RU	852	557	351	415	404	507	474
JS	11	87	121	79	92	105	66
SN	2652	4230	6109	4566	5898	4718	3505
WK	2	2	20	12	34	15	6
BW	25058	28731	16964	20441	20569	18301	18842
BA	32030	22900	30645	35328	40450	45923	22237
WM	153	33	11	6	4	8	15
CU	78225	80584	55410	56709	82153	69565	49610
DR	128	126	90	55	52	82	54
RK	76335	92382	68768	68025	83372	70703	56588
GK	1909	1086	391	277	281	246	222
LY	0	2	1	1	1	1	1
GE	346	262	174	109	103	78	78
OD	5	0	0	0	0	0	0
CS	405	71	47	59	32	26	20
TT	8249	10087	9592	11110	10765	10055	7445
NK	2	0	0	0	0	0	0
PL	0	4	0	1	0	0	0
	788157	**1024124**	**1360837**	**1528606**	**1613174**	**1175903**	**544996**

Table 3. continued

	Species	Apr	May	Jun	Jul	Aug
	Number of sites visited	*715*	*610*	*633*	*646*	*702*
MU	Mediterranean Gull	41	15	15	53	90
LU	Little Gull	260	54	29	66	418
BH	Black-headed Gull	55880	29983	23207	72419	107167
IN	Ring-billed Gull	1	0	0	0	0
CM	Common Gull	6358	3745	3844	12162	19105
LB	Lesser Black-backed Gull	39467	22284	27730	38829	40307
HG	Herring Gull	30838	19313	26936	29483	43897
YM	Western Yellow-legged Gull	0	0	0	0	19
YC	Caspian Gull	0	0	0	0	0
YG	Unidentified Yellow-legged Gull	4	1	2	14	81
IG	Iceland Gull	1	0	0	0	0
GZ	Glaucous Gull	1	0	0	0	0
GB	Great Black-backed Gull	2428	1223	1529	2648	4588
KI	Kittiwake	635	1021	1667	3905	5948
ZU	Hybrid gull	0	0	1	0	0
UU	Unidentified gull	0	0	0	0	0
VU	Unidentified large gull	25	0	0	0	0
	TOTAL GULLS	**135945**	**77641**	**84960**	**159580**	**221622**

	Species	Apr	May	Jun	Jul	Aug
	Number of sites visited	*728*	*630*	*645*	*655*	*711*
TE	Sandwich Tern	5548	7768	8108	10674	10381
RS	Roseate Tern	0	0	1	1	36
CN	Common Tern	929	2393	2882	4897	6265
AE	Arctic Tern	205	393	523	2245	347
UI	Common/Arctic Tern	0	0	0	0	1
AF	Little Tern	52	320	647	914	333
BJ	Black Tern	14	3	0	0	1
WJ	White-winged Black Tern	0	0	1	1	1
UT	Unidentified tern	0	0	0	0	0
	TOTAL TERNS	**6748**	**10877**	**12162**	**18732**	**17365**

Table 3. continued

	Sep	Oct	Nov	Dec	Jan	Feb	Mar
sites	*1172*	*1303*	*1331*	*1298*	*1385*	*1365*	*1287*
MU	69	71	25	31	51	51	72
LU	166	72	4	8	1	3	450
BH	151067	131220	162576	191006	223715	196660	99426
IN	0	2	2	3	4	2	0
CM	24374	34489	48893	37596	64678	55374	26109
LB	19744	17214	10765	10844	5554	7124	21506
HG	39062	39622	41421	40582	52874	44131	38215
YM	40	30	7	5	0	1	13
YC	0	0	2	3	0	2	0
YG	38	17	16	15	20	5	0
IG	0	0	0	1	1	2	2
GZ	0	2	3	1	8	2	2
GB	9807	12948	8206	6716	6409	4289	2773
KI	1847	633	134	337	207	76	499
ZU	0	0	0	0	0	0	0
UU	1001	3	0	40	18000	192	1
VU	0	0	0	0	200	50	40
	247221	**236327**	**272054**	**287188**	**371722**	**307964**	**189108**

	Sep	Oct	Nov	Dec	Jan	Feb	Mar
sites	*1168*	*1281*	*1303*	*1269*	*1252*	*1223*	*1163*
TE	3581	358	6	7	4	6	77
RS	1	0	0	0	0	0	0
CN	1560	69	4	0	0	0	0
AE	37	4	0	0	0	0	0
UI	0	0	0	0	0	0	0
AF	52	0	0	0	0	0	0
BJ	66	0	0	0	0	0	0
WJ	0	0	0	0	0	0	0
UT	9	0	0	0	0	0	0
	5306	**431**	**10**	**7**	**4**	**6**	**77**

Table 4. Total numbers of waterbirds recorded by WeBS Core Counts in Northern Ireland in 2003/04

	Species	Apr	May	Jun	Jul	Aug
	Number of sites visited	*5*	*3*	*4*	*3*	*4*
RH	Red-throated Diver	19	0	0	0	0
BV	Black-throated Diver	0	0	0	0	0
ND	Great Northern Diver	1	0	0	0	0
LG	Little Grebe	6	9	9	4	37
GG	Great Crested Grebe	6	13	3	3	0
SZ	Slavonian Grebe	0	0	0	0	0
CA	Cormorant	96	58	71	55	205
SA	Shag	4	0	0	0	0
XU	Unidentified Cormorant/Shag	0	0	0	0	0
ET	Little Egret	0	0	0	0	0
H.	Grey Heron	15	24	35	15	35
MS	Mute Swan	94	42	52	13	39
BS	Bewick's Swan	0	0	0	0	0
WS	Whooper Swan	5	0	0	0	0
BE	Bean Goose	0	0	0	0	0
PG	Pink-footed Goose	0	0	0	0	0
NW	Greenland White-fronted Goose	0	0	0	0	0
JE	Re-established Greylag Goose	194	69	52	61	59
CG	Canada Goose	0	0	0	0	0
YE	Naturalised Barnacle Goose	0	0	0	0	0
QN	Nearctic Light-bellied Brent Goose	187	0	0	0	9
SU	Shelduck	285	143	138	9	28
WN	Wigeon	27	0	5	0	89
GA	Gadwall	0	0	0	0	0
T.	Teal	33	0	0	0	20
MA	Mallard	113	69	271	142	785
PT	Pintail	0	0	0	0	0
SV	Shoveler	0	0	0	0	0
PO	Pochard	5	6	8	1	3
TU	Tufted Duck	93	28	31	39	61
SP	Scaup	0	0	0	0	0
E.	Eider	30	78	220	4	436
LN	Long-tailed Duck	0	0	0	0	0
CX	Common Scoter	1	0	0	0	0
VS	Velvet Scoter	0	0	0	0	0
GN	Goldeneye	21	1	2	0	1
SY	Smew	0	0	0	0	0
RM	Red-breasted Merganser	20	12	26	0	7
GD	Goosander	1	0	0	0	0
RY	Ruddy Duck	0	0	1	1	1
WA	Water Rail	0	0	0	0	0
MH	Moorhen	10	8	7	6	13
CO	Coot	18	21	12	22	27
KF	Kingfisher	0	0	0	0	0
	TOTAL WILDFOWL	**1284**	**581**	**943**	**375**	**1855**

Table 4. continued

	Sep	Oct	Nov	Dec	Jan	Feb	Mar
sites	*15*	*22*	*25*	*23*	*27*	*24*	*26*
RH	1	18	150	24	21	25	11
BV	0	0	3	0	0	0	0
ND	0	1	50	3	1	21	1
LG	406	558	597	758	491	437	163
GG	3571	2742	2555	1380	1453	1220	1747
SZ	1	2	61	12	3	10	0
CA	2843	2748	1416	2006	1650	1130	1250
SA	115	256	341	304	434	93	256
XU	157	234	133	0	0	49	0
ET	0	0	0	0	1	0	1
H.	439	450	236	310	272	260	135
MS	1231	1491	1345	1819	1411	1240	1033
BS	0	0	3	22	32	6	0
WS	8	742	1538	1905	2321	1704	1268
BE	0	0	0	0	2	0	0
PG	0	3	0	1	2	0	2
NW	0	1	0	0	27	60	0
JE	204	298	564	1034	1594	2394	1098
CG	91	323	117	260	828	433	195
YE	232	228	177	226	227	155	227
QN	1081	21129	18806	5688	4451	2604	3293
SU	228	1207	2876	3957	6349	3749	2474
WN	1128	6574	8730	7876	5882	6342	3039
GA	93	187	157	156	179	211	208
T.	3021	3292	4489	7527	4395	4337	2167
MA	7858	7419	6290	7007	5543	4091	1889
PT	20	50	261	297	595	256	49
SV	31	75	106	175	241	121	42
PO	333	720	4312	8348	5780	4775	767
TU	3143	4897	6845	11129	8197	7665	5306
SP	17	128	334	1300	1498	3029	2160
E.	2597	2622	1207	575	1518	1565	1091
LN	0	0	13	2	21	27	10
CX	0	4	95	11	0	0	0
VS	0	0	3	0	0	0	0
GN	95	264	4091	5004	3764	5178	3439
SY	0	0	1	0	0	5	0
RM	271	508	563	452	388	253	450
GD	0	0	0	3	1	5	1
RY	37	42	56	3	14	2	37
WA	0	1	3	2	1	2	0
MH	200	258	225	250	249	257	199
CO	4407	3458	2609	4841	4131	3066	1514
KF	0	0	2	2	0	0	2
	33859	**62930**	**71360**	**74669**	**63967**	**56777**	**35524**

Table 4. continued

	Species	Apr	May	Jun	Jul	Aug
	Number of sites visited	*5*	*3*	*4*	*3*	*4*
OC	Oystercatcher	1142	619	574	434	4594
RP	Ringed Plover	66	21	0	27	8
GP	Golden Plover	950	0	0	0	266
GV	Grey Plover	2	0	0	0	0
L.	Lapwing	45	82	27	167	84
KN	Knot	2	8	8	1	37
SS	Sanderling	32	44	0	12	3
CV	Curlew Sandpiper	0	0	0	0	0
PS	Purple Sandpiper	0	0	0	0	0
DN	Dunlin	32	463	45	256	76
RU	Ruff	0	0	0	0	4
JS	Jack Snipe	0	0	0	0	0
SN	Snipe	4	2	2	0	0
WK	Woodcock	0	0	0	0	0
BW	Black-tailed Godwit	0	0	3	31	20
BA	Bar-tailed Godwit	76	17	72	11	16
WM	Whimbrel	20	23	0	5	5
CU	Curlew	1057	68	221	668	1689
DR	Spotted Redshank	0	0	0	0	0
RK	Redshank	580	3	6	778	1018
GK	Greenshank	2	0	4	21	58
CS	Common Sandpiper	1	1	1	5	2
TT	Turnstone	160	0	0	2	8
	TOTAL WADERS	**4171**	**1351**	**963**	**2418**	**7888**

	Species	Apr	May	Jun	Jul	Aug
	Number of sites visited	*5*	*3*	*4*	*3*	*4*
MU	Mediterranean Gull	0	0	0	0	0
LU	Little Gull	0	0	0	0	0
BH	Black-headed Gull	145	28	295	491	908
IN	Ring-billed Gull	0	0	0	0	0
CM	Common Gull	35	14	62	85	6012
LB	Lesser Black-backed Gull	9	4	5	0	43
HG	Herring Gull	21	1	29	25	62
IG	Iceland Gull	0	0	0	0	0
GZ	Glaucous Gull	0	0	0	0	0
GB	Great Black-backed Gull	242	228	60	37	22
KI	Kittiwake	0	0	0	0	0
	TOTAL GULLS	**452**	**275**	**451**	**638**	**7047**

	Species	Apr	May	Jun	Jul	Aug
	Number of sites visited	*4*	*3*	*4*	*3*	*4*
TE	Sandwich Tern	361	30	30	296	125
CN	Common Tern	8	0	0	38	5
	TOTAL TERNS	**369**	**30**	**30**	**334**	**130**

Table 4. continued

	Sep	Oct	Nov	Dec	Jan	Feb	Mar
sites	*15*	*22*	*25*	*23*	*27*	*24*	*26*
OC	14950	16272	15166	12989	16875	12398	9326
RP	482	730	458	235	470	239	128
GP	526	15369	15276	12673	14967	8757	10575
GV	0	144	167	180	227	113	50
L.	2100	4672	12969	21392	18710	8860	1104
KN	104	535	5352	1018	1555	2129	1455
SS	24	0	0	14	1	2	2
CV	4	1	0	0	0	0	0
PS	1	1	0	0	100	0	31
DN	939	1186	4885	9676	12257	8420	2707
RU	9	3	0	1	1	2	1
JS	0	0	0	1	0	1	0
SN	21	73	383	433	152	151	113
WK	1	0	1	0	0	0	0
BW	647	834	653	605	509	327	538
BA	128	477	1248	2815	1341	2360	921
WM	3	0	0	1	0	0	3
CU	4756	5135	3906	4989	5697	5188	2743
DR	0	0	0	1	1	0	0
RK	7335	9527	7781	6269	7359	5802	5567
GK	165	158	115	95	94	76	88
CS	3	0	0	0	0	0	0
TT	767	1436	566	576	1962	661	1266
	32965	**56553**	**68926**	**73963**	**82278**	**55486**	**36618**

	Sep	Oct	Nov	Dec	Jan	Feb	Mar
sites	*13*	*15*	*16*	*17*	*20*	*16*	*18*
MU	0	0	2	0	3	0	1
LU	0	0	0	0	0	0	1
BH	9451	7676	9392	11644	16178	13589	11691
IN	0	0	1	0	0	0	0
CM	4322	6005	1293	2160	3979	4493	1953
LB	1545	894	349	859	37	182	371
HG	2644	3239	5662	6460	8673	9064	5687
IG	0	0	0	1	0	0	4
GZ	0	0	0	0	2	2	2
GB	393	424	361	366	775	763	598
KI	15	0	0	0	0	0	0
	18370	**18238**	**17060**	**21490**	**29647**	**28093**	**20308**

	Sep	Oct	Nov	Dec	Jan	Feb	Mar
sites	*11*	*9*	*9*	*10*	*11*	*10*	*10*
TE	326	6	0	0	0	0	2
CN	0	0	0	0	0	0	0
	326	**6**	**0**	**0**	**0**	**0**	**2**

Table 5. Total numbers of waterbirds recorded by I-WeBS in the Republic of Ireland in 2003/04

Species	Sep	Oct	Nov	Dec	Jan	Feb	Mar
Number of sites visited	*89*	*120*	*140*	*138*	*187*	*142*	*138*
Red-throated Diver	57	6	30	62	56	109	38
Black-throated Diver	0	0	34	0	4	2	1
Great Northern Diver	10	6	242	60	321	219	153
Little Grebe	579	434	813	698	702	323	346
Great Crested Grebe	205	238	530	515	608	453	272
Slavonian Grebe	0	0	1	4	6	7	7
Cormorant	2033	1596	2100	2107	1993	1426	770
Grey Heron	531	487	598	402	498	306	169
Little Egret	233	199	144	111	92	115	62
Mute Swan	1054	1498	1943	1251	2426	1449	1058
Black Swan	0	0	0	0	2	3	0
Bewick's Swan	0	2	2	59	247	149	18
Whooper Swan	1	430	2678	2726	3645	1359	811
Bean Goose	0	0	1	1	0	2	0
Pink-footed Goose	10	6	6	10	9	7	2
European White-fronted Goose	0	0	0	0	0	0	3
Greenland White-fronted Goose	52	7255	7619	7385	7178	9447	260
Greylag Goose	118	182	1216	1778	1787	2642	1266
Snow Goose	0	1	1	1	0	1	0
Canada Goose	16	23	21	2	332	33	11
Barnacle Goose	5	7	8	607	3214	61	801
Dark-Bellied Brent Goose	0	0	0	3	4	2	0
Black Brant	0	0	0	0	1	0	1
Light-bellied Brent Goose	340	1616	3705	10285	11010	7571	8429
Feral/hybrid Goose	37	14	20	23	82	70	56
Shelduck	94	549	3033	2833	5787	5173	3778
Unidentified Duck	0	0	0	250	96	0	0
Wigeon	856	9302	20458	25439	36387	23506	9232
American Wigeon	0	0	1	2	4	4	2
Gadwall	51	92	147	367	247	210	135
Teal	2151	6078	9500	10264	15726	11083	5293
Green-winged Teal	0	0	0	1	4	1	0
Mallard	8043	7627	6273	6003	8186	4837	2224
Pintail	31	201	231	615	676	744	287
Shoveler	25	138	514	1208	742	1327	220
Pochard	3	6603	16324	5822	2527	806	237
Lesser Scaup	0	0	0	0	1	0	0
Ring-necked Duck	1	0	10	2	1	0	0
Tufted Duck	465	1692	6876	6057	5020	1484	1459
Scaup	13	234	63	34	507	307	68
Eider	2	0	1	1	7	20	0
Long-tailed Duck	0	0	7	17	12	20	0
Common Scoter	1902	32	870	3318	2418	2019	1815
Velvet Scoter	0	0	2	0	0	0	0
Goldeneye	6	50	626	1114	1044	540	482
Smew	0	1	1	3	5	2	1
Red-breasted Merganser	234	262	723	464	577	635	312
Goosander	0	10	0	0	5	7	0
Ruddy Duck	0	0	0	1	5	0	0
Feral/hybrid Mallard type	0	0	0	0	1	0	0
Coot	1775	12019	26589	4761	6935	1154	566
Moorhen	340	422	384	309	400	371	283
Crane	0	3	0	0	0	0	0
Water Rail	13	15	18	21	12	24	22
Kingfisher	14	10	9	11	13	11	8
TOTAL WILDFOWL	**21300**	**59340**	**114372**	**97007**	**121562**	**80041**	**40958**

Table 5. continued

Species	Sep	Oct	Nov	Dec	Jan	Feb	Mar
Oystercatcher	15777	14307	16205	11701	19901	24060	15546
Little Ringed Plover	0	0	0	0	1	0	0
Ringed Plover	2375	1241	2992	2209	3482	2214	753
Golden Plover	2727	28288	45982	65452	78287	54219	28305
Grey Plover	874	720	1422	1783	1470	1846	1103
Lapwing	921	9663	34075	46029	62150	29961	1700
Knot	687	548	3995	4451	15405	15140	12814
Sanderling	803	832	1630	758	1431	1011	959
Little Stint	1	1	0	0	0	0	0
Pectoral Sandpiper	4	0	0	0	0	0	0
Curlew Sandpiper	5	2	0	0	0	0	0
Purple Sandpiper	21	12	55	68	65	59	47
Dunlin	4762	5928	20942	20490	36760	28910	14578
Ruff	7	1	0	4	21	8	0
Jack Snipe	0	4	10	24	25	22	23
Snipe	79	377	855	739	832	658	404
Woodcock	0	0	0	0	0	6	0
Black-tailed Godwit	5642	7444	6423	4532	8247	8296	4306
Bar-tailed Godwit	2602	2826	5336	5749	5755	6656	3378
Whimbrel	59	1	0	0	38	3	0
Curlew	9991	8135	8212	9807	13800	15091	5911
Spotted Redshank	1	7	4	10	7	6	1
Redshank	8452	8759	11394	5969	8234	11041	8113
Greenshank	364	331	371	214	330	322	146
Lesser Yellowlegs	0	2	0	0	0	0	0
Green Sandpiper	3	2	0	1	11	1	3
Common Sandpiper	5	4	3	2	5	26	1
Turnstone	975	941	2091	1303	1767	1510	1177
TOTAL WADERS	**57137**	**90376**	**161997**	**181295**	**258024**	**201066**	**99268**

Species	Sep	Oct	Nov	Dec	Jan	Feb	Mar
Mediterranean Gull	22	12	23	12	6	13	15
Little Gull	0	6	0	0	0	2	0
Sabine's Gull	0	0	1	0	0	0	0
Black-headed Gull	14247	8133	14013	14276	18504	13893	6764
Ring-billed Gull	2	1	0	3	6	0	2
Common Gull	2928	1806	4485	4607	5932	4582	2747
Lesser Black-backed Gull	10475	1389	1325	364	369	1008	1025
Herring Gull	1255	784	1424	862	1180	1119	1784
American Herring Gull	1	0	0	0	0	0	0
Iceland Gull	0	0	8	0	0	1	0
Glaucous Gull	0	0	0	0	2	1	1
Great Black-backed Gull	1116	1017	1037	845	939	955	409
TOTAL GULLS	**30046**	**13148**	**22316**	**20969**	**26938**	**21574**	**12747**

Species	Sep	Oct	Nov	Dec	Jan	Feb	Mar
Unidentified Tern	0	0	0	0	0	0	3
Sandwich Tern	434	37	4	0	7	0	10
Roseate Tern	8	0	0	0	0	0	0
Common Tern	102	3	0	1	0	31	17
Little Tern	0	0	0	0	0	0	0
TOTAL TERNS	**544**	**40**	**4**	**1**	**7**	**31**	**30**

SPECIES ACCOUNTS

Key to symbols commonly used in the species accounts.

As footnotes to thresholds:

?   population size not accurately known

+   population too small for meaningful threshold

*   where 1% of the national population is fewer than 50 birds, 50 is normally used as a minimum threshold for national importance

**   a site regularly holding more than 20,000 waterbirds (excluding non-native species) qualifies as internationally important by virtue of absolute numbers

†   denotes that a qualifying level different to the national threshold has been used for the purposes of presenting sites in this report

To denote WeBS alerts status in headers:

++   >100% increase

+   33-100% increase

o   stable trend

-   25-50% decrease

--   >50% decrease

In tables of important sites:

-   no data available

( )   incomplete count

†   same meaning as used for thresholds

▲   site was of a higher importance status in the previous five-year period

▼   site was of a lower importance status in the previous five-year period

1,2   count obtained using different survey methodology from WeBS Core Counts (see table below)

S   short term (5 years)

M   medium term (10 years)

L   long term (25 years or maximum period if <25 years)

Sources of additional information used in compiling tables of important sites are listed below. Non-WeBS counts are identified in the tables by the relevant number below given in superscript following the count.

1	RSPB/Talisman Energy studies, *e.g.* Stenning (1998)	25	Dorset Bird Report
2	M. Howe (*in litt.*)	26	Judith Smith, Gr. Manchester County recorder
3	WWT studies, *e.g.* Rees *et al.* (2000)	27	BTO/ Lucy Smith
4	Bean Goose Working Group, Simpson and Maciver (2004)	28	Paul Daw, County recorder for Argyll
5	RSPB (*pers comm.*)	29	Steve Percival's counts of Lindisfarne - Svalbard Light-bellied Brents
6	Lancashire Goose Report, *e.g.* Forshaw (1998)		
7	SNH 'adopted' counts	30	JNCC report of aerial and shore-based surveys for seaducks, divers and grebes (Dean *et al.* 2004)
8	WWT data		
9	Greenland White-fronted Goose Study, *e.g.* Fox and Francis (2004)	31	WWT report to DTI. Aerial survey of Thames strategic area.
10	SOTEAG reports, *e.g.* Heubeck and Mellor (2005)	32	WWT report to DTI. Aerial survey of Greater Wash strategic area.
11	WeBS Low Tide Counts	33	All Wales Common Scoter Survey. WWT reports to CCW.
12	Roost counts		
13	Supplementary daytime counts	34	All-Ireland Light-bellied Brent Goose Census
14	WWT/JNCC National Grey Goose Census	35	Cormorant Roost Survey 2003
15	Firth of Clyde Eider counts, *e.g.* Waltho, C.M. (2004)	36	Scottish Bird Report records
16	R. Godfrey (*in litt.*)	37	Worden *et al.* (2004)
17	Argyll Bird Report	38	RSPB data
18	SNH Greenland Goose Census	39	SNH data
19	R. MacDonald (*in litt.*)	40	WWT UK-breeding Greylag Goose Survey
20	Little Egret Roost counts	41	Frank Mawby (*in litt.*)
21	D Carrington (*in litt.*)	42	Shetland coordinated swan count
22	P Reay (*in litt.*)	43	CSL supplementary Ruddy Duck counts
23	WWT unpublished data	44	Winter Gull Roost Survey
24	Woolmer *et al.* (2001), Common Scoter count in Carmarthen Bay	45	BTO/CCW Carmarthen Bay surveys

Red-throated Diver
Gavia stellata

International threshold: 10,000
Great Britain threshold: 49*
All-Ireland threshold: 10*

GB max: 456 Oct
NI max: 150 Nov

50 is normally used as a minimum threshold

The Red-throated Diver is a scarce breeding species in Scotland, but outside the breeding season is much more numerous and widespread, with numbers augmented by arrivals from northern Europe. However, our knowledge of the status of Red-throated Divers in UK waters has been changing dramatically in recent years. Always the most numerous and widespread of the divers, and by far the most likely to be encountered along the English east and south coasts and in the Irish Sea, the numbers now thought to be present offshore are much higher than previously imagined. Earlier hints of this came from sea-watching observations between Suffolk and Kent, later backed up by aerial and boat-based offshore surveys, which have revealed thousands of birds using the relatively shallow waters of the outer Greater Thames region. The same pattern, although involving smaller numbers, has also been found in the Irish Sea. For further details, see the previous volume of *Wildfowl and Wader Counts*.

Despite this discovery, numbers recorded during WeBS core counts in Britain during the 2003/04 winter were the lowest for some years. Conversely, the Northern Ireland peak was by far the highest to date. The extent to which WeBS totals reflect the actual numbers in UK waters is clearly very much open to question, given the fact that only a small proportion of the total is counted and that numbers counted on a given date depend so strongly on the conditions at the time. Interestingly, the peak numbers were rather early, both British and Northern Irish peaks being in autumn rather than mid-winter as usual.

Looking at individual sites, counts at Cardigan Bay were very low for the second year running. Within this broad area, most birds are generally found off Borth and the mouth of the Dyfi Estuary. It is possible that the apparent decline is due to count conditions on the days in question, but with two years of poor counts further investigation may well be called for at this important location. Similarly low totals at Minsmere, Lade Sands and the Thames Estuary should not necessarily be considered an immediate cause for concern. Perhaps of more interest, though, is the low count on the Inner Firth of Clyde, which should be less affected by visibility issues. The most noteworthy high site count was at Lough Foyle, a site that also saw large numbers of other offshore fish-eating species during winter 2003/04. Loch Ryan and Lunan Bay were also sites at which numbers were above recent core counts. The highest count submitted to WeBS of this winter, however, has not been included in any of the above national totals or the table below; a series of counts off Ness House, Thorpeness (Suffolk) included an incredible peak of 4,710 flying past on 4th January 2004.

	99/00	00/01	01/02	02/03	03/04	Mon	Mean
Sites of national importance in Great Britain							
Cardigan Bay	(229)	460	732	32	22	Nov	312
Minsmere	717 [13]	700 [13]	4	3	57	Dec	296
Nigg Bay to Cruden Bay	(101)	(33)	(15)	(35)	225 [30]	Mar	225
Lade Sands	100 [13]	0	800	100	10	Dec	202
Thames Estuary	(11)	13	(211) [30]	(344) [31]	(16)	Dec	146
Moray Firth	103 [1]	(150) [30]	(74) [30]	126 [1]	166	Oct	136
Inner Firth of Clyde	123	145	112	151	54	Oct	117
Forth Estuary	75	104	93	106	(40)	Oct	95
Dengie Flats	92	145	51	114	50	Jan	90
Lavan Sands	(90)	72 [13]	13	202 [13]	30	Feb	81
Pegwell Bay	1	4	54	215			69
Loch Ryan	26	35	47	111 [13]	89	Feb	62
Sites of all-Ireland importance in Northern Ireland							
Lough Foyle	15	5	7	29	147	Nov	41
Belfast Lough	39	14	41	31	13	Oct	28
Strangford Lough	6 [11]		57 [11]	1 [11]			21

	99/00	00/01	01/02	02/03	03/04	Mon	Mean
Sites no longer meeting table qualifying levels in WeBS-Year 2003/2004							
Alt Estuary		21	33	101	59	26	Oct	48
The Wash		24	14	3	11	6	Dec	12
Dundrum Bay		(0)	(1)	(0)	(0)	(1)	Nov	(1)
Other sites attaining table qualifying levels in WeBS-Year 2003/2004 in Great Britain							
Lunan Bay				30	20	50	Jan	33

Black-throated Diver
Gavia arctica

International threshold: 10,000
Great Britain threshold: 7*
All-Ireland threshold: 1*

GB max: 66 Mar
NI max: 3 Nov

50 is normally used as a minimum threshold

Black-throated Divers are relatively unfamiliar birds to most WeBS counters. Overall numbers in UK waters are low and birds tend to occur in a dispersed fashion along the coast, especially in the west and north, although unlike Great Northern Diver relatively few winter in Shetland. The large numbers of divers recently discovered offshore in the outer Thames do not appear to include many Black-throated. Although identification from the air is difficult, boat surveys have indicated that the majority are Red-throated. Our wintering Black-throated Divers are derived from a combination of Scottish and Scandinavian breeders and, although monitoring of this species is not straightforward, peak numbers generally fall between November and March.

Several of the key sites in the table are only counted occasionally, due to their remote nature. However, regular monitoring at Gerrans Bay in south Cornwall has revealed consistently high numbers, although the 2003/04 peak was down from the high total during the previous winter. The high site count at the Moray Firth 'complex' in October included 36 at Inver Bay in the Dornoch Firth. At Girvan to Turnberry, the high peak of the previous year was maintained throughout the 2003/04 winter. In Northern Ireland, this species is most consistently recorded from Belfast Lough and the count of four here was the highest at the site to date.

	99/00	00/01	01/02	02/03	03/04	Mon	Mean
Sites of national importance in Great Britain							
Gerrans Bay		35	33	53	37	Feb	40
Loch Ewe	(29)	(15)					(29)
Loch Gairloch	(5)	23					23
Moray Firth	14[1]	17[1]	9	18[1]	48	Oct	21
Gruinard Bay	(14)	(11)					(14)
Bay of Sandoyne - Holme Sound	14[13]						14
Girvan to Turnberry	7		8	20	19	Mar	12
Forth Estuary	6	(2)	24	9	5	Nov	11
Red Point to Port Henderson	9	11					10
Little Loch Broom	1	17					9
Sites of all-Ireland importance in Northern Ireland							
Outer Ards Shoreline	2	(3)		(0)	(0)		3
Belfast Lough	3	(2)	2	1	4[11]	Nov	3

Great Northern Diver
Gavia immer

International threshold: 50
Great Britain threshold: 30*[†]
All-Ireland threshold: ?[†]

GB max: 111 Jan
NI max: 50 Nov

50 is normally used as a minimum threshold

Great Northern Divers are an exciting find in the southeast of the UK but become a much more expected part of the offshore avifauna the further north and west one gets. Particular concentrations are found around the Northern Isles, west Scotland, Northern Ireland and, in smaller numbers, the southwest peninsula. Our wintering birds come from breeding grounds in Iceland and Greenland, most birds arriving through October and numbers then staying at a relatively high level even as late as April; a handful even remain throughout the summer each year. Due to the variable nature of coverage of key sites coupled with the difficulties of surveying offshore waters, trends are difficult to detect for this species. However, peak counts were similar to the previous two winters in Britain, whereas the peak Northern Ireland total was the second highest ever for the province.

The table shows that many of the key sites for this species are counted on an irregular basis, due to their remote nature and the need for specialist (often boat-based) surveys. A program of counts carried out by the Shetland Oil Terminal Environmental Advisory Group (SOTEAG) does provide regular information for some key Shetland coastal stretches. For example, the peak at Kirkabister to Wadbister Ness was the highest in the UK during winter 2003/04 and is a recovery of numbers after a low total the previous winter. In contrast, the numbers found between Whiteness and Skelda Voes were on the low side compared to recent years and just one was noted along the regular Hacosay/Bluemull/Colgrave route. As with all offshore counts, numbers can be strongly affected by conditions on the day and longer-term trends are more important than one-off peaks and troughs. Moreover, some of the counts in the table below refer to aerial surveys flown using distance sampling methodology (Bibby et al. 2000, Buckland et al. 2001, 2004) and thus the numbers presented are very much underestimates. The key sites for the species during the standard core counts remain Loch Indaal (Islay), Broadford Bay (Skye) and the Moray Firth. There were high counts at both ends of the Northern Irish coast, at Carlingford Lough and Lough Foyle. Gerrans Bay in Cornwall and Portland Harbour in Dorset remain the top south coast sites.

	99/00	00/01	01/02	02/03	03/04	Mon	Mean
Sites of international importance in the UK							
Entrance Deer/Shapinsay Snds	375 [13]	225 [13]					300
Outer Hebrides					266 [30]	Feb	266
Coll/Tiree					175 [30]	Feb	175
Sound of Gigha	104 [28]						104
Scapa Flow	82			9 [30]	156 [30]	Feb	82
Moray Firth	12 [1]	38 [1]	(54) [30]	60 [1]	109 [30]	Feb	55
Sites of national importance in Great Britain							
Loch Indaal	31	19	74	68	18	Nov	42
Kirkabister to Wadbister Ness	45 [10]	46 [10]	49 [10]	22 [10]	50 [10]	Jan	42
Broadford Bay			(25)	35	(43)	Feb	39
East Unst			37 [10]				37
Whiteness to Skelda Ness	47 [10]	30 [10]	34 [10]	34 [10]	27 [10]	Jan	34
Sites with mean peak counts of 5 or more birds in Great Britain†							
Scalloway Islands			58 [10]		19 [10]	Dec	30 ▼
Pontllyfni to Aberdesach					28 [13]	Mar	28
Quendale to Virkie	15 [10]	19 [10]	30 [10]	22 [10]	24 [10]	Jan	22
Rova Head to Wadbister Ness	18 [10]	23 [10]	38 [10]	19 [10]	30 [10]	Jan	22
Scousburgh to Maywick	22 [10]						22
Island of Papa Westray			6	20	22	Jan	16
Loch Eriboll	(15)	(1)					(15)
Gerrans Bay		13	6	17	15	Mar	13
Uyea Sound	26	13	6	10	5	Jan	12
Kirkabister to Dury Voe		11 [10]					11
Island of Egilsay	6	28	4	3	(0)		10
Balnakeil Bay Durness					9 [13]	Mar	9
Gruinard Bay	(9)	(7)					(9)
Little Loch Broom	2	16					9
West Whalsay and Sounds			9 [10]				9
Fleet and Wey	8	14	5	4	3	Jan	7
Hacosay/Bluemill/Colgrave		10 [10]	19 [10]	3 [10]	1 [10]	Feb	7
Loch Ewe	8	6					7
Lunning and Lunna Holm			7 [10]				7
Traigh Luskentyre	8	6	8				7
Burra and Trondra			10 [10]		1 [10]	Dec	6
Forth Estuary	17	2	4	2	(2)	Jan	6
Lochs Beg and Scridain (East)	(8)	4					6
South Fetlar			6 [10]				6
South Havra			6 [10]				6
South Unst			8 [10]		5 [10]	Feb	6
South Yell Sound	9 [10]	6 [10]	8 [10]	7 [10]	4 [10]	Feb	6
Cleddau Estuary	(2)	7	1	7	3	Jan	5
Easting and Sand Wick	5						5
Kyle of Durness	(0)	5					5

	99/00	00/01	01/02	02/03	03/04	Mon	Mean
Quendale Bay			5 [10]				5
Sullom Voe	8 [10]	5 [10]	5 [10]	6 [10]	4 [10]	Feb	5
Sites with mean peak counts of 5 or more birds in Northern Ireland[†]							
Carlingford Lough	(7)	(16)	(3)	(15)	25	Nov	25
Lough Foyle	2	0	4	26	24	Nov	11
Strangford Lough	17 [11]	1 [11]		1 [11]	2 [11]	Nov	5

[†] as few sites exceed the British threshold and no All-Ireland threshold has been set, a qualifying level of 5 has been chosen to select sites for presentation in this report

Little Grebe
Tachybaptus ruficollis

			International threshold:	3,400
			Great Britain threshold:	78
			All-Ireland threshold:	?[†]

				S	M	L
GB max:	5,162	Oct				
NI max:	758	Dec				
			GB change:	o	+	++
			NI change:	o	o	+

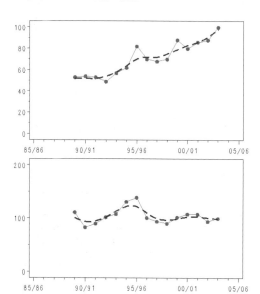

Figure 3.a, Annual indices & trend for Little Grebe for GB (above) & NI (below).

— ● — Annual Index
- - - - - Trend

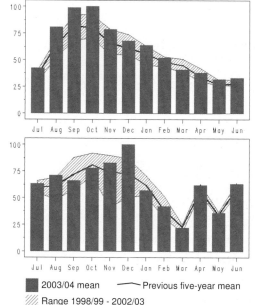

■ 2003/04 mean   ⁀ Previous five-year mean
▨ Range 1998/99 - 2002/03

Figure 3.b, Monthly indices for Little Grebe for GB (above) & NI (below).

The Little Grebe is a widespread resident species in the UK, winter numbers being supplemented to an unknown degree by incoming migrants from northern Europe. Although many are recorded on WeBS sites, the species is widely dispersed on other small waterbodies and in riverine habitats and thus some care should be taken when interpreting national trends on the basis of WeBS data alone.

The British index shows a species which appears to be doing very well, numbers having roughly doubled since monitoring began and having increased by 14% since the previous year alone, although this was not reflected in the peak national recorded total which fell slightly since the previous year. Numbers peaked in early autumn as usual. The Northern Ireland index is more stable, although fluctuating, whilst the peak recorded total for Northern Ireland was the highest ever for the Province.

In line with the increase nationally, numbers were higher than usual at several sites including the neighbouring sites of Chew Valley Lake and Blagdon Lake, as well as Old Moor, Draycote Water, Larne Lough and Upper Lough Erne. However, numbers remained low for the third year running at the Swale Estuary and were also disappointing at Holme Pierrepont. At Loughs Neagh and Beg, the most important site in the UK, numbers remained stable despite large declines in other species at the site in recent years.

	99/00	00/01	01/02	02/03	03/04	Mon	Mean
Sites of national importance in Great Britain							
Thames Estuary	217	348	351	378	(198)	Oct	324
Swale Estuary	238	195	64 [11]	43	49	Oct	118
Holme Pierrepont Gravel Pits	158	107			55	Jan	107
Chichester Harbour	58	78	150 [11]	111	125	Dec	104
King`s Dyke Pits Whittlesey	92				(6)	Sep	92
Bewl Water	38	54	132	136	94	Aug	91
Chew Valley Lake	65	95	100	70	110	Sep	88
Rutland Water	120	87	77	58	87	Oct	86
Sutton and Lound Gravel Pits	45		109	86			80
Tees Estuary	56	82	(59)	104	70	Aug	78 ▲
Sites no longer meeting table qualifying levels in WeBS-Year 2003/2004							
North Norfolk Coast	74	77	100 [11]	42	60	Jan	71
Sites with mean peak counts of 30 or more birds in Northern Ireland[†]							
Loughs Neagh and Beg	413	400	412	430	430	Dec	417
Upper Lough Erne	67	94	122	75	131	Feb	98
Strangford Lough	87	72	103	113	83	Jan	92
Lower Lough Erne				39	(57)	Dec	48
Lough Money	55	48	53	41	39	Feb	47
Larne Lough	35	36	27	32	65	Oct	39
Hillsborough Main Lake	25	40	45	37	27	Sep	35
Belfast Lough	31	41	29	37	30	Oct	34
Other sites attaining table qualifying levels in WeBS-Year 2003/2004 in Great Britain							
Blagdon Lake	46	42	127	18	127	Aug	72
Old Moor	56	52	45	(49)	112	Aug	66
Hamford Water	41	52	105	68	(92)	Jan	72
Draycote Water	24	44	60	71	85	Oct	57
Lee Valley Gravel Pits	(37)	55	59	71	83	Sep	67
Blackwater Estuary	70	53	58	59	80	Sep	64

[†] as no All-Ireland threshold has been set a qualifying level of 30 has been chosen to select sites for presentation in this report

Great Crested Grebe
Podiceps cristatus

International threshold:		4,800		
Great Britain threshold:		159		
All-Ireland threshold:		30*		

		S	M	L
GB max:	9,569 Oct			
NI max:	3,571 Sep			
GB change:		o	o	+
NI change:		o	+	+

*50 is normally used as a minimum threshold

Great Crested Grebes are a familiar sight throughout much of the UK. The species is widespread on inland waterbodies and rivers during the summer, but there is a tendency then for many birds to congregate at favoured sites, both inland and coastal, during the autumn and winter. There is known to be interchange between UK birds and those elsewhere in Europe, but the extent to which this occurs is not well understood.

The British index rose in 2003/04 to its second highest ever value, numbers peaking in the autumn as usual but again not quite breaking 10,000. In Northern Ireland, despite a greater level of fluctuation in annual indices the underlying trend suggests a stable picture over the last decade. However, the peak Northern Ireland total was the highest ever recorded in the province.

Notably in 2003/04, four-figure counts were recorded from four different sites. In Northern Ireland, the usual key sites of Loughs Neagh and Beg (where there was the highest count since 1995) and Belfast Lough were also joined by an exceptional count at Lough Foyle, the highest ever here and linked to high numbers also of other fish-eaters such as Red-throated Diver, Slavonian Grebe and Red-breasted Merganser. The three key Northern Ireland sites peaked in separate months, suggesting that some of the same birds may have been involved. In Britain, peak supplementary counts at Lade Sands exceeded 1,000 for the fourth time in the last five years making this the top British site by a considerable margin. There were also high offshore counts at Minsmere and Rye Harbour but lower than average ones at Pegwell Bay, Lavan Sands and the Solway Estuary. However, at coastal sites birds may be present a fair way offshore which can have a major effect on the numbers recorded when viewing conditions are anything less than ideal and such ups and downs should be treated with caution. Inland, the Pitsford Reservoir count

was relatively high but Chew Valley Lake numbers were much lower than normal.

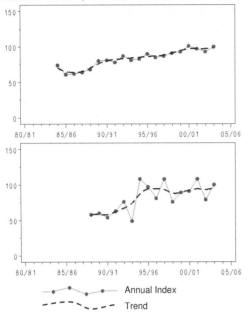

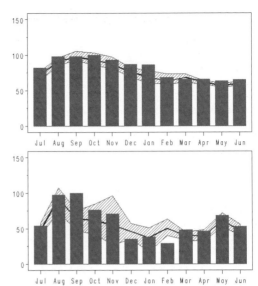

Figure 4.a, Annual indices & trend for Great Crested Grebe for GB (above) & NI (below).

Figure 4.b, Monthly indices for Great Crested Grebe for GB (above) & NI (below).

	99/00	00/01	01/02	02/03	03/04	Mon	Mean	
Sites of national importance in Great Britain								
Lade Sands	1,100 [13]	1,012 [13]	755	1,600	1,080 [13]	Jan	1,109	
Rutland Water	726	997	600	607	619	Oct	710	
Chew Valley Lake	550	690	480	320	330	Oct	474	
Queen Mary Reservoir	312	246	671	267	495	Dec	398	
Grafham Water	150	98	619	311	463	Jan	328	
Forth Estuary	297	(290)	224	(389)	295	Sep	299	
Cotswold Water Park (West)	(225)	306	(258)	(188)	244	Nov	275	
Minsmere	500 [13]	350 [13]	5	19	463	Jan	267	
Pitsford Reservoir	195	241	268	203	341	Jan	250	
Pegwell Bay	68	370	146	604	20	Feb	242	
Bewl Water	104	261	292	356	190	Jul	241	
Loch Ryan	258	147	(121)	(300)	210	Dec	229	
Morecambe Bay	239	245	222	187	218	Jan	222	
Lavan Sands	165 [2]	388 [13]	113	308	114	Jan	218	
Draycote Water	200	219	221	255	151	Jul	209	
Swale Estuary	75	64	311 [11]	(42)	316	Jan	192	▲
Solway Firth	251 [11]	336 [11]	164 [11]	119	88	Jan	192	
Lee Valley Gravel Pits	201	191	181	169	204	Nov	189	
Rye Harbour and Pett Level	299	68	160	48	365	Jan	188	▲
Stour Estuary	290 [11]	222 [11]	139 [11]	136	139 [11]	Feb	185	
Blithfield Reservoir	240	231	110	98	202	Jul	176	
Loch Leven	170	131	222	127	204	Sep	171	▲
Abberton Reservoir	207	77	198	144	176	Oct	160	
Sites of all-Ireland importance in Northern Ireland								
Belfast Lough	1,508	1,338	1,995	1,214	1,832	Oct	1,577	
Loughs Neagh and Beg	847	1,547	336	930	1,695	Sep	1,071	
Lough Foyle	24	38	278	782	1,030	Nov	430	
Carlingford Lough	249	326	284	174	184	Oct	243	
Upper Lough Erne	243	113	190	110	112	Feb	154	
Larne Lough	140	204	80	105	115	Sep	129	
Lower Lough Erne				71	(66)	Feb	71	
Outer Ards Shoreline	1	199		9	(7)	Jan	70	
Strangford Lough	70	141	50	36	43	Oct	68	

	99/00	00/01	01/02	02/03	03/04	Mon	Mean
Sites no longer meeting table qualifying levels in WeBS-Year 2003/2004							
Wraysbury Gravel Pits	202	167	130	150	113	Oct	152
Dundrum Bay	(0)	(4)	(1)	(1)	(1)	Nov	(4)
Other sites attaining table qualifying levels in WeBS-Year 2003/2004 in Great Britain							
Poole Harbour	76	151	171	127	202	Jan	145
Bough Beech Reservoir	30	160	128	149	196	Sep	133
Staines Reservoirs	72	61	68	51	168	Sep	84
Blagdon Lake	(98)	80	110	113	161	Aug	116

Red-necked Grebe
Podiceps grisegena

International threshold:	1,000
Great Britain threshold:	2*
All-Ireland threshold:	?

GB max:	16 Aug
NI max:	0

*50 is normally used as a minimum threshold

Red-necked Grebe is a scarce wintering species in the UK. Unlike the other grebes, only sporadic attempts at breeding occur and the majority of birds are seen between August and March, originating from breeding areas in eastern and northern Europe.

By far the highest numbers in the UK occur at the Forth Estuary, mostly along the south side of the outer firth. As shown in the table counts on the Forth were the lowest of the past five years, indeed the lowest since 1992/93. As a result, the total for Great Britain was similarly low. Elsewhere, the North Norfolk Coast remains the only other site to feature every year in the table, with no birds recorded from Lindisfarne for the first time. The lack of any records from Northern Ireland was not unusual.

	99/00	00/01	01/02	02/03	03/04	Mon	Mean
Sites of national importance in Great Britain							
Forth Estuary	55	29	39	44	15	Aug	36
Bay of Sandoyne - Holme Sound	8 [13]						8
North Norfolk Coast	6	3	9	2	(2)	Oct	5
Lindisfarne	2	3 [11]	5	4 [11]	(0)		4
Other sites attaining table qualifying levels in WeBS-Year 2003/2004 in Great Britain							
Loch Ryan	0	0	(1)	(0)	3	Dec	1

Slavonian Grebe
Podiceps auritus

International threshold:	35
Great Britain threshold:	7*
All-Ireland threshold:	?[†]

GB max:	227 Jan
NI max:	61 Nov

*50 is normally used as a minimum threshold

The Slavonian Grebe breeds in the Scottish Highlands albeit in small numbers and is also scarce, but somewhat more widespread, in the winter. Although non-breeding birds have the potential to appear on many WeBS sites, there are certain favoured coastal sites that host high numbers of the species each winter. Interestingly, the key sites are found from the north of Shetland to the south coast of England, although more are in the north. Our wintering birds are thought to involve birds from a variety of breeding areas, with south coast birds thought to originate from Fenno-Scandia but the birds in the north being local breeders or from Iceland and Greenland.

The British peak of 227 was about average for recent years but the Northern Ireland peak was exceptionally high, being almost entirely due to numbers at Lough Foyle, which following 103 at the same location in 1995 was the second highest ever total for a single Northern Irish site. The count from the Forth Estuary in November 2003, mostly involving birds along the south shore between Eastfield and Musselburgh, was the third highest site total ever recorded by WeBS. The Blackwater Estuary peak was almost twice as high as previous peaks whilst Pagham Harbour showed a recovery in numbers after recent poor years. There were few signs of clear declines anywhere, except perhaps Lindisfarne, although monitoring this species in choppy offshore waters can often be problematic.

	99/00	00/01	01/02	02/03	03/04	Mon	Mean	
Sites of international importance in the UK								
Forth Estuary	67	44	61	80	110	Nov	72	
Moray Firth	29	86	75	69 [1]	62 [1]	Dec	64	
Whiteness to Skelda Ness	30 [10]	43 [10]	29 [10]	55 [10]	55 [10]	Jan	45	
Loch Ashie		41 [13]					41	
Traigh Luskentyre	38	48	19				35	▲
Sites of national importance in Great Britain								
Sound of Gigha	44 [28]	9 [28]					27	
Loch Ryan	10	19	31	31 [13]	32	Feb	25	
Inner Firth of Clyde	22	20	10	45	(20)	Jan	24	
Loch Indaal	27	23	11	31	30	Oct	24	
Loch of Harray	(24)	8	25	25	23	Nov	21	
Jersey Shore		5	(31)				18	
Blackwater Estuary	8	9	22	9 [11]	41	Jan	18	
Pagham Harbour	34	1	6	6	28	Jan	15	
Scapa Flow	14						14	
Kirkabister to Wadbister Ness	11 [10]	23 [10]	5 [10]	13 [10]	17 [10]	Jan	14	
Lindisfarne	1	9	14	23 [11]	(2)	Jan	12	
Rova Head to Wadbister Ness	4 [10]	5 [10]	15 [10]	11 [10]	6 [10]	Jan	10	
Lavan Sands	(4)	6	(4)	15 [13]	6	Jan	9	▲
Upper Loch Torridon	(0)	9					9	
North West Solent	(8)	8	10	(4)	5	Dec	8	
Broadford Bay		8	10	6	Nov	8		
Sullom Voe		8 [10]	8 [10]	6 [10]	6 [10]	Feb	8	▲
Loch of Swannay	3	7	4	10	11	Dec	7	
Sites with mean peak counts of 4 or more birds in Northern Ireland[†]								
Lough Foyle	2	9	6	13	61	Nov	18	

[†] as no All-Ireland threshold has been set a qualifying level of 4 has been chosen to select sites for presentation in this report

Black-necked Grebe (Mark Collier)

Black-necked Grebe
Podiceps nigricollis

International threshold:	2,800
Great Britain threshold:	1*[†]
All-Ireland threshold:	?[†]

GB max: 40 Nov
NI max: 0

*50 is normally used as a minimum threshold

The Black-necked Grebe is a scarce wintering species in Britain and is generally absent from Northern Ireland. Although most wintering birds occur in coastal areas, at many inland sites the species is more likely to be recorded on spring or autumn passage. Although WeBS is primarily concerned with non-breeding waterbirds, the submission of summer counts from many sites does mean that breeding locations for this rare species are included within the database. The only such sites published in *Wildfowl and Wader Counts* are those where the Rare Breeding Birds Panel (Ogilvie 2004) and/or local counters have deemed it acceptable to do so.

The British peak of 40 was the lowest since 1992/93. This total seems to have been driven by low site counts at several south western sites, notably the Fal Complex, Tamar Complex and the Fleet and Wey. Whilst this species can be easily overlooked on offshore waters and even within Estuaries, the geographical location of these declines is worthy of note and it will be interesting to see if this trend continues into 2004/05. Further along the south coast, at both Poole Harbour and Langstone Harbour, numbers were also below average. William Girling Reservoir, in contrast, supported its highest ever numbers in October 2003 and now becomes the top-ranked site in the country. As usual, the species was not recorded in Northern Ireland.

	99/00	00/01	01/02	02/03	03/04	Mon	Mean
Sites of national importance in Great Britain							
William Girling Reservoir	11	14	16	16	21	Oct	16
Langstone Harbour	12	15	22 [11]	15	11	Nov	15
Fal Complex		(1)	16	15	7	Jan	13
Woolston Eyes	15	1	41	6	1	Mar	13
Holme Pierrepont Gravel Pits	14	10			0		8
Confidential Northumberland site			2	11	10	Jul	8
Fleet and Wey	11	9	13	3	1	Jan	7
Confidential Hertfordshire site	7	5	8	7	9	Jul	7
Kilconquhar Loch	5	8	8	6	2	Jul	6
Tamar Complex	(6)	9	3	6 [11]	2	Jan	5
Other sites attaining table qualifying levels in WeBS-Year 2003/2004 in Great Britain							
Gerrans Bay		0	4	5	6	Feb	4
Abberton Reservoir	2	2	2	1	5	Sep	2

[†] as the British threshold for national importance is so small, and as no All-Ireland threshold has been set a qualifying level of 5 has been chosen to select sites for presentation in this report

Cormorant
Phalacrocorax carbo

International threshold: 1,200
Great Britain threshold: 230
All-Ireland threshold: ?[†]

			S	M	L
GB max:	18,792	Oct			
NI max:	2,843	Sep			
		GB change:	o	o	+
		NI change:	o	+	+

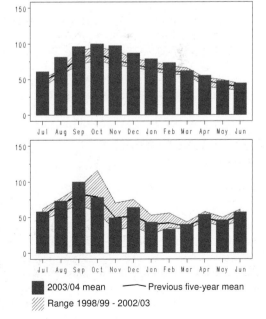

Annual Index
Trend

2003/04 mean   Previous five-year mean
Range 1998/99 - 2002/03

Figure 5.a, Annual indices & trend for Cormorant for GB (above) & NI (below).

Figure 5.b, Monthly indices for Cormorant for GB (above) & NI (below).

Cormorants are a widespread and familiar waterbird throughout the whole of the UK. Traditionally thought of as a coastal bird, Cormorants have increasingly been using inland habitats in recent winters. This is due in part (although not entirely) to an expansion of the more typically freshwater continental race *sinensis*, both as a breeding and non-breeding bird. However, the native *carbo* certainly does occur inland also.

The British maximum of 18,792 was the highest on record, albeit only about 3% higher than in autumn 2002. However, the British annual index showed a much larger increase, also to its highest ever value. Recent work (Baylis *et al.* 2005) has been carried out to clarify the Cormorant index in the early years following its inclusion as a WeBS species, as variable timing of take-up by different counters caused particularly low (and incorrect) index values for 1986/87 and 1987/88. This problem has now been addressed and it has been found most sensible to remove the value for the first of these winters, due to low coverage of Cormorants then, and to correct the value for 1987/88, as shown in the plot above. Clearly, there has been a substantial increase during this period, the British index increasing by 85% during the period 1987/88 to 2003/04. The Northern Ireland maximum was the second highest on record and the annual indices appear to show a generally increasing trend in the province also; the initial decrease is probably an artefact relating to a very small number of sites being involved. However, as with all WeBS species to a greater or lesser degree, it is important to remember that the indices refer only to sites counted for WeBS and not necessarily for the British or Northern Ireland populations as a whole, as many Cormorants occur on sites not counted for the scheme.

In Britain, monthly indices suggest that numbers peaked in September 2003, a month earlier than usual (and earlier than the peak actual count, due to lower coverage in September). January counts were also particularly high compared to previous years but there was then a major decline to February with more typical numbers present from then on. A similar pattern, of an autumn peak and declining numbers from February, was also seen in Northern Ireland.

Only one site, Loughs Neagh and Beg, currently supports internationally important numbers of Cormorant and numbers here remained at a high level. Numbers at Carlingford Lough were possibly higher than shown below but due to a January count of 234 involving unidentified Cormorant/Shag, these were not included in the table below. At the top British site, Morecambe Bay, low numbers were probably more a result of incomplete coverage in the peak month. Individual sites that supported notably high counts included the Tees, Exe, Ribble, Blackwater and Colne Estuaries, Rutland Water and a cluster of west London sites: Wraysbury Gravel Pits, Wraysbury Reservoir, Staines Reservoirs, Queen Mary Reservoir and Queen Elizabeth II Reservoir. Whilst these latter sites may have been sharing birds over different months, there was certainly evidence of an increase in this general area. There were relatively few sites exhibiting sizeable declines, such as those at Abberton Reservoir and the Firths of Clyde and Forth.

	99/00	00/01	01/02	02/03	03/04	Mon	Mean
Sites of international importance in the UK							
Loughs Neagh and Beg	1,643	1,416	722	1,383	1,468	Sep	1,326
Sites of national importance in Great Britain							
Morecambe Bay	1,030	1,223	398	(657)	(539)	Sep	884
Forth Estuary	681	(744)	761	(982)	595	Oct	753
Dee Estuary (England/Wales)	541	864	(692)	668	718	Oct	698
Alt Estuary	574	574	960	569	(456)	Jan	669
Thames Estuary	(437)	(740)	578	722	591	Jan	658
Solway Estuary	(628)	(678)	378	500	(591)	Nov	555
Walthamstow Reservoirs	580	551	(531)	570	505	Jul	552
Tees Estuary	451	647	429	438	773	Aug	548
Abberton Reservoir	600	318	780	600	420	Mar	544
Rutland Water	330	425	520	529	788	Aug	518
Inner Firth of Clyde	466	606	528	553	425	Oct	516
Queen Mary Reservoir	678	112	580	342	768	Nov	496

	99/00	00/01	01/02	02/03	03/04	Mon	Mean	
Poole Harbour	298	338	585	558	(412)	Sep	445	
The Wash	462	401	233	502	449	Sep	409	
Hanningfield Reservoir	539	221	585	189 [35]	411	Oct	389	
North Norfolk Coast	278	294	(268)	581	(276)	Sep	384	
Loch Leven	608	488	421	68	310	Nov	379	
Besthorpe and Girton Gravel Pits	304	(10)	386	415	364	Mar	367	
Ribble Estuary	(163)	219	358	398	(456)	Dec	358	
Dungeness Gravel Pits	344	294	625	235 [35]	251	Feb	350	
Little Paxton Gravel Pits	303 [13]			362 [35]			333	
Wraysbury Gravel Pits	276	264	306	181	607	Nov	327	
Ranworth and Cockshoot Broads	317	298 [12]	398 [12]	270 [12]	324 [12]	Dec	321	
Blackwater Estuary	190	(209)	450	104	473	Jan	304	
Rye Harbour and Pett Level	211	324	218	340	382	Aug	295	
Staines Reservoirs	39	499	77	41	773	Sep	286	▲
Ouse Washes	287 [12]	225 [12]	213 [12]	347	252	Feb	265	
Colne Estuary	(176)	103	(151)	(29)	423	Jan	263	▲
Queen Mother Reservoir	535	360	50	91			259	▲
Pagham Harbour	234	244	247	240	303	Nov	254	▲
Herne Bay		250 [13]					250	
Wraysbury Reservoir	39	59	93	132	899	Sep	244	▲
Lee Valley Gravel Pits	206	220	271	231	286	Dec	243	
Medway Estuary	(271)	220	167	(136)	305	Oct	241	▲
Thorpeness Offshore					239	Dec	239	▲
Rostherne Mere	273	281	31	293	306	Jan	237	▲
Sites no longer meeting table qualifying levels in WeBS-Year 2003/2004								
Grafham Water	212	71	204	349	193	Feb	206	
Sites with mean peak counts of 130 or more birds in Northern Ireland[†]								
Belfast Lough	321	499	528	388	348	Oct	417	
Outer Ards Shoreline	303	121		652	563	Oct	410	
Strangford Lough	285	275	245	358	400	Oct	313	
Carlingford Lough	(209)	(166)	208	206	154	Oct	194	
Dundrum Bay	(90)	(120)	(104)	(124)	(162)	Sep	(162)	
Upper Lough Erne	104	109	199	124	225	Dec	152	
Other sites attaining table qualifying levels in WeBS-Year 2003/2004 in Great Britain								
Exe Estuary	113	140	209	199	415	Oct	215	
William Girling Reservoir	210	60	95	240	400	Aug	201	
Queen Elizabeth II Reservoir	172	90	115	308 [35]	340	Aug	205	
Inner Moray and Inverness Firth	71	88 [1]	90	236	276	Oct	152	
Loch Kindar	64	41	46	3	247	Dec	80	
Tay Estuary	196	165	197	233	236	Oct	205	

[†] *as no All-Ireland threshold has been set a qualifying level of 130 has been chosen to select sites for presentation in this report*

Shag
Phalacrocorax aristotelis

International threshold: 2,400
Great Britain threshold: ?[†]
All-Ireland threshold: ?[†]

GB max: 2,903   Oct
NI max: 434   Jan

The Shag has only recently been added to the list of standard WeBS species, although some counters have recorded them for some time now and the species is also well covered by supplementary surveys such as those around Shetland and in the Moray Firth. Shags are almost entirely restricted to coastal waters, being scarce both inland and far offshore. Globally, the species' distribution is limited with the UK supporting approximately one-third of the total world population. Movements tend to be relatively local although birds from northern Norway and Russia are truly migratory.

In 2003/04, Shags were recorded from 93 different sites during WeBS Core Counts, with further important sites recorded by non-WeBS surveys. There is a clear concentration in the north, particularly Shetland. Overall UK core count numbers peaked in October when 3,183 were noted. Clearly, WeBS only covers a relatively small proportion of the population. The number of Shags wintering around the UK coast is not well known, but likely to be of the order of 100,000 birds. On this basis, the Forth Estuary and South Yell Sound would both be nationally important for the species. Moreover, the counts from the Forth Estuary to date are only just below the level of international importance. Numbers at Carlingford Lough were possibly higher than shown below but due to a January count of 234 involving unidentified Cormorant/Shag, these were not included in the table below.

	99/00	00/01	01/02	02/03	03/04	Mon	Mean
Sites with mean peak counts of 50 or more birds in Great Britain[†]							
Forth Estuary				2,315	(1,664)	Oct	2,315
South Yell Sound	1,419 [10]	1,006 [10]	1,690 [10]	710 [10]	893 [10]	Dec	1,046
Hacosay/Bluemill/Colgrave		301 [10]	1,132 [10]	423 [10]	709 [10]	Feb	559
North-west Yell Sound	561 [10]	620 [10]	495 [10]				559
Scalloway Islands			760 [10]		424 [10]	Dec	480
Burra and Trondra			478 [10]		476 [10]	Dec	465
Moray Firth				636 [1]	413 [1]	Dec	413
West Whalsay and Sounds			383 [10]				383
West Yell			349 [10]				349
North Bressay	198 [10]			53 [10]			326
Widewall Bay				68	580	Dec	324
Kirkabister to Wadbister Ness	100 [10]	355 [10]	73 [10]	172 [10]	778 [10]	Jan	296
Bressay Sound		282 [10]	657 [10]	114 [10]	100 [10]	Jan	285
Kirkabister to Dury Voe		250 [10]					250
East Unst			246 [10]				246
South Havra			428 [10]				244
Quendale to Virkie	360 [10]	98 [10]	605 [10]	123 [10]	176 [10]	Jan	243
South Unst			339 [10]		206 [10]	Feb	203
Anstruther Harbour		4	639	64	8	Oct	179
Inner Firth of Clyde			139	(213)	(159)	Sep	170
South Yell			157 [10]				157
Lunning and Lunna Holm		156 [10]					156
Rova Head to Wadbister Ness	200 [10]	214 [10]	83 [10]	166 [10]	132 [10]	Jan	154
Broadford Bay				150	(100)	Nov	150
Scousburgh to Maywick	144 [10]						144
Linga Beach			133 [13]				133
Whiteness to Skelda Ness	101 [10]	51 [10]	142 [10]	149 [10]	169 [10]	Jan	125
Ayr to North Troon			63	184	(26)	Jan	124
Island of Papa Westray			47	107	210	Mar	121
South-east Yell			120 [10]				120
Arran			86	100	125	Dec	104
Girvan to Turnberry			111	80	117	Dec	103
Thurso Bay					100	Dec	100
Camas Shallachain			90				90
Sullom Voe	81 [10]	62 [10]	50 [10]	106 [10]	104 [10]	Feb	89
Lindisfarne		27 [11]	118 [11]	156 [11]	48 [11]	Nov	87
South Fetlar			84 [10]				84
North Fetlar			79 [10]				79
Loch Ryan		30	(90)	(110)	79	Dec	77
Island of Egilsay				78	62	Jan	70
Hunterston Sands					64	Oct	64
Kingsbridge Estuary			60	47	(72)	Dec	60
Quendale Bay			60 [10]				60
Ardrossan-West Kilbride			53	78	41	Feb	57
Sites with mean peak counts of 50 or more birds in Northern Ireland[†]							
Outer Ards Shoreline				227	187	Jan	207
Strangford Lough	44 [11]	17 [11]	166	193	226	Jan	129
Carlingford Lough			294	48	37	Mar	126
Belfast Lough		39 [11]	30 [11]	215	194 [11]	Dec	120

[†] as no British or All-Ireland thresholds have been set a qualifying level of 50 has been chosen to select sites for presentation in this report

Bittern
Botaurus stellaris

International threshold:	65	
Great Britain threshold:	?	
All-Ireland threshold:	?	

GB max: 36   Jan
NI max: 0

In line with the improving fortunes of the British breeding population, it was another good year for Bitterns, which were recorded from a total of 45 different sites during 2003/04. Despite above average temperatures, peak numbers were in the winter, especially January when 36 birds were found. Most summer records referred to booming birds at known breeding sites, with up to eight recorded for Minsmere, from which site relatively few were reported in the winter months, although this could be due to problems of detection. No Bitterns have ever been recorded by WeBS in Northern Ireland.

Little Egret
Egretta garzetta

International threshold:	1,300	
Great Britain threshold:	?[†]	
All-Ireland threshold:	?[†]	

GB max: 2,777 Sep
NI max: 1 Jan

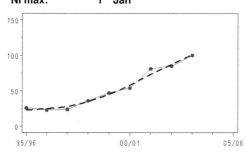

Figure 6.a, Annual indices & trend for Little Egret for GB.

The Little Egret continues to go from strength to strength. The plot of the British index, published here for the first time, shows the phenomenal rate of increase for a species still on the British Birds Rarities Committee list until the end of 1990. A review of the status of the species (Musgrove 2002) estimated the 1999 post-breeding population to be of the order of 1,700 birds, over 50% more than the peak WeBS core count total that year. Since then, autumn peaks from core counts have increased by a factor of 2.7 and thus if such a scaling factor still holds true there may actually have been closer to 4,400 Little Egrets present in the UK in autumn 2003. Whilst this is an approximate calculation, and the underlying assumptions could be questioned, continued evidence of the discrepancies between core counts and dedicated roost counts at sites such as the Medway Estuary, where a roost of 413 compared with a core count total of 101 in September 2003, shows that this is a species which can still be easy to overlook. A recent review by Voisin *et al.* (2005) showed that over 8,000 Little Egrets were present in western France in January 2001.

Unsurprisingly, many individual sites exhibited increases over previous years. Whilst the species is still common in its previous core areas of the Solent, Poole and the southwest peninsula, there are a number of sites here where numbers seem to have levelled out and much of the national increase is fuelled by the extremities of the British range, notably around the 'greater Thames', along the east coast of Essex, Suffolk and Norfolk, around the North Norfolk Coast and into the Wash. On the west coast, the Dyfi Estuary, Lavan Sands and the Dee Estuary also hold increased numbers. The cut-off beyond the Dee and the Wash is, however, striking. Counts have yet to exceed three birds on the Humber Estuary or two birds on the Ribble Estuary. Whether this remains the northwards limit for the Little Egret or whether it will continue to push northwards remains to be seen. The species also remains scarce on WeBS counts in Scotland and Northern Ireland.

	99/00	00/01	01/02	02/03	03/04	Mon	Mean
Sites with mean peak counts of 10 or more birds in Great Britain[†]							
Medway Estuary	(71)	(19)	106	(125)	413 [12]	Sep	260
Chichester Harbour	271 [12]	220 [12]	255 [12]	218	228	Oct	238
Thames Estuary	(30)	83	132	197	255 [12]	Aug	167
Poole Harbour	156 [20]	118	197 [12]	(140)	(179)	Sep	163
Tamar Complex	143 [22]	121	141	129	143	Sep	135
Longueville Marsh	(70)	(85)	132	145	105	Oct	127
Portsmouth Harbour	(51)	64	123 [12]	12 [110]	(34)	Sep	99
Exe Estuary	58	71	149	67	131	Sep	95
Jersey Shore		64	126				95
Kingsbridge Estuary	58	72	100	105	(99)	Sep	87
North Norfolk Coast	8	15 [12]	50 [11]	81	149 [12]	Nov	86
Burry Inlet	(86)	58	99	87	(90)	Sep	84
Langstone Harbour	51	51	99	88	90	Oct	76
Pagham Harbour	51 [20]	76	81 [12]	76	63	Aug	69
Taw-Torridge Estuary	77 [20]	71	64	60	(74)	Aug	69
Camel Estuary	55 [20]	(77)	48	64	65	Sep	62
Colne Estuary	27 [12]	26	118 [12]	(2)	(35)	Sep	57
Swale Estuary	10 [20]	22	44	(59)	131	Oct	53
Fowey Estuary	40 [20]	49	79	48	35	Sep	50
Fal Complex	(34)	39	(30)	55	52	Jul	49
R. Avon: Salisbury-Fordingbridge	(20)	(38)	49	(79)	19	Oct	46
Guernsey Shore	31	46	50	(48)	(51)	Sep	45
Cleddau Estuary	(17)	25	66	48	36	Sep	44
North West Solent	45 [20]	(30)	(44)	(25)	42	Sep	44
Severn Estuary	(10)	13	59	41	47	Sep	40
Southampton Water	(11)	25	45 [12]	(19)	(51)	Sep	40
Newtown Estuary	46 [20]	38	44 [12]	22	41	Sep	38
Orwell Estuary	(0)	11 [12]	43 [12]	12 [37]	56 [12]	Aug	37
Helford Estuary	(24)	30	33	47	35	Sep	36
Blackwater Estuary	4	15	(35)	(51)	66	Sep	34
Fleet and Wey	30	37	37	38	25	Sep	33
Lavan Sands	(4)	(6)	6	15	67	Sep	29
Avon Estuary	20 [20]	21	33 [12]	24	35	Aug	27
Stour Estuary	5	10	29	32	57	Sep	27
The Wash	2	5	(6)	29	72	Oct	27
Crouch-Roach Estuary	4	15	24	42	43	Sep	26
R. Avon: R'gwood - Christchurch	(12)	26	(28)	26	22	Jan	26
Christchurch Harbour	9	(20)	24	21	38	Sep	23
Hamford Water	2	9	31	20	53	Sep	23
Teign Estuary	30 [20]	25	16	31	15	Sep	23
Beaulieu Estuary	(7)	19	6	42	22	Oct	22
Erme Estuary	26 [20]	17	32	14	(18)	Dec	22
Axe Estuary (Devon)	6	10	35	24	32	Jan	21
Cuckmere Estuary	7	15	12	27	41	Oct	20
Alde Complex	(4)	(12)	15	20	(23)	Nov	19
Allington Gravel Pit	0	0	21 [12]	12 [37]	35 [12]	Jan	19
Dee Estuary (England/Wales)	(5)	7	18 [11]	20	32 [12]	Nov	19
Pegwell Bay	7	17	20	23	26	Aug	19
Rye Harbour and Pett Level	16 [20]	9	25	19	27	Aug	19
Dart Estuary	6	12	9	20	44	Sep	18
Yar Estuary	10	19	44 [12]	12	5	Jul	18
Yealm Estuary	16	9	19	25	18	Aug	17
Brading Harbour	3	9	15	26	23	Oct	15
Dengie Flats	3	3	18 [11]	15	(27)	Sep	13
Hayle Estuary	13	13	12	12	15	Jul	13
Bardolf Water Meadows	6	9	10	22	11	Nov	12
Carmarthen Bay	4	(7)	13	9	23	Feb	12
Looe Estuary	(9)	9	5	13	19	Jul	12
Somerset Levels	1	2	14	26	(12)	Jan	11
Breydon Water / Berney Marshes	2	2	7	19	20	Jul	10
Dyfi Estuary	(2)	6	5	10	20	Jan	10

[†] *as no British or All-Ireland thresholds have been set a qualifying level of 10 has been chosen to select sites for presentation in this report*

Great White Egret
Ardea alba

Vagrant
Native Range: S Europe, Africa, Asia and N & C America

GB max: 1   Aug
NI max: 0

Singles were recorded at Rutland Water in August and September, Drakelow Gravel Pit in October and on the Humber Estuary in November.

Grey Heron
Ardea cinerea

International threshold:	**2,700**
Great Britain threshold:	**?[†]**
All-Ireland threshold:	**?[†]**

GB max: 4,496   Sep
NI max: 450   Oct

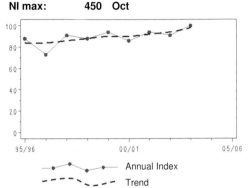

Annual Index
- - - - Trend

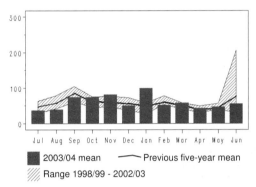

■ 2003/04 mean   ⌢ Previous five-year mean
▨ Range 1998/99 - 2002/03

Figure 7.a, Annual indices & trend for Grey Heron for GB.

Figure 7.b, Monthly indices for Grey Heron for GB.

Grey Herons are widely distributed waterbirds, generally occurring in low numbers at any given site. As a result, for many of the sites holding larger numbers this is principally a function of their larger size. Although the majority of UK Grey Herons are rather sedentary, some dispersal does occur and in the winter as resident birds are joined by immigrants from northern Europe.

The 2003/04 peak core count total in Britain was the highest yet recorded by WeBS; the annual trend suggests a small rise over the last decade. The Northern Ireland peak also remained at a relatively high level, following an increasing trend in the late 1990s. As would be expected for a largely resident species, the monthly indices suggest relative stability throughout the year.

In line with the small overall increase, there were no spectacular rises in numbers at individual sites but higher numbers than usual at several sites including the Forth Estuary and Cromarty Firth. Lower than usual peaks were noted from Hanningfield Reservoir, Walthamstow Reservoirs and the Ouse Washes. Numbers at the two key Northern Ireland sites remained stable.

	99/00	00/01	01/02	02/03	03/04	Mon	Mean
Sites with mean peak counts of 50 or more birds in Great Britain[†]							
R. Avon: Salisbury-Fordingbridge	(102)	326	(100)	(83)	(150)	Oct	326
Somerset Levels	143	148	125	134	(130)	Feb	138
Thames Estuary	(118)	145	(129)	124	(94)	Aug	135
Dee Estuary (England/Wales)	80	124	63 [11]	(111)	87	Sep	93
Walthamstow Reservoirs	44	117	91	133	56	Feb	88
Inner Firth of Clyde	93 [11]	81	90	87	81	Sep	86
Severn Estuary	(51)	(67)	69	104 [11]	73	Sep	82
Morecambe Bay	88	69	51	101	91	Aug	80
Ouse Washes	61	70 [13]	100	104 [13]	55	Feb	78
Taw-Torridge Estuary	78	69	(20)	(41)	77	Aug	75
Coombe Country Park	11			159	37	Feb	69
Colne Valley Gravel Pits	(25)	(21)	(36)	(33)	68	Mar	68
Tees Estuary	57	83	58	66	63	Aug	65
The Wash	91	56	49	54	76	Aug	65
Humber Estuary	85	(40)	(31)	43	(39)	Nov	64

	99/00	00/01	01/02	02/03	03/04	Mon	Mean
Inner Moray and Inverness Firth	48	44	56	91	67	Oct	61
Montrose Basin	83	87	55	24	54	Sep	61
Whinney Loch	61						61
Forth Estuary	46	59	47	62	78 [11]	Dec	58
Durham Coast	60	63	60	41	41	Mar	53
North Norfolk Coast	75	51	39	47	(38)	Oct	53
Ribble Estuary	88	(48)	27	40	(31)	Sep	52
Hanningfield Reservoir	137	57	20	21	18	Sep	51
Solway Estuary	63	(48)	28 [11]	(69)	(49)	Oct	51
Cromarty Firth	45	41	48	44	73	Oct	50
Poole Harbour	50	49	50	49	(47)	Sep	50
Sites with mean peak counts of 50 or more birds in Northern Ireland[†]							
Loughs Neagh and Beg	269	267	87	225	208	Sep	211
Strangford Lough	96	92	113	103	102	Oct	101

[†] as no British or All-Ireland thresholds have been set a qualifying level of 50 has been chosen to select sites for presentation in this report

Purple Heron
Ardea purpurea

Scarce

GB max: 1   Aug
NI max: 0

One was recorded at Ormesby Reservoir in August.

White Stork
Ciconia ciconia

Vagrant and escape
Native Range: Europe, Africa and Asia

GB max: 3   Mar
NI max: 0

The usual free-flying White Storks of Harewood Lake were noted there throughout the year, the maximum being three in March.

Glossy Ibis
Plegadis falcinellus

Vagrant
Native Range: S Europe, Africa, Asia, Australia and N & C America

GB max: 1   May
NI max: 0

The long-staying and well-watched bird remained on the Exe Estuary, being noted in six months between May 2003 and March 2004; this bird was originally recorded on the November 2002 WeBS count.

Sacred Ibis
Threskiornis aethiopicus

Escape
Native Range: Africa and Middle East

GB max: 1   Apr
NI max: 0

One was recorded every month at Outwood Swan Sanctuary, where this species was also noted back during the 1998/99 winter, presumably the same individual. Whilst most likely a local escape, the increasing naturalised population in western France is also a potential source.

Spoonbill
Platalea leucorodia

International threshold: 100

GB max: 10   May
NI max: 0

Spoonbills were recorded from 14 sites in 2003/04, with a peak of 10 in May and up to five birds throughout the winter months. The Exe Estuary was the most reliable site for this species in 2003/04, with records from nine months.

Sites with two or more birds in 2003/04

Benacre Broad	4	Oct
Exe Estuary	4	Apr
Poole Harbour	3	Feb
Taw-Torridge Estuary	3	Dec
Beaulieu Estuary	2	May
Humber Estuary	2	Jun
Otter Estuary	2	May

Greater Flamingo
Phoenicopterus ruber

Escape
Native Range: S Europe, Africa and C America

GB max: 1   Jan
NI max: 0

One was recorded at Mersea Island on the Colne Estuary in January and March.

Fulvous Whistling Duck
Dendrocygna bicolor

Escape
Native Range: C & S America, Africa and S Asia

GB max: 2   Feb
NI max: 0

One was at Walland Marsh from April to June, one at Godmanchester Gravel Pit in September and two were at Chichester Harbour in February.

Lesser Whistling Duck
Dendrocygna javanica

Escape
Native Range: S & E Asia

GB max: 1   Apr
NI max: 0

One was recorded at Bittell Reservoirs in April.

Mute Swan
Cygnus olor

International threshold (British population):	380
International threshold (Irish population):	100

GB max: 20,299   Oct
NI max: 1,819   Dec

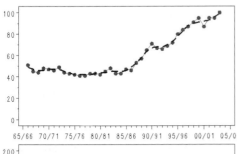

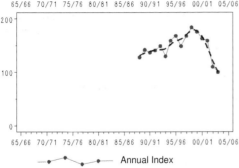

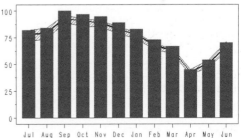

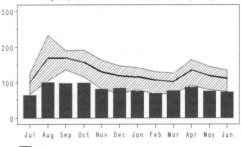

Figure 8.a, Annual indices & trend for Mute Swan for GB (above) & NI (below).

Figure 8.b, Monthly indices for Mute Swan for GB (above) & NI (below).

57

Mute Swans are widespread, being found in a variety of wetland habitats and showing tolerance to human activity. The majority of birds are thought to be sedentary although post-natal dispersal and winter movements, mainly southwest or towards coastal regions, are common.

Although British and Northern Irish maxima were both comparable to previous years, very different patterns were evident in annual indices. The British index rose 5% to its highest ever level, whilst in contrast the fifth consecutive decline in the Northern Irish indices equates to current values being almost half of those five years ago. Furthermore, monthly indices were below the range of the previous five years in all months except

December, February and March, although these still failed to reach average levels. Conversely, British monthly indices peaked above average throughout the year.

Counts at Lough Neagh and Beg were well below average for the site, although the five-year mean for the site still exceeds any other in the UK. The Fleet and Wey remained the top site in Britain with the 2003/04 peak over 20% higher than that for any other site. As during 2002/03 current counts for Abberton Reservoir exceeded the international qualifying threshold levels, however, mean values fell to just below this level. The second year of below average counts recorded at Lough Foyle have resulted in a mean peak below the international qualifying threshold.

	99/00	00/01	01/02	02/03	03/04	Mon	Mean
Sites of international importance in the UK							
Loughs Neagh and Beg	1,887	1,931	1,346	1,391	920	Sep	1,495
Fleet and Wey	1,177	1,150	1,228	1,368	1,092	Oct	1,203
Somerset Levels	(1,011)	(1,110)	(1,121)	(1,039)	(883)	Dec	(1,121)
Ouse Washes	662	726 [13]	1,110 [13]	782 [13]	530 [13]	Jan	762
Loch of Harray	(495)	597	597	672	522	Feb	597
Rutland Water	617	547	590	594	542	Jul	578
Loch Leven	406	496	506	550	526	Sep	497
Tweed Estuary	580	575	464 [13]	414	446	Jul	496
R. Avon: Salisbury-Fordingbridge	(263)	(395)	(229)	(162)	(311)	Oct	(395)
Hornsea Mere	364	346	217	486	527 [13]	Aug	388 ▲
Upper Lough Erne	328	445	306	323	272	Dec	335
Lower Lough Erne				199	(286)	Dec	243
Strangford Lough	225	174	183	180	193	Oct	191
Broad Water Canal		113	77	172	152	Oct	129
Sites no longer meeting table qualifying levels in WeBS-Year 2003/2004							
Lough Foyle	115	98	101	77	66	Jan	91
Other sites attaining table qualifying levels in WeBS-Year 2003/2004 in Great Britain							
Loch Bee (South Uist)	341	343	200	297	407	Aug	318
Abberton Reservoir	520	328	187	387	379	Aug	360 ▼
Other sites attaining table qualifying levels in WeBS-Year 2003/2004 in Northern Ireland							
Upper Quoile River	88	32	117	(71)	108	Oct	86

Black Swan
Cygnus atratus

Escape
Native Range: Australia

GB max: 49   Nov
NI max: 0

The GB maximum count of 49 was similar to that recorded by WeBS in recent years. None were noted in Northern Ireland. The species was recorded from a total of 73 sites, slightly up on recent years, as was the summed site maxima of 128. Twelve sites held three or more birds, compared to eight and 10 in the previous two years. Overall, this suggests consolidation or stabilisation of this relatively regular escape/feral bird.

Sites with three or more birds in 2003/04

Woburn Park Lakes	8	Sep
Walthamstow Reservoirs	6	May
Nene Washes	4	Jan
R.Kennet: R'bury-Chilton Foliat	4	Jun
Abberton Reservoir	3	Apr
Cassington & Yarnton GPs	3	Oct
Dungeness Gravel Pits	3	Jan
Fleet and Wey	3	Aug
Hill Ridware Lake	3	Nov
King George V Reservoirs	3	Oct
Mersey Estuary	3	Sep
R. Cam: Owlstone - Baits Bite	3	Oct

Bewick's Swan
Cygnus columbianus

GB max:	6,691	Jan
NI max:	32	Jan
% young: 7.9		

International threshold (*bewickii*): 290
Great Britain threshold: 81
All-Ireland threshold: 25*

	S	M	L
GB change:	--	--	--
NI change:	--	--	--

50 is normally used as a minimum threshold

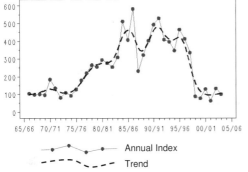

Annual Index
Trend

Figure 9.a, Annual indices & trend for Bewick's Swan for GB.

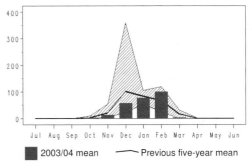

2003/04 mean — Previous five-year mean
Range 1998/99 - 2002/03

Figure 9.b, Monthly indices for Bewick's Swan for GB.

Bewick's Swans breed across the far northern tundra of Russia, the western population, which breed on the Kanin Peninsula, migrate southwest in the autumn to winter mainly in Britain and the Netherlands.

Peak GB numbers in 2003/04 were slightly higher than the previous year, although the total is heavily influenced by roost counts from a single site, the Ouse Washes. A high roost count early in January at the Ouse Washes (in fact, the highest single site total ever recorded in the UK), although not synchronised with WeBS Core Counts elsewhere in Britain, perhaps suggests that the true peak was even higher, perhaps about 7,000. The annual indices suggest that numbers remain low but are similar to the last few years; the indices are, however, based on core counts alone and so may well be somewhat unrepresentative. Productivity was low during the summer of 2003, with 7.9% young being the lowest since 1997.

Elsewhere, numbers of birds using the Nene Washes, Severn Estuary and Martin Mere appeared to be similar to recent winters, whilst counts at Breydon Water, St Benet's Levels and Walmore Common were higher than their recent averages.

Whilst the peak count in Northern Ireland was higher than during the two previous winters, it was still extremely small compared to the early 1990s, when a peak count of 805 was recorded. There remains uncertainty as to whether overall numbers of this population have declined, or whether birds have redistributed and are mostly wintering further east, closer to the breeding grounds. An international census carried out in early 2005 should help to provide answers.

A bird identified as being of the nominate race, known as Whistling Swan, was present at Gadloch between April and October, with presumably the same bird also recorded from nearby Bridgend Farm Pool in May.

	99/00	00/01	01/02	02/03	03/04	Mon	Mean
Sites of international importance in the UK							
Ouse Washes	5,649 [8]	4,693 [12]	5,735 [8]	5,177 [8]	6,330 [8]	Dec	5,517
Nene Washes	327	1,100	347 [12]	1,068	790	Feb	726
Sites of national importance in Great Britain							
Severn Estuary	216 [8]	272 [8]	310 [8]	345 [8]	230	Jan	275
Martin Mere and Ribble Estuary	163 [8]	322 [8]	296 [8]	315	221	Jan	263
St Benet's Levels	209	(206)	147	287	280	Jan	231
Breydon Water / Berney Marshes	132	186	85	240	220	Feb	173
Old Romney	160 [8]				184 [13]	Jan	172
Somerset Levels	(117)	(146)	(108)	(69)	(112)	Jan	(146)
Confidential SE England Site	64	10	180	220	148	Jan	124
Dee Estuary (England/Wales)	56 [8]	(118)	(78)	(70)	(92)	Feb	83 ▲

	99/00	00/01	01/02	02/03	03/04	Mon	Mean
Sites of all-Ireland importance in Northern Ireland							
Loughs Neagh and Beg	16	102	19	6	5	Dec	30
Sites no longer meeting table qualifying levels in WeBS-Year 2003/2004							
Medway Estuary	(42)	(0)	(0)	(0)	(0)		(42)
Other sites attaining table qualifying levels in WeBS-Year 2003/2004 in Great Britain							
Walmore Common	41 [8]	7	51	99	95	Feb	59
Other sites attaining table qualifying levels in WeBS-Year 2003/2004 in Northern Ireland							
Lough Foyle	6 [8]	10	12	8	27	Jan	13

Whooper Swan
Cygnus cygnus

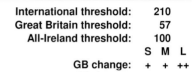

International threshold:		210
Great Britain threshold:		57
All-Ireland threshold:		100

		S	M	L
GB max:	7,558 Jan			
NI max:	2,321 Jan			
% young: 14.9				
	GB change:	+	+	++
	NI change:	o	+	o

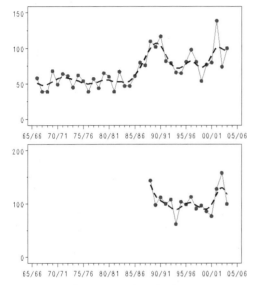

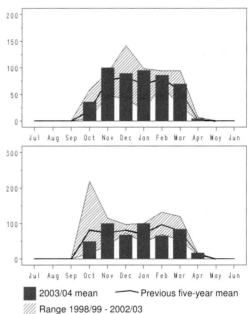

— Annual Index
- - - - Trend

■ 2003/04 mean ⌒ Previous five-year mean
/// Range 1998/99 - 2002/03

Figure 10.a, Annual indices & trend for Whooper Swan for GB (above) & NI (below).

Figure 10.b, Monthly indices for Whooper Swan for GB (above) & NI (below).

Almost the entire Icelandic breeding population of Whooper Swan winters in Britain and Ireland, although significant numbers remain in Iceland and small numbers continue on to the Netherlands, Denmark and southern Scandinavia (Brazil, 2003). With the UK regularly hosting the majority of this population it is unsurprising that a total of nine sites held internationally and a further 29 nationally important numbers in the five years up to 2003/04.

The Ouse Washes and Martin Mere/Ribble Estuary remained the only sites outside Northern Ireland or Scotland to hold internationally important numbers; and while peak numbers at the latter were lower than those of the past three years supplementary counts at the Ouse Washes helped boost the 2003/04 peak. This trend was reflected across sites of international importance that, with the exception of Loch of Strathbeg, all held peak numbers below average. The five-year mean for Black Cart Water fell below the international qualifying level, while in contrast, mean peaks at four sites Lindisfarne, Loch Connell, Barons Folly and Clatto Reservoir each surpassed 57 birds.

Stark differences were also evident at the national level with the Northern Irish index falling and that of Britain rising. Following its highest ever peak in 2002/03 the Northern Irish index fell by over a third, however, numbers remain comparable to those of the past decade. Conversely, the British rose by a third contributing to the increase witnessed over the past 20 years.

Previous *Wildfowl and Wader Counts* have suggested the possibility of winter movements between Britain and Northern Ireland. However, with November and January counts above average in both Britain and Northern Ireland, and December counts below average, no evidence of this interchange was seen during 2003/04. The overall productivity of 14.9% was similar to that of 2002/03.

	99/00	00/01	01/02	02/03	03/04	Mon	Mean
Sites of international importance in the UK							
Ouse Washes	2,120 [12]	1,797 [8]	2,894 [8]	2,745 [12]	3,624 [8]	Jan	2,636
Martin Mere and Ribble Estuary	1,335 [8]	1,650	1,762 [8]	1,770 [8]	1,597	Dec	1,623
Loughs Neagh and Beg	(641)	(735)	(1,532)	1,514	867	Jan	1,304
Lough Foyle	657	434	548	3,284	680	Nov	1,121
Upper Lough Erne	985	1,010	1,228 [13]	658	855	Dec	947
Loch of Strathbeg	262	424	(223)	(67)	794	Nov	493
Solway Estuary	223 [8]	466 [8]	(309)	340 [8]	(188)	Nov	343
R. Clyde: Carstairs - Thankerton	393	142	242	(101)	91	Feb	217
Black Cart Water	187 [3]	299	238 [3]	176 [3]	151 [3]	Mar	210
Sites of national importance in Great Britain							
Loch Eye and Cromarty	180 [8]	(39)	230	141	322	Oct	205
Nene Washes	9	111	110 [12]	663 [12]	111	Feb	201
Loch of Wester	45	(86)	341				193
Wigtown Bay	134	(110)	156	(135)	255	Mar	182
Lower Teviot Valley	(12)	(179)	(50)	(29)			(179)
R. Nith: Keltonbank to Nunholm	(146)	131	125	(108)	165	Feb	142
Killimster Loch			135				135
Ravenstruther		347		0	48	Mar	132
Loch a` Phuill (Tiree)	142	36		168	118	Nov	116
Dornoch Firth	84	307	53 [11]	23	94	Oct	112
Loch Insh and Spey Marshes	125 [13]	96	92	91			101
Caistron Quarry		71	71	67	164	Dec	93
Loch of Lintrathen	68	96	10	166	93	Jan	87
Inner Moray and Inverness Firth	17	1	173	60	165	Feb	83
Vasa Loch Shapinsay				68	96	Nov	82
Lower Derwent Ings	81						81
Forth Estuary	(20)	(95)	(20)	(24)	62 [11]	Feb	79
Milldam and Balfour Mains Pools	53 [13]	112	98	41	86	Jan	78
R. Tweed: Kelso to Coldstream	50	47	60	116	109	Dec	76
Warkworth Lane Ponds	113 [8]	62	25	128	47	Mar	75
Threave Estate	(117)	74	21				71
Lindisfarne	47	45 [11]	15	(90)	(139)	Mar	67 ▲
Loch Leven	144	144	0	13	19	Dec	64
Loch of Spiggie	24	73	47	86	89	Nov	64
Loch Connell	63						63 ▲
Kinnordy Loch	17		116	82	35	Feb	63
Barons Folly	71	107	3	4	126	Jan	62 ▲
Clatto Reservoir	52	108	62	10	58	Nov	58 ▲
Sites of all-Ireland importance in Northern Ireland							
Strangford Lough	177	220 [11]	212	191	150	Jan	190
Other sites attaining table qualifying levels in WeBS-Year 2003/2004 in Great Britain							
Tyninghame Estuary	76 [8]	15	49	3	135	Feb	56
Loch Moraig	37	15	12	20	121	Nov	41
St Benet`s Levels	27	(26)	6	58	108	Jan	50
Douglas Estate Ponds	13	30	21	22	100	Nov	37
Fergus Loch	32	31	38	36	73	Nov	42
Wilkhaven to Rockfield	70	1	60	0	70	Feb	40
Martnaham Loch	1	34	37	32	67	Dec	34

Chinese Goose
Anser cygnoides

Escape
Native Range: E Asia

GB max: 11   Oct
NI max: 0

Chinese Geese (the domestic equivalent of the Swan Goose) were reported from seven sites during 2003/04, far fewer than in previous years. Singles were at Eccup Reservoir, Little Weighton Pond, Nafferton Mere and Torside Reservoir, two were at Dagenham Chase Gravel Pit, up to three were present all year at Harrow Lodge Park and up to seven were counted throughout the year at Diss Mere. The regular birds at both Etherow Country Park and Esthwaite Water have been absent from WeBS counts since winter 2002/03.

Bean Goose
Anser fabalis

International threshold (*fabalis*):   1,000
Great Britain threshold: 4*
All-Ireland threshold: +

GB max: 149   Jan
NI max: 2   Jan

*50 is normally used as a minimum threshold

Bean Geese are an extremely local wintering species in the UK with only two regular flocks occurring, both involving the nominate Taiga Bean Goose. There are a few records from other, mostly southeasterly sites, each year, these sporadic sightings generally attributable to the smaller Tundra Bean Goose (*rossicus*).

For the second year running, the Slamannan Plateau area south of Falkirk again held the highest numbers of Bean Geese in the country and, indeed, exceeded any other recent previous Bean Goose site totals outside Norfolk. As seen previously, the Slammanan peak was in October, well before the usual later arrival of the Norfolk flock. Numbers around Cantley in the Yare Valley of east Norfolk were low again this year, indeed the lowest for many years. A single Tundra Bean Goose was recorded among the flock at Buckenham Marshes in November and another was at North Warren and Thorpeness Mere in December.

Away from these two key locations, there was a scattering of records as usual. The Ouse Washes remains the only other site at which Bean Geese have been recorded during every winter of the last five, whilst Dungeness Gravel Pits and the Humber Estuary also had return visits in 2003/04. Away from the east, however, records from the Severn/Vyrnwy confluence (12 in February), Balnakeil Bay (5 in March) and two at Lough Foyle in January were particularly noteworthy; the latter being the second WeBS record in Northern Ireland, following one at the same location in October 1997.

	99/00	00/01	01/02	02/03	03/04	Mon	Mean
Sites of national importance in Great Britain							
Middle Yare Marshes	227 [5]	276	272 [5]	183 [5]	140	Jan	220
Slamannan Area	188 [4]	187	192 [4]	231 [4]	235 [4]	Oct	207
Fleet and Wey	0	(0)	(26)	6	0		8
Medway Estuary	(7)						(7)
Lower Derwent Ings	7						7
Ouse Washes	9	4 [12]	4 [13]	8 [13]	4	Dec	6
Balnakeil Bay Durness					5 [13]	Mar	5 ▲
Other sites attaining table qualifying levels in WeBS-Year 2003/2004 in Great Britain							
Dungeness Gravel Pits	0	0	0	7	7	Jan	3
Severn Vyrnwy Confluence	0	0	0	0	(12)	Feb	2
Tophill Low Reservoirs	0	0	0	0	6	Nov	1

Pink-footed Goose
Anser brachyrhynchus

International threshold: 2,400
Great Britain threshold: 2,400
All-Ireland threshold: +

GB max: 274,594 Nov
NI max: 3 Oct
% young: 19   Brood size: 2.2

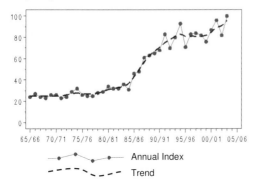

Figure 11.a, Annual indices & trend for Pink-footed Goose for GB.

Apart from a smaller population breeding on Svalbard and wintering on the near-continent, most of the world's Pink-footed Geese breed in Iceland and Greenland and then make their way to Britain for the winter. Birds arrive in northern Scotland from late September, and filter their way south through traditional areas elsewhere in Scotland and northern England, especially Lancashire, and make their way as far south as Norfolk. Despite the numbers of birds involved, Pink-footed Geese remain scarce in Northern Ireland, Wales and most of central and southern England.

The British maximum count of 274,954 was obtained during dedicated roost counts in November, by which month over 50% of this total was in England; compared to about 30% during similar counts in October. The census total was the highest yet recorded, albeit similar to that of two years ago, and supports the notion put forward in the previous *Wildfowl and Wader Counts* that the autumn 2002 census total was probably unreliably low. Such roost counts are required as many geese disperse over farmland away from usual core count sites at the time that core counts are usually carried out. However, nearly 150,000 Pink-footed Geese were counted during core counts in October. Productivity, which is rather consistent between years, compared to some other goose populations, was slightly higher than average in autumn 2003 (19%

young and mean brood size 2.2), which will have helped contribute to the record census total.

As shown in the sites table, numbers at Scolt Head have continued to increase, peak counts doubling there in the past two years. In the last *Wildfowl and Wader Counts* it was pointed out that the count there of 62,500 was the highest ever single site count; this has now risen by a further 28% in the course of a single year. Scolt may have benefited at the expense of Snettisham, where the peak count fell by 26%. The peak numbers using Holkham also increased by a large amount, whilst proportionally even larger increases were seen at Horsey Mere in December then at Breydon Water in January, the most southerly regular site. Pink-footed Geese from this roost are now regularly feeding in Suffolk as well as Norfolk during the day and it remains to be seen how far south this species will go over the coming years. Proposed reforms of the subsidy regime for sugar beet from the Common Agricultural Policy may have a significant impact on this species in East Anglia. The monthly differences in peaks between Norfolk roosts suggest a great deal of interchange between the network of sites, backed up by daytime observations of movements throughout the winter in the county.

Further north, the arrival of a flock of 66,000 birds at Loch of Strathbeg as early as September was exceptional, whilst numbers at West Water Reservoir also peaked this early in the autumn with another good showing. The number of birds roosting at Findhorn Bay has increased massively over five years and Loch Spynie has maintained recent increased numbers. Other sites with relatively high numbers included Wigtown Bay and Holburn Moss, but Montrose Basin and the Tay Estuary supported lower counts than normal. The small number of birds recorded in Northern Ireland, from Lough Foyle and the Outer Ards, was typical for the province.

	99/00	00/01	01/02	02/03	03/04	Mon	Mean
Sites of international importance in the UK							
Scolt Head	35,180 [14]	41,000 [14]	33,900 [14]	62,500 [14]	80,000 [12]	Dec	50,516
Loch of Strathbeg	31,031	42,615 [14]	46,898 [14]	39,900	66,000 [14]	Sep	45,289
Holkham Bay	31,190 [14]	33,750 [14]	45,000 [14]	33,800 [14]	47,750 [14]	Nov	38,298
West Water Reservoir	28,000 [14]	26,500 [14]	23,270 [14]	(40,000) [14]	34,210 [14]	Sep	30,396
Southwest Lancashire	29,955 [14]	16,885 [14]	33,180 [14]	31,645 [14]	27,025 [14]	Oct	27,738
Snettisham	19,450 [14]	18,250 [14]	35,000 [14]	37,050 [14]	27,350 [14]	Dec	27,420
Montrose Basin	18,480 [14]	29,922 [14]	38,669 [14]	11,500 [14]	10,149 [14]	Nov	21,744
Ythan Estuary & Slains Lochs	15,500 [14]	23,500 [14]	13,900 [14]	19,600 [14]	19,200 [14]	Oct	18,340
Dupplin Lochs	22,800 [14]	15,530 [14]	17,500 [14]	9,500 [14]	14,100 [14]	Oct	15,886
Aberlady Bay	4,840 [14]	16,750 [14]	13,740 [14]	22,200 [14]	15,040 [14]	Oct	14,514
Loch Leven	11,540 [14]	14,700 [14]	16,200 [14]	(12,874) [14]	15,120 [14]	Oct	14,390
Carsebreck and Rhynd Lochs	15,400 [14]	16,500 [14]	14,500 [14]	10,320 [14]	11,450 [14]	Feb	13,634
Loch of Skene	(60) [14]	13,550 [12]	13,175 [14]	(8,420) [14]	(8,500) [14]	Oct	13,363
Hule Moss	19,100 [13]	14,700 [14]	8,600 [14]	5,850 [14]	14,200 [13]	Oct	12,490
Findhorn Bay	750 [14]	5,500 [14]	14,000 [14]		25,000 [14]	Oct	11,313
Morecambe Bay	2,347	7,143	14,100 [14]	14,600 [6]	17,050 [14]	Jan	11,048
Loch Spynie	1,000 [14]	8,000 [14]	9,100 [14]	11,700 [14]	11,100 [14]	Nov	8,180
Breydon Water / Berney Marshes	6,600	5,500 [14]	4,380	7,100	17,100	Jan	8,136
Loch of Lintrathen	10,400 [14]	2,220 [14]	5,920 [14]	(6,440) [14]	11,100 [14]	Oct	7,410
Cameron Reservoir	3,168 [14]	5,000	15,823	3,000	8,900 [14]	Nov	7,178
R. Clyde: Carstairs – Thankerton	5,650	(4,850)	11,000	3,350	5,300	Oct	6,325
Solway Estuary	6,434 [14]	2,541 [14]	(5,550)	(4,075)	(10,133)	Mar	6,165
Tay Estuary	4,630 [14]	8,930 [14]	11,385 [14]	2,700 [14]	2,425 [14]	Oct	6,014
Fala Flow	7,550 [14]	4,910 [14]	7,500 [14]	2,790 [14]	5,450 [14]	Sep	5,640
Loch Eye & Cromarty Firth	12,000 [13]	126 [14]	367 [14]	14,050 [14]	546	Dec	5,418
Wigtown Bay	6,459	50	5,316 [14]	(4,747)	8,662 [14]	Mar	5,122
Holbeach St Matthew	(1,700) [14]	(5,000) [14]					(5,000)
Humber Estuary	2,410 [14]	(2,700) [14]	4,300 [14]	4,620 [14]	6,562	Dec	4,473
Horsey Mere	1,027	3,620 [14]	(5,000) [14]	4,000 [14]	8,200 [14]	Dec	4,369
Strathearn (West)				4,100 [14]			4,100
Loch Tullybelton		4,050 [14]					4,050
Lindisfarne	1,500 [14]	5,881	6,450 [14]	(3,679)	1,496	Oct	3,832
R. Nith: Keltonbank to Nunholm	(1,835)	(1,850)	(1,200)	(470)	(3,710)	Feb	(3,710) ▲
Gladhouse Reservoir	6,000 [14]	1,520 [14]	3,200	700	4,570 [14]	Oct	3,198 ▲
Holburn Moss	2,000 [14]	(1,500) [14]	20	4,250 [14]	6,500 [14]	Oct	3,193 ▲
Thornham		5,180 [14]			950 [14]	Nov	3,065
Lake of Menteith	2,190 [14]	(4,500) [14]	3	4,515 [14]	4,026 [14]	Oct	3,047 ▲
Tarbat Ness	(3,000) [13]						(3,000)
Heigham Holmes	3,236		2,500 [14]				2,868 ▲
Tay-Isla Valley	2,700 [14]	(2,000) [14]	2,133 [14]	2,497 [14]	4,134 [14]	Oct	2,866 ▲
Skinflats	2,030 [14]	2,750 [14]	3,800 [14]	1,900 [14]	3,250 [14]	Oct	2,746
Loch Mullion	5,500 [14]	(660) [14]	900 [14]	1,600 [14]			2,667
Orchardton / Auchencairn Bays	(160)	(990)		2,000	3,100	Oct	2,550 ▲

Pink-footed Geese (Dawn Balmer)

European White-fronted Goose
Anser albifrons albifrons

International threshold: 10,000
Great Britain threshold: 58
All-Ireland threshold: +

GB max: 2,208 Jan
NI max: 0
% young: 24 Brood size: 2.2

GB change: S   M   L
           -    -   --

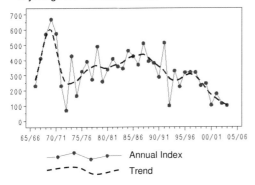

— ● — Annual Index

- - - - Trend

Figure 12.a, Annual indices & trend for European White-fronted Goose for GB.

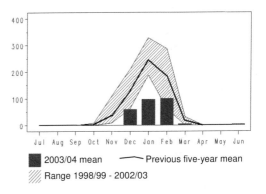

■ 2003/04 mean   ⌒ Previous five-year mean

▨ Range 1998/99 - 2002/03

Figure 12.b, Monthly indices for European White-fronted Goose for GB.

European White-fronted Geese (*albifrons*), breeding on the Taimyr Peninsula winter mostly in the Netherlands with a relatively small proportion of the total migrating to southern Britain. In recent years, the numbers here have been declining, probably as birds remain in continental Europe rather than continuing further west. This trend has been reflected in the Netherlands, which has recorded an increase in numbers during recent years (van Roomen *et al.* 2004).

In support of this theory, both the British total and the national trend reached their lowest ever levels. However, with the flock at Slimbridge containing 24% young birds, and having exceeded 10% for at least the last seven years, this is clearly not a result of poor productivity. The estimated mean brood size of 2.2 during 2003 was slightly below that of the past two years. Furthermore, the period during

which birds remain in Britain appears to be shortening. Monthly indices for 2003/04 clearly show that very few birds appeared before December and virtually all had left by March.

In winter 2003/04, the count at Slimbridge on the Severn Estuary was particularly low and, indeed, for the first time ever the peak during standard Core Counts at the Severn was exceeded by that from the North Norfolk Coast. At the latter site the species was found exclusively at Holkham and Burnham Overy Marshes. Other noteworthy high counts were at Breydon Water and Minsmere, both being some of the most easterly sites in Britain. With the continuing declines at key sites, and the possibility of a shift in wintering distribution, the future of this bird in Britain does not seem particularly rosy.

	99/00	00/01	01/02	02/03	03/04	Mon	Mean
Sites of national importance in Great Britain							
Severn Estuary	1,931	996	1,250 [13]	990 [11]	780 [13]	Jan	1,189
Swale Estuary	(455)	(432)	(360)	(655)	(327)	Jan	(655)
Heigham Holmes	(415)						(415)
North Norfolk Coast	343	240	380	347	540	Jan	370
Dungeness Gravel Pits	340 [13]	234 [13]	355	460	205 [13]	Mar	319
North Warren / Thorpeness Mere	350 [13]		250	310 [13]	190 [13]	Jan	275
Confidential SE England Site	230	26	450	300	140	Feb	229
Breydon Water / Berney Marshes	51	112	110	181	455	Jan	182
Alde Complex	323	0	5 [11]	385	54	Jan	153
Middle Yare Marshes	155	298	74	89	120	Jan	147
Minsmere		200 [13]	120	1	175	Feb	124
Sites no longer meeting table qualifying levels in WeBS-Year 2003/2004							
Sizewell Belts			66	(0)	43	Feb	55

Greenland White-fronted Goose
Anser albifrons flavirostris

International threshold:	300
Great Britain threshold:	209
All-Ireland threshold:	140

GB max: 17,449 Dec
NI max: 60 Feb
% young: 7.6   Brood size: 3.1

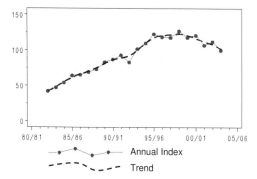

Figure 13.a, Annual indices & trend for Greenland White-fronted Goose for GB.

The 22nd biannual census organised by Greenland White-fronted Goose Study took place in 2003/04 (Fox and Francis 2004). The autumn census totals in Britain were lower than for recent years. Although Islay remained by far the most important UK site, the steady

decline of recent years continued on the island and peak numbers were the lowest since the 1992/93 winter.

There was excellent coverage of the other key areas, but the findings were consistently worrying. Significantly, every single listed site had numbers lower than its five-year mean, albeit the declines at some sites were small. At many locations, the fall in numbers has been steady over recent years. Proportionately, the greatest declines were at Coll, Stranraer Lochs and Rhunahaorine, at all of which peak counts were 20% below their five-year peak means. This downwards trend is presumably due, in large part, to a long run of poor productivity. The percentage young recorded in 2002/03 was the lowest it had been for at least seven years, and the last five consecutive years have seen less than 10% young each year.

	99/00	00/01	01/02	02/03	03/04	Mon	Mean
Sites of international importance in the UK							
Island of Islay	14,474 [9]	13,281 [9]	12,261 [18]	12,253 [9]	11,272 [7]	Dec	12,708
Rhunahaorine	1,585 [9]	1,551 [9]	1,594 [9]	1,450 [9]	1,156 [7]	Dec	1,467
Machrihanish	1,322 [9]	1,386 [9]	1,448 [9]	1,501 [9]	1,377 [7]	Dec	1,407
Tiree	1,347 [9]	1,221 [9]	1,076 [9]	1,093 [9]	1,093 [18]	Dec	1,166
Isle of Coll	1,014 [7]	721 [9]	705 [9]	611 [9]	370 [7]	Dec	684
Stranraer Lochs	440 [9]	550 [9]	500 [9]	365 [9]	249 [9]	Dec	421
Keills Peninsula / Isle of Danna	290 [9]	443 [9]	403 [9]	411 [9]	377 [7]	Dec	385
Loch Ken	330 [9]	325 [9]	326 [9]	275 [9]	250 [9]	Nov	301
Sites of national importance in Great Britain							
Isle of Lismore		275 [9]	295 [9]	310 [9]	277 [9]	Nov	289
Loch Lomond	200 [9]	200 [9]	294 [9]	450 [9]	260 [9]	Dec	281
Loch of Mey	280 [9]	232 [9]	260 [9]	208 [9]	196 [9]	Nov	235
Clachan and Whitehouse	232 [9]	366 [9]	100 [9]	250 [9]	215 [7]	Dec	233
Sites no longer meeting table qualifying levels in WeBS-Year 2003/2004							
Westfield Marshes	255 [9]	171 [9]	228 [9]	196 [9]	170 [9]	Nov	204

Lesser White-fronted Goose
Anser erythropus

Vagrant and escape
Native Range: SE Europe and Asia

GB max: 2 Aug
NI max: 0

Whilst wild birds and individuals from reintroduction programmes can and do occur in the UK, none of the birds recorded during WeBS counts this year would seem especially good candidates. Singles were recorded from Llyn Traffwll, Dee Estuary (England/Wales),

Besthorpe and Girton Gravel Pits, Grindon Lough, River Avon (Ringwood to Christchurch), River Cam (Kingfishers Bridge) and WWT Martin Mere, all records falling between June and November.

Greylag Goose
Anser anser

Icelandic Population

International threshold: 1,000
Great Britain threshold: 819
All-Ireland threshold: 40*

GB max: 78,070 Nov
NI max: 0
% young: 20.5 Brood size: 2.7

*50 is normally used as a minimum threshold

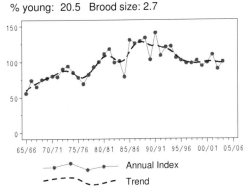

Annual Index

- - - - Trend

Figure 14.a, Annual indices & trend for Icelandic Greylag Goose for GB.

The autumn 2003 census of Icelandic Greylag Geese found a total of 80,143 birds in November, of which 75,007 were in Scotland, 3,063 in England and the remainder in Iceland, the Faeroes and the Republic of Ireland. This was well above the numbers recorded in 2002, although as discussed in the previous *Wildfowl and Wader Counts* that figure was thought to be an underestimate. Even so, the 2003 total represents a fall of about 10% from 2001. Productivity was relatively high in 2003 (mean brood size 2.7) and at 20.5% the percentage of young was similar to that seen in 2000 and 2001.

The northwards shift of wintering Icelandic Greylag Geese discussed in the previous *Wildfowl and Wader Counts* has continued. There was a major increase in the numbers of birds on Orkney in the 2003/04 winter, to such an extent that the islands now support over 50% of the total. The majority of Orkney birds were found on Mainland, particularly the west of the island. The Orkney peak did not occur until November, when numbers were about three times higher than in October.

Conversely, numbers wintering at Caithness Lochs have declined greatly in recent years and it is tempting to conclude that many birds have not felt the need to continue southwards past Orkney in the autumn. However, movements of marked birds suggest that many continue to arrive at key arrival sites further south before moving north to Orkney (Swann *et al.* 2005). There have been large declines at many of the roosts around the Moray Firth basin, at Lochs Davan and Kinord and on the Tay Estuary. However, the picture is not clear-cut as numbers have been maintained at some of the sites in the south of the range, such as at Bute, Kilconquar and the Tay-Isla valley. There are increasing numbers of re-established birds in at least the latter area, however, which may be clouding the issue.

The picture is somewhat clouded by overlap between different populations of Greylag Geese at some of the key locations, including Orkney where birds from the native Northwest Scotland population occur, and further south where there may be an increasing degree of encroachment by re-established birds. In Northern Ireland, there is certainly overlap with the latter group of birds. It is hoped that forthcoming surveys of the NW Scotland population will shed further light on this issue.

	99/00	00/01	01/02	02/03	03/04	Mon	Mean
Sites of international importance in the UK							
Orkney	20,475 [14]	15,914 [14]	22,665 [14]	26,505 [14]	43,097 [14]	Nov	25,731
Caithness Lochs	10,017 [14]	8,326 [14]	(7,854)	2,792 [14]	2,971 [14]	Oct	6,392
Loch Eye & Cromarty Firth	5,674 [14]	(6,192)	5,680 [14]	(7,028) [14]	6,523 [14]	Nov	6,219
Loch of Skene	6,110 [14]	9,660 [14]	2,100 [14]	(1,021) [14]	(2,600) [14]	Oct	5,957
Lochs Davan and Kinord	(10,000) [14]	4,560 [14]	5,277 [14]	2,700 [14]	920 [14]	Oct	4,691
Loch Spynie	3,000 [13]	5,500 [14]	5,300 [14]	3,200 [14]	2,200 [14]	Nov	3,840
Dornoch Firth	3,351 [14]	3,339	2,386 [14]	2,916	2,259	Feb	2,850
Tay-Isla Valley	2,075 [14]	2,490 [14]	2,092 [14]	1,700	2,425 [14]	Nov	2,156
Lower Teviot Valley	509	3,500 [13]	(598)	(1,800)			2,005
R. Eden: Warcop - Little Salkeld		1,900					1,900
Loch Garten	1,650 [14]	2,700 [14]	2,800 [14]	1,000 [14]	1,000 [14]	Nov	1,830

	99/00	00/01	01/02	02/03	03/04	Mon	Mean
Bute	1,780 [14]	1,530 [14]	2,300 [14]	1,380 [14]	2,000 [14]	Feb	1,798
Loch Ken	(1,742)	(971)	(1,368)	(1,106)	(1,280)	Dec	(1,742)
River Earn - Lawhill Oxbows		2,316	1,138				1,727
Loch Fleet Complex	980 [14]	1,700 [14]	4,210 [14]	817 [14]	905 [14]	Nov	1,722
Munlochy Bay	1,050 [14]	424 [14]	3,500 [14]	3,130 [14]	110 [14]	Nov	1,643
Threipmuir / Harlaw Reservoirs	(5,000)	1,390	530 [14]	350 [14]	447	Dec	1,543
Findhorn Bay	2,600 [14]	620 [14]	1,950 [14]		190 [14]	Nov	1,340
Beauly Firth	400 [14]	2,980 [14]	840 [14]	2,010 [14]	280 [14]	Oct	1,302
Kilconquhar Loch	844 [14]	1,096	1,380 [14]	1,552	1,620	Jan	1,298
Tay Estuary	2,221 [14]	1,116 [14]	1,950 [14]	80 [14]	754 [14]	Nov	1,224
Strathearn (West)				1,050 [14]	1,050 [14]	Nov	1,050
Sites of national importance in Great Britain							
Haddo House Lakes	670 [14]	1,100 [14]	980	975	1,100 [14]	Nov	965 ▲
Gadloch	902 [14]	1,550 [14]	685	994	650	Sep	956 ▼
Loch of Lintrathen	1,440 [14]	(905) [14]	1,330 [14]	400 [14]	616 [14]	Nov	947
Upper Tay	376 [14]	1,189 [14]	1,022 [14]	943 [14]	1,197 [14]	Nov	945
R. Eamont/Eden: H'pot-Edenhall	1,300	(920)		(1,400)	100	Nov	930 ▼
East Chevington Pools		598	700	1,500	650	Feb	862
Carsebreck and Rhynd Lochs	1,060 [14]	1,160 [14]	953 [14]	610 [14]	494 [14]	Jan	855 ▲
Whitrig Bog	700			1,000 [14]			850
Forth Estuary	217	(321)	826	1,564	792	Dec	850 ▲
Cochrage Loch			850 [14]				850
Sites no longer meeting table qualifying levels in WeBS-Year 2003/2004							
Lindisfarne	500 [14]	1,050 [14]	1,060	(1,000)	400	Dec	802
Loch of Strathbeg	325 [14]	993	1,744 [14]	415 [14]	295 [14]	Nov	754

Northwest Scottish Population

International threshold: **90**
Great Britain threshold: **90**

GB max: **5,322** Aug
NI max: **0**
% young: 29.5   Brood size: 2.7

The coordinated August counts of Northwest Scotland Greylag Geese found a total of 5,063 birds on the Uists, whilst a further 259 birds in suitable areas were noted on WeBS Core Counts during the same month. This compared well with recent years. Productivity estimates from examining flocks on Coll and Tiree during August showed another good year for the geese (percentage young 29.5 and mean brood size 2.7), at least on those two islands.

Peak counts on Tiree, North Uist and South Uist were all high and above recent averages. The lack of data for other sites is a result of the effort required to monitor often remote areas, leading to sporadic information.

One particular problem with monitoring this population, however, is that it can be difficult to decide whether particular birds should be assigned to this group, or to the ever-increasing re-established birds from the south. A survey of north and west Scotland is planned to help resolve some of these issues.

	99/00	00/01	01/02	02/03	03/04	Mon	Mean
Sites of international importance in the UK							
Tiree	3,109 [18]	3,535 [5]	2,040 [18]	2,154 [18]	3,516 [18]	Dec	2,871
North Uist	1,808 [19]	2,877 [19]	2,076 [19]	2,261 [19]	2,642 [19]	Aug	2,333
South Uist	1,362 [19]	1,862 [19]	2,303 [19]	2,095 [19]	2,102 [19]	Aug	1,945
Isle of Coll	587 [18]	679 [18]		675 [18]	411 [7]	Dec	588
Benbecula	374 [19]	431 [19]	376 [19]	488 [19]	319 [19]	Aug	398
Tayinloan	267 [7]			175 [18]			221
Melbost / Tong / Broad Bay	64	(394)	197				218
Machrihanish	12 [7]			388 [18]			200
Loch Broom		(197)					(197)
Clachan and Whitehouse				184 [18]			184
Moine Mhor and Add Estuary	165 [7]	137 [18]	192 [18]				165
Isle of Colonsay	121 [7]	112 [7]			116 [7]	Dec	116
Loch Urrahag	40	(167)	(27)				104
Branahuie Saltings			101				101
Other sites attaining table qualifying levels in WeBS-Year 2003/2004 in Great Britain							
Kentra Moss & Lower Loch Shiel	59	79	90	93	102	Jan	85

Re-established Population

GB max: 27,382 Nov
NI max: 2,394 Feb

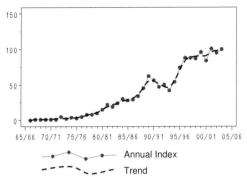

Figure 15.a, Annual indices & trend for Re-established Population for GB.

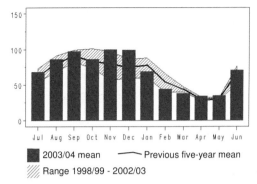

Figure 15.b, Monthly indices for Re-established Population for GB.

Greylag Geese in most of England and Wales, and increasingly also in Northern Ireland and parts of Scotland, are termed "re-established". The species used to be a widespread resident but was hunted to extinction (aided by habitat modification) throughout most of its range. However, birds were released in a number of locations and the size of this population has grown substantially. Recent estimates of the numbers of this population in Britain have been of the order of 25-30,000 birds (Kershaw & Cranswick 2003, Rehfisch *et al.* 2004, Rowell *et al.* 2004). However, with WeBS core counts now at the current level, which are known to miss birds on smaller unsurveyed waterbodies and rivers, the number may be increasing well past this level.

The peak core count total for Britain was the highest yet recorded, although that in Northern Ireland fell slightly from 2002/03. The plot of the British index suggests a continued increase, although at a reduced rate since the mid-1990s. This could, however, be due to a saturation of favoured large (mostly surveyed) waterbodies and continued increase on unsurveyed smaller sites. The monthly indices are much as would be expected for a resident bird, highest in the autumn and declining through the winter.

The number of British sites from which peak means of over 400 were recorded has continued to increase, with 40 this winter. At the North Norfolk Coast the numbers were down a little but counts were assessed as incomplete due to omission of a number of sections, especially Holkham Lake. Whilst numbers fluctuate at many sites, more sustained increases over the last five years are apparent for Eccup Reservoir, Baston/Langtoft Gravel Pits, Kirkby-on-Bain Gravel Pits, Tattershall Pits, Clifford Hill Gravel Pits, Wynyard Lake, Breydon Water, the Tees Estuary and the Wash. Against the national trend, however, there were declines at Abberton Reservoir, Langtoft West End, Southill Lake, Windermere and the Beaulieu Estuary. In Northern Ireland, a sustained increase was evident at Loughs Neagh and Beg where, intriguingly, there remains a complete absence of Canada Geese.

	99/00	00/01	01/02	02/03	03/04	Mon	Mean
Sites with mean peak counts of 300 or more birds in Great Britain[†]							
North Norfolk Coast	(1,837)	3,431	1,850	1,657	(1,767)	Nov	2,313
Nosterfield Gravel Pits	993	678	1,084	1,746	1,338	Jul	1,168
Sutton and Lound Gravel Pits	800		1,057	1,176			1,011
Tophill Low Reservoirs	850	1,126	1,183	828	683	Dec	934
Bolton-on-Swale Gravel Pits	880	1,110	699	1,060	710	Dec	892
Humber Estuary	(553)	(590)	648	1,053	(769)	Aug	851
Eccup Reservoir	600	742	760	1,000	1,084	Sep	837
Ouse Washes	596 [13]	964	958	691 [13]	883 [13]	Dec	818
Baston and Langtoft Gravel Pits	(380)	(152)	(330)	(600)	(803)	Nov	(803)
Lavan Sands	(146)	903	609	1,037	623	Aug	793
The Wash	476	563	967	895	1,011	Oct	782

	99/00	00/01	01/02	02/03	03/04	Mon	Mean
Swale Estuary	653	(907)	830	760	718	Jan	774
Lower Derwent Ings	763						763
Kirkby-on-Bain Gravel Pits	541	562	635	900	1,072	Dec	742
Abberton Reservoir	589	469	(2,500)	80	50	Sep	738
Hornsea Mere	834	625	745	465	642	Aug	662
Orwell Estuary	989 [11]	449	604 [11]	587 [11]	677 [11]	Jan	661
Llyn Traffwll	746	450	700	769	489	Jul	631
Tattershall Pits	570	403	400	730	1,015	Nov	624
Morecambe Bay	411	327	867	741	629	Jan	595
Heigham Holmes	865		300 [14]				583
Dungeness Gravel Pits	517	(472)	554	(502)	667	Dec	579
Alton Water	550	624	490	577	571	Oct	562
Little Paxton Gravel Pits	399	457	467	746	652	Oct	544
WWT Martin Mere	460	440	438	580	600	Oct	504
Livermere	655	249	490	806	280	Jan	496
Hay-a-Park Gravel Pits	501	696	529	183	560	Oct	494
Cranwich Gravel Pits	328	722		408			486
Derwent Reservoir	285 [14]	530	482	544	(568)	Jan	482
Breydon Water / Berney Marshes	219	335	340	723	720	Nov	467
Dee Flood Meadows	(310)	295	480	540	480	Jan	449
Langtoft West End Gravel Pits	(165)	401	901	441	54	Mar	449
Hardley Flood		307		515	487	Jan	436
Middle Yare Marshes	340	442	340	569	473	Sep	433
Ardleigh Reservoir	271	610	286	560			432
Bough Beech Reservoir	95	543	428	488	597	Aug	430
Stodmarsh & Collards Lagoon	276	521	454	599	274	Sep	425
Billing Sewage Treatment Works			420				420
Llyn Alaw	384	328	275	538	557	Sep	416
River Ure - Givendale to Ripon		230	620	772	2	Aug	406
Sites with mean peak counts of 50 or more birds in Northern Ireland[†]							
Loughs Neagh and Beg	(71)	785	915	1,179	1,270	Feb	1,037
Lough Foyle	1,282	0	786	1,207	518	Feb	759
Strangford Lough	367	166	405	577	373	Dec	378
Belfast Lough	116 [11]	242	188	144	132	Jan	164
Lower Lough Erne				(71)	(54)	Feb	(71)
Ballysaggart Lough				70	66	Dec	68

[†] as no British or All-Ireland thresholds have been set qualifying levels of 400 and 50 have been chosen to select sites, in Great Britain and Northern Ireland respectivley, for presentation in this report

Bar-headed Goose

Anser indicus

Escape

Native Range: S Asia

GB max: 44   Sep
NI max: 0

Bar-headed Geese were recorded from 40 sites in 2003/04, none of which were in Northern Ireland. Most records were of single birds, but multiple occurrences were noted from 13 sites, the highest being 12 at Chichester Harbour, 11 at Spade Oak Gravel Pit and 10 at Stodmarsh and Collards Lagoon. The summed site maxima was 87, which was almost half that of 2002/03 but similar to 2001/02.

Snow Goose

Anser caerulescens

Vagrant and escape

Native Range: N America

GB max: 49   Oct
NI max: 0

Snow Geese were noted at 21 sites this year, none in Northern Ireland. Most records, if not all, referred to escaped or feral birds. This represents a decline in the number of sites over the past few years and unsurprisingly the summed site maximum of 77 was also down. Most records involved single birds, with more than one at only seven sites. Most noteworthy were up to 30 at Eversley Cross and Yateley Gravel Pits, up to 15 at Blenheim Park Lake and up to nine at the Lower Windrush Gravel Pits.

Ross's Goose
Anser rossii

Escape and possible vagrant
Native Range: N America

GB max: 3   Jul
NI max: 0

This species was recorded from four sites during the year. Three at Sennowe Park Lake in July were clearly of captive origin, but given recent massive increases in the native Nearctic population of this species, the origins of the other records are perhaps more open to question. One such individual was at Ardrossan-West Kilbride between September and December, up to two were noted along the North Norfolk Coast between September and January, and one was at the Mersey Estuary in January.

Emperor Goose
Anser canagicus

Escape
Native Range: Alaska and NE Siberia

GB max: 23   Oct
NI max: 0

Birds were recorded from nine sites, all within Britain. Most noteworthy is the continued occurrence of a flock of up to 21 birds at South Walney Island, Morecambe Bay, which have been present during recent years. Otherwise, singles were noted at Cowden Loch and Pools, Eccup Reservoir, Harewood Lake (presumably the same individual as at the previous site), Livermere, Middle Tame Valley Gravel Pits, Ramsbury Lake, Reedham Water and Walthamstow Reservoirs.

Canada Goose
Branta canadensis

Naturalised introduction[†]
Native Range: N America

GB max: 51,882   Sep
NI max: 828   Jan

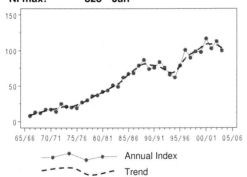

Figure 16.a, Annual indices & trend for Canada Goose for GB.

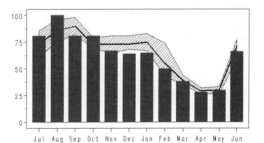

Figure 16.b, Monthly indices for Canada Goose for GB.

The Canada Goose is one of the best-known UK waterbirds, albeit not a native one. They are to be found over the whole of England and Wales, through the southern and central lowlands of Scotland and more sporadically north to Orkney. The species is still more local in Northern Ireland however. Apart from the naturalised population, occasional birds are found accompanying flocks of wintering geese arriving from the northwest and these are presumed to be wild birds from the Nearctic populations. The precise identity of these vagrant birds will come under increased scrutiny in the future following the recent announcement by the British Ornithologists' Union of a split into two species, the Greater Canada Goose *Branta canadensis* and the Lesser Canada Goose *Branta hutchinsii* (Sangster *et al.* 2005).

Numbers have increased dramatically since the 1960s. However, the British total in 2002/03 was the lowest since 1999/00 and the index similarly shows that the population growth has apparently slowed. This pattern was seen back in the late 1980s and early 1990s also, just before another large increase occurred. The index in Northern Ireland is more variable but the January peak of 828 was the second highest in the province. However, it should be remembered that this is a widely dispersed species which occurs on many rivers and smaller waterbodies that are not covered by WeBS; analysis has shown that trends based upon WeBS data alone do not show the full picture, with many large sites reaching saturation point but increases continuing on many smaller, unsurveyed, sites (Rehfisch *et al.* 2004, Rowell *et al.* 2004, Jackson *et al.* in press.) As expected for a resident species, the monthly indices show numbers are highest in late summer (the August value in 2003/04 was particularly high) and then decrease through the winter.

There were five sites at which counts of Canada Geese exceeded 1,000 in 2003/04, most notably the Stour Estuary where a steady increase has been apparent in recent years. In 2003/04, the Dyfi Estuary was again the site with the highest count but at a lower level than the previous winter. Sites with lower counts than normal included the Dee Estuary, Arun Valley, Abberton, Colliford, Cleddau Estuary and Old Moor. In Northern Ireland, most Canada Geese are found at Strangford Lough and Upper and Lower Loughs Erne; the continued absence of the species from Loughs Neagh and Beg is striking.

	99/00	00/01	01/02	02/03	03/04	Mon	Mean
Sites with mean peak counts of 600 or more birds in Great Britain[†]							
Dee Estuary (England/Wales)	(1,347)	(1,664)	(2,268)	(2,568)	(1,529)	Oct	(2,568)
Dyfi Estuary	1,884	2,180	2,156 [11]	3,029	2,421	Jul	2,334
Rutland Water	1,365	1,539	1,120	1,276	1,369	Sep	1,334
Arun Valley	967	1,139	1,550	(1,754)	860	Nov	1,254
Mersey Estuary	308	1,738	737	1,437	1,177	Jul	1,079
Middle Tame Valley Gravel Pits	1,173	889	(456)	(402)	(334)	Aug	1,031
Abberton Reservoir	928	1,217	(2,000)	270	639	Aug	1,011
Colliford Reservoir	858	946	894	1,884	350	Nov	986
Bewl Water	1,200	1,078	500	885	960	Sep	925
Cleddau Estuary	(1,108)	1,080	1,000	765	655	Dec	922
Fairburn Ings	1,177	950	709	823	893	Jul	910
Ellesmere Lakes	737	912	906	751	812	Sep	824
Stour Estuary	785	485	713	983	1,135	Oct	820
Southampton Water	675	735	(1,084)	609	777	Oct	776
King`s Bromley Gravel Pits	814	850	669	712	776	Jul	764
Chew Valley Lake	660	720	810	830	785	Jul	761
Harewood Lake	943	750	700	700	686	Feb	756
Taw-Torridge Estuary	587	591	888	1,179	526	Aug	754
Walthamstow Reservoirs	(500)	781	662	945	606	Jul	749
Tring Reservoirs	593	626	893	962	560	Oct	727
Lee Valley Gravel Pits	498	591	955	678	699	Sep	684
Pitsford Reservoir	451	516	722	967	727	Sep	677
Somerset Levels	275	(704)	417	1,378	555	Dec	666
Blithfield Reservoir	1,140	570	321	386	756	Aug	635
Carsington Water	484		511	848	680	Jul	631
Lower Derwent Ings	627						627
Old Moor	480	670	768	(730)	380	Aug	606
Brown Moss					600	Oct	600
Sites with mean peak counts of 50 or more birds in Northern Ireland[†]							
Strangford Lough	307 [11]	310	238	323	307	Oct	297
Upper Lough Erne	222	289	347	293	263	Feb	283
Lower Lough Erne				110	343	Jan	227
Drumgay Lough	110	70					90

[†] as no British or All-Ireland thresholds have been set qualifying levels of 600 and 50 have been chosen to select sites, in Great Britain and Northern Ireland respectivley, for presentation in this report

Hawaiian Goose
Branta sandvicensis

Escape
Native Range: Hawaii

GB max: 1   Nov
 NI max: 0

One recorded on Harewood Lake in November and January.

Barnacle Goose
Branta leucopsis

Greenland Population

GB max: 45,296 Mar
NI max: 0
% young: 6.4 Brood size: 1.6

International threshold: 540
Great Britain threshold: 450
All-Ireland threshold: 75

Barnacle Geese nesting in Greenland winter mostly on islands off the west coasts of Scotland and Ireland. The most important site by far is Islay, and this and some of the other key islands are well monitored each year. However, smaller numbers occur widely over more remote areas and these are only censused every five years, involving a combination of aerial and land-based survey. The most recent census in March 2003 estimated a total wintering population of 56,386 birds (Worden *et al.* 2004).

The GB core count total in 2003/04 was typically low, peaking at just 601 in November with most of these found at Lochs Paible, Eaval and Hosta on North Uist. Dedicated surveys were carried out at several sites in December and March, however. In general, numbers were similar to other counts in recent years, although the Colonsay/Oronsay counts were somewhat higher than usual. Productivity this year was low (6.4% young, mean brood size 1.6), although the range of variation in this population is much smaller than for some other geese. Away from the main sites, the small flock at the Dyfi Estuary peaked at 120 in December.

	99/00	00/01	01/02	02/03	03/04	Mon	Mean
Sites of international importance in the UK							
Island of Islay	40,054 [7]	38,022 [39]	35,213 [18]	36,478 [39]	40,018 [39]	Mar	37,957
North Uist	1,495 [19]	1,957 [19]	3,326 [19]	2,732 [19]			2,378
South Walls (Hoy)			2,600 [39]	1,800 [39]			2,200
Tiree	1,607 [38]	1,442 [38]	2,132 [38]	2,786 [38]	2,752 [18]	Mar	2,144
Sound of Barra (Barra)		1,326 [36]					1,326
Isle of Coll	788 [38]	718 [38]	933 [38]	1,010 [38]	792 [7]	Dec	848
Islands South of Barra	1,491 [36]	500 [36]		271 [37]			754
Sound of Harris (NW) (Harris)				706 [37]			706
North Sutherland				669 [37]			669
Sites of national importance in Great Britain							
Colonsay/Oronsay	576 [36]	244 [7]		510 [38]	793 [7]	Dec	531 ▲

Svalbard Population

GB max: 28,318 Jan
NI max: 0
% young: 4.1 Brood size: 2.0

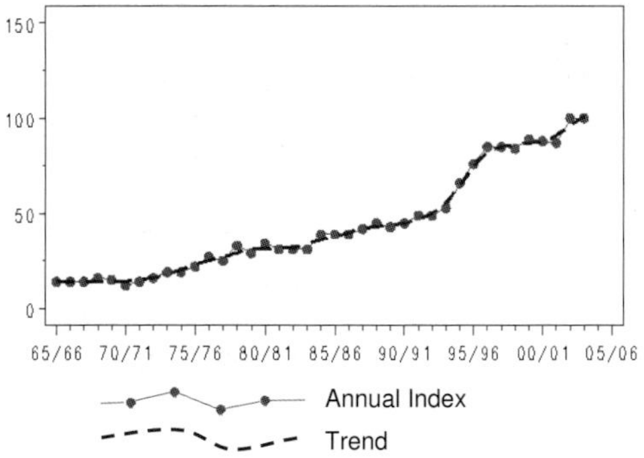

International threshold: 230
Great Britain threshold: 220

Figure 17.a, Annual indices & trend for Svalbard Population for GB.

The Barnacle Geese breeding on Svalbard winter almost exclusively around the Solway Firth, although new arrivals are often first detected along the east coasts of Scotland and northern England. In 2003/04, early arriving flocks were noted at Tyninghame Estuary, Lindisfarne and Eden Estuary, as well as smaller numbers at many other sites, but few remained for long. However, small numbers remained throughout the winter at Loch of Strathbeg and East Chevington Pools. Interestingly, a small flock later took up residence at Montrose Basin between January and March.

Even in October, 95% of birds on WeBS core counts were on the Solway, increasing to over 99% during the remainder of the winter. The peak census total of 28,256 for the Solway Firth, which included 'Outer Solway' sites such as Wigtown, Auchencairn and Orchardton Bays, revealed continued high numbers after the previous winter's record peak. Productivity was poor (4.1% young, mean brood size 2.0), however, with less than 10% young for the third time in the last four winters.

Whilst Caerlaverock and Mersehead were consistently favoured areas on the Solway, large flocks did use other parts of the firth more sporadically. Auchencairn Bay was used by up to 3,100 birds between October and January but geese were not found at Wigtown Bay until late in the winter, peaking at 690 in March.

	99/00	00/01	01/02	02/03	03/04	Mon	Mean
Sites of international importance in the UK							
Solway Firth	25,750 [8]	23,783 [8]	23,524 [8]	28,447 [8]	28,256 [8]	Jan	25,952
Loch of Strathbeg	217 [5]	(244)	10,390 [38]	138	95	Nov	2,710
Lindisfarne	0	93	(400)	140	786	Oct	284 ▲
Other sites attaining table qualifying levels in WeBS-Year 2003/2004 in Great Britain							
Tyninghame Estuary	1	0	239	7	277	Sep	105

Barnacle Geese (Mike Weston)

Naturalised Population

Naturalised establishment[†]

GB max: 1,011 Dec
NI max: 232 Sep

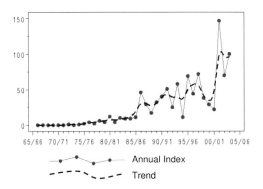

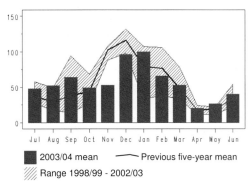

Annual Index
Trend

2003/04 mean — Previous five-year mean
Range 1998/99 - 2002/03

Figure 18.a, Annual indices & trend for Naturalised Population for GB.

Figure 18.b, Monthly indices for Naturalised Population for GB.

Barnacle Geese are becoming an increasingly regular feature of many waterbodies in the UK. Away from the regular wintering sites for the wild, migratory birds on the Solway and the Western Isles, the majority of records are derived from escapes from collections, or indeed birds still part of collections but remaining free flying. Increasingly, such birds are now breeding in the wild. Large numbers of wild Barnacle Geese winter on the east side of the North Sea in the Netherlands and it seems highly likely that occasional birds make it to the British east coast in the winter. However, naturalised birds are now so widespread that such incoming birds would be all but impossible to detect, unless ringed or otherwise marked.

The peak core count total in Britain was the highest yet recorded by WeBS and naturalised Barnacle Geese were recorded from nearly 200 locations. At four of these sites, three-figure counts were recorded with those at Benacre Broad, Willington and Roxton Gravel Pits representing notable increases. However, at Hornsea Mere counts seem to have been declining steadily in recent years against the national trend. In Northern Ireland, virtually all birds are found at Strangford Lough where numbers reached a new peak.

	99/00	00/01	01/02	02/03	03/04	Mon	Mean
Sites with mean peak counts of 50 or more birds in Great Britain[†]							
Hornsea Mere	(326)	241	202	132	96	Nov	199
Eversley Cross / Yateley GPs	187	183	236	219	158	Feb	197
Thwaite Flat / Roanhead Ponds			152 [13]				152
Willington	0	47	115	84	298	Dec	109
Roxton Gravel Pits	6	18	105	107	262	Oct	100
Benacre Broad	56	26	42	120	250	Oct	99
Middle Yare Marshes	80	20	141	104	72	Nov	83
Duddon Estuary	155	2	(0)	(1)	(65)	Sep	79
Barcombe Mills Reservoir	(47)	60	76	64	73	Oct	68
Frampton Pools	46	37	(75)	79	98	Jul	67
Severn Estuary	0	41	73	96	(94)	Dec	61
Humber Estuary	11	42	(53)	(74)	(80)	Nov	52
Sites with mean peak counts of 50 or more birds in Northern Ireland[†]							
Strangford Lough	136	158	214	223	232	Sep	193

[†] *as no British or All-Ireland thresholds have been set a qualifying level of 50 has been chosen to select sites for presentation in this report*

Dark-bellied Brent Goose
Branta bernicla bernicla

International threshold: 2,200
Great Britain threshold: 981
All-Ireland threshold: +

GB max: 64,366 Jan
NI max: 0
% young: 10 Brood size: 2.2

S M L
GB change: o - +

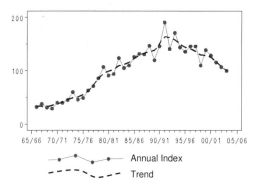

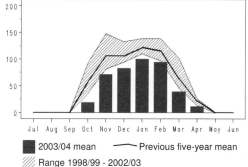

- - - Annual Index

- - - - - Trend

■ 2003/04 mean ⟋ Previous five-year mean

▨ Range 1998/99 - 2002/03

Figure 19.a, Annual indices & trend for Dark-bellied Brent Goose for GB.

Figure 19.b, Monthly indices for Dark-bellied Brent Goose for GB.

Dark-bellied Brent Geese are a familiar site on estuaries in the south, mostly from the Humber to the outer Bristol Channel. The birds nest in the high Arctic tundra of Russia and winter in northwest Europe, with British estuaries supporting about a third of the world population. Although traditionally the most exclusively coastal of our wintering geese, in recent years there has been an increasing tendency in some areas for Dark-bellied Brent Geese to feed inland (Rowell & Robinson 2004).

In winter 2003/04, the British index continued its decline to the lowest level since 1981/82 and the peak core count total was also the lowest since the same winter. Whilst the percentage of young birds (10%) was up slightly on the previous two winters, and the

highest since 1999/00, it was still below the estimated 15% required to balance the average mortality rate. The estimated mean brood size of 2.2 was similar to that of 2002/03.

Not surprisingly, numbers at most key sites were down. The most serious declines were evident from the North Norfolk Coast, Blackwater Estuary, Pagham Harbour, the Beaulieu Estuary and the Medway Estuary. However, numbers at the Wash appear to be holding up, as are those at Chichester and Langstone Harbours and the Stour Estuary. Interestingly, numbers at the two extremities of the British range, the Humber Estuary and Burry Inlet, have also not shown a notable decline yet. Not surprisingly, there were no sites exhibiting noteworthy increases in numbers.

	99/00	00/01	01/02	02/03	03/04	Mon	Mean
Sites of international importance in the UK							
The Wash	28,811	19,518	17,924	20,314	18,734	Jan	21,060
North Norfolk Coast	12,969 [12]	10,201	8,033	(9,180)	5,722	Jan	9,231
Thames Estuary	7,346	7,371	12,157	(8,589)	(6,445)	Nov	8,958
Chichester Harbour	(9,267)	7,412	7,470	7,358	8,290	Feb	7,959
Blackwater Estuary	9,838	(9,860)	(7,195)	6,100	4,892	Jan	7,577
Langstone Harbour	6,928	5,080	4,813	4,686	5,804 [11]	Feb	5,462
Crouch-Roach Estuary	(5,488)	4,446	3,471	3,083	2,914	Jan	3,880
Hamford Water	3,879	4,047	4,331	3,567	3,336	Jan	3,832
Colne Estuary	(3,614)	3,310	2,572	(409)	(1,959)	Jan	3,165
Pagham Harbour	2,438 [11]	2,520	3,178	2,252	1,210	Feb	2,320
Sites of national importance in Great Britain							
Deben Estuary	2,139	2,890	2,218	1,251	2,234	Dec	2,146
Portsmouth Harbour	(2,661)	1,827	1,682	2,185	2,293	Dec	2,130
Southampton Water	2,480 [11]	1,742 [11]	(1,455)	(1,326)	(1,274)	Jan	2,111
Humber Estuary	2,404	(1,649)	1,432	(2,351)	2,118 [11]	Dec	2,076

	99/00	00/01	01/02	02/03	03/04	Mon	Mean
Swale Estuary	(1,800)	2,149	1,690 [11]	(1,278)	(1,210)	Feb	1,920
North West Solent	(2,114)	1,616	2,350	1,500	1,790	Jan	1,874
Newtown Estuary	(1,727)	1,800	1,660	1,779	(1,235)	Dec	1,746
Dengie Flats	(1,550)	2,455	1,798	1,160	1,507	Feb	1,730
Stour Estuary	1,769	1,716 [11]	1,412	1,753	1,914	Mar	1,713
Poole Harbour	1,354	1,708	(599)	(740)	(868)	Dec	1,531
Exe Estuary	1,806	1,345	1,183	1,714	1,368	Oct	1,483
Orwell Estuary	1,799 [11]	1,228 [11]	1,215 [11]	1,525 [11]	1,396 [11]	Feb	1,433
Beaulieu Estuary	1,458	1,334	2,015	1,512	835	Dec	1,431
Fleet and Wey	1,404	1,813	2,188	398	1,337	Nov	1,428
Medway Estuary	(1,845)	(1,041)	(1,725)	(1,179)	836	Oct	1,325 ▼
Burry Inlet	(1,195)	1,158	1,174	917	(1,255)	Nov	1,140

Light-bellied Brent Goose
Branta bernicla hrota

East Canadian High Arctic population

GB max: 371 Dec
NI max: 21,129 Oct
% young: 17.8   Brood size: 3.2

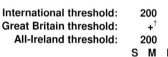

International threshold: 200
Great Britain threshold: +[†]
All-Ireland threshold: 200

	S	M	L
NI change:	-	-	-

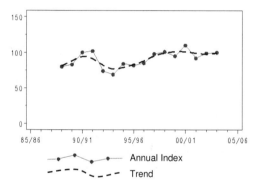

Annual Index
Trend

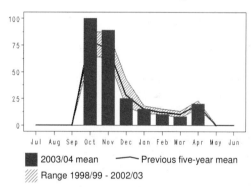

2003/04 mean   Previous five-year mean
Range 1998/99 - 2002/03

Figure 20.a, Annual indices & trend for East Canadian High Arctic population for NI.

Figure 20.b, Monthly indices for East Canadian High Arctic population for NI.

Light-bellied Brent Geese breeding on the high-Arctic islands of northeastern Canada migrate eastwards across the Greenland ice cap, cross to Iceland and then make their way to Ireland. Most arrive first at Strangford Lough or Lough Foyle in the autumn, before dispersing more widely as the winter progresses elsewhere in Ireland, as well as to western Britain and south to the Channel Islands, France and Spain.

Over recent years, the annual index for this population has remained fairly level, but the peak core count total for winter 2003/04 was the highest ever recorded for WeBS. Moreover, the international Light-bellied Brent Goose census in October 2003 estimated the highest ever population size of almost 29,000 birds. These high numbers were clearly due, in part at least, to a good breeding season (percentage young estimated at 17.8 and mean

brood size 3.2) following two where very few young were produced. As usual, the majority (over 85%) were found at Strangford Lough with most of the rest at Lough Foyle. Later in the winter birds were typically more widespread around the other Northern Irish coastal sites, with numbers relatively high at Carlingford and the Outer Ards but somewhat low at Dundrum Bay.

There was also a continued presence in western Britain. The peak British count of 371 birds, made up of small flocks between Loch Ryan and the Cleddau Estuary, was the highest ever British total of birds considered to be derived from this population. However, in the absence of ringing or marking recoveries, it is not possible to be entirely sure that some of these birds were not from the Svalbard population.

	99/00	00/01	01/02	02/03	03/04	Mon	Mean
Sites of international importance in the UK							
Strangford Lough	14,074 [11]	16,162	19,583 [34]	17,520 [34]	21,500 [34]	Oct	17,768
Lough Foyle	1,934	3,469	1,841	1,563 [34]	3,277 [34]	Oct	2,417
Carlingford Lough	(437)	(498)	(259)	319	(570)	Mar	456
Killough Harbour			489 [11]	472	383	Mar	448
Outer Ards Shoreline	(215)	120	210 [34]	700	642	Mar	418
Dundrum Bay	(148)	(205)	(320)	(242)	(188)	Dec	(320)
Larne Lough	253	266	235	139	235	Dec	226
Sites with mean peak counts of 25 or more birds in Great Britain[†]							
Jersey Shore		86	127				107
Inland Sea / Alaw Estuary	51	95	80	76	95	Mar	79
Dee Estuary (England/Wales)	14	75	32 [11]	25	66	Feb	42
Cleddau Estuary	(4)	12	(4)	3	106	Feb	40
Foryd Bay	27	8	43	9	96	Mar	37
Morecambe Bay	5	3	(7)	62 [11]	53	Feb	31
Loch Gruinart	46	60		2	0		27
Loch Ryan	6	24	28 [13]	25 [13]	45	Dec	26

[†] as no British threshold has been set a qualifying level of 25 has been chosen to select sites for presentation in this report

Svalbard population

International threshold:	50
Great Britain threshold:	30*

GB max:	3,745	Dec
NI max:	0	

	S	M	L
GB change:	+	++	++

50 is normally used as a minimum threshold

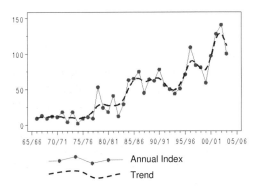

Annual Index
Trend

Figure 21.a, Annual indices & trend for Svalbard Light-bellied Brent Goose for GB.

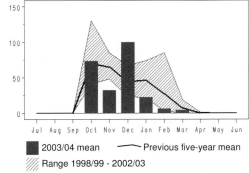

2003/04 mean   Previous five-year mean
Range 1998/99 - 2002/03

Figure 21.b, Monthly indices for Svalbard Light-bellied Brent Goose for GB.

The population of Light-bellied Brent Geese breeding on Svalbard (as well as in northeast Greenland and Franz Josef Land) is currently fairly stable although numbers are lower than a century ago. Lindisfarne is by far the key British site, where numbers vary between years in a manner at least partly dependent upon conditions in their other key wintering area in Denmark.

The numbers at Lindisfarne during the 2003/04 winter were well within their usual range for recent winters. The first arrivals were in September increasing to a peak in December but numbers then declined rapidly in the new year. Away from Lindisfarne, the birds on the Inner Moray Firth were present only between December and February. The only areas with a sustained presence of more than a few birds considered likely to be from this population were the Eden Estuary, with up to 15, and the Cromarty Firth, with up to 12.

	99/00	00/01	01/02	02/03	03/04	Mon	Mean
Sites of international importance in the UK							
Lindisfarne	(1,767)	3,184	(4,845)	(3,150)	3,716	Dec	3,915
Inner Moray and Inverness Firth	(39)	10	41	100	55	Jan	52 ▲

Black Brant
Branta bernicla nigricans

Vagrant
Native Range: N America and E Asia

GB max: 1   Dec
NI max: 0

Singles were recorded at East Head in Chichester Harbour in December and Moonfleet to Chickerell Hive Point, Chesil Fleet (Fleet and Wey) in January.

Red-breasted Goose
Branta ruficollis

Vagrant and escape
Native Range: SE Europe and Asia

GB max: 5   Jun
NI max: 0

Birds were recorded at 12 sites during the year compared to 13 the previous. The increasing number of escaped birds makes it even more difficult to judge the provenance of potentially wild birds. Two were present all year at Harewood Lake, with two also at Nosterfield Gravel Pits in June. Singles were recorded from Barrow upon Trent Gravel Pit, Diss Mere, Fleet and Wey, Foremark Reservoir, Minsmere, Ribble Estuary, Rutland Water, Swarkestone Gravel Pits, Tyberton Pools and WWT Martin Mere.

Egyptian Goose
Alopochen aegyptiaca

Naturalised introduction[†]
Native Range: Africa

GB max: 313   Jul
NI max: 0

Egyptian Geese remain uncommon outside eastern England and, although partial migrants in their native range, the introduced British population is essentially sedentary or at most locally dispersive. Coinciding with the aggregation of moulting and young birds, peak numbers are commonly recorded during late summer. Of the seventy-one sites at which the species was recorded during 2003/04, 80% of these held single figures. This is another species for which WeBS is likely to miss a sizeable proportion of the population. Many inland sites in East Anglia, (such as wet corners of fields) may hold cumulatively a lot of birds, albeit often in low numbers at any one site.

Five key sites reached their highest ever totals during 2003/04. Of these, only Rutland Water, peaking in September, falls outside the East Anglia stronghold.

	99/00	00/01	01/02	02/03	03/04	Mon	Mean
Sites with mean peak counts of 10 or more birds in Great Britain[†]							
North Norfolk Coast	197	218	318	233	(126)	Aug	242
Sennowe Park Lake Guist				98	85	Jul	92
Rutland Water	52	54	60	58	70	Sep	59
Middle Yare Marshes	44	(45)	45	72	24	Oct	46
Breydon Water / Berney Marshes	12	25	48	63	65	Jul	43
St Benet`s Levels	0	(51)	52	88	23	Dec	43
Cranwich Gravel Pits	92	23		8			41
Nunnery Lakes	22	20	19	21	51	Oct	27
Snetterton Gravel Pits	29	24					27
Trinity Broads	58	11	18	20	10	Jul	23
Lynford Gravel Pit	33	11					22
Stanford Training Area	30 [13]	(7)	13				22
Weybread Pits		0	18	31	21	Jul	18
Spade Oak Gravel Pit	1	18	23	33	6	Sep	16
Barton Broad	8	13	15	18	14	Aug	14
Didlington Lakes	6	17					12
Ampton Water	2			2	25	Jul	10
Colney Gravel Pits			10				10
Ranworth and Cockshoot Broads	4	12 [13]	12	14	7	Jul	10
Whitlingham Country Park	9	6	10	7	18	Oct	10

[†] *as no British or All-Ireland thresholds have been set a qualifying level of 10 has been chosen to select sites for presentation in this report*

Upland Goose *(formerly Magellan Goose)*
Chloephaga picta

Escape
Native Range: S America

GB max: 1 Apr
NI max: 0

One was present on Auchlochan Pond throughout the year.

Paradise Shelduck
Tadorna variegata

Escape
Native Range: New Zealand

GB max: 1 Jul
NI max: 0

One was recorded monthly from Par Sands Pool between July and March.

Cape Shelduck
Tadorna cana

Escape
Native Range: S Africa

GB max: 4 May
NI max: 0

Up to four were recorded at Ince Bank on the Mersey Estuary between April and January, and one was at Ellesmere Lakes in September and October.

Ruddy Shelduck
Tadorna ferruginea

Escape and possible vagrant
Native Range: Asia, N Africa and S Europe

GB max: 11 Jul
NI max: 0

This species was recorded from 23 sites throughout the year, the summed site maxima being 39 (compared to 33 in 2002/03). Birds were recorded every month, with a slight peak in July. All sites maxima of one or two birds except for three at the North Norfolk Coast and five at Killington Reservoir in July, and six at Cassington and Yarnton Gravel Pits in December.

Shelduck (Paul Collier)

Shelduck
Tadorna tadorna

GB max:	56,339	Jan
NI max:	6,349	Jan

International threshold:		3,000
Great Britain threshold:		782
All-Ireland threshold:		70

	S	M	L
GB change:	o	o	o
NI change:	o	+	+

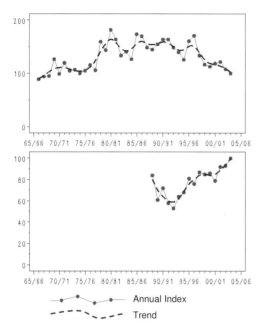

Figure 22.a, Annual indices & trend for Shelduck for GB (above) & NI (below).

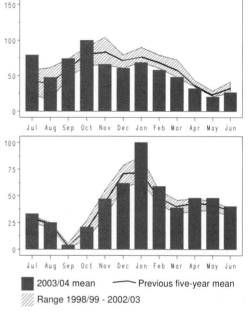

Figure 22.b, Monthly indices for Shelduck for GB (above) & NI (below).

Although essentially a coastal species Shelduck also occur inland, mainly on larger wetlands. Birds in northern Europe are centred on the North Sea with the German and Dutch coasts constituting the most important moulting and wintering areas.

Shelduck have shown an unquestionable increase in Northern Ireland with numbers at Strangford Lough being the highest for eight years. This rise has been evident at other WeBS sites in the region and was reflected in the Northern Irish trend, which has risen consecutively for the past eleven years. British totals showed a different pattern however, with numbers being at their lowest since 1970/71 and although Shelduck numbers have fluctuated a fair amount during this time, totals for the past five years indicated a fall in numbers.

Indices peaked in Britain in October and in Northern Ireland in January, both of which were well above the range of the previous five years. The lag between national peaks may be due to cold weather movements, which has been suggested to be a major factor influencing wintering numbers across UK. Following the October peak, numbers at British sites were below average, while indices in Northern Ireland were more analogous with those of the past five years.

At most sites, average counts were recorded during 2003/04 and there were few changes in the five-year means at the main sites. Peak counts at the Mersey and Dee Estuaries and Martin Mere surpassed their mean peaks for the second consecutive year. Mean peaks at the Alde Complex, Blackwater, Swale and Severn Estuaries all fell by at least 10% on previous figures.

81

	99/00	00/01	01/02	02/03	03/04	Mon	Mean
Sites of international importance in the UK							
Mersey Estuary	15,070	10,084	5,740	19,810	17,823	Jul	13,705
Dee Estuary (England/Wales)	8,814	11,563	10,200	10,533	12,630	Oct	10,748
The Wash	7,608	10,074	11,783	7,834	7,341	Jan	8,928
Morecambe Bay	6,225	(6,707)	6,137	7,164	8,228	Dec	6,939
Humber Estuary	4,020	6,918	3,655	(4,819)	6,426 [11]	Dec	5,255
Strangford Lough	4,251 [11]	3,067 [11]	4,162	4,199 [11]	4,475	Jan	4,031
Solway Estuary	3,270 [11]	(4,626)	(2,213)	(4,324)	3,131	Oct	3,838
Forth Estuary	3,775	3,009	(2,920)	3,531	3,452	Sep	3,442
Severn Estuary	(1,996)	(2,912)	3,776	3,495 [11]	2,579	Sep	3,283
Thames Estuary	(2,711)	(3,385)	2,940	3,040	(1,478)	Feb	3,122
Ribble Estuary	2,908	2,536	3,190	(3,063)	3,829	Oct	3,116 ▲
Sites of national importance in Great Britain							
Medway Estuary	(2,627)	(1,912)	(2,045)	(1,257)	(2,170)	Dec	(2,627)
Blackwater Estuary	(3,093)	(2,873)	(1,808)	(2,572)	1,904	Feb	2,611 ▼
Swale Estuary	2,929	(2,047)	2,342	2,290	1,818	Jan	2,345
Poole Harbour	2,192	1,748	2,221	2,385	(2,072)	Jan	2,137
Stour Estuary	2,351 [11]	2,164 [11]	1,441 [11]	1,916	1,569 [11]	Dec	1,888
Hamford Water	1,369	2,003	1,737 [11]	1,903	(1,657)	Dec	1,753
Lindisfarne	1,224	1,751	1,546 [11]	1,826	1,323 [11]	Nov	1,534
North Norfolk Coast	955	938	2,012 [11]	(1,182)	1,112	Jan	1,254
Alde Complex	1,707	1,328	881	945	1,124	Dec	1,197
Burry Inlet	(1,557)	1,233	963	570	(847)	Dec	1,081
WWT Martin Mere	913	743	950	1,435	1,150	Feb	1,038
Montrose Basin	1,071	907	776	1,191	(1,240)	Dec	1,037
Chichester Harbour	(1,040)	990	1,014 [11]	1,019	810	Feb	975
Colne Estuary	(963)	773	920	(263)	(804)	Feb	885
Crouch-Roach Estuary	836	(483)	(478)	(385)	(342)	Feb	836
Deben Estuary	952	772	676	864	802	Mar	813
Sites of all-Ireland importance in Northern Ireland							
Larne Lough	414	710	776	637	633	Jan	634
Carlingford Lough	321	326	(365)	493	423	Jan	391
Lough Foyle	419	278	536	232	(315)	Mar	366
Belfast Lough	250	319 [11]	437	199 [11]	494 [11]	Feb	340
Loughs Neagh and Beg	157	74	102	146	205	Feb	137
Dundrum Bay	104	79	93	99	138	Jan	103
Bann Estuary	48	50	138	87	71	Mar	79

Muscovy Duck

Cairina moschata

Escape[†]

Native Range: S America

GB max: 48   Jan
NI max: 0

There was no noticeable rise in Muscovy Duck numbers this year compared to 2002/03. Birds were recorded from 34 sites, three fewer than previous, and the summed site maximum of 85 was only one below that of 2002/03.

	99/00	00/01	01/02	02/03	03/04	Mon	Mean
Sites with mean peak counts of 5 or more birds in Great Britain[†]							
Buxton Pavilion Gardens		25					25
Derwent Water	7	21	10	6	6	Nov	10
Par Sands Pools	6	4	20	6	8	Feb	9
Nafferton Mere	12	12	7	1	4	Nov	7
Redwell Fishery	7						7
River Devon - Kersiepow Ponds	7	13	16	0	0		7
Wilderness Pond	0	6	10	12	7	Jul	7
Ft Henry Ponds / Exton Pk Lake	0	15	14	0	0		6
Stanley Park Lakes				5			5

[†] as no British or All-Ireland thresholds have been set a qualifying level of 5 has been chosen to select sites for presentation in this report

Wood Duck
Aix sponsa

Escape
Native Range: N America

GB max:	9 Aug
NI max:	0

Wood Ducks were recorded from eight sites this year. Most notable was a count of eight at Loch Gelly, whilst as during 2002/03 up to six birds were noted throughout the year at Stanton Lake. Singles were at Allestree Park Lakes, Castle Park Lochan, Hay-a-Park Gravel Pits, Middle Pool Shropshire, Plym Estuary and Stour Estuary.

Mandarin
Aix galericulata

Naturalised introduction[†]
Native Range: E Asia

GB max:	551 Dec
NI max:	0

Although Mandarin were introduced to Britain over 250 years ago there has been little dispersal from their stronghold in southern and central England. Numbers recorded by WeBS have reached record levels during 2003/04, continuing the rise seen in recent years. Typically the winter months witness an increase in national totals, which usually peak in December. The British maximum followed this pattern and also exceeded the previous year's peak during November.

Peaks recorded at many key sites were similar to average, but several, notably Bradley Pools, Passfield Pond, Headley Mill Pond, Darwell Reservoir, Harewood Lake and Strawberry Hill Lake, held counts well above their five-year means.

	99/00	00/01	01/02	02/03	03/04	Mon	Mean
Sites with mean peak counts of 10 or more birds in Great Britain[†]							
Forest of Dean Ponds	195 [16]						195
Bradley Pools	26	43	85	55	188	Nov	79
Cuttmill Ponds	65	104	98	51	59	Jul	75
Wraysbury Pond		83	78	63 [12]	61	Dec	71
Stockgrove Country Park	66	80	54	70			68
Dean Heritage Museum Lake				59 [13]			59
Busbridge Lakes		57	54	47	72	Jan	58
Passfield Pond	(10)	61	14	67	73	Sep	54
Headley Mill Pond	18	16	70	76	76	Dec	51
Dee Flood Meadows	36	31	79	49	32	Sep	45
Severn Estuary	32	72	65	28	3	Mar	40
Soudley Ponds				39 [13]			39
Darwell Reservoir	6	46	43	25	56	Oct	35
Arun Valley	36	31	28	41	32	Aug	34
Bough Beech Reservoir	2	40 [13]	63	27	(40)	Nov	34
Connaught Water	27	54	26	31	33	Nov	34
Sutton Place			44	21	32	Aug	32
Lost / Golding Hill / Baldwins Hill	6	45	10	78	18	Feb	31
River Thames at Staines Bridge				31			31
Harewood Lake	6	10	11	53	35	Dec	23
Paultons Bird Park			21	20			21
Fonthill Lake	23	23	17	18	20	Dec	20
Woburn Park Lakes	18	25	12	24	8	Jul	17
Cannop Ponds				15 [13]			15
Osterley Park Lakes	23	8	13	20	13	Jul	15
Strawberry Hill Ponds	1	8	7	30	23	Nov	14
Gatton Park	7	15	20	18	5	Oct	13
Panshanger Estate	6	8	16	24	12	Aug	13
Bramshill Park Lake	19	(14)	4	15 [13]	8	Sep	12

[†] *as no British or All-Ireland thresholds have been set a qualifying level of 10 has been chosen to select sites for presentation in this report*

Wigeon
Anas penelope

International threshold: 15,000
Great Britain threshold: 4,060
All-Ireland threshold: 1,250

GB max: 447,675   Jan
NI max: 8,730   Nov

	S	M	L
GB change:	o	o	++
NI change:	o	o	-

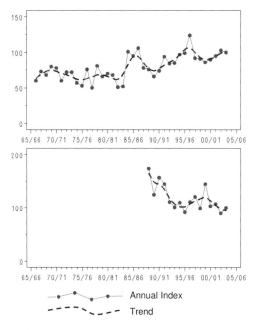

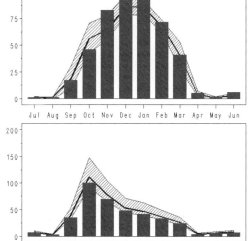

Annual Index

Trend

2003/04 mean   Previous five-year mean

Range 1998/99 - 2002/03

Figure 23.a, Annual indices & trend for Wigeon for GB (above) & NI (below).

Figure 23.b, Monthly indices for Wigeon for GB (above) & NI (below).

The UK's wintering population of Wigeon includes birds from Iceland, Scandinavia, northern Europe and eastern Russia, as well as birds from the small breeding population centred in northern England and Scotland. Wigeon are highly sociable and large wintering flocks are typical around British Estuaries and large inland waters.

Wintering numbers of Wigeon are characteristically variable due to movements in response to cold weather. Nevertheless the variation between years has been slight during recent years, yet the British indices have shown a definite rise. Britain witnessed a subtle fall in the index during 2003/04, which was well within the expected level of between-year variation. In contrast, the 2003/04 Northern Irish index was higher than in 2002/03, although the overall trend suggests a steady decline.

As usual Britain's key sites held peak numbers of Wigeon during January and between November and February indices were above average. Again this pattern was reversed in Northern Ireland, which held below average numbers in all months. However, the indices did follow the usual trend of an October peak followed by a steady decrease in subsequent months.

There were few changes at the main sites and the Ribble Estuary clearly remains the most important site for this species. Following high counts during 2003/04 an additional four sites hold nationally important numbers; these were predominately in the west.

	99/00	00/01	01/02	02/03	03/04	Mon	Mean
Sites of international importance in the UK							
Ribble Estuary	50,678	(63,921)	68,661	75,617	82,627	Jan	69,396
Somerset Levels	(21,965) [13]	28,366	28,779	(39,492)	29,397	Jan	31,509
Ouse Washes	24,540	14,874 [13]	26,623	26,753 [13]	33,773 [13]	Jan	25,313
North Norfolk Coast	18,950	20,083	19,078	16,056	20,694	Jan	18,972

	99/00	00/01	01/02	02/03	03/04	Mon	Mean
Swale Estuary	11,725	(17,637)	15,303	20,827	20,772	Jan	17,253
Breydon Water / Berney Marshes	14,130	15,700	21,700	15,999 [11]	16,811	Jan	16,868
Sites of national importance in Great Britain							
Dornoch Firth	9,305	(17,445)	17,967	16,979	12,485	Oct	14,836
Cromarty Firth	14,956 [11]	14,027	11,987	(6,041)	12,877	Dec	13,462
Lindisfarne	5,006	14,141	(12,435)	(20,016)	(12,321)	Nov	12,784
Lower Derwent Ings	8,600						8,600
Nene Washes	6,994	10,808	5,053	11,866	8,190	Jan	8,582
Inner Moray and Inverness Firth	9,746	7,260	7,070	7,820	(7,568)	Dec	7,974
Blackwater Estuary	4,296	6,507	(5,789)	10,976	7,057	Feb	7,209
Alde Complex	6,676	7,145	6,647 [11]	7,387	(4,956)	Jan	6,964
Severn Estuary	3,459	(5,789)	(5,579)	7,019	9,110	Jan	6,529
Mersey Estuary	8,731 [11]	8,279	9,150	4,280	2,044	Jan	6,497
Morecambe Bay	5,289	7,746	5,861	5,634	7,151	Jan	6,336
Loch of Harray	(5,092)	9,476	4,255	(2,682)	4,823	Dec	6,185
Thames Estuary	2,975	5,392	5,808	9,784	5,345	Jan	5,861
R. Avon: R'gwood - Christchurch	(3,051)	4,945 [13]	(1,450)	6,394	(1,783)	Jan	5,670
Solway Estuary	(2,146)	(2,778)	(3,085)	(5,497)	(3,671)	Dec	(5,497)
Middle Yare Marshes	5,387	4,794	5,668	5,508	4,998	Feb	5,271
Arun Valley	4,173	5,343	4,010	6,237	5,073	Jan	4,967
Montrose Basin	4,402	3,446	4,381	4,752	5,488	Nov	4,494
Dee Estuary (England/Wales)	2,751	4,681	4,941 [11]	3,979	(5,658)	Nov	4,402 ▲
Cleddau Estuary	(3,532)	(3,604)	3,192	3,720	6,045	Dec	4,319 ▲
Fleet and Wey	1,889	3,062	5,337	5,360	(5,105)	Dec	4,151 ▲
Cassington / Yarnton Gravel Pits	(758)	(377)	(437)	(530)	4,144	Jan	4,144 ▲
Sites of all-Ireland importance in Northern Ireland							
Lough Foyle	11,496	8,051	5,696	2,609	3,978	Oct	6,366
Loughs Neagh and Beg	5,743	2,375	2,707	1,908	3,045	Dec	3,156
Strangford Lough	2,469	2,509	2,414	3,400	4,299	Nov	3,018

American Wigeon
Anas americana

Vagrant
Native Range: N & C America

GB max: 5 Jan
NI max: 0

Birds were recorded at ten sites this year, mostly likely to be genuine vagrants between September and February although one at Dorchester Gravel Pits in April was a long-staying bird considered an escape. Apart from two at Loch of Hillwell in December, where single birds were present in January and February, all other sites held just one bird: Crowdy Reservoir, Dee Estuary (England/Wales), Hayle Estuary, Loch Ardnave, Loch Bee, Moine Mhor & Add Estuary, North Norfolk Coast and Stour Estuary.

Chiloe Wigeon
Anas sibilatrix

Escape
Native Range: S America

GB max: 1 Jul
NI max: 0

Singles were recorded at Harewood Lake in July, Eyebrook Reservoir in September and Cloddach Gravel Pit in December.

Gadwall
Anas strepera

	International threshold:	600
	Great Britain threshold:	171
	All-Ireland threshold:	+[†]

GB max: 16,527   Dec
NI max: 211   Feb

	S	M	L
GB change:	o	+	++
NI change:	o	o	o

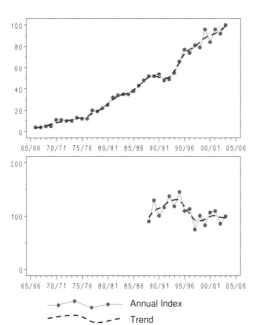 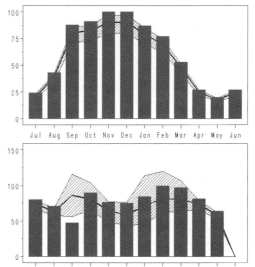

Annual Index
Trend

2003/04 mean   Previous five-year mean
Range 1998/99 - 2002/03

Figure 24.a, Annual indices & trend for Gadwall for GB (above) & NI (below).

Figure 24.b, Monthly indices for Gadwall for GB (above) & NI (below).

The Gadwall is a widespread and increasing species throughout much of Great Britain, although the stronghold remains central and southern England. The wintering population includes birds from north and east Europe, whilst some of the British breeding population, which is currently estimated at less than 1,000 breeding pairs, winter in southern Europe.

The long-term success of Gadwall in Great Britain continues with both 2003/2004 counts and index values being the highest ever recorded. Despite the slight fluctuation of recent years there has been an approximate doubling of the numbers recorded by WeBS during the last ten years. Similar growth in this population has been reported across Europe (Wetlands International 2002). Numbers recorded in Northern Ireland were slightly higher than the previous winter, although the

species is still much more scarce here than in England.

Numbers recorded by WeBS increased during winter and, in Great Britain, peaked in November and December. Some of the key sites, however, had their maximum counts recorded during August. Most other sites, however, as well as those in Northern Ireland supported the greatest numbers during the autumn and winter months, likely to be due to an influx of birds moving in from northern and eastern Europe and dispersal of moulting aggregations.

Rutland Water remains the top site for Gadwall and is the only site to surpass 1,000 birds in more than one reporting year. Other notable counts include unusually high numbers at Pitsford Reservoir and a low peak count for Brent Reservoir.

	99/00	00/01	01/02	02/03	03/04	Mon	Mean
Sites of international importance in the UK							
Rutland Water	1,529	967	747	867	1,096	Aug	1,041
R. Avon: F'bridge - Ringwood	612	897 [13]	525	824	701	Dec	712
Somerset Levels	(527)	453	754	(1,077)	430	Dec	679
Lee Valley Gravel Pits	(764)	526	717	808	560	Dec	675

	99/00	00/01	01/02	02/03	03/04	Mon	Mean
Thames Estuary	(439)	(535)	512	815	(543)	Feb	664
Ouse Washes	808 [13]	393	433 [13]	782	889 [13]	Mar	661 ▲
Wraysbury Gravel Pits	612	713	552	745	516	Oct	628
Sites of national importance in Great Britain							
Abberton Reservoir	549	746	173	730	519	Aug	543
Loch Leven	544	270	320	840	635	Sep	522
Thrapston Gravel Pits	668	531	(98)	(218)	207	Dec	469
Pitsford Reservoir	204	259	581	164	898	Oct	421
Hoveton Great Broad	230	283	310		667	Jan	373
Chichester Gravel Pits	289	307	569	349	279	Dec	359
Horsey Mere	316						316
Cotswold Water Park (West)	282	194	267	403	375	Dec	304
Chew Valley Lake	145	310	230	360	410	Aug	291
Fen Drayton Gravel Pits	186	345	362	336	219	Dec	290
Eversley Cross / Yateley GPs	248	323	292	305	230	Jan	280
Little Paxton Gravel Pits	132	360	287	275	339	Jan	279
Hornsea Mere	(380)	265	240	285	219	Aug	278
Severn Estuary	294	298	250	253	292	Jan	277
Orwell Estuary	165 [11]	150	160 [11]	465 [11]	446	Nov	277
Stodmarsh & Collards Lagoon	276	222	259	360	264	Sep	276
North Norfolk Coast	(294)	250	(221)	215	262	Aug	255
Lower Derwent Ings	255						255
Colne Valley Gravel Pits	(155)	(412)	(211)	149	238	Dec	253
Lackford GPs			68	432			250
Thorpe Water Park	(249)	(157)	(55)	(74)	(74)	Dec	(249)
Fairburn Ings	342	220	150	154	367	Oct	247
Burghfield Gravel Pits	175			312			244
Minsmere	0	366 [13]	212	394	239	Sep	242
Sutton and Lound Gravel Pits	274		370	58			234
Alton Water	168	92	268	270	360	Dec	232
Lakenheath Fen				179	263	Feb	221
Whitlingham Country Park	187	145	177	222	358	Dec	218 ▲
Buckden and Stirtloe Pits	257	284	118	208			217
Hickling Broad	198	229					214 ▲
Dinton Pastures	204		291	144			213
Woolston Eyes	165	211	124	182	297	Aug	196 ▲
Meadow Lane Gravel Pits St Ives	59	195	211	321	190	Jan	195
Blagdon Lake	175	178	257	17	335	Aug	192 ▲
Alde Complex	78	(106)	277	163	(244)	Jan	191 ▲
Ravensthorpe Reservoir	144	42	372	288	98	Dec	189
Brent Reservoir	180	306	295	109	33	Jan	185
Earls Barton Gravel Pits	279	159	140 [13]	(207)	124	Sep	182
Blatherwyke Lake	236	174	116	188			179 ▲
Middle Tame Valley Gravel Pits	127	(113)	(100)	(156)	(255)	Oct	179 ▲
Ditchford Gravel Pits	230	104	(118)		192	Feb	175
Sites no longer meeting table qualifying levels in WeBS-Year 2003/2004							
Eyebrook Reservoir		101	162	250	134	Sep	162
Humber Estuary	(64)	(73)	(102)	176	104	Dec	140
Hampton / Kempton Reservoirs	273	113	100	122	91	Aug	140
Sites with mean peak counts of 10 or more birds in Northern Ireland[†]							
Loughs Neagh and Beg	138	155	178	149	173	Mar	159
Strangford Lough	62	72	58	57	73	Jan	64
Hillsborough Main Lake	53	3	27	12	41	Jan	27
Other sites attaining table qualifying levels in WeBS-Year 2003/2004 in Great Britain							
Swithland Reservoir	59	117	(46)	243	237	Dec	164
Tring Reservoirs	68	102	111	94	217	Jan	118
Radwell Gravel Pits	74	58	58	93	215	Feb	100
Llyn Traffwll	62	47	48	45	208	Nov	82
Tees Estuary	(136)	76	(107)	201	206	Nov	161
Lower Windrush Valley GPs	55	188	81	142	205	Nov	134
Frampton Pools	8	120	130	148	192	Nov	120
Hanningfield Reservoir	159	159	217	69	180	Oct	157
Swale Estuary	94	(119)	158	157	176	Mar	146

[†] as no All-Ireland threshold has been set a qualifying level of 10 has been chosen to select sites for presentation in this report

Cape Teal
Anas capensis

Escape
Native Range: S & C Africa

GB max: 1 Mar
NI max: 0

One was recorded at Stanton Lake in March.

Teal
Anas crecca

International threshold:	4,000
Great Britain threshold:	1,920
All-Ireland threshold:	650

GB max: 174,438 Jan
NI max: 7,527 Dec

	S	M	L
GB change:	o	o	++
NI change:	o	o	o

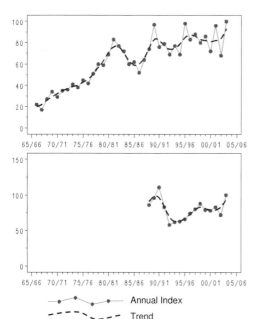

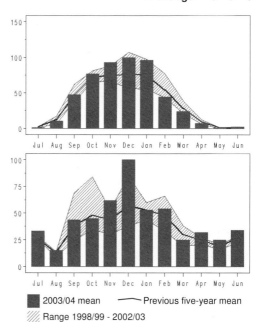

Figure 25.a, Annual indices & trend for Teal for GB (above) & NI (below).

Figure 25.b, Monthly indices for Teal for GB (above) & NI (below).

Although the breeding range of the Teal extends through most of northern Europe and across Russia, the UK wintering population consists primarily of birds from the nearby continent, Scandinavia and Iceland. Additionally, local breeding birds are generally resident although cold weather movements from and to the UK are commonly recognised.

Indices for Teal in Northern Ireland have increased by over a third on the previous year, being the highest for over 12 years. In spite of this, the mean peaks at the four top sites varied little and totals at Lough Foyle and Upper Lough Erne even fell by three-quarters compared to the previous year.

British sites have experienced high levels of annual fluctuation in Teal numbers during recent years; a trend that continued into 2003/04. The annual index rose by almost 50% during 2003/04 to reach its highest ever level. Noteworthy totals were recorded at the Ribble, the Humber, Martin Mere, the Wash and Minsmere, all of which exceeded their five-year means. Monthly indices were slightly above average during the early part of the winter but numbers fell below average after January. December was the only remarkable month in Northern Ireland with Teal numbers being twice the average for the past five-years.

	99/00	00/01	01/02	02/03	03/04	Mon	Mean	
Sites of international importance in the UK								
Somerset Levels	13,641	(19,040) [13]	29,586	(33,350)	17,225	Jan	23,451	
Mersey Estuary	11,700	8,777	17,660	7,855	8,364	Jan	10,871	
Thames Estuary	(4,007)	(4,610)	6,994	9,780	6,361	Jan	7,712	
Ribble Estuary	5,748	7,874	5,316	4,671	7,421	Jan	6,206	
Dee Estuary (England/Wales)	5,185	5,622	6,887 [11]	4,361	5,459	Nov	5,503	
Hamford Water	1,514	2,510	9,055 [11]	3,628	6,579	Dec	4,657	
North Norfolk Coast	(3,133)	4,186	5,718	5,281	3,436	Jan	4,655	
Loch Leven	4,320	2,940	4,100	6,562	4,847	Oct	4,554	
WWT Martin Mere	3,710	6,700	4,460	2,750	5,100	Dec	4,544	
Severn Estuary	(4,719)	5,151	(4,449)	3,748	(3,006)	Jan	4,539	
Swale Estuary	2,388	4,385	4,297	5,752	5,428	Oct	4,450	▲
Ouse Washes	3,212	2,429	5,757	4,433 [13]	5,102	Dec	4,187	▲
Lower Derwent Ings	4,100						4,100	
Sites of national importance in Great Britain								
Breydon Water / Berney Marshes	3,150	4,237	6,487	3,124	1,982	Feb	3,796	
R. Avon: R'gwood - Christchurch	(104)	2,178 [13]	(654)	4,841	(695)	Feb	3,510	
Blackwater Estuary	2,598	(4,867)	2,517	3,721	(2,873)	Jan	3,426	
Mersehead RSPB Reserve	970	4,180	4,390	3,100	2,850	Jan	3,098	
Humber Estuary	2,765	3,370	1,300	2,681	(5,111)	Oct	3,045	
Arun Valley	2,438	4,276	2,194	3,934	1,912	Jan	2,951	
Inner Moray and Inverness Firth	2,921	2,794	2,289	2,948 [11]	3,439	Oct	2,878	
Solway Estuary	(1,387)	(2,101)	(750)	(2,813)	(1,266)	Sep	(2,813)	
Alde Complex	1,837	(2,234)	3,690	2,609	(2,530)	Dec	2,712	
Abberton Reservoir	5,450	488	(1,871)	736	3,863	Nov	2,634	
Morecambe Bay	1,719	(2,956)	2,519	(2,261)	(2,808)	Jan	2,453	
Dornoch Firth	2,039	2,261	2,797	2,502	2,619	Oct	2,444	
Woolston Eyes	(1,800)	2,100	3,675	1,320	2,072	Jan	2,292	
Cleddau Estuary	(2,438)	2,427	(1,621)	2,095	2,129	Dec	2,272	
Otmoor		(1,313)	856	3,633			2,245	
Nene Washes	1,548	1,592	940	4,046	2,730	Jan	2,171	
Horsey Mere	2,143						2,143	
The Wash	1,418	808	2,217	1,918	4,223	Jan	2,117	▲
Minsmere	21	1,700 [13]	2,227	2,189	4,381	Dec	2,104	▲
Forth Estuary	1,419	(2,359)	(1,585)	1,984	(2,511)	Jan	2,068	
Sites of all-Ireland importance in Northern Ireland								
Loughs Neagh and Beg	1,487	2,002	1,633	1,887	2,732	Dec	1,948	
Strangford Lough	1,627	1,189	2,121	2,177	2,232	Dec	1,869	
Lough Foyle	577	2,888	684	2,275	582	Oct	1,401	
Upper Lough Erne	1,379	308	333	1,635	407	Dec	812	

Green-winged Teal
Anas carolinensis

Vagrant
Native Range: N America

GB max:	6	Dec
NI max:	0	

Green-winged Teals were noted from 13 sites this year, records coming from eight months but with a peak of six in December. All records involved single birds, the sites being Carsebreck and Rhynd Lochs, Dee Estuary (England/Wales), Duns Dish, Earls Barton Gravel Pits, Garths Loch Scatness, Hayle Estuary, Inner Moray Firth, Linford Gravel Pits, Loch Gruinart Floods, Loch Leven, Minsmere, Woodhorn Flashes and WWT Martin Mere.

Speckled Teal
Anas flavirostris

Escape
Native Range: S America

GB max:	2	May
NI max:	0	

Two were noted at Woburn Park Lakes in May.

Mallard
Anas platyrhynchos

GB max: 142,045   Dec
NI max: 7,858   Sep

International threshold: 20,000**
Great Britain threshold: 3,520†
All-Ireland threshold: 500

	S	M	L
GB change:	o	o	o
NI change:	o	o	o

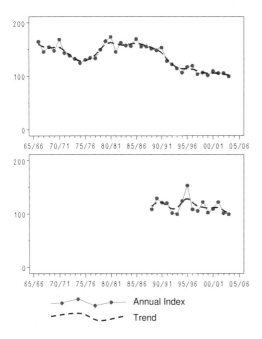

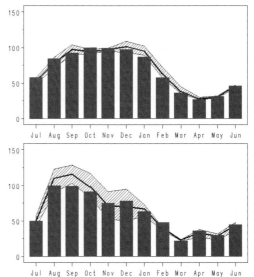

2003/04 mean — Previous five-year mean

/// Range 1998/99 - 2002/03

Figure 26.a, Annual indices & trend for Mallard for GB (above) & NI (below).

Figure 26.b, Monthly indices for Mallard for GB (above) & NI (below).

Mallard are undoubtedly the most frequently recorded species during WeBS, being confirmed at nearly 2,000 sites during 2003/04. Much of the Mallard's success is due to the wide range of habitats utilised by this species, which range from large inland waterbodies, marshes, Estuaries, small ponds, rivers and, to a lesser extent, open coasts, as well as their tolerance of humans. Around 150,000 pairs are estimated to breed in Britain and Ireland with the majority of these being sedentary. During the winter months, birds from Iceland and nearby Europe join the resident population, with cold weather movements bringing in additional birds from the Baltic and northeastern Europe.

Although the year-to-year changes in the British index have in themselves been small, the underlying trend has suffered its 15th consecutive drop and the current value is the lowest that has been recorded by WeBS. This decline was mirrored in the national maxima, which were 4% lower than in the previous year. A similar decline was experienced in both the summed totals and annual index for Northern Ireland and although the index reached its second lowest level the annual change was within the expected fluctuation of recent years.

With such a widespread and abundant species it is not surprising that only six sites held nationally important numbers, four of which were in Northern Ireland; reflecting the lower threshold value. In line with national figures 2003/04 totals at these four sites were below average. Despite this, the highest total from a single site in the UK was of 4,774 in September at Loughs Neagh and Beg. Key sites in Britain fared slightly better with approximately half of the sites averaging over 1,000 birds exceeding their five-year mean. Monthly indices revealed a contrast between Britain, which were above average during early winter and below later, and Northern Ireland, where the pattern was reversed.

	99/00	00/01	01/02	02/03	03/04	Mon	Mean
Sites of national importance in Great Britain							
Lower Derwent Ings	4,250						4,250
Ouse Washes	4,168 [13]	3,657	4,457	3,580 [13]	3,988 [13]	Dec	3,970
Sites of all-Ireland importance in Northern Ireland							
Loughs Neagh and Beg	3,828	6,431	4,242	4,753	4,774	Sep	4,806
Strangford Lough	1,514	1,807	2,227	1,851	1,568	Dec	1,793
Lough Foyle	1,336	1,298	1,181	705	791	Sep	1,062
Lower Lough Erne				533	(494)	Dec	533
Sites no longer meeting table qualifying levels in WeBS-Year 2003/2004							
Upper Lough Erne	603	323	514	730	211	Dec	476
Sites with mean peak counts of 2,000 or more birds in Great Britain[†]							
WWT Martin Mere	2,230	2,400	3,800	3,280	3,350	Oct	3,012
Severn Estuary	(2,767)	3,265	2,761	2,936	2,701	Sep	2,916
Morecambe Bay	3,334	(3,126)	(1,683)	2,455	2,208	Sep	2,781
Ampton Water	1,746			2,535	3,735	Aug	2,672
Humber Estuary	2,001	3,460	1,626	2,957	(2,347)	Oct	2,511
The Wash	2,350	3,264	1,781	2,384	2,639	Jan	2,484
Tring Reservoirs	(1,500)	(1,700)	1,834	2,800	2,000	Aug	2,211
Solway Estuary	2,176 [11]	(1,856)	(1,033)	(1,954)	(1,400)	Dec	2,176
Somerset Levels	(1,615)	2,681	1,932	2,587	1,335	Jan	2,134

[†] *as few sites exceed the British threshold a qualifying level of 2,000 has been chosen to select sites for presentation in this report*

Chestnut Teal
Anas castanea

Escape
Native Range: S Australia

GB max: 2   Sep
NI max: 0

Two were at Liden Lagoon in September with   another at Spade Oak Gravel Pit in January.

Pintail
Anas acuta

International threshold: 600
Great Britain threshold: 279
All-Ireland threshold: 60

	S	M	L
GB max: 27,418 Jan	GB change:	o o o
NI max: 595 Jan	NI change:	o + +

GB max: 27,418   Jan
NI max: 595   Jan

GB change: o   o   o
NI change: o   +   +

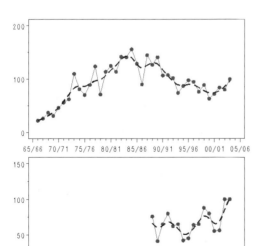

Annual Index
Trend

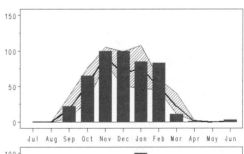

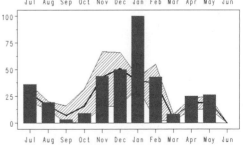

2003/04 mean   Previous five-year mean
Range 1998/99 - 2002/03

Figure 27.a, Annual indices & trend for Pintail for GB (above) & NI (below).

Figure 27.b, Monthly indices for Pintail for GB (above) & NI (below).

The main breeding areas for the Pintail include northern and Baltic Europe, Scandinavia and Russia. Birds from these areas winter across a large geographical range, which covers northern Europe, west and equatorial Africa to the Middle East. Northern Europe is an important area for this species with a large proportion of the key wintering sites occurring around the North Sea. Breeding records in the UK are scarce with most of the UK wintering population breeding in Iceland, or eastwards from Scandinavia and Eastern Europe.

Pintail numbers typically start to build up across Britain in late autumn and include passage birds en route towards southern Europe or Ireland. Accordingly, 2003/04 saw numbers triple between September and October and another rise of a half by November. Numbers between September and February were above average, and above the range of the previous five years during December and February. Conversely, March values were comparable to the lower limit of the same period.

The high numbers between October and January correspond to the increase in the British indices, which rose 25% on the previous year. The British index reached its highest level for over ten years and rose by over a third in the last four years, following a sustained decline. A similar trend has been observed in Northern Ireland, 2003/04 values being the highest ever recorded. Although Pintail numbers in Northern Ireland are typically variable, the underlying trend has highlighted a rise over the past 15 years, most of which has been due to increasing numbers being recorded at Strangford Lough.

Peak counts at the majority of British sites were unremarkable with few changes in five-year means. A handful of sites held numbers exceeding their five-year means, almost all of which were west coast sites and included the Dee Estuary, the Ribble Estuary, Burry Inlet and the Duddon Estuary. One exception, however, was the Wash, which held numbers in excess of 1,000 birds for the second year running.

	99/00	00/01	01/02	02/03	03/04	Mon	Mean
Sites of international importance in the UK							
Dee Estuary (England/Wales)	(2,356)	4,216	6,023	6,000 [13]	6,317	Nov	5,639
Solway Estuary	(3,067)	2,818 [11]	(8,070)	(3,357)	(4,183)	Jan	4,299
Morecambe Bay	4,161	2,387	3,471	3,628	(3,942)	Nov	3,518
Burry Inlet	(3,609)	1,328	1,305	4,410	5,772	Feb	3,285
Ouse Washes	3,804	1,498 [13]	2,606 [13]	2,844 [13]	2,277 [13]	Jan	2,606
Nene Washes	(353)	2,671	1,250	3,478	1,779	Jan	2,295
Ribble Estuary	747	819	619	1,405	(2,562)	Nov	1,230
North Norfolk Coast	1,235	987	1,296	(475)	(767)	Nov	1,173
Medway Estuary	(463)	(475)	(1,118)	(333)	(95)	Dec	(1,118)
Somerset Levels	570	1,546	1,084	(1,315)	494	Jan	1,002
Dee Flood Meadows	(472)	(990)	1,050	(628)	580	Feb	873
R. Avon: R'gwood - Christchurch	30	1,385 [13]	(280)	2,013	25	Nov	863
Severn Estuary	778	(981)	(780)	(891)	(354)	Jan	858
Swale Estuary	395	952	998	946	962	Jan	851
Duddon Estuary	810	(628)	391	(415)	(1,299)	Jan	782
The Wash	200	70	516	1,253	1,086	Feb	625 ▲
Stour Estuary	629 [11]	691	629	613 [11]	467	Jan	606
Sites of national importance in Great Britain							
Arun Valley	199	(1,171)	(413)	(775)	403	Dec	592 ▼
Alde Complex	495	(506)	705	403	(330)	Jan	534
Mersehead RSPB Reserve	46	480	410	1,140	480	Jan	511
Ashleworth Ham	52	291	2,000 [13]	40	121	Feb	501
Blackwater Estuary	(295)	(325)	(352)	(498)	461	Feb	480
WWT Martin Mere	313	344	635	487	463	Jan	448
Coombe Hill Canal	(36)	(90)	800 [13]	70	(190)	Jan	435
Pagham Harbour	434 [11]	340	587	304	477	Jan	428
Mersey Estuary	1,100	491	134	220	152	Jan	419
Breydon Water / Berney Marshes	204	446	329	571	271 [11]	Feb	364
Lower Derwent Ings	347						347
Otmoor		396 [13]	160 [13]	481 [13]			346
Thames Estuary	(128)	(244)	(223)	335 [11]	(114)	Feb	335
Orwell Estuary	115 [11]	179 [11]	473 [11]	372 [11]	325 [11]	Jan	293 ▲
Poole Harbour	227	296	424	191	316	Jan	291

	99/00	00/01	01/02	02/03	03/04	Mon	Mean
Blyth Estuary (Suffolk)		202	368				285
Inner Moray and Inverness Firth	227	307	313	310	258	Dec	283
Sites of all-Ireland importance in Northern Ireland							
Strangford Lough	303	249	348	378	582	Jan	372
Other sites attaining table qualifying levels in WeBS-Year 2003/2004 in Great Britain							
North West Solent	(250)	100	233	96	391	Feb	214
Lindisfarne	92	196	272 [11]	330	384	Jan	255
Cromarty Firth	340 [11]	60	66 [13]	204	375	Dec	209
Loch Leven	102	112	32	275	302	Oct	165
Bayfield Loch	190	195	229	137	300	Jan	210
Dyfi Estuary	245	235	304 [11]	196 [11]	282	Jan	252
Other sites attaining table qualifying levels in WeBS-Year 2003/2004 in Northern Ireland							
Belfast Lough	0	0	1	1	66	Dec	14

Bahama Pintail

Anas bahamensis

Escape
Native Range: S America

GB max: 10 Jan
NI max: 0

Single birds were noted at the Dee Estuary (England/Wales) in May and at Doddington Pool from January to March, whilst at Woodford Ponds there was an exceptional record of nine present in January.

Red-billed Teal

Anas erythrorhyncha

Escape
Native Range: Africa

GB max: 2 Jan
NI max: 0

Two were noted at Copped Hall Pond in January.

Garganey

Anas querquedula

International threshold: 20,000**
Great Britain threshold: +[†]
All-Ireland threshold: +[†]

GB max: 42 Sep
NI max: 0

Garganey are unique among UK wildfowl species, their occurrence being almost exclusively restricted to the summer months. A small breeding population, concentrated in central and eastern England, is estimated to number fewer than 125 pairs. Favouring freshwater marshes with a dense fringe of vegetation, Garganey are found less often in coastal waters. Garganey migrate to south of the Sahara with the main wintering area for birds of northwest Europe being West Africa.

Garganey numbers peaked in September with a national total that was slightly down on the previous year. Unsurprisingly, nearly all site counts were in single figures and were during the main months for migration, April and September. A single bird was present at Rutland Water in November, which was the latest record for the UK until 12, including eight at Breydon Water / Berney Marshes and two at Ingrebourne Valley, appeared the following March.

	1999	2000	2001	2002	2003	Mon	Mean
Sites with mean peak counts of 4 or more birds in Great Britain[†]							
Stodmarsh & Collards Lagoon	7	12	30	5	7	Jun	12
Thames Estuary	6	9	(2)	(5)	(1)	May	8
Wraysbury Gravel Pits	10	2	0	15	12	Sep	8
Ouse Washes	7	9	3	7	2	Mar	6
Breydon Water / Berney Marshes	8	6	4	4	4	Jun	5
Dungeness Gravel Pits	3	2	12	(0)	3	Sep	5
North Norfolk Coast	7	3	(4)	(4)	(3)	Jul	5
Dee Estuary (England/Wales)	(2)	(4)	(0)	(3)	(1)	Oct	(4)

	1999	2000	2001	2002	2003	Mon	Mean
Fairburn Ings	10	4	0	2	2	May	4
Nene Washes	7	2	2	0	8	Mar	4
Rye Harbour and Pett Level	2	1	7	9	2	Mar	4
Severn Estuary	(2)	4	4	(7)	2	Mar	4
Tees Estuary	8	3	(0)	1	2	May	4

† *as no British or All-Ireland thresholds have been set a qualifying level of 4 has been chosen to select sites for presentation in this report*

Blue-winged Teal
Anas discors

Vagrant and escape
Native Range: America

GB max: 1   Aug
NI max: 0

One was recorded at Chew Valley Lake in August.

Cinnamon Teal
Anas cyanoptera

Escape
Native Range: America

GB max: 1   Jan
NI max: 0

One was seen at the Lower Windrush Valley Gravel Pits in January.

Shoveler
Anas clypeata

International threshold:		400
Great Britain threshold:		148
All-Ireland threshold:		65

	S	M	L
GB change:	o	o	+
NI change:	o	o	o

GB max: 9,761   Feb
NI max: 241   Jan

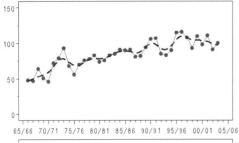

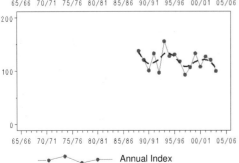

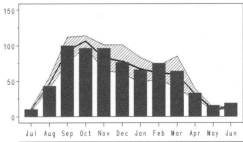

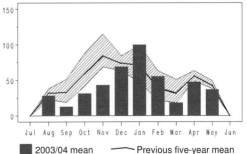

Figure 28.a, Annual indices & trend for Shoveler for GB (above) & NI (below).

Figure 28.b, Monthly indices for Shoveler for GB (above) & NI (below).

Shoveler winter throughout Europe and as far south as West Africa. The UK wintering population is made up primarily of birds from Scandinavia and northeastern Russia. During harsh winters, cold weather can bring in birds from the Wadden Sea, although movements to southwest Europe are not uncommon. Current breeding estimates exceed 1,000 pairs, which are mainly found in south and east Britain. Many of these birds appear to move south in the winter.

In line with the high level of recent fluctuations seen across Britain, the index rose on the previous year. The longer-term trend suggests a slight decline, however, current values are still higher than ten years ago. Northern Irish totals have also shown high variation during the past few years, however, in contrast to the British index the 2003/04 values fell for the second year running.

With the exception of a low count during October, usually the peak month for Shoveler in Britain, and a high February count, monthly indices were within the normal range of variation.

Mean peaks at nine sites surpassed the international qualifying threshold and due to the fall in the Burry Inlet's average this was one less than previously. Five sites failed to maintain nationally important numbers while mean peaks at Walthamstow, Hampton/Kempton and Pitsford Reservoirs as well as at the Middle Yare Marshes all surpassed nationally important levels. Strangford Lough remained the only Northern Irish site to hold nationally important numbers.

	99/00	00/01	01/02	02/03	03/04	Mon	Mean
Sites of international importance in the UK							
Somerset Levels	635	1,343	1,170	(2,190)	784	Jan	1,224
Ouse Washes	980 [13]	396 [13]	968 [13]	1,125	1,104 [13]	Mar	915
Rutland Water	1,154	401	608	504	475	Sep	628
Chew Valley Lake	425	270	805	535	565	Sep	520
Thames Estuary	187	564	(605)	697	353	Jan	481
Breydon Water / Berney Marshes	356	620	679	415	322	Mar	478
Swale Estuary	498	511	587	440	330	Dec	473
Loch Leven	420	480	400	550	295	Sep	429
Abberton Reservoir	375	352	440	422	488	Nov	415
Sites of national importance in Great Britain							
Burry Inlet	(573)	368	215	397	327	Feb	376 ▼
Dungeness Gravel Pits	269	398	504	320	378	Sep	374
Lee Valley Gravel Pits	(241)	374	321	(308)	(246)	Dec	348
Severn Estuary	(206)	306	366	368 [11]	325	Feb	341
Staines Reservoirs	312	(130)	356	377	261	Oct	327
Nene Washes	406	190	374	262	200	Feb	286
Medway Estuary	(122)	(71)	(280)	(20)	(26)	Dec	(280)
Stodmarsh & Collards Lagoon	(280)	(409)	206	244	202	Mar	268
Alde Complex	161	(181)	(407)	229	(106)	Nov	266
Llynnau Y Fali	92	464	176	337	233	Mar	260
Confidential SE England Site	320	164	520	125	120	Jan	250
Arun Valley	163	392	227	259	195	Jan	247
Ribble Estuary	173	393	179	197	231	Jan	235
Chichester Gravel Pits	112	160	317	238	321	Feb	230
Wraysbury Gravel Pits	399	154	260 [13]	221	97	Sep	226
Blithfield Reservoir	443	341	58	148	60	Aug	210
North Norfolk Coast	153	203	289	182	212	Mar	208
Fairburn Ings	144	289	153	159	221	Nov	193
Rye Harbour and Pett Level	130	160	282	167	204	Oct	189
R. Avon: F'bridge - Ringwood	81	182	117	361	188	Dec	186
Tees Estuary	131	(260)	114	245	164	Oct	183
Morecambe Bay	86	57	380	(82)	184	Jan	177
Fen Drayton Gravel Pits	92	378	157	128	115	Jan	174
Solway Estuary	(77)	(174)	(59)	(144)	(27)	Nov	(174)
Blagdon Lake	95	145	400	75	146	Sep	172
Minsmere	0	241 [13]	207	233	180	Feb	172
Walthamstow Reservoirs	143	157	179	135	212	Sep	165 ▲
Hampton / Kempton Reservoirs	147	118	208	(88)	165	Feb	160 ▲
Brent Reservoir	241	183	230	125	20	Jan	160
Pitsford Reservoir	47	114	153	91	378	Nov	157 ▲
Middle Yare Marshes	123	(175)	151	169	(96)	Feb	155 ▲

	99/00	00/01	01/02	02/03	03/04	Mon	Mean
Malltraeth RSPB	145	(157)	(145)	186	124	Jan	153
Humber Estuary	195	146	(78)	109	(127)	Oct	150
Sites of all-Ireland importance in Northern Ireland							
Strangford Lough	168	159	182	199	201	Jan	182
Sites no longer meeting table qualifying levels in WeBS-Year 2003/2004							
Grafham Water	265	128	143	51	112	Mar	140
King George VI Reservoir	114	141	241	163	54	Jan	143
Fleet and Wey	(118)	73	(183)	142	54	Nov	114
Leighton Moss	146						146
Lower Derwent Ings	122						122
Other sites attaining table qualifying levels in WeBS-Year 2003/2004 in Great Britain							
Hanningfield Reservoir	184	42	55	73	224	Oct	116
Woolston Eyes	(176)	210	103	71	175	Oct	147
Langstone Harbour	74	49	135	105	162	Feb	105
WWT Martin Mere	77	103	92	43	162	Oct	95
Chetwynd Pool	64	91	67	166	156	Nov	109

Ringed Teal
Callonetta leucophrys

Escape

Native Range: S America

GB max: 3 Sep
NI max: 0

Singles were recorded during the year at Hanningfield Reservoir, Cresswell Pond, Gresford Flash, Outwood Swan Sanctuary and Cotswold Water Park (East), with two at the latter site in September.

Red-crested Pochard
Netta rufina

International threshold: 500
Great Britain threshold: ?[†]
All-Ireland threshold: ?[†]

GB max: 164 Dec
NI max: 0

Red-crested Pochard have a fragmented distribution through central Europe and are thought to be mainly sedentary. Britain's naturalised populations, the core being at the Cotswold Water Park, are likely to have originated from escaped birds.

Peak numbers were recorded from October to February with the 2003/04 peak recorded in December. The high count of 114 at the Cotswold Water Park West was almost double the site's previous five-year mean and reiterates the importance of this site for this species.

	99/00	00/01	01/02	02/03	03/04	Mon	Mean
Sites with mean peak counts of 10 or more birds in Great Britain[†]							
Cotswold Water Park (West)	63	56	58	(74)	114	Dec	73
Cotswold Water Park (East)	22	33	72	40	33	Mar	40
Baston and Langtoft Gravel Pits	(4)	17	16	8	(23)	Mar	16

[†] as no British or All-Ireland thresholds have been set a qualifying level of 10 has been chosen to select sites for presentation in this report

Pochard
Aythya ferina

International threshold: 3,500
Great Britain threshold: 595
All-Ireland threshold: 400

GB max: 30,675 Jan
NI max: 8,348 Dec

	S	M	L
GB change:	o	o	o
NI change:	-	--	--

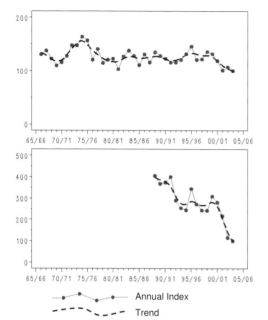

Figure 29.a, Annual indices & trend for Pochard for GB (above) & NI (below).

— Annual Index
--- Trend

2003/04 mean — Previous five-year mean
Range 1998/99 - 2002/03

Figure 29.b, Monthly indices for Pochard for GB (above) & NI (below).

Pochard breed in small numbers in parts of eastern Scotland and England, but are much more abundant outside the breeding season. An estimated 84,000 birds winter in the UK, which represents a quarter of the northwest European population. The majority of this wintering population is thought to breed in Scandinavia, Germany, Baltic Europe and western Russia.

Pochard numbers across the UK have declined during the past five years and 2003/04 saw the British index reach a record low. This decline has been more prevalent in Northern Ireland where current numbers are a third of those three years ago. This is largely due to the change in numbers at Loughs Neagh and Beg, which have fallen by two thirds over the past three years. Although monthly indices were below the five-year average peak numbers were typical in occurring during December and January. No surprises were evident in any of the key sites for this species, which are mainly inland waterbodies, numbers being similar to the previous five-year means. The Nene Washes typically experiences high annual fluctuation in Pochard numbers so the apparent low count during 2003/04 is in line with the longer-term pattern for this site.

	99/00	00/01	01/02	02/03	03/04	Mon	Mean
Sites of international importance in the UK							
Loughs Neagh and Beg	22,681	24,388	16,138	9,080	7,831	Dec	16,024
Ouse Washes	6,345 [13]	4,602 [13]	4,206	4,583	3,304 [13]	Feb	4,608
Abberton Reservoir	4,744	5,296	3,125	4,325	5,290	Aug	4,556
Sites of national importance in Great Britain							
Loch Leven	1,320	1,330	4,074	2,934	2,548	Oct	2,441
Middle Tame Valley Gravel Pits	1,167	1,733	1,423	(442)	(203)	Feb	1,441
Nene Washes	27	4,102	48	2,853	66	Feb	1,419
Hornsea Mere	1,065	580	1,115	1,415	1,325	Dec	1,100
Severn Estuary	1,473	1,008	1,064	772	(905)	Feb	1,079

	99/00	00/01	01/02	02/03	03/04	Mon	Mean
Cotswold Water Park (West)	(670)	988	(512)	(377)	(499)	Jan	988
Fleet and Wey	850	928	1,072	926	850	Dec	925
Loch of Boardhouse	1,156	711	822	605	705	Jan	800
WWT Martin Mere	905	861	860	750	565	Feb	788
Cotswold Water Park (East)	1,225	723	826	371	629	Dec	755
Dungeness Gravel Pits	889	669	595	765	855	Jul	755
Lower Windrush Valley GPs	1,150	681	600	(384)	505	Dec	734
Hickling Broad	945	390					668 ▲
Woolston Eyes	(630)	537	570	637	663	Feb	607
Sites of all-Ireland importance in Northern Ireland							
Upper Lough Erne	188	185	780	916	801	Jan	574
Other sites attaining table qualifying levels in WeBS-Year 2003/2004 in Great Britain							
Cheddar Reservoir	724	33	138	203	778	Dec	375
Eyebrook Reservoir		475	113	352	742	Oct	421
Rutland Water	620	318	630	411	645	Aug	525
Pitsford Reservoir	654	357	224	251	634	Sep	424
Loch of Harray	(416)	457	187	715	606	Dec	491

Ring-necked Duck

Aythya collaris

Vagrant

Native Range: N America

GB max: 5   Sep
NI max: 0

Birds were recorded from 12 sites during the year, all records involving single birds except for an exceptional count of five at Loch Leven in September. Other sites were Barrow Gurney Reservoir, Chew Valley Lake, Dungeness Gravel Pits, Foxcote Reservoir, Loch Gelly, Loch Oire, Papil Water (Fetlar), Severn Estuary, Tees Estuary, Upper Rivington Reservoir and Wintersett and Cold Hiendley Reservoirs. The species was noted in every month except May.

New Zealand Scaup

Aythya novaeseelandiae

Escape

Native Range: New Zealand

GB max: 1   Apr
NI max: 0

One was recorded from Connaught Water in April, October and December, following other records here in recent years.

Ferruginous Duck

Aythya nyroca

Vagrant and escape

Native Range: N America and Asia

GB max: 4   Aug
NI max: 0

Birds were recorded from eight sites this year, with some birds present for extended periods. Up to three were noted from Pitsford Reservoir and two were at Loch Leven, with singles at Elstow Clay Pit, Loch Bhasapoll, Loch Gelly, Minsmere, Ouse Washes and River Cam (Kingfishers Bridge).

Tufted Duck
Aythya fuligula

		International threshold:	12,000	
		Great Britain threshold:	901	
		All-Ireland threshold:	400	

GB max: 57,149 Nov
NI max: 11,129 Dec

	S	M	L
GB change:	o	o	o
NI change:	-	-	-

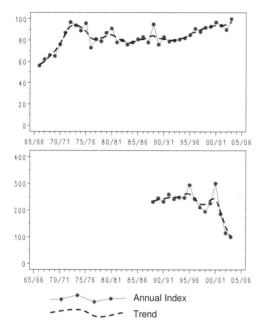

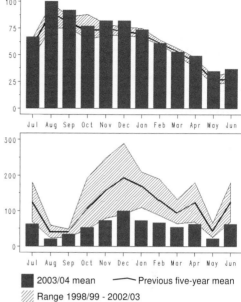

Figure 30.a, Annual indices & trend for Tufted Duck for GB (above) & NI (below).

Figure 30.b, Monthly indices for Tufted Duck for GB (above) & NI (below).

Large flocks of Tufted Duck are a common sight on many larger inland water bodies during winter. Although favouring freshwater habitats, birds can also occur in large numbers on estuaries and some coastal waters. Cold weather movements can bring influxes of birds from the Baltic, which can hold almost half of the northwest European population.

British indices peaked during August and maintained steady numbers through the winter, which were above average until February. 2003/04 saw the annual index rise by 11% to its highest level yet, following two years of declines. The current value builds on the long-term increase revealed by the indices.

Although Northern Ireland typically holds peaks a fifth those of Britain, the majority of these birds are found at Loughs Neagh and Beg. Numbers at this internationally important site have fallen for the third consecutive year to the extent that the 2003/04 peak was almost half the current five-year mean. With Loughs Neagh and Beg being such an important site it is unsurprising that this decline is reflected in the Northern Irish index, which fell by 13%.

In general wintering numbers were variable between sites. Peak counts during 2003/04 were below average at Abberton Reservoir and the Ouse Washes, whilst Rutland Water, Hanningfield and Pitsford Reservoirs surpassed their five-year means. Peaks at Upper Lough Erne surpassed 1,000 for the second year running.

	99/00	00/01	01/02	02/03	03/04	Mon	Mean
Sites of international importance in the UK							
Loughs Neagh and Beg	20,039	26,360	13,303	9,769	8,946	Dec	15,683
Sites of national importance in Great Britain							
Rutland Water	3,325	3,313	5,115	7,496	6,818	Sep	5,213
Loch Leven	3,550	3,900	3,650	4,872	3,913	Oct	3,977
Abberton Reservoir	4,654	4,414	1,418	2,487	2,067	Aug	3,008

	99/00	00/01	01/02	02/03	03/04	Mon	Mean
Middle Tame Valley Gravel Pits	2,370	2,547	2,164	(915)	(325)	Aug	2,360
Hanningfield Reservoir	1,534	2,183	1,160	1,641	3,109	Sep	1,925
Pitsford Reservoir	1,312	1,202	1,263	2,441	2,226	Oct	1,689
Walthamstow Reservoirs	1,194	1,691	1,838	1,867	1,772	Aug	1,672
Wraysbury Gravel Pits	1,812	785	2,091	2,422	846	Dec	1,591
Ouse Washes	1,361	2,214	1,395 [13]	1,192	973 [13]	Feb	1,427
Staines Reservoirs	1,250	1,243	1,026	1,971	1,133	Jul	1,325
Lee Valley Gravel Pits	1,065	1,085	1,027	1,248	1,404	Nov	1,166
Alton Water	736	1,389	961	815	1,440	Sep	1,068
Chew Valley Lake	965	785	1,020	1,080	1,465	Sep	1,063
Besthorpe and Girton Gravel Pits	983	(462)	(418)	(10)	(200)	Nov	983
Draycote Water	1,007	744	740 [13]	1,030	1,251	Nov	954
Tophill Low Reservoirs	1,208	920	720	898	853	Aug	920 ▲
Sites of all-Ireland importance in Northern Ireland							
Upper Lough Erne	546	745	998	1,065	1,236	Dec	918
Lower Lough Erne				635	580	Dec	608
Other sites attaining table qualifying levels in WeBS-Year 2003/2004 in Great Britain							
Wraysbury Reservoir	85	25	151	653	954	Sep	374

Scaup
Aythya marila

GB max: 4,714 Dec
NI max: 3,029 Feb

International threshold: 3,100
Great Britain threshold: 76
All-Ireland threshold: 30*

	S	M	L
GB change:	-	o	-
NI change:	-	o	+

*50 is normally used as a minimum threshold

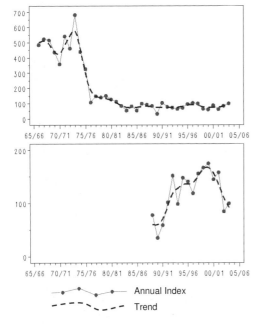

Figure 31.a, Annual indices & trend for Scaup for GB (above) & NI (below).

— Annual Index
--- Trend

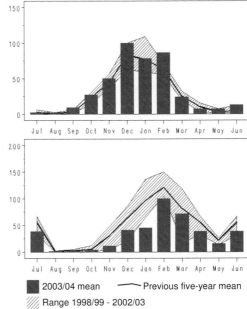

Figure 31.b, Monthly indices for Scaup for GB (above) & NI (below).

■ 2003/04 mean — Previous five-year mean
▨ Range 1998/99 - 2002/03

Scaup are not uncommon wintering birds in the UK, but most occur on a relatively small number of key sites from the northern Irish Sea and the Firth of Forth northwards. South of here, whilst the species can occur anywhere, numbers are usually low and occurrence often sporadic. All of the key sites apart from

Loughs Neagh and Beg are coastal. Although evidence from ringing studies is fairly limited, wintering birds in the UK are known to be derived both from Icelandic and Fenno-Scandian breeders.

The British index shows a massive decline since the early 1970s, followed by small flucutations which are probably mostly due to the practical difficulties of monitoring offshore seaducks reliably. The British index reached its highest value for seven years and the peak core total was the highest since 1999/00. In Northern Ireland, the index fell significantly in 2002/03 and remained at the same level this winter; the Northern Ireland peak core count total was the lowest since 1993/94. As usual the peak for Northern Ireland was recorded in February.

The decline in diving ducks on Loughs Neagh and Beg has been seen for Scaup as well as for Pochard, Tufted Duck and Goldeneye, although the rate of decrease has not been quite so dramatic. However, the numbers in 2003/04 were low enough to bring the five-year average below the threshold for

international importance, leaving no such sites any more in the UK. There has also been a big decline at Carlingford Lough, although an apparent concurrent increase at Belfast Lough along the coast. In Britain, several of the key sites are not so far away as the duck flies. The Solway is still by far the pre-eminent British site although monitoring of the offshore flock at Carse Bay is not always straightforward. Numbers at Loch Indaal and Loch Ryan were relatively high whilst further north on Orkney, the peak at Loch of Harray was the highest recorded by WeBS although this may have been linked to lower than average numbers at Loch of Stenness. On the east coast, counts from the Firth of Forth and the Cromarty Firth were very low.

	99/00	00/01	01/02	02/03	03/04	Mon	Mean
Sites of national importance in Great Britain							
Solway Estuary	(3,001)	1,818 [11]	2,367 [11]	(1,077)	(1,782)	Dec	2,395
Loch Ryan	(637)	631	766 [13]	907 [13]	986	Dec	823
Loch Indaal	900	1,200	241	755	1,003	Jan	820
Inner Moray and Inverness Firth	480	313	323	923	518	Jan	511
Loch of Stenness	(250)	211	513	309	266	Mar	325
Loch of Harray	(201)	311	97	(185)	420	Nov	276
Cromarty Firth	117 [1]	424	353 [13]	160 [1]	126 [1]	Jan	236
Forth Estuary	157	240	189	130	14 [11]	Feb	146
Rough Firth	204	204	88	0	107	Feb	121
Ayr to North Troon	60	100	200	120	(12)	Jan	120
Auchenharvie Golf Course	107	98			145	Feb	117
Dornoch Firth	0	56	107	163	70	Dec	79 ▲
Sites of all-Ireland importance in Northern Ireland							
Loughs Neagh and Beg	3,874	2,633	3,389	2,565	2,674	Feb	3,027 ▼
Carlingford Lough	700	800	618	168	(158)	Jan	572
Belfast Lough	244	493	270	642	669 [11]	Feb	464

Lesser Scaup

Aythya affinis

Vagrant

Native Range: N America

GB max: 1   Feb
NI max: 0

Singles were recorded at the Exe Estuary in February and Spade Oak Gravel Pit in March.

Eider

Somateria mollissima

International threshold: 15,500
Great Britain threshold: 730
All-Ireland threshold: 20*

GB max: 23,390   Sep
NI max: 2,622   Oct

	S	M	L
GB change:	o	o	+
NI change:	+	++	++

*50 is normally used as a minimum threshold

Eiders are widespread around UK coasts throughout the year, particularly from Northumberland and Cumbria northwards and with relatively few along the south coast. The species is very seldom encountered inland. Our

Eiders are sedentary or make fairly short-distance movements, but some continental birds do visit the east coast in winter. Scott & Rose (1996) have suggested that the nominate race is separated into a number of separate

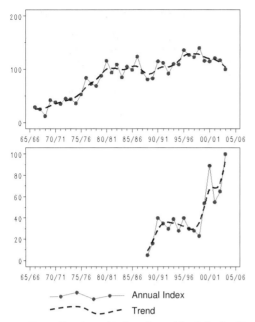

Annual Index

- - - - Trend

Figure 32.a, Annual indices & trend for Eider for GB (above) & NI (below).

WeBS core counts have tended to be fairly consistent between years recently, although the 2003/04 peak was the second-lowest of the last decade. The British index also suggests a slight fall. However, this species is widespread away from core count sites and such trends thus need to be treated with some caution. In Northern Ireland, both the peak core count total and the index reached their highest ever values.

Supplementary September count data supplied from the Firth of Clyde (Waltho 2004) shows that this composite area, tabulated in upper case below and including the Inner Clyde, Gare Loch, Lochs Long, Goil, Striven & Fyne, Isles of Bute & Arran, the east Kintyre coast and the Ayrshire coast down to Loch Ryan, still (just) supports a five-year peak mean that qualifies as internationally important. These counts are made in September. Within this area, Eiders were found throughout but were most numerous in the north, between Gare Loch and Largs. The overlap of this dedicated survey with standard WeBS Core Count boundaries is not entirely straightforward but the importance of the overall area is clear from the table below.

Elsewhere, there were high counts at Belfast Lough (representing a large proportion of the Northern Ireland total) and at Lough Foyle. Conversely, somewhat lower totals than normal were found at Montrose Basin, Lindisfarne, Larne Lough and the Wash.

populations, of which British and Irish birds are one. Additionally, more northerly races are also split into several populations, of which the birds of Shetland and Orkney are one. Such population delineation has implications for 1% thresholds and thus for listing sites as internationally important. However, the UK Special Protection Area Scientific Working Group has decided that the current evidence for such a split is, as yet, insufficient and that a combined 1% level of 15,500 should be used for the time being.

Numbers of Eiders recorded in Britain by

	99/00	00/01	01/02	02/03	03/04	Mon	Mean
Sites of international importance in the UK							
FIRTH OF CLYDE	17,596 [15]	14,679 [15]	15,692 [15]	14,297 [15]	15,276 [15]	Sep	15,508
Sites of national importance in Great Britain							
Forth Estuary	6,283	8,893	5,684	7,616	7,014	Aug	7,098
Tay Estuary	(32)	(3,861) [30]	7,500 [13]	(6,000)	5,974 [30]	Nov	6,737
Morecambe Bay	6,713	5,306	3,903	(4,541)	(3,940)	Jul	5,307
Inner Firth of Clyde	4,454	6,126	3,901	4,730	6,194	Sep	5,081
Montrose Basin	2,214	(2,500)	3,013	3,051	2,075	Jan	2,588
Ythan Estuary	3,800	583	3,531	2,082	2,003	Sep	2,400
Lindisfarne	1,407	1,841 [11]	2,024	2,043	1,241	Oct	1,711
Moray Firth	(963)	(1,491)	(749)	(747)	1,639 [1]	Jan	1,639
Loch Ryan	1,400	2,037	(1,031)	1,188 [15]	1,803	Aug	1,607
Loch Long and Loch Goil	2,164 [15]	1,539 [15]	1,299 [15]	1,459 [15]	1,390 [15]	Sep	1,570
Loch Fyne	1,510 [15]	1,297 [15]	1,874 [15]	1,505 [15]	1,363 [15]	Sep	1,510
Farne Islands	200	2,434	(671)	(293)			1,317
The Wash	258	1,370	1,344	2,546	703	Jul	1,244
Holy Loch to Toward Point	1,504 [15]	1,319 [15]	615 [15]	1,146 [15]	1,114 [15]	Sep	1,140
Girvan to Turnberry	1,083	957	(151)	1,198	(330)	Oct	1,079
Outer Hebrides					1,078 [30]	Feb	1,078
Bute	1,367 [15]	771 [15]	1,143 [15]	944 [15]	457 [15]	Sep	936
Wemyss Bay to Fairlie	744	561	1,246	733	(247) [15]	Sep	821

	99/00	00/01	01/02	02/03	03/04	Mon	Mean
Sites of all-Ireland importance in Northern Ireland							
Belfast Lough	1,076	2,219 [11]	906	1,016 [11]	1,813	Sep	1,406
Outer Ards Shoreline	382	241		428	(256)	Jan	350
Lough Foyle	11	28	344	551	645	Oct	316
Strangford Lough	122	279	283	165	259	Jan	222
Larne Lough	157	128	107	120	55	Sep	113
Sites no longer meeting table qualifying levels in WeBS-Year 2003/2004							
Ayr to North Troon	775 [15]	504 [15]	321	387	1,064	Oct	610
Alnmouth	(12)	(6)	(9)	(7)	(3)	Oct	(12)
Isle of Cumbrae	577						577

King Eider
Somateria spectabilis

Vagrant
Native Range: Arctic

GB max: 1 Dec
NI max: 0

The only record was one on Loch Ryan in December.

Long-tailed Duck
Clangula hyemalis

International threshold: 20,000
Great Britain threshold: 160[†]
All-Ireland threshold: +[†]

GB max: 3,015 Dec
NI max: 27 Feb

Long-tailed Ducks are, for most WeBS counters, somewhat unfamiliar and enigmatic birds. They are rather more everyday (although surely never mundane) to counters from the Forth northwards to Shetland where the species is widespread. Our Long-tailed Ducks are presumed to originate from breeding grounds in Fenno-Scandia, although direct evidence from ringing studies is limited. Numbers in UK waters are, however, a tiny fraction of those found in the Baltic Sea to the east.

Total numbers recorded during WeBS core counts in 2003/04, both in Britain and Northern Ireland, were unexceptional compared to recent years. The key site remains the Moray Firth where dedicated sea-duck surveys located more Long-tailed Ducks than standard core counts found in the whole of the UK combined. The January survey here found the highest number since counts of over 10,000 in winter 1993/94 (Heubeck and Mellor 2005). Moray birds were widespread but with particular concentrations between Nairn and Culbin Bars and Spey Bay. Elsewhere, Forth Estuary counts were rather low but there were relatively high core counts from Tyninghame Estuary and the North Norfolk Coast. In Shetland, supplementary counts on behalf of the Shetland Oil Terminal Environmental Advisory Group illustrated the continued ubiquity of the species around the islands.

	99/00	00/01	01/02	02/03	03/04	Mon	Mean
Sites of national importance in Great Britain							
Moray Firth	1,389 [1]	(3,991)	(1,501)	3,585 [1]	5,446 [1]	Jan	3,603
Forth Estuary	783	(319)	413	435	(238)	Dec	544
Hacosay/Bluemill/Colgrave		169 [10]	201 [10]	59 [10]	249 [10]	Feb	196
South Yell Sound	317 [10]	222 [10]	136 [10]	108 [10]	201 [10]	Dec	179
Sites with mean peak counts of 30 or more birds in Great Britain[†]							
St Andrews Bay	(16)	(7)	(10)	(97)	159 [30]	Mar	159
Loch of Stenness	(173)	75	226	182	105 [13]	Mar	152
West Whalsay and Sounds			152 [10]				152
Tay Estuary	9	(546) [30]	(116) [30]	1 [13]		Dec	134
Quendale to Virkie	110 [10]	203 [10]	117 [10]	122 [10]	103 [10]	Jan	126
Island of Papa Westray			4	182	184	Mar	123
Water Sound	120	179	68	155	80	Jan	120
Burra and Trondra			109 [10]		97 [10]	Dec	108
Bressay Sound		31 [10]	130 [10]	176 [10]	66 [10]	Jan	99
Rova Head to Wadbister Ness	210 [10]	84 [10]	131 [10]	63 [10]	34 [10]	Jan	91
Dee Mouth to Don Mouth	88						88
Outer Hebrides					84 [30]	Feb	84

	99/00	00/01	01/02	02/03	03/04	Mon	Mean
Traigh Luskentyre	49	49	126				75
Kirkabister to Wadbister Ness	93 [10]	74 [10]	90 [10]	21 [10]	73 [10]	Jan	70
Coll & Tiree					61 [30]	Feb	61
Whiteness to Skelda Ness	87 [10]	60 [10]	40 [10]	45 [10]	37 [10]	Jan	52
Loch Indaal	8	231	0	6	5	Jan	50
Thurso Bay	(60)			30	43	Nov	44
Loch of Tankerness	79	7					43
Scapa Flow				43 [30]			43
North Bressay	70 [10]			43 [10]			40
Lunan Bay			59	30	29	Dec	39
North Norfolk Coast	49	31	34	15	50	Feb	36
Quendale Bay			34 [10]				34
East Unst			31 [10]				31
Tyninghame Estuary	5	16	4	7	124	Dec	31
North-west Yell Sound		45 [10]	14 [10]				30
Sites with mean peak counts of 30 or more birds in Northern Ireland[†]							
Lough Foyle	4	161	0	1	(0)		42
Other sites attaining table qualifying levels in WeBS-Year 2003/2004 in Great Britain							
Island of Papa Westray			4	182	184	Mar	123

[†] as few sites exceed the British threshold and no All-Ireland threshold has been set, a qualifying level of 30 has been chosen to select sites for presentation in this report

Common Scoter
Melanitta nigra

International threshold:	16,000
Great Britain threshold:	500
All-Ireland threshold:	40*

GB max:	11,425	Feb
NI max:	95	Nov

	S	M	L
GB change:	++	++	+
NI change:	++	++	++

*50 is normally used as a minimum threshold

Common Scoters are widespread in UK coastal waters, both in the winter but also in the summer when non-breeding birds are joined by post-breeding birds to moult. As a result of recent offshore surveys, the numbers of birds present is now known to be substantially higher than estimates of just a few years ago, although precise estimation remains problematic. It is clear, however, that many birds are missed from land-based surveys alone. The approach presented here in *Wildfowl and Wader Counts* attempts to include as much supplementary data as possible. However, it should be remembered that most aerial surveys use a distance sampling approach, whereby transects are flown and the numbers of birds seen at varying distances from the transect can be used to estimate the numbers missed, and thus the total number present. As *Wildfowl and Wader Counts* presents counts, not estimates, the numbers tabulated are the actual numbers of birds counted rather than estimates derived from distance sampling. However, these actual counts are bracketed as undercounts where they are from distance sampling.

Peak total numbers on core counts in Britain are highly variable between years, due to the high dependency on viewing conditions at key sites. The peak of over 11,000 was about average for recent years, but this national total is well short of numbers known to be actually present in Carmarthen Bay alone. The numbers on core counts in Northern Ireland were up a little compared to recent years, but still well down on counts from the late 1980s and early 1990s. These earlier high counts were mostly due to birds off Dundrum Bay, an area still used by Common Scoter but not currently surveyed during core counts.

Carmarthen Bay and the Liverpool Bay 'super-site' (the latter tabulated in upper case below) clearly remain the two most important areas for Common Scoter in British waters. Distance sampling estimates from Carmarthen Bay suggested estimates of up to 18,000 in November 2003, whereas the peak figure shown in the table is derived from a 'census' aerial survey method and may be high due to movements of birds between closely spaced transect cells (Banks *et al.* 2005). Away from these two areas, land-based counts on the Moray Firth remained relatively high but counts off North Norfolk and the Wash were relatively low.

	99/00	00/01	01/02	02/03	03/04	Mon	Mean
Sites of international importance in the UK							
LIVERPOOL BAY			(13,207) [33]	(24,301) [33]			(24,301)
Carmarthen Bay	21,592 [24]	19,506 [24]	20,078 [33]	23,288 [45]	20,271 [45]	Jan	20,947
Sites of national importance in Great Britain							
Liverpool Bay - Shell Flat				(14,002) [33]			(14,002)
Colwyn Bay	(735)	(500)	(5,194) [33]	(7,436) [33]	(1,737)	Oct	(7,436)
Liverpool Bay - Blackpool Ribble			(7,278) [33]				(7,278)
Moray Firth	2,281 [1]	(3,848)	(3,072)	(8,351)	(7,987)	Feb	5,108
Cardigan Bay	(126)	(3,767) [30]	4,045 [33]	(4,219) [33]	(198)	Oct	4,132
North Norfolk Coast	3,014	606	8,008	5,051	1,710	Jan	3,678
Liverpool Bay - Formby Burbo			(3,611) [33]				(3,611)
Forth Estuary	3,764	(841) [30]	(2,557) [30]	3,255	(1,115)	Nov	3,510
Conwy Bay			(3,336) [33]	(1,424) [33]			(3,336)
Squires Gate				3,000 [13]			3,000
The Wash Strategic Area				(2,042) [32]			(2,042)
St Andrews Bay	880	2,300	1,705	(584)	1,170	Dec	1,514
Liverpool Bay - Ribble				(1,238) [33]			(1,238)
The Wash	(166)	2,650	150	452	(15)	Nov	1,084
Alt Estuary	572	399	1,900 [13]	1,818	462	Oct	1,030
Dee Estuary (England/Wales)	11	24	4,000 [11]	5	26	Oct	813
Liverpool Bay - Formby				(715) [33]			(715)
Red Wharf				(571) [33]			(571)
Tay Estuary	0	(1,687) [30]	(865) [30]	0	(1)	Mar	511
Sites of all-Ireland importance in Northern Ireland							
Dundrum Bay	(0)	(0)	828 [23]	(0)	(0)		828
Sites no longer meeting table qualifying levels in WeBS-Year 2003/2004							
Lindisfarne	220	(0)	844 [11]	450 [11]	103 [11]	Nov	404
Swale Estuary	2	18	(20)	(2,000)	3	Nov	409

Surf Scoter
Melanitta perspicillata

Vagrant
Native Range: N America

GB max: 4 Dec
NI max: 0

Birds were recorded from typical northern localities, with singles at the Dornoch Firth and Forth Estuary and three at the Inner Moray Firth. Most notable, however, was a series of records from Carrick Roads at the Fal Complex, with two in April, three in December and one from January to March.

Velvet Scoter
Melanitta fusca

International threshold: 10,000
Great Britain threshold: 30*
All-Ireland threshold: +

GB max: 2,332 Feb
NI max: 3 Nov

*50 is normally used as a minimum threshold

Velvet Scoters nest as close to the UK as Norway and yet are one of the most localised species recorded by WeBS. Almost all of the birds recorded in any given month can be found on just a handful of Scottish sites, generally between the Moray Firth and the Firth of Forth. The Winter Atlas, however, suggests that more complete coverage of the waters around Orkney would reveal more birds.

The British core count peak total of 2,385 was less than half that recorded in 2002/03 but similar to the peaks during the two preceding winters. The total of three in Northern Ireland was fairly typical for this species in the province. Much of the reduction in the British total was due to lower numbers found in the Moray Firth, from both core counts and supplementary counts, where the main concentration was found off Nairn and Culbin Bars and in Burghead Bay. Numbers in St Andrews Bay appeared to be low for a second year running. There is, of course, the usual proviso about the difficulty of monitoring offshore birds from the land, and the counts will have depended greatly on the conditions on the day.

	99/00	00/01	01/02	02/03	03/04	Mon	Mean
Sites of national importance in Great Britain							
Moray Firth	401 [1]	744 [1]	610	4,398	2,103 [1]	Jan	1,651
Forth Estuary	751	(542)	1,923	1,487	(888)	Mar	1,387
St Andrews Bay	845	(1,870)	800	2	90	Dec	721
Lunan Bay			400	105	(300)	Sep	268

Goldeneye
Bucephala clangula

GB max:	13,087	Jan
NI max:	5,178	Feb

International threshold: 4,000
Great Britain threshold: 249
All-Ireland threshold: 110

	S	M	L
GB change:	o	o	+
NI change:	-	--	--

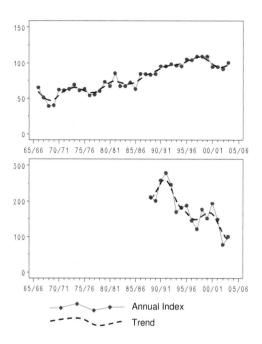

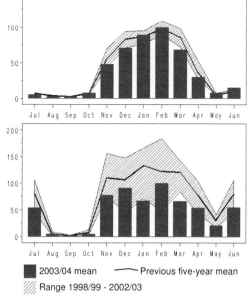

Annual Index
Trend

2003/04 mean
Previous five-year mean
Range 1998/99 - 2002/03

Figure 33.a, Annual indices & trend for Goldeneye for GB (above) & NI (below).

Figure 33.b, Monthly indices for Goldeneye for GB (above) & NI (below).

Goldeneye are found throughout the whole UK in the winter. Most sites support only small numbers but some hold very large concentrations. The species is at home both in coastal and inland situations. Although small numbers breed in Scotland, the vast majority of UK wintering Goldeneye arrive from abroad, probably mostly Fenno-Scandia. Arrival is somewhat later than for many other wintering ducks with few here until November.

The British index has shown a sustained and major increase since the late 1960s, although the last few years have seen somewhat lower numbers than the peaks of the late 1990s and the peak core count total was the lowest of the last decade. Conversely, the Northern Ireland index depicts one of the most striking declines

of any waterbird in the province and whilst the 2003/04 index is slightly higher than that of the previous year, the situation is still clearly of major concern.

The picture in Northern Ireland is heavily dependent upon Loughs Neagh and Beg, by far the most important site in the UK and accounting for over 85% of the Northern Ireland peak core count total in February 2004. Numbers of Goldeneye here rallied somewhat following the very low count the previous winter but remained low. Elsewhere in the province, numbers at Larne and Carlingford Loughs also appear to be showing a downward trend. In Britain, a low peak was noted from the Inner Moray Firth, whilst low counts at the Blackwater Estuary, Loch of Stenness and Loch Leven meant these sites no longer qualify as nationally important for Goldeneye based on their five-year peak means. More positively, higher numbers than usual were recorded from Rutland Water, the Tweed Estuary and Loch of Strathbeg.

	99/00	00/01	01/02	02/03	03/04	Mon	Mean
Sites of international importance in the UK							
Loughs Neagh and Beg	7,026	8,482	6,454	3,661	4,497	Feb	6,024
Sites of national importance in Great Britain							
Forth Estuary	1,653	(2,414)	1,113	(1,241)	(718)	Dec	1,727
Inner Moray and Inverness Firth	894	1,141	993	1,352 [11]	707 [1]	Jan	1,017
Abberton Reservoir	651	448	(619)	469	431	Feb	524
Inner Firth of Clyde	858	468	321	264	(514)	Mar	485
Rutland Water	354	353	450	428	511	Feb	419
Humber Estuary	410	498	208	618	296	Dec	406
Hornsea Mere	(505)	85	294	(480) [13]	235	Mar	320
Stour Estuary	146	291	205	573	262	Jan	295
Tweed Estuary	302	151	312	240	390	Feb	279
Morecambe Bay	288	346	221	280	204	Jan	268
Loch of Skene	244	225	270	(192)	298	Feb	259 ▲
R. Tweed: Kelso to Coldstream	220	285	345	180	246	Dec	255 ▲
Sites of all-Ireland importance in Northern Ireland							
Lower Lough Erne				218	337	Dec	278
Strangford Lough	238	108	256	295	253	Jan	230
Belfast Lough	161	276	140 [11]	249	242 [11]	Dec	214
Larne Lough	247	136	189	130	95	Dec	159
Carlingford Lough	(139)	163	(68)	103	68	Dec	118
Sites no longer meeting table qualifying levels in WeBS-Year 2003/2004							
Blackwater Estuary	265	(341)	197	181	143	Jan	225
Loch of Stenness	(310)	261	227	237	142	Dec	235
Loch Leven	256	215	249	153	86	Dec	192
Other sites attaining table qualifying levels in WeBS-Year 2003/2004 in Great Britain							
Loch of Strathbeg	101	99	192	(126)	294	Nov	172
Other sites attaining table qualifying levels in WeBS-Year 2003/2004 in Northern Ireland							
Ballysaggart Lough				54	118	Nov	86

Smew
Mergellus albellus

International threshold:	400	
Great Britain threshold:	4*	
All-Ireland threshold:	+	

GB max:	258	Jan
NI max:	5	Feb

50 is normally used as a minimum threshold

Most British wintering Smew originate from the Scandinavian breeding population, where they occur along tree-lined rivers and pools. Outside the breeding season Smew are most commonly seen on inland lakes and sheltered coastal areas.

As usual British totals peaked during January, although the 2003/04 maximum was the second lowest for ten years. The majority of key sites held peak numbers between December and February. Key sites are focused around the south and east of Britain and most are inland sites. There were few changes in the five-year means at key sites, Wraysbury Gravel Pits remaining the top site. The only records from Northern Ireland were counts of one and five at Lower Lough Erne in November and February respectively.

	99/00	00/01	01/02	02/03	03/04	Mon	Mean
Sites of national importance in Great Britain							
Wraysbury Gravel Pits	56	53	66	63	55	Dec	59
Dungeness Gravel Pits	29	27	32	18	33	Dec	28
Cotswold Water Park (West)	28	17	31	32	20	Jan	26
Lee Valley Gravel Pits	(22)	20	23	29	23	Jan	24
Rye Harbour and Pett Level	7	2	20	28	19	Jan	15
Fen Drayton Gravel Pits	14	7	15	11	16	Dec	13
Twyford Gravel Pits	17		7	12			12
Seaton Gravel Pits and River	9	7	11	7 [13]	14	Feb	10
Thorpe Water Park	9	6	6	11	18	Jan	10
Cassington / Yarnton Gravel Pits	(1)	(1)	(0)	(0)	10	Jan	10 ▲

	99/00	00/01	01/02	02/03	03/04	Mon	Mean	
Rutland Water	8	8	12	8	8	Dec	9	
R. Avon: R'gwood - Christchurch	(7)						(7)	▲
Horsey Mere	7						7	
Middle Tame Valley Gravel Pits	5	8	(8)	(5)	(1)	Dec	7	
Chew Valley Lake	5	11	3	7	4	Feb	6	
Bedfont and Ashford Gravel Pits	(1)	5	6	(6)			6	
Little Mollands Farm Pits		0	2	11	11	Jan	6	▲
Thrapston Gravel Pits	(7)	2	(2)	2	11	Jan	6	▲
Little Paxton Gravel Pits	5	10	4	8	4	Jan	6	
Hickling Broad	2	10					6	
Hoveringham and Bleasby GPs	6	(0)	(0)				6	
Fairburn Ings	6	8	6	6	4	Mar	6	
Meadow Lane Gravel Pits St Ives	0	3	1	17	3	Feb	5	▲
Eyebrook Reservoir		7	7	1	3	Jan	5	
Pitsford Reservoir	2	2	9	2	3	Feb	4	
Leybourne and New Hythe GPs		7	7	3	0		4	
Earls Barton Gravel Pits	3	(2)	0	7	7	Feb	4	
Colne Valley Gravel Pits	2	3	0	6	(8)	Jan	4	
Abberton Reservoir	0	0	(9)	4	5	Feb	4	
Sites no longer meeting table qualifying levels in WeBS-Year 2003/2004								
Tees Estuary	3	2	3	5	3	Jan	3	
Hornsea Mere	1	3	7	4	2	Jan	3	
Loch of Strathbeg	3	5	2	(1)	2	Nov	3	
Other sites attaining table qualifying levels in WeBS-Year 2003/2004 in Great Britain								
Belhus Woods Country Park	0	0	0	7	7	Feb	3	
Tophill Low Reservoirs	1	1	3	5	6	Jan	3	
Chilham and Chartham GPs	0	0	0	2	5	Feb	1	
Llangorse Lake	1	1	1	1	5	Dec	2	

Red-breasted Merganser
Mergus serrator

GB max: 3,458 Jan
NI max: 563 Nov

International threshold: 1,700
Great Britain threshold: 98
All-Ireland threshold: 20*

	S	M	L
GB change:	o	o	+
NI change:	o	o	o

50 is normally used as a minimum threshold

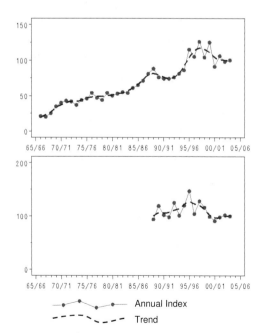

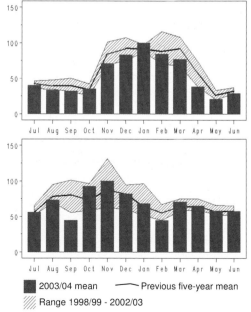

Annual Index
Trend

2003/04 mean
Previous five-year mean
Range 1998/99 - 2002/03

Figure 34.a, Annual indices & trend for Red-breasted Merganser for GB (above) & NI (below).

Figure 34.b, Monthly indices for Red-breasted Merganser for GB (above) & NI (below).

The Red-breasted Merganser is a widespread breeding species in Scotland and parts of Northern Ireland, Wales and northern England. In the autumn, almost all move to the coast and many move south, such that the species can be seen around almost the entire UK coastline. Birds from the Icelandic and Greenland populations are thought to winter in large numbers off the north of Scotland. However, no single site covered by WeBS holds anywhere near the level required to attain international importance for this species.

The British index shows a species that has increased greatly since the 1960s but has shown a slight decline since the late 1990s; this is borne out by the British core count peak, which fell below 4,000 for the fourth consecutive year. In Northern Ireland, peak numbers were not dissimilar to other recent years.

Of the nationally important sites, the only site where substantially higher numbers than usual were noted was Lough Foyle. These high numbers coincided with high numbers of other fish-eating birds: Great Crested and Slavonian Grebes and Red-throated Divers. There were also few strikingly low site totals, those at Portsmouth Harbour, Strangford and Larne Loughs being slightly lower than usual but remaining within the expected level of fluctuation of these sites. Away from the key listed sites, increased numbers at the Fal Complex over the last two winters, reaching 101 in 2003/04, point to a potential new nationally important site if such counts are maintained in future.

	99/00	00/01	01/02	02/03	03/04	Mon	Mean
Sites of national importance in Great Britain							
Forth Estuary	(601)	459	599	769	(661)	Mar	622
Poole Harbour	466	336	(417)	469	(392)	Jan	424
Fleet and Wey	530	283	366	358	425	Jan	392
Morecambe Bay	475	338	229	(265)	(170)	Nov	347
Moray Firth	302	(295)	(234)	355	338	Oct	332
Lavan Sands	255 [2]	317	164	170	264	Aug	234
Duddon Estuary	240	(148)	136	220	(167)	Jul	199
Chichester Harbour	(212)	180	(159)	(184)	191	Dec	194
Inner Firth of Clyde	159	125	(196)	141	(164)	Mar	157
Langstone Harbour	116	122	192	158	127	Dec	143
Loch Indaal	185	163	40	172	138	Aug	140
Solway Firth	(127)	(111)	(58)	(55)	(92)	Dec	(127)
Tay Estuary	(27)	(127)	(30)	(39)	(98)	Oct	(127)
Exe Estuary	130	139	94	112	(132)	Feb	121
Cardigan Bay	(113)	(109)	118 [33]	(47)	(76)	Jan	118
North Norfolk Coast	128	103	(102)	(109)	105	Mar	112
Portsmouth Harbour	(104)	(63)	125	100	85	Jan	104
Loch Ryan	80	94	(113)	133 [13]	74	Dec	99 ▲
Arran	64	108	(94)	(126)	103	Aug	99 ▲
Sites of all-Ireland importance in Northern Ireland							
Strangford Lough	211	148	342	187	188	Jan	215
Belfast Lough	166	169	162	228	216	Oct	188
Larne Lough	243	188	176	123	135	Oct	173
Outer Ards Shoreline	(52)	(35)		62	48	Mar	55
Lough Foyle	27	15	73	37	122	Nov	55
Carlingford Lough	41	44	24	106	40	Sep	51
Sites no longer meeting table qualifying levels in WeBS-Year 2003/2004							
Loughs Neagh and Beg	9	21	19	29	14	Mar	18
Dundrum Bay	(10)	(13)	(11)	(3)	(3)	Nov	(13)
Other sites attaining table qualifying levels in WeBS-Year 2003/2004 in Great Britain							
Montrose Basin	99	120	16	33	139	Sep	81
Fal Complex	(14)	(26)	64	95	101	Jan	87

Goosander
Mergus merganser

International threshold: 2,700
Great Britain threshold: 161
All-Ireland threshold: +

GB max: 3,216 Jan
NI max: 5 Feb

S M L
GB change: - o +

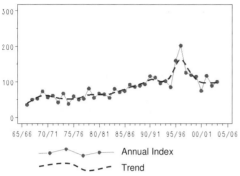

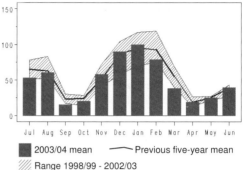

— ● — Annual Index

- - - - Trend

■ 2003/04 mean ⎯ Previous five-year mean

▨ Range 1998/99 - 2002/03

Figure 35.a, Annual indices & trend for Goosander for GB.

Figure 35.b, Monthly indices for Goosander for GB.

Goosanders breed in the north and west of Britain but are found more widely in the winter. Unlike Red-breasted Mergansers, they are largely found on inland waterbodies in the UK. Following the breeding season, most male British Goosanders make their way to the northern fjords of Norway to moult, following which they make their way back more gradually. Our wintering birds are thought to be largely British breeders, although some in the southeast may be derived from continental populations.

The British index has shown a steady increase from the 1960s to the mid-1990s, when there was an exceptional peak in 1996/97 as a result of a cold snap on the continent, which drove many birds to southern Britain. After this, numbers appear to have declined somewhat and the 2003/04 British core count peak was at the lower end of the range of recent years. The monthly indices clearly show the exodus to the moulting grounds in late summer, a gradual return to a peak in January and then a decline as birds disperse to breeding sites. The Northern Ireland peak core count total of just five was actually the highest total for the province for 15 years, involving birds at Belfast Lough and the Bann Estuary.

Relatively few sites now qualify as nationally important for Goosander, and counts on the Tay Estuary and the Tweed between Kelso and Coldstream were relatively low in 2003/04. Loch Lomond counts have suffered from incomplete coverage in recent winters. Hirsel Lake has dropped out of the table following much reduced counts in 2003/04. Of the listed sites, only the numbers at Tyninghame Estuary increased on 2002/03. Other sites supporting three-figures counts of Goosanders in 2003/04 were Eccup Reservoir (137 in February), Castle Loch (Lochmaben) (137 in November), Inner Moray Firth (137 in July), Talkin Tarn (115 in December), Solway Estuary (105 in August) and Montrose Basin (101 in August). From the English Midlands southwards, however, the only counts of 50 or more were from Cotswold Water Park (West), Blithfield Reservoir, Abberton Reservoir, Chew Valley Lake and Clumber Park Lake.

Goosander is a species that is widely dispersed in the day, although birds often return to communal roosts late in the afternoon. Therefore, the precise timing of counts at key sites can have a major effect on the numbers recorded. Submission of roost counts at key sites is welcomed.

	99/00	00/01	01/02	02/03	03/04	Mon	Mean
Sites of national importance in Great Britain							
Tay Estuary	268	230	245	248	192 [13]	Aug	237
Loch Lomond	176	(12)	(37)	(84)	(23)	Nov	176 ▲
R. Tweed: Kelso to Coldstream	158	111	371	179	61	Oct	176
Tyninghame Estuary	130	(300)	161	97	177	Aug	173 ▲
Sites no longer meeting table qualifying levels in WeBS-Year 2003/2004							
Hirsel Lake	87 [13]	145			6	Nov	79

Ruddy Duck
Oxyura jamaicensis

Naturalised introduction[†]
Native Range: N & S America

GB max: 3,580 Jan
NI max: 56 Nov

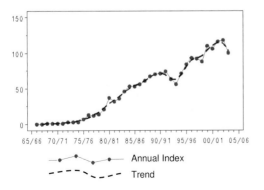

Figure 36.a, Annual indices & trend for Ruddy Duck for GB.

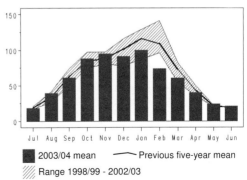

Figure 36.b, Monthly indices for Ruddy Duck for GB.

Ruddy Duck naturally occur throughout continental America and have become established in the UK after escaping from collections during the 1950s. Since first breeding at Chew Valley Lake several years later the British population has rapidly increased, doubling in the eight years up to its peak in 2002/03. In Northern Ireland the index plot (not shown here) is subject to a high level of fluctuation, being largely dependent upon the relatively few birds at Loughs Neagh and Beg.

The 2003/04 maximum was the lowest since 1995/96 and corresponded to a 15% fall in the annual index since the unsurpassed peak of the preceding year. The slowed rate of increase and then decline must surely be attributable to the government's control program.

British totals peaked in January and were mirrored by monthly indices, which were below average throughout the year. Despite fewer birds being recorded at several of the key sites, including Rutland Water, Hanningfield Reservoir, Blithfield Reservoir, Blagdon Lake and Pitsford Reservoir, 55 sites held mean peaks of at least 30 birds, three more than previously. The two main centres of concentration were the central midlands and southeast England. The use of an increasing number of sites may be an indication of the suggested range expansion outlined in the previous report, although disturbance caused by control measures may also lead to greater dispersal.

	99/00	00/01	01/02	02/03	03/04	Mon	Mean
Sites with mean peak counts of 30 or more birds in Great Britain[†]							
Rutland Water	1,345	1,187	911	482	200	Oct	825
Staines Reservoirs	127	(244)	444	(696)	694	Dec	531
Chew Valley Lake	390 [43]	647 [43]	491 [13]	427 [13]	488 [43]	Dec	444
Abberton Reservoir	443	389	456	493	678	Nov	426
Hanningfield Reservoir	22	287	553	(664)	285 [43]	Jan	371
Blithfield Reservoir	449	600 [43]	265	187	180 [43]	Jan	309
Blagdon Lake	360	152	463	394	249	Jan	295
Pitsford Reservoir	167	135	293	358	103	Sep	211
Hilfield Park Reservoir	298	206	159	125	187	Feb	203
Stanford Reservoir	212	(67)	274	97	277 [43]	Dec	186
Dungeness Gravel Pits	110	134	224	264	222	Jan	180
Middle Tame Valley Gravel Pits	185 [43]	125	146 [43]	(120)	(96)	Feb	129
Tophill Low Reservoirs	113	117	173	89	110 [43]	Feb	116
Colwick Country Park	181 [13]		69 [43]		88 [43]	Jan	110
Holme Pierrepont Gravel Pits	102	106			115	Feb	108
King George V Reservoirs	20	46	156	135	268	Feb	105

	99/00	00/01	01/02	02/03	03/04	Mon	Mean
Cotswold Water Park (West)	34	(115)	128	(60)	127	Dec	101
Eyebrook Reservoir		116 [43]	236	56	84	Jan	99
Blackwater Estuary	80	106	152	53	69	Jan	92
Hollowell Reservoir	60	91	76	39	191	Jan	91
Carsington Water	96		141 [43]	132	0		90
Angler`s Country Park Lake	69	70 [13]	58	76	78	Dec	89
Bolton-on-Swale Gravel Pits	66	79	97	108	118 [43]	Jan	87
Clumber Park Lake	66	123	122	72	76	Nov	79
Belvide Reservoir	100	170	30		6 [43]	Nov	77
Humber Estuary	54	99	45	55	116	Feb	74
Fairburn Ings	45	100	69	94	115	Oct	71
Llyn Traffwll	92	61	36 [43]	80	83	Sep	70
Church Wilne Reservoir			68 [43]				68
Sutton and Lound Gravel Pits	38		132	26			65
Walthamstow Reservoirs	32	(41)	40 [43]	(67)	118	Feb	64
Thames Estuary	29	63	34	106	(82)	Sep	63
Tees Estuary	56	71	40	77	68	Oct	62
King George VI Reservoir	0	0	283 [13]	0	2	Nov	57
Llyn Alaw	159	18 [43]	54 [43]	44	0		55
Brent Reservoir	44	61	73	104	2	Jan	50
Great Pool Westwood Park	47	90	59	57	22	Jul	48
Wigan Flashes	16	39	78	49	60	Dec	48
Llynnau Y Fali	30 [43]	20	32	86	57	Oct	45
Kilconquhar Loch	56	80 [43]	30	42	12	Jul	44
Knight / Bessborough Reservoirs	10	31	122	29	23	Jan	43
Newsham Park					42 [43]	Jul	42
Thoresby Lake	74	22	30 [43]	3 [43]	69 [43]	Oct	41
Hule Moss	38	53 [13]	68 [13]	28 [13]	11 [13]	Sep	40
Pugneys Country Park Lakes	35	49	57	7	63	Dec	38
Hampton / Kempton Reservoirs	40	20	47	(30)	39	Mar	37
Ravensthorpe Reservoir	58	44	40	26	6	Dec	35
Rostherne Mere	88	66	7 [43]	26	5	Jan	35
Woolston Eyes	48	43	23	29	32	Aug	35
Hogganfield Loch	44	39	27	26	34	Oct	34
Old Moor	31	26	40	47	28	Jul	34
Loch Gelly	3	16 [43]	58	24 [13]	66	Sep	33
Barrow Gurney Reservoir	0	16	59	38	49	Nov	32
Houghton Green Pool	28	37	36	36	40	Dec	32
Barn Elms Reservoirs	12	24	39	36	43	Jan	31
Grafham Water	4	3	121	10	10	Dec	30
Sites with mean peak counts of 30 or more birds in Northern Ireland[†]							
Loughs Neagh and Beg	(14)	53	59	67	56	Nov	59

[†] as no British or All-Ireland thresholds have been set a qualifying level of 30 has been chosen to select sites for presentation in this report

Argentine Bluebill
Oxyura vittata

Escape
Native Range: S America

GB max: 1 Jul
NI max: 0

One was recorded at Netherfield Gravel Pits in July and August.

White-headed Duck
Oxyura leucocephala

Escape
Native Range: S Europe and W Asia

GB max: 2 Oct
NI max: 0

Single birds were recorded at Little Paxton Gravel Pits in September and at both Chew Valley Lake and Swithland Reservoir in October.

Water Rail
Rallus aquaticus

International threshold: ?
Great Britain threshold: ?[†]
All-Ireland threshold: ?[†]

GB max: 420 Nov
NI max: 3 Nov

Water Rails are notoriously difficult to monitor, due to their preference for dense vegetation. The UK breeding population is thought to be largely resident, with the wintering population bolstered by birds from continental Europe.

The November peak of 422 birds is a considerable underestimate of birds actually present on WeBS sites, although numbers at the top sites remain consistent between years.

The highest count from a single site was recorded in January, 45 at the Somerset Levels, which was about average for this site. This was closely followed by an exceptional March count at North Warren and Thorpeness Mere, which was over three times higher than the site average. Northern Ireland peaks remain in single figures the highest single counts being two at Belfast Lough and Upper Lough Erne.

	99/00	00/01	01/02	02/03	03/04	Mon	Mean
Sites with mean peak counts of 10 or more birds in Great Britain[†]							
Somerset Levels	34	43	45	(45)	45	Jan	42
Grouville Marsh	(40)	(30)	30	25	20	Nov	29
Stodmarsh & Collards Lagoon	41	25	27	28	20	Sep	28
Rye Harbour and Pett Level	40	31	13	8	16	Nov	22
Kenfig Pool	2	7	30	39	27	Nov	21
Middle Yare Marshes	(0)	(4)	23	17	18	Nov	19
Kenfig NNR	24 [21]	12 [21]					18
Lee Valley Gravel Pits	22	18	18	18	12	Dec	18
Marston Sewage Treatment Wks	18						18
Poole Harbour	16	15	15	24	(10)	Sep	18
Southampton Water	16	13	20	18	(7)	Feb	17
Fleet Pond	20	25		6	10	Dec	15
Leighton Moss	15						15
Longueville Marsh	(10)	(10)	15	15	15	Nov	15
North Norfolk Coast	10	13	22	(10)	(10)	Dec	15
North Warren / Thorpeness Mere	4		4	2 [13]	44	Mar	14
Thames Estuary	(7)	(6)	12	21	8	Dec	14
Burry Inlet	9	9	16	10	18	Dec	12
Dee Estuary (England/Wales)	(7)	16	8 [11]	13	(5)	Oct	12
Ingrebourne Valley	10	14	10	14	12	Dec	12
Kilconquhar Loch	14	15	8	14	11	Dec	12
Chichester Harbour	8	12	14	16	6	Dec	11
Drakelow Gravel Pit	9	7	11	20	6	Nov	11
Brent Reservoir	22	7	6	7	10	Jan	10
Doxey Marshes SSSI	11	8	8	(14)	7	Sep	10
Llangorse Lake	8	8	10	15	7	Jan	10
Loe Pool	(8)	4	1	19	(16)	Feb	10

[†] *as no British or All-Ireland thresholds have been set a qualifying level of 10 has been chosen to select sites for presentation in this report*

Spotted Crake
Porzana porzana

Scarce

GB max: 1 Oct
NI max: 0

The only record this year was of one at Inner Marsh Farm on the Dee Estuary (England/Wales) in October.

Corncrake
Crex crex

Scarce

GB max: 1 Aug
NI max: 0

The single bird found at Doxey Marshes in August was the first ever record for WeBS.

Moorhen
Gallinula chloropus

International threshold: 20,000
Great Britain threshold: 7,500[†]
All-Ireland threshold: ?[†]

GB max:	14,728 Oct
NI max:	258 Oct

Moorhens are widely distributed and occur throughout a range of wetland habitats, which means that the proportion of birds recorded by WeBS is limited. During the five years up to 2003/04 36 sites in Britain held mean counts in excess of 100 birds. Although the UK breeding population is by and large sedentary, birds from Iceland and northwest Europe supplement numbers during winter and accordingly national totals exceeded 10,000 in Britain between September and March and reached around 200 in Northern Ireland during the same period.

In line with recent years' peaks, numbers at the Severn Estuary continued to fall. In general peak counts across a number of key sites were below average.

	99/00	00/01	01/02	02/03	03/04	Mon	Mean
Sites with mean peak counts of 100 or more birds in Great Britain[†]							
Severn Estuary	679	735	557	476	443	Feb	578
WWT Martin Mere	570	510	485	490	440	Sep	499
Lower Derwent Ings	419						419
Thames Estuary	(269)	(268)	345	448	(317)	Sep	397
Somerset Levels	407	310	308	322	276	Feb	325
North Norfolk Coast	441	309	334	243	280	Jan	321
Lee Valley Gravel Pits	278	315	357	312	340	Nov	320
Durham Coast	307	240	225	160	(0)		233
Pitsford Reservoir	172	175	267	209	326	Oct	230
Rutland Water	229	252	211	189	191	Oct	214
Bewl Water	122	230	200	254	215	Jul	204
Burry Inlet	213	196	209	175	169	Mar	192
Arun Valley	(240)	202	148	172	163	Aug	185
Chew Valley Lake	130	185	165	105	245	Sep	166
Dee Estuary (England/Wales)	(120)	134	199	(116)	121	Jan	151
Colne Valley Gravel Pits	(66)	(51)	(149)	(110)	(58)	Sep	(149)
Chichester Gravel Pits	138	132	157	149	161	Feb	147
R. Avon: Salisbury-Fordingbridge	(55)	(69)	(79)	(56)	(143)	Sep	(143)
Orwell Estuary	157 [11]	160 [11]	117 [11]	100 [11]	164 [11]	Feb	140
Humber Estuary	64	87	101	215	224	Jan	138
Sutton and Lound Gravel Pits	136		(160)	118			138
Barn Elms Reservoirs	62	95	170	131	137	Aug	119
Marston Sewage Treatment Wks	118						118
Blackwater Estuary	138	96	(75)	(51)	(54)	Nov	117
Ouse Washes	141	206 [13]	61	70	95	Nov	115
Tring Reservoirs	90	149	110	106	115	Jan	114
River Wye - Bakewell to Haddon	114	101	89	131	126	Dec	112
Rye Harbour and Pett Level	162	99	107	71	116	Jan	111
Thanet Coast	83	87	95	123	169	Dec	111
Hamford Water	82	68	(72)	134	(156)	Dec	110
Fairburn Ings	113	(115)	86	73	154	Dec	108
Stodmarsh & Collards Lagoon	136	152	105	78	70	Sep	108
Grouville Marsh	(140)	(120)	120	122	35	Nov	107
Ingrebourne Valley	107	76	122	116	116	Feb	107
Ribble Estuary	141	(59)	(74)	(94)	73	Mar	107
Southampton Water	(73)	(102)	(81)	81	125	Jan	103
Sites with mean peak counts of 30 or more birds in Northern Ireland[†]							
Loughs Neagh and Beg	124	183	374	155	160	Sep	199
Upper Lough Erne	67	59	60	46	(32)	Feb	58
Broad Water Canal		55	19	69	50	Oct	48
Belfast Lough	46 [11]	44	47	62	27	Oct	45
Upper Quoile River	38	(9)	(27)	(4)	(21)	Jan	38

[†] as few sites exceed the British threshold and no All-Ireland threshold has been set qualifying levels of 100 and 30 have been chosen to select sites, in Great Britain and Northern Ireland respectivley, for presentation in this report

Coot
Fulica atra

International threshold: 17,500
Great Britain threshold: 1,730
All-Ireland threshold: 250

GB max: 106,969 Nov
NI max: 4,841 Dec

	S	M	L
GB change:	o	o	o
NI change:	-	o	o

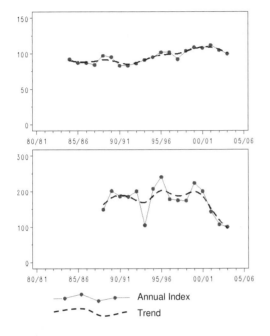

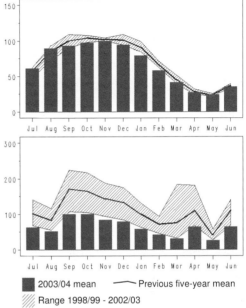

Figure 37.a, Annual indices & trend for Coot for GB (above) & NI (below).

Figure 37.b, Monthly indices for Coot for GB (above) & NI (below).

Within the UK Coots favour large bodies of fresh water, although have a widespread distribution on smaller ponds and rivers. Coots gather to moult during early autumn, which is well reflected by the monthly WeBS indices, which increase in August and September. Typically, peak numbers occur in subsequent months and in 2003/04 British totals peaked in November, a month earlier than in Northern Ireland. The timing of winter peaks can be attributed to the influx of wintering birds from northwest Europe, which can increase further in response to cold weather.

National indices for both Britain and Northern Ireland have suffered declines, mirroring the fall in the national totals of both. Although this corresponds to only a 10% fall in the British index since its highest ever peak in 2001/02, the Northern Irish index has halved in only three years and is currently at its lowest ever mainly due to declines at Loughs Neagh and Beg. This dramatic decrease was witnessed throughout the year with monthly indices each falling below the range of the previous five years. Much the same pattern was true in Britain, indices being below average throughout the year and below the five-year minima from October onwards.

Eighteen British sites held numbers exceeding the national threshold, two more than previously. These sites were almost exclusively in the southern half of England with only Loch Leven outside this area. Furthermore, with the exception of the Fleet and Wey, key sites consisted of reservoirs, gravel pits and natural inland wetlands. Trends varied between British sites with five key locations exceeding their means and six below by more than 10%. Similar mixed fortunes were evident in Northern Ireland, where the mean peak of Upper Lough Erne rose and that of Lower Lough Erne fell, to below the national qualifying threshold.

	99/00	00/01	01/02	02/03	03/04	Mon	Mean	
Sites of national importance in Great Britain								
Abberton Reservoir	9,673	11,645	7,610	6,885	6,166	Aug	8,396	
Cotswold Water Park (West)	3,980	(3,806)	4,161	(2,528)	4,042	Dec	4,061	
Rutland Water	3,759	3,375	3,283	3,969	4,021	Nov	3,681	
Lee Valley Gravel Pits	3,559	2,751	3,245	3,250	3,213	Dec	3,204	
Hanningfield Reservoir	2,809	4,282	1,369	3,426	3,791	Nov	3,135	
Hickling Broad	4,993	1,021					3,007	
Cheddar Reservoir	2,500	3,410	2,950	2,975	3,100	Dec	2,987	
Chew Valley Lake	1,980	3,500	2,360	3,715	3,285	Aug	2,968	
Fleet and Wey	1,862	2,346	3,418	2,353	(2,923)	Dec	2,580	
Cotswold Water Park (East)	2,944	2,227	2,634	2,365	2,296	Dec	2,493	
Loch Leven	2,340	2,100	1,818	3,205	2,650 [13]	Sep	2,423	
Ouse Washes	3,803	2,062 [13]	2,488 [13]	1,349	2,039	Mar	2,348	
Pitsford Reservoir	2,415	2,331	2,746	1,949	1,823	Nov	2,253	
Lower Windrush Valley GPs	2,188	2,274	1,720	2,016	2,341	Dec	2,108	
Middle Tame Valley Gravel Pits	(1,368)	1,674	(2,106)	(1,284)	(559)	Nov	1,890	▲
Alton Water	3,090	655	2,536	2,491	649	Oct	1,884	
Little Paxton Gravel Pits	1,235	3,014	1,679	1,831	1,334	Nov	1,819	▲
Dungeness Gravel Pits	2,085	1,564	1,573	1,528	1,943	Aug	1,739	▲
Sites of all-Ireland importance in Northern Ireland								
Loughs Neagh and Beg	7,307	6,579	2,535	4,269	4,124	Sep	4,963	
Upper Lough Erne	646	899	1,660	1,447	2,062	Dec	1,343	
Strangford Lough	703	400	581	420	230	Oct	467	
Sites no longer meeting table qualifying levels in WeBS-Year 2003/2004								
Blithfield Reservoir	1,946	1,731	890	1,830	1,621	Aug	1,604	
Lower Lough Erne				272	197	Feb	235	

American Coot
Fulica americana

Vagrant
Native Range: N America

GB max:	1 Dec
NI max:	0

One was at the Loch of Clickimin in December, January and March, the first ever recorded during a WeBS count and the third for Britain.

Oystercatchers (Tommy Holden)

Oystercatcher
Haematopus ostralegus

International threshold: 10,200
Great Britain threshold: 3,200
All-Ireland threshold: 500

GB max:	248,815	Oct
NI max:	16,875	Jan

	S	M	L
GB change:	o	o	o
NI change:	o	o	o

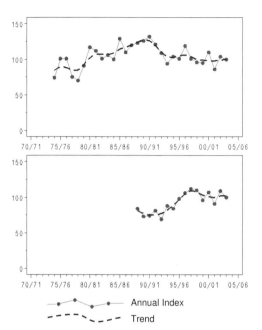

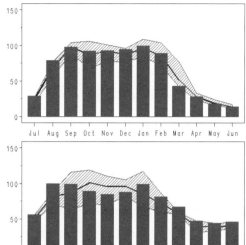

* Annual Index
- - - Trend

2003/04 mean — Previous five-year mean
Range 1998/99 - 2002/03

Figure 38.a, Annual indices & trend for Oystercatcher for GB (above) & NI (below).

Figure 38.b, Monthly indices for Oystercatcher for GB (above) & NI (below).

The conspicuous Oystercatcher is widespread across the UK and whilst breeding birds occur inland, outside the breeding season Oystercatcher are found almost exclusively in coastal areas. Coastal breeders may stay locally throughout the year whilst other individuals winter in southern Europe. During winter the UK's estuaries also provide refuge for birds from Iceland and Scandinavia.

The British maximum remained at levels similar to recent years; the slight fall from the 2002/03 peak was reflected in the annual indices. Following the decline of the early 1990s, the underlying trend in subsequent years has been more stable, although actual index values have fluctuated. In Northern Ireland, recent fluctuating indices and a stable underlying trend follow the increase witnessed during the 1990s.

British indices revealed similar monthly numbers to average with high numbers from September to February, which halved during March. Despite numbers in Northern Ireland being above average throughout most of the year, indices between October and December, the months in which peaks typically occur, were below the mean of the previous five years.

Numbers at key sites remain stable with peak means similar to previous. High numbers on the Thames in 2002/03 were maintained in 2003/04. Although totals for the Medway have fallen below the national threshold level this only represents a 12% decline in the five-year peak.

	99/00	00/01	01/02	02/03	03/04	Mon	Mean
Sites of international importance in the UK							
Morecambe Bay	50,990	50,831	47,286	48,752	(48,600)	Nov	49,465
Solway Estuary	(36,752)	(34,196)	(35,035)	(47,415)	(33,993)	Feb	(47,415)
Dee Estuary (England/Wales)	12,506	21,326	31,851 [11]	20,373	23,906	Dec	21,992
Thames Estuary	12,760	(14,938)	18,814	25,958	23,856	Feb	20,347

	99/00	00/01	01/02	02/03	03/04	Mon	Mean
Ribble Estuary	19,535	(17,784)	23,072	12,395	19,915	Jan	18,729
Burry Inlet	(17,867)	13,347	15,253	14,570	13,831 [11]	Feb	14,974
The Wash	15,701	13,457	13,371	16,760	14,684	Jan	14,795
Sites of national importance in Great Britain							
Forth Estuary	8,744	6,814	(6,631)	9,279	7,802	Nov	8,160
Duddon Estuary	6,890	(4,867)	6,907	(6,476)	8,683	Nov	7,493
Lavan Sands	(5,781)	6,897	7,831	7,612	6,796	Dec	7,284
Inner Moray and Inverness Firth	4,785	6,049	5,153	6,087	7,624	Jan	5,940
Swale Estuary	5,539	5,427	6,270	5,058	5,858	Jan	5,630
Inner Firth of Clyde	4,878	5,060	5,488	5,386	4,627	Jan	5,088
Carmarthen Bay	4,851 [11]	(4,154)	(5,575)	4,530	4,597	Jan	4,888
Humber Estuary	5,292	3,834	(3,318)	2,963	3,305 [11]	Jan	3,849
North Norfolk Coast	3,980	3,755	3,990	3,011	3,858	Mar	3,719
Swansea Bay	2,826	3,500	3,563	3,797	2,857 [11]	Nov	3,309
Sites of all-Ireland importance in Northern Ireland							
Strangford Lough	7,781 [11]	7,149	8,298	8,625	7,412	Jan	7,853
Belfast Lough	6,216 [11]	5,647	4,276 [11]	5,542 [11]	4,248 [11]	Nov	5,186
Lough Foyle	3,087	2,730	2,294	2,326	2,231	Feb	2,534
Outer Ards Shoreline	1,872	1,621		1,968	1,812	Jan	1,818
Dundrum Bay	1,103	1,707	(1,428)	(1,250)	(1,425)	Nov	1,416
Carlingford Lough	1,289	(1,184)	986	1,289	(1,414)	Jan	1,245
Sites no longer meeting table qualifying levels in winter 2003/2004							
Medway Estuary	(4,452)	2,448	2,294	(3,034)	(2,216)	Dec	3,057

Sites attaining international passage threshold in the UK in 2003

Morecambe Bay	56,745	Oct	Dee Estuary (England/Wales)	22,833	Sep
Solway Estuary	37,907	Oct	Ribble Estuary	16,042	Oct
The Wash	28,795	Sep	Burry Inlet	10,910	Oct

Sites attaining national passage threshold in Great Britain in 2003

Inner Moray and Inverness Firth	9,644	Oct	Swale Estuary	5,004	Sep
Forth Estuary	8,930	Sep	Inner Firth of Clyde	4,982	Oct
Carmarthen Bay	5,747	Oct	Thames Estuary	4,248	Oct
Lavan Sands	5,364	Oct	North Norfolk Coast	3,806	Aug
Duddon Estuary	5,203	Oct			

Sites attaining national passage threshold in Northern Ireland in 2003

Strangford Lough	7,459	Sep	Outer Ards Shoreline	1,822	Oct
Belfast Lough	4,321	Oct	Carlingford Lough	1,525	Oct
Lough Foyle	3,219	Aug	Dundrum Bay	1,295	Aug

Black-winged Stilt
Himantopus himantopus

Vagrant
Native Range: Worldwide

GB max: 1 Apr
NI max: 0

The long-staying bird was still present at Titchwell on the North Norfolk Coast, being noted in nine months, for two of which it was at nearby Thornham.

Avocet
Recurvirostra avosetta

International threshold: 730
Great Britain threshold: 35*

	S	M	L
GB change:	+	++	++

GB max: 5,921
NI max: 0

50 is normally used as a minimum threshold

As elsewhere across northern Europe, Avocet are on the increase in Britain as both a breeding and a wintering species. Many British breeding birds winter between southern Europe and West Africa, whilst our wintering population is comprised of the remaining breeders as well as birds from the nearby continent. The recent status of the species in western Europe is well summarised by Hötker & West (2005).

Britain has experienced a large increase in Avocet numbers over the past 15 years, the current maximum being just below the all time peak of 2001/02. Mirroring this rise, annual indices have more than doubled in the last decade, 2003/04 seeing a 12% increase on the preceding year. Of the 18 sites that held numbers exceeding the national threshold 14 were in eastern England, underlining this region's status as the heart of the UK range.

Monthly indices revealed a peak during July, which inevitably will have included a number of juvenile birds. The December peak exceeded the range of the previous five years.

The majority of key sites held peaks above average; these included totals 67% and 89% above their five-year means at the Deben and Blackwater Estuaries respectively. Winter peaks for the Exe and Colne Estuaries have fallen for the second year running, although the latter may be accounted for by a recent reduction in coverage. The post-breeding build-up at Breydon Water reached a new four-figure peak, well above either breeding or mid-winter levels here. As usual, no Avocets were recorded during core counts in Northern Ireland.

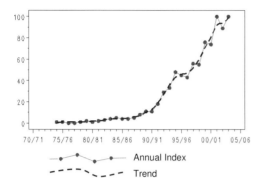

Figure 39.a, Annual indices & trend for Avocet for GB.

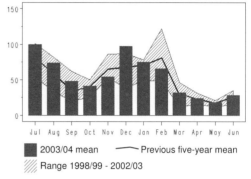

Figure 39.b, Monthly indices for Avocet for GB.

	99/00	00/01	01/02	02/03	03/04	Mon	Mean
Sites of international importance in the UK							
Poole Harbour	823	1,491	1,893	1,007	(1,493)	Dec	1,341
Alde Complex	1,330	1,007	1,174	1,089	1,073	Feb	1,135
Thames Estuary	766	563	1,447	839	658	Jan	855
Sites of national importance in Great Britain							
Medway Estuary	(374)	301	860	(650)	(615)	Dec	607
Blyth Estuary (Suffolk)		524	463				494
Exe Estuary	544	366	528	436	353	Dec	445
Swale Estuary	402	(145)	532	318	451	Feb	426
Hamford Water	532	242	485	(406)	433	Nov	423
Colne Estuary	417	351	465	(383)	205 [13]	Jan	364
Tamar Complex	(207)	452	277	317 [11]	394	Jan	360
North Norfolk Coast	321	(72)	228	334	508	Mar	348
Breydon Water / Berney Marshes	177	272	172	224	268	Dec	223
Deben Estuary	172	165	193	170	353	Feb	211
Humber Estuary	82	(126)	121	281	(271)	Mar	189
The Wash	183	6	347	130	180	Mar	169
Blackwater Estuary	44	167	125	151 [11]	295	Dec	156
Minsmere		120	10	1	107	Mar	60
Other sites attaining table qualifying levels in winter 2003/2004 in Great Britain							
Ouse Washes	11	0	14	43	68	Mar	27
Orwell Estuary	4	1 [11]	3 [11]	36	63	Mar	21
Abberton Reservoir	0	0	0	0	42	Nov	8

Sites attaining international passage threshold in the UK in 2003			
Breydon Water/Berney Marshes	1,069	Aug	Swale Estuary	731	Oct
Medway Estuary	757	Oct			

Table continued:

Breydon Water/Berney Marshes	1,069	Aug	Swale Estuary	731	Oct
Medway Estuary	757	Oct			

Sites attaining national passage threshold in Great Britain in 2003

Alde Complex	694	Oct	Exe Estuary	181	Oct
Thames Estuary	571	Aug	Minsmere	158	Apr
Hamford Water	461	Oct	Blackwater Estuary	122	Apr
Poole Harbour	443	Oct	Ouse Washes	81	Apr
The Wash	417	Jul	Deben Estuary	72	Oct
Humber Estuary	364	Apr	Colne Estuary	64	Oct
North Norfolk Coast	363	Apr	Orwell Estuary	63	May

Stone-curlew
Burhinus oedicnemus

Scarce

GB max: 1   Jun
NI max: 0

The only record was of one at a site in eastern England close to a known breeding location.

Little Ringed Plover
Charadrius dubius

International threshold:	2,400
Great Britain threshold:	?[†]
All-Ireland threshold:	?[†]

GB max: 295 Apr
NI max: 0

The British maximum of Little Ringed Plover far exceeded that of the preceding year and is the highest peak since 1995. In accordance with the rise in the national totals the number of sites from where this species was recorded also rose to 158, almost twice as many as during the previous year. The 27 recorded at the Mersey Estuary represents the highest total for a single site during 2003/04; peaks at this site have never previously exceeded single figures.

Sites with ten or more birds in Great Britain in 2003[†]

Mersey Estuary	27	Apr	Tyttenhanger Gravel Pits	12	Jul
Old Moor	20	May	Fairburn Ings	11	May
Rutland Water	18	Jul	Ouse Washes	11	Apr
North Norfolk Coast	13	Jul	Upton Warren LNR	11	Jun
Sandbach Flashes	12	Apr	Barn Elms Reservoirs	10	May

[†] as no British or All-Ireland thresholds have been set a qualifying level of 10 has been chosen to select sites for presentation in this report

Ringed Plover
Charadrius hiaticula

International threshold:	730
Great Britain winter threshold:	330
Great Britain passage threshold:	300
All-Ireland threshold:	125

	S	M	L
GB change:	o	o	o
NI change:	o	-	-

GB max: 15,513 Aug
NI max: 730 Oct

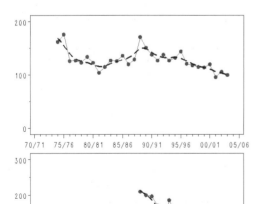

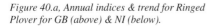

Figure 40.a, Annual indices & trend for Ringed Plover for GB (above) & NI (below).

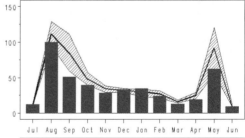

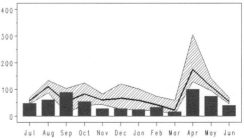

■ 2003/04 mean   ⌒ Previous five-year mean
▨ Range 1998/99 - 2002/03

Figure 40.b, Monthly indices for Ringed Plover for GB (above) & NI (below).

As usual Northern Irish totals peaked during October, this figure, however, was considerably lower than in the previous year. A similar decline was evident in the British maximum, which was attained earlier in the autumn than during recent years. These changes were reflected in the annual indices of Britain and Northern Ireland, both of which reached their second lowest ever value.

Britain has witnessed 15 years of decline in this species, numbers being recorded at WeBS sites in 2003/04 being two thirds of those in 1988/89, whilst the underlying trend suggests that numbers in Northern Ireland have halved during the same period. During most months in 2003/04 British index values fell below the range of the last five years, although numbers appeared slightly above average during December and January. Only in September did the Northern Irish indices exceed the mean, values falling short in all other months.

At the level of individual WeBS sites, a decreased five-year peak mean at the Solway Estuary now falls below the international threshold. Numbers at the Thanet Coast also continued to decline steadily and the peak core count at Langstone Harbour of 193 in December was the lowest in the last decade. Peak numbers at the Blackwater Estuary continued to rise. In Northern Ireland, the low tide count at Belfast Lough was the highest total here of recent years.

	99/00	00/01	01/02	02/03	03/04	Mon	Mean
Sites of international importance in the UK							
Thames Estuary	(775)	954	765	768	(654)	Dec	829
Sites of national importance in Great Britain							
Hamford Water	365	678	1,302 [11]	201	(576)	Nov	637
Thanet Coast	558	528	407	412	389	Jan	459
North Norfolk Coast	373	369	(471)	262	464	Mar	388
South Ford	570	341		373	250	Dec	384
Langstone Harbour	605	413	268	394	201 [11]	Nov	376
Solway Estuary	(276)	(330)	(289)	(599)	286	Nov	376 ▼
Humber Estuary	466	409	350	225	418 [11]	Nov	374
Morecambe Bay	522	(473)	298	246	303	Dec	368
Medway Estuary	(351)	(126)	(89)	(249)	(136)	Jan	(351)
Forth Estuary	441	(356)	266	343	303 [11]	Nov	342
Sites of all-Ireland importance in Northern Ireland							
Strangford Lough	278 [11]	494 [11]	618 [11]	236 [11]	277 [11]	Nov	381
Outer Ards Shoreline	223	313		315	(198)	Jan	284
Carlingford Lough	(125)	(116)	(203)	(240)	161	Nov	201
Belfast Lough	192	142	188	189	234 [11]	Nov	189
Other sites attaining table qualifying levels in winter 2003/2004 in Great Britain							
Blackwater Estuary	209	243	215	362	374	Nov	281
The Wash	169	(124)	242	195	347	Jan	238

Sites attaining international passage threshold in the UK in 2003					
Ribble Estuary	4,300	May	Thames Estuary	1,045	Oct
North Norfolk Coast	1,744	Aug	Alt Estuary	770	Aug
The Wash	1,194	May	Solway Estuary	740	May
Humber Estuary	1,169	Aug			
Sites attaining national passage threshold in Great Britain in 2003					
Tyninghame Estuary	717	May	Forth Estuary	469	Aug
Dee Estuary (England/Wales)	658	Aug	Hamford Water	455	Sep
Severn Estuary	595	Aug	Tees Estuary	436	May
Morecambe Bay	561	Aug	Swale Estuary	414	Oct
Stour Estuary	556	Sep	Ardivachar Point (South Uist)	400	Aug
Blackwater Estuary	493	Sep	South Ford	350	Aug
Colne Estuary	479	Oct	Duddon Estuary	337	May
Sites attaining national passage threshold in Northern Ireland in 2003					
Outer Ards Shoreline	344	Oct	Carlingford Lough	165	Sep
Strangford Lough	189	Sep			

Dotterel

Charadrius morinellus

Scarce

GB max: 15   May
NI max: 0

A fine 'trip' of 15 at Donna Nook on the Humber Estuary in May were followed by two autumn singles, at Scolt Head on the North Norfolk Coast in August and Minnis Bay, Reculver on the Thanet Coast in September.

American Golden Plover

Pluvialis dominica

Vagrant
Native Range: America

GB max:	1	Nov
NI max:	0	

One was recorded at Marshside on the Ribble Estuary in November.

Golden Plover

Pluvialis apricaria

International threshold:	9,300
Great Britain threshold:	2,500
All-Ireland threshold:	2,000

GB max:	169,007	Jan
NI max:	15,369	Oct

	S	M	L
GB change:	o	+	++
NI change:	-	o	o

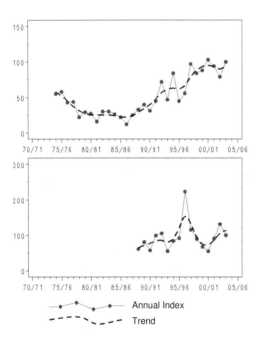

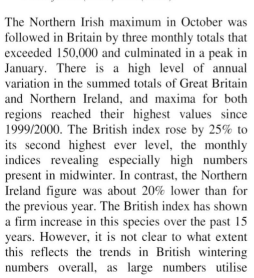

- — • — Annual Index
- – – – Trend

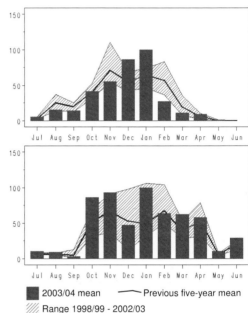

■ 2003/04 mean ——— Previous five-year mean
/// Range 1998/99 - 2002/03

Figure 41.a, Annual indices & trend for Golden Plover for GB (above) & NI (below).

Figure 41.b, Monthly indices for Golden Plover for GB (above) & NI (below).

The Northern Irish maximum in October was followed in Britain by three monthly totals that exceeded 150,000 and culminated in a peak in January. There is a high level of annual variation in the summed totals of Great Britain and Northern Ireland, and maxima for both regions reached their highest values since 1999/2000. The British index rose by 25% to its second highest ever level, the monthly indices revealing especially high numbers present in midwinter. In contrast, the Northern Ireland figure was about 20% lower than for the previous year. The British index has shown a firm increase in this species over the past 15 years. However, it is not clear to what extent this reflects the trends in British wintering numbers overall, as large numbers utilise terrestrial habitats away from sites covered by WeBS. These trends are largely driven by increases on the English east coast and may reflect redistribution perhaps in response to milder winters, but the precise mechanisms are unclear.

Reflecting this variability, changes in status were noted at nine key sites. Unusually high peaks were observed at Carmarthen Bay and Strangford Lough, taking the mean peaks for these sites beyond the international threshold. Similarly, counters at the Mersey Estuary witnessed their highest count for over ten years. Both the Nene Washes and the Crouch-Roach Estuary held numbers well below their five-year means.

	99/00	00/01	01/02	02/03	03/04	Mon	Mean	
Sites of international importance in the UK								
Humber Estuary	42,381	25,133	29,607	40,585	(50,662)	Dec	37,674	
The Wash	42,761	13,740	14,109	19,089	25,817	Jan	23,103	
Blackwater Estuary	14,902	18,826	(8,082)	12,455 [11]	6,986	Jan	13,292	
Breydon Water / Berney Marshes	10,600	13,280	10,200	8,900	10,464	Jan	10,689	
Strangford Lough	7,076	6,948 [11]	11,726 [11]	8,766	15,988 [11]	Dec	10,101	▲
Carmarthen Bay	(9)	(5,001)	(800)	(500)	(9,832)	Feb	(9,832)	▲
Sites of national importance in Great Britain								
Swale Estuary	7,010	(6,217)	13,898	3,282	10,935	Jan	8,781	
Blyth Estuary (Suffolk)		10,000	3,510				6,755	
Pegwell Bay	3,800	4,000	7,000	7,229 [11]	8,000	Jan	6,006	
Old Moor	4,100	4,700	5,500	(7,700)	7,000	Jan	5,800	
Lynemouth Ash Lagoons					5,700	Nov	5,700	▲
Solway Estuary	3,984 [11]	8,065 [11]	(3,333)	(3,708)	4,409	Jan	5,486	
Stour Estuary	2,160 [11]	6,620 [11]	8,531 [11]	2,567 [11]	7,083 [11]	Dec	5,392	
Thames Estuary	4,166	7,911	3,538	(3,268)	(1,823)	Nov	5,205	
Morecambe Bay	3,628	(4,121)	(5,649)	(3,349)	(7,304)	Nov	5,176	
Somerset Levels	5,401	5,077	5,169	1,260	8,609	Jan	5,103	
Medway Estuary	(4,500)	(30)	(14)	(75)	(15)	Dec	(4,500)	
Taw-Torridge Estuary	3,440	(1,900)	(4,500)	(2,612)	(3,300)	Dec	3,970	
Lindisfarne	4,830	(3,598)	2,881	(3,383)	3,822 [11]	Nov	3,844	
Clifford Hill Gravel Pits	5,500	4,500	3,560	2,500	2,740	Jan	3,760	
Forth Estuary	(1,316)	1,027	2,419	(4,632)	6,940 [11]	Nov	3,755	
North Norfolk Coast	3,442	3,386	4,917	1,919	5,039	Jan	3,741	
Ribble Estuary	3,546	(4,341)	3,075	(2,671)	(3,300)	Nov	3,654	
Colne Estuary	(5,000)	4,045	1,820	(82)	(1,480)	Jan	3,622	
Lower Derwent Ings	3,400						3,400	
Mersey Estuary	2,440	(2,227)	(2,000)	(600)	(4,200)	Dec	3,320	▲
Hamford Water	2,245	4,164	2,464	2,384	3,204	Jan	2,892	
Ouse Washes	4,201	216	4,035	2,828 [13]	2,844	Dec	2,825	▲
St Mary`s Island	2,000	(1,000)	(2,000)	3,000	3,200	Nov	2,733	▲
Stanwick Gravel Pits	(0)		4,504		880	Jan	2,692	
Sites of all-Ireland importance in Northern Ireland								
Loughs Neagh and Beg	(6,675)	7,621	(2,817)	(3,767)	7,091	Dec	7,356	
Lough Foyle	2,600	2,590	4,100	3,320	5,719	Nov	3,666	
Outer Ards Shoreline	2,095	1,411		3,164	1,369	Mar	2,010	
Sites no longer meeting table qualifying levels in winter 2003/2004								
Crouch-Roach Estuary	1,730	3,889	2,602	2,165	1,354	Feb	2,348	
Nene Washes	2,260	500	4,440	4,320	650	Mar	2,434	
Confidential SE England Site	5,000	1,600	2,600	500	600	Dec	2,060	

Sites attaining national passage threshold in Great Britain in 2003

Site			Site		
Solway Estuary	5,063	Oct	Breydon Water / Berney Marshes	3,190	Oct
Humber Estuary	4,587	Jul	Ribble Estuary	2,980	Oct
The Wash	4,148	Aug	Blackwater Estuary	2,918	Oct
Lindisfarne	3,528	Oct	North Norfolk Coast	2,781	Oct
Forth Estuary	3,248	Oct			

Sites attaining national passage threshold in Northern Ireland in 2003

Site			Site		
Lough Foyle	7,647	Oct	Loughs Neagh and Beg	4,930	Oct

Grey Plover
Pluvialis squatarola

International threshold:	2,500
Great Britain threshold:	530
All-Ireland threshold:	40*

					S	M	L
GB max:	34,678	Jan					
NI max:	227	Jan		GB change:	o	o	++
				NI change:	-	+	+

50 is normally used as a minimum threshold

Grey Plover are almost entirely confined to the coast and even during the breeding season do not occur as far inland as other arctic tundra species. Birds migrating through Western Europe in autumn travel as far south as West Africa. Many European estuaries, south and west from the Wadden Sea, sustain large numbers throughout winter.

Since reaching their highest peak in the mid-1990s, Grey Plover have undergone a decline in both Great Britain and Northern Ireland. The British index is currently at a similar level to 1987/88, at which time however, the species was increasing. This decline is mirrored in Northern Ireland, where the 2003/04 index fell to its lowest value for over ten years. Interestingly, despite the recent declines, winter numbers at the most important site, the Wash, were the highest of recent years.

Monthly indices were lower than their respective five-year mean values in all months, with the exception of July and August in Britain. Although most individual sites held average numbers during 2003/04, peak means at four sites fell below the national threshold for this species. Although these relate to declines of less than 25% at Forth Estuary, Burry Inlet and Beaulieu Estuary, the five-year mean for the Mersey Estuary has halved following the incorporation of the counts from 2003/04.

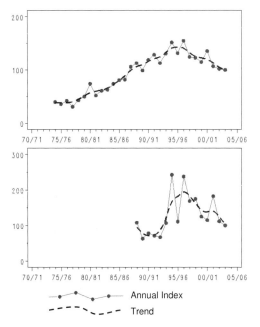

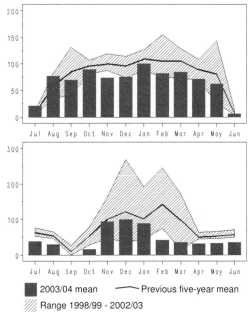

	Annual Index
	Trend

	2003/04 mean		Previous five-year mean
	Range 1998/99 - 2002/03		

Figure 42.a, Annual indices & trend for Grey Plover for GB (above) & NI (below).

Figure 42.b, Monthly indices for Grey Plover for GB (above) & NI (below).

	99/00	00/01	01/02	02/03	03/04	Mon	Mean
Sites of international importance in the UK							
The Wash	7,432	7,495	8,395	7,778	10,447	Jan	8,309
Thames Estuary	5,871	6,923	(5,160)	3,188	(3,812)	Feb	5,327
Ribble Estuary	3,234	5,139	6,285	1,658	5,568	Mar	4,377
Dengie Flats	3,252	7,826	3,640	3,610	2,943	Feb	4,254
Stour Estuary	3,739	(3,130)	3,084	3,013	2,975	Feb	3,203
Blackwater Estuary	4,649	2,920	2,228	3,230	2,011	Dec	3,008
Hamford Water	1,672	2,803	3,267	2,984	(1,746)	Jan	2,682
Sites of national importance in Great Britain							
Chichester Harbour	(2,145)	2,180	(3,180)	1,700	1,515	Dec	2,144
Swale Estuary	1,858	(2,992)	1,745	2,181	1,892	Jan	2,134
Alt Estuary	1,877	1,538	2,500	1,099	3,098	Nov	2,022
Medway Estuary	(2,631)	3,221	1,616	938	1,544	Dec	1,990
Humber Estuary	1,446	(1,320)	1,567	(1,300)	2,285 [11]	Feb	1,766
North Norfolk Coast	1,637	1,382	1,720	1,374	1,316	Dec	1,486
Dee Estuary (England/Wales)	742	(823)	2,201 [11]	966	(1,851)	Dec	1,440
Colne Estuary	898	1,331	1,357	(141)	(705)	Jan	1,195
Lindisfarne	(1,165)	(1,230)	1,016	(635)	(656)	Jan	1,137
Langstone Harbour	1,454	1,405	504	982	1,119	Nov	1,093
Pagham Harbour	1,139 [11]	979	713	704	1,348	Jan	977
Morecambe Bay	1,072	1,288	1,043	657	778	Dec	968

	99/00	00/01	01/02	02/03	03/04	Mon	Mean
Eden Estuary	514	646	812	690	371	Nov	607
Orwell Estuary	1,034	484	323 [11]	413	710	Nov	593
Solway Estuary	678 [11]	520 [11]	(482)	(466)	509	Feb	569
Sites of all-Ireland importance in Northern Ireland							
Strangford Lough	320	268	273	398 [11]	137	Dec	279
Dundrum Bay	(14)	(28)	(19)	(72)	(27)	Jan	(72)
Carlingford Lough	35	(17)	45	52	(57)	Jan	47
Sites no longer meeting table qualifying levels in winter 2003/2004							
Forth Estuary	554	517	420	549	425	Mar	493
Burry Inlet	(284)	417	392	774	236	Feb	455
Mersey Estuary	630 [11]	60	260	201	205	Dec	271
Beaulieu Estuary	547	600	708	188	46	Jan	418
Other sites attaining table qualifying levels in winter 2003/2004 in Great Britain							
Deben Estuary	239	308	340	344	656	Feb	377

Sites attaining international passage threshold in the UK in 2003

The Wash	15,056	May	Alt Estuary	3,756	Apr
Humber Estuary	6,135	Apr	Stour Estuary	2,893	Oct
Ribble Estuary	4,580	May			

Sites attaining national passage threshold in Great Britain in 2003

Blackwater Estuary	2,415	Sep	Thames Estuary	1,048	Oct
Swale Estuary	1,953	Oct	Langstone Harbour	960	Sep
Hamford Water	1,551	Oct	Medway Estuary	735	Oct
North Norfolk Coast	1,421	Sep	Chichester Harbour	670	Oct
Lindisfarne	1,412	Apr	Morecambe Bay	630	Oct
Dengie Flats	1,300	Sep			

Sites attaining national passage threshold in Northern Ireland in 2003

Belfast Lough	120	Oct

Lapwing
Vanellus vanellus

International threshold: 20,000**
Great Britain threshold: 20,000**[†]
All-Ireland threshold: 2,500

GB max: 373,202 Dec
NI max: 21,392 Dec

	S	M	L
GB change:	o	o	++
NI change:	-	o	-

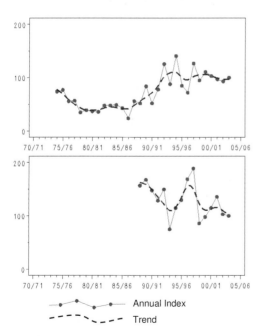

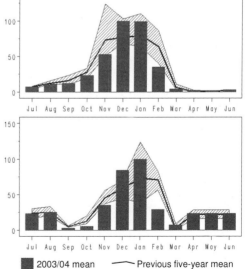

Figure 43.a, Annual indices & trend for Lapwing for GB (above) & NI (below).

Figure 43.b, Monthly indices for Lapwing for GB (above) & NI (below).

Lapwing are widespread throughout the UK, occurring from upland moors through farmland and down to both freshwater and coastal habitats. Whilst part of the British breeding population undertakes winter movement southwards to continental Europe, birds from Scandinavia, eastern Europe and Russia supplement the remaining numbers. Cold weather movements bring in additional birds as well as forcing British birds south and west and to the coast.

Both British and Northern Irish maxima were higher than in recent years, amounting to the greatest total since 1999/2000. The slight rise in the Northern Irish index was overshadowed by continued decline indicated by the underlying trend, however, the variability of the numbers using WeBS sites coupled with an extensive use of non-WeBS habitats promotes caution when considering changes at the population level. Furthermore, numbers in Northern Ireland are typically subject to a high level of fluctuation, even between months, as birds respond to changes in weather conditions.

Similarly, British indices have previously shown a large amount of variation between years although they have been less variable during the past five years. The rise witnessed during 2003/04 follows three years of slight declines contributing to an overall trend that is more stable than in Northern Ireland.

Monthly indices were similar for Great Britain and Northern Ireland, which with the exception of the peaks in December and January were below average in all other months; December values exceeding the previous five-year maximum. The coincidence of peak counts in Britain and Northern Ireland may indicate a response to harsh conditions in northwest Europe, although with a large proportion of UK wintering population utilising agricultural habitats cold weather movements may be more local.

The three sites holding internationally important numbers over the five years up to 2003/04 are all similar in being large sites. In accordance with the fluctuation at the national level numbers at key sites vary greatly between years and during 2003/04 the Humber Estuary, Pegwell Bay and Lough Foyle witnessed totals that exceeded their five-year means.

	99/00	00/01	01/02	02/03	03/04	Mon	Mean
Sites of international importance in the UK							
The Wash	86,129	31,165	43,558	43,672	29,350	Dec	46,775
Somerset Levels	28,895	50,328	41,675	(16,036)	(23,641)	Dec	40,299
Humber Estuary	32,720	16,870	10,719	(36,309)	(39,865)	Dec	27,297
Sites of all-Ireland importance in Northern Ireland							
Loughs Neagh and Beg	10,968	(6,281)	(4,264)	(2,980)	6,282	Dec	8,625
Strangford Lough	5,736	6,214	10,527	6,977	8,884 [11]	Jan	7,668
Lough Foyle	2,990	(2,277)	(3,320)	2,629	4,240	Nov	3,295
Sites with mean peak counts of 5,000 or more birds in Great Britain[†]							
Breydon Water / Berney Marshes	20,500	18,300	19,380	15,230	15,890	Dec	17,860 ▾
Morecambe Bay	18,796	16,213	13,504	(13,714)	(20,750)	Nov	17,316
Swale Estuary	18,641	13,585	14,804	14,974	16,523	Jan	15,705
Thames Estuary	(11,850)	(19,073)	(10,282)	16,036	10,229	Feb	15,113
Ouse Washes	29,913	1,289	19,219 [13]	8,125 [13]	13,577	Dec	14,425
Mersey Estuary	(13,620)	(1,930)	(5,284)	(5,675)	(12,150)	Dec	(13,620)
Ribble Estuary	11,022	(12,405)	(9,579)	(14,500)	(15,374)	Dec	13,325
Blackwater Estuary	14,154	20,309	(9,005)	11,053 [11]	7,472	Jan	13,247
Severn Estuary	19,034	(9,817)	(7,439)	12,129 [11]	6,273	Jan	12,479
Nene Washes	13,080	7,100	4,230	21,016	3,870	Jan	9,859
Solway Estuary	8,345	8,596 [11]	(5,211)	(7,340)	(7,218)	Nov	8,471
Dee Estuary (England/Wales)	8,278	6,270	9,206	6,470	7,853	Dec	7,615
Confidential SE England Site	17,500	5,000	11,000	1,800	1,700	Dec	7,400
Colne Estuary	7,500	6,430	(2,182)	(765)	(1,950)	Dec	6,965
North Norfolk Coast	8,744	5,799	7,830	5,124	6,801	Feb	6,860
Pegwell Bay	2,100	5,900	6,000	10,282 [11]	10,000	Jan	6,856
Medway Estuary	(6,728)	(1,055)	(2,488)	(1,755)	(661)	Dec	(6,728)
Taw-Torridge Estuary	5,895	(3,053)	(3,237)	(2,339)	(1,270)	Dec	5,895
R. Avon: R'gwood - Christchurch	(2,692)	4,650 [13]	(1,564)	6,660	(1,125)	Jan	5,655
Tees Estuary	3,468	5,562	(3,196)	6,017	6,588	Dec	5,409
Crouch-Roach Estuary	5,962	6,537	3,697	4,939	5,386	Jan	5,304
Stour Estuary	6,192	4,264	5,204 [11]	4,137 [11]	5,244	Jan	5,008

[†] as few sites exceed the British threshold a qualifying level of 5,000 has been chosen to select sites for presentation in this report

Knot
Calidris canutus

GB max:	238,567	Nov
NI max:	5,352	Nov

International threshold:	4,500
Great Britain threshold:	2,800
All-Ireland threshold:	375

	S	M	L
GB change:	o	o	+
NI change:	--	-	o

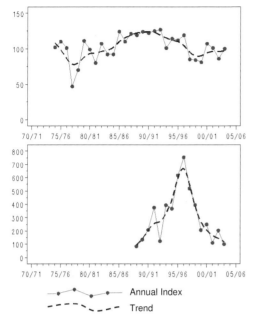

Annual Index
Trend

2003/04 mean — Previous five-year mean
Range 1998/99 - 2002/03

Figure 44.a, Annual indices & trend for Knot for GB (above) & NI (below).

Figure 44.b, Monthly indices for Knot for GB (above) & NI (below).

Knot breed in the high Arctic, across Siberia, Greenland and Canada. Birds from the *islandica* race, which breed in Greenland and northeast Canada, constitute the wintering population for the UK. Knot typically occur in large flocks and are almost exclusively coastal. During passage, numbers are supplemented by birds of the nominate race, which breed in western Siberia and winter along the west coast of Africa.

Knot numbers in Britain appear to be stable with indices currently at a similar level to five years ago, although there has been evidence of a slight decline since record levels during the late 1980s. In contrast, Northern Ireland indices reveal a more obvious trend and since reaching an unprecedented peak in 1996/97 Knot numbers have declined steadily and continue to do so albeit more slowly.

However, with only three sites within Northern Ireland attaining nationally important numbers this area is prone to a high level of variation.

Monthly indices for Great Britain were similar to recent years with numbers steady from October to February. Northern Ireland indices were less analagous with numbers between December and February being below average, whilst in contrast the November peak was the highest since January 2001.

Peak counts at Lindisfarne, Cromarty Firth and Blackwater Estuary surpassed the international threshold during 2003/04. Other sites worthy of note include the Inner Moray Firth, Tees Estuary and Lough Foyle, all of which newly qualify for national importance, and the Thames Estuary, where the highest count since 1997 was recorded.

	99/00	00/01	01/02	02/03	03/04	Mon	Mean
Sites of international importance in the UK							
Morecambe Bay	59,530	72,908	66,031	(61,968)	67,959	Nov	66,607
The Wash	60,711	72,939	80,452	51,642	48,372	Dec	62,823
Humber Estuary	25,719	34,888	49,991	18,936	50,557 [11]	Nov	36,018

	99/00	00/01	01/02	02/03	03/04	Mon	Mean
Ribble Estuary	22,010	(20,331)	36,202	(23,691)	44,947	Mar	34,386
Thames Estuary	21,942	(38,357)	27,425	28,060	43,873	Feb	31,931
Alt Estuary	20,000	31,219	44,012	25,045	27,904	Nov	29,636
Dee Estuary (England/Wales)	8,683	5,672	52,792	26,769	38,070	Dec	26,397
North Norfolk Coast	3,356	29,636	16,214	9,224	7,523	Dec	13,191
Dengie Flats	(5,800)	19,400	13,600	10,550	8,000	Nov	12,888
Solway Estuary	(8,544)	9,159 [11]	(3,784)	(9,620)	8,725	Dec	9,168
Stour Estuary	9,677	8,036 [11]	6,998 [11]	8,648 [11]	6,564 [11]	Dec	7,985
Forth Estuary	6,345	5,807	7,232	8,936	6,907 [11]	Feb	7,045
Strangford Lough	5,238 [11]	5,863	4,000 [11]	10,340 [11]	4,058	Nov	5,900
Sites of national importance in Great Britain							
Lindisfarne	(1,954)	3,130 [11]	2,858	(4,512)	(6,751)	Jan	4,313
Montrose Basin	1,824	2,800	5,000	5,800	(2,562)	Dec	3,856
Hamford Water	3,533	5,431	1,957	2,935	4,160	Dec	3,603
Burry Inlet	(3,562)	4,800	2,000	3,800	3,500	Jan	3,532
Cromarty Firth	1,685 [11]	5,050	2,621	3,132	4,932	Dec	3,484
Blackwater Estuary	2,565	(4,470)	(2,495)	1,700 [11]	(5,982)	Jan	3,442
Swale Estuary	3,400	(4,200)	2,900	1,500	4,050	Jan	3,210
Medway Estuary	(5,055)	1,370	1,950	4,085	1,817	Dec	2,855
Inner Moray and Inverness Firth	3,251	3,373	1,980	1,873	3,663	Jan	2,828 ▲
Tees Estuary	1,671	2,356	4,416	2,604	3,012	Jan	2,812 ▲
Sites of all-Ireland importance in Northern Ireland							
Dundrum Bay	1,000	(981)	(555)	(603)	320	Nov	767
Lough Foyle	180	490	20	345	942	Feb	395 ▲
Sites no longer meeting table qualifying levels in winter 2003/2004							
Belfast Lough	600	120	153	155	4	Mar	206

Sites attaining international passage threshold in the UK in 2003

The Wash	76,346	Oct	Humber Estuary	8,794	Aug
Ribble Estuary	45,989	Apr	Solway Estuary	6,466	Oct
North Norfolk Coast	37,124	Oct	Morecambe Bay	5,891	Oct
Alt Estuary	15,000	Aug	Dengie Flats	5,100	Oct

Sites attaining national passage threshold in Northern Ireland in 2003

Lough Foyle	397	Oct

Sanderling
Calidris alba

GB max: 17,262 May
NI max: 44 May

International threshold: 1,200
Great Britain winter threshold: 210
Great Britain passage threshold: 300
All-Ireland threshold: 35*

	S	M	L
GB change:	o	+	+
NI change:	--	--	o

*50 is normally used as a minimum threshold

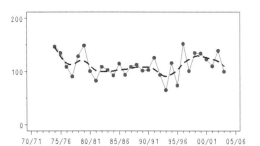

Figure 45.a, Annual indices & trend for Sanderling for GB.

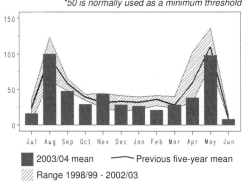

Figure 45.b, Monthly indices for Sanderling for GB.

Sanderling breed almost exclusively in the high Arctic, with individuals from both the Greenland and Siberian populations migrating through northwest Europe. Sanderling undertake long non-stop flights during this time and despite favouring coastal habitats can traverse large areas of land. The Baltic represents the northern limit of the wintering range within the East Atlantic Flyway, which extends down to southern Africa. Sanderling are widespread around the UK's coasts favouring sandy sediments and open shores.

The British maximum was 25% lower than in the preceding year. This decline was reflected in the British index, which fell by 30%. Conversely, the Northern Irish peak, which was typical in being recorded during spring, was the highest count recorded by WeBS.

Peak counts were recorded during passage when over four times the mean winter total were recorded in Britain. With the exception

of August and November British monthly indices were below average in all months.

Interestingly, two of the greatest changes in five-year means were recorded in the Uists with Ardivachar Point and Balranald undergoing a 50% increase and 23% decline respectively. Ardivachar Point currently holds nationally important numbers whilst numbers at Balranald have fallen below this threshold. Other notably low counts were at the Alt Estuary, North Norfolk Coast, Thanet Coast and Lade Sands.

	99/00	00/01	01/02	02/03	03/04	Mon	Mean
Sites of international importance in the UK							
Ribble Estuary	2,501	1,290	3,004	2,680	2,400	Nov	2,375
Alt Estuary	1,320	967	1,556	1,431	778	Nov	1,210
Sites of national importance in Great Britain							
Carmarthen Bay	592	730	1,600	1,770	833	Feb	1,105
North Norfolk Coast	881	1,179	1,319	1,150	601	Mar	1,026
Thames Estuary	(127)	334	552	875	385	Dec	537
Thanet Coast	610	677	434	444	342	Jan	501
Duddon Estuary	485	606	486	287	(585)	Mar	490
Humber Estuary	496	546	358	440	370 [11]	Dec	442
The Wash	(441)	317	504	496	317	Jan	415
Solway Estuary	(125)	(117)	(218)	(266)	(370)	Feb	(370)
Jersey Shore	443	253	391				362
Tees Estuary	456	373	259	280	240	Nov	322
Dee Estuary (England/Wales)	246	100	550	286	(379)	Dec	312
Forth Estuary	(184)	(262)	274	389	269 [11]	Feb	311
Swansea Bay	(235)	234	356	410	200	Nov	300
Morecambe Bay	235	391	275	240	306	Feb	289
South Ford	540	228		120	250	Dec	285
Durham Coast	(250)	(0)	(0)		(0)		(250) ▲
Pegwell Bay	65	375	123	373 [11]	(115)	Dec	234
Ardivachar Point (South Uist)	61	0		398	460	Dec	230 ▲
Lade Sands	330	320 [13]	236	140	118	Mar	229
Sites of all-Ireland importance in Northern Ireland							
Dundrum Bay	(65)	(132)	(0)	(30)	(0)		(132)
Killough Harbour			76 [11]				76
Sites no longer meeting table qualifying levels in winter 2003/2004							
Balranald RSPB Reserve		(0)	(290)	170	72	Dec	177
Other sites attaining table qualifying levels in winter 2003/2004 in Great Britain							
North Bay (South Uist)	180	302 [13]		67	235	Jan	196
Lindisfarne	129	58	321 [11]	283 [11]	221	Dec	202

Sites attaining international passage threshold in the UK in 2003					
Ribble Estuary	8,203	May	The Wash	2,563	Aug
Alt Estuary	6,894	Aug	Thames Estuary	1,394	Oct
Sites attaining national passage threshold in Great Britain in 2003					
North Norfolk Coast	1,029	Aug	Solway Estuary	577	May
Ardivachar Point (South Uist)	700	Aug	Tees Estuary	461	May
Morecambe Bay	640	Aug	Tay Estuary	409	Sep
North Bay (South Uist)	600	Sep	Carmarthen Bay	325	Oct
Humber Estuary	594	Aug			

Little Stint
Calidris minuta

International threshold: 2,000
Great Britain threshold: ?[†]
All-Ireland threshold: ?[†]

GB max: 78 Sep
NI max: 0

Predominantly a passage migrant in the UK, Little Stints breed from Scandinavia through Siberia and winter around the Mediterranean and throughout Africa. Typically, peak

numbers occur during autumn as juvenile birds follow adults on their southward migration.

The British maximum, recorded during September, was slightly higher than that of the previous year but lower than in other recent years being surpassed by all other maxima back to 1997/98. Interestingly, that was the same year in which no Little Stints appeared on Northern Irish WeBS sites, an event not repeated until this year.

Throughout Britain, Little Stints were recorded from 33 sites, the peak total being nine at the Fal Complex during September.

Wintering birds were less abundant, being present on five sites between November and February, all of which were in the southern half of Britain. Although most winter records were of single birds, five were present on the Severn Estuary during January, four in November at Abberton Reservoir and three each at Rutland Water and Chichester Harbour in November and February respectively.

Sites with five or more birds in Great Britain in 2003/2004[†]

Fal Complex	9	Sep	Humber Estuary	6	Sep
Thames Estuary	8	Sep	Severn Estuary	5	Jan
North Norfolk Coast	7	Sep	Benacre Broad	5	Sep
The Wash	6	Sep			

[†] as no British or All-Ireland thresholds have been set a qualifying level of five has been chosen to select sites for presentation in this report

Baird's Sandpiper

Calidris bairdii

Vagrant
Native Range: America

GB max: 1   Sep
NI max: 0

One was recorded at Bavelaw Marsh (Threipmuir and Harlow Reservoirs) in September.

Pectoral Sandpiper

Calidris melanotos

Vagrant
Native Range: America, N Siberia and Australia

GB max: 16   Sep
NI max: 0

Pectoral Sandpipers were recorded from a record 17 sites this year, with a wide geographical spread to the records. Singles were the norm, but there were two at Wyver Lane Marsh in September and at Ripon Race Course Gravel Pit in October, and a record four during a single WeBS count at Cliffe Pits and Pools on the Thames Estuary in September. As usual, records fell between July and October, with a strong peak in September.

Curlew Sandpiper

Calidris ferruginea

International threshold: 7,400
Great Britain threshold: ?
All-Ireland threshold: ?

GB max: 150   Sep
NI max: 4   Sep

Curlew Sandpipers typically occur in peak numbers during autumn passage. British maxima have exceeded 200 birds for the past five years making September's 150 total below average.

With the exception of 12 birds at the Dysynni Estuary all counts exceeding 10 birds were along the east coast and all were during August or September. The only 'winter' record refers to the presence of a single bird on the Severn Estuary during November.

Sites with ten or more birds in Great Britain in 2003/2004[†]

Pegwell Bay	25	Sep	Breydon Water / Berney Marshes	11	Sep
Humber Estuary	22	Sep	The Wash	11	Aug
Thames Estuary	14	Sep	North Norfolk Coast	10	Aug
Dysynni Estuary	12	Sep			

[†] as no British or All-Ireland thresholds have been set a qualifying level of 10 has been chosen to select sites for presentation in this report

Purple Sandpiper
Calidris maritima

GB max:	1,667	Jan
NI max:	100	Jan

International threshold: 750
Great Britain threshold: 180[†]
All-Ireland threshold: 10*

	S	M	L
GB change:	o	-	o
NI change:	o	o	-

50 is normally used as a minimum threshold

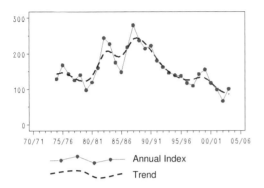

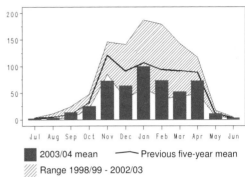

●━━● Annual Index	■ 2003/04 mean
- - - - Trend	⬆️ Previous five-year mean
	▨ Range 1998/99 - 2002/03

Figure 46.a, Annual indices & trend for Purple Sandpiper for GB.

Figure 46.b, Monthly indices for Purple Sandpiper for GB.

The UK wintering population of Purple Sandpiper is made up of birds from western areas in Iceland, Greenland and eastern Canada, and eastern areas in Scandinavia and Svalbard. The summed British maximum reached its highest total since 1992/93, increasing some 49% on the previous year's total. Conversely the Northern Irish maximum fell during 2003/04, although with the majority of these being on the Outer Ards, numbers at this site greatly influence the total for the province. The rise seen in Britain was mirrored in the annual indices, which were similar to those in 2001/02. The longer term trend, however, is less favourable being at its lowest ever level. This decline was also recorded in the monthly indices, which were below average throughout the year.

With the majority of Purple Sandpipers occurring along open rocky coastlines it is unsurprising that only five WeBS sites, all consisting of this habitat, currently hold numbers exceeding national thresholds; this is two fewer than in 2002/03. In line with recent years, annual peaks at Seahouses to Budle Point continued to fall well below the five-year mean to the extent that numbers were below the national qualifying level. The preference for rocky and open shores means that the proportion of the population counted during WeBS is severely limited; more focused monitoring of these areas (such as during the Non-estuarine Coastal Waterbird Survey in 1997/98) are needed to understand fully the changes recorded by WeBS.

	99/00	00/01	01/02	02/03	03/04	Mon	Mean
Sites of national importance in Great Britain							
Island of Papa Westray			330	120	216	Jan	222
Farne Islands		207	194	(185)			201
Balranald RSPB Reserve				190	180	Jan	185
Sites of all-Ireland importance in Northern Ireland							
Outer Ards Shoreline	100	82		122	83	Jan	97
Belfast Lough	19	(13)	16	15	17	Jan	17
Sites no longer meeting table qualifying levels in winter 2003/2004							
Dundrum Bay		(9)	(5)				(9)
Sites with mean peak counts of 100 or more birds in Great Britain[†]							
Island of Egilsay	136	334	4	141	195	Mar	162
Forth Estuary	128	159	172	248	72	Dec	156
Seahouses to Budle Point	310	205	151	25	64	Feb	151 ▼
Moray Coast	129	(158)	144	89	127	Jan	129
Durham Coast	122	(21)	(1)		(21)	Jan	122

	99/00	00/01	01/02	02/03	03/04	Mon	Mean
Ardivachar Point (South Uist)	112	100		120	110	Feb	111
East Unst			110 [10]				110
Tees Estuary	137	118	89	93	110	Dec	109
Other sites attaining table qualifying levels in winter 2003/2004 in Great Britain							
Island of Egilsay	136	334	4	141	195	Mar	162

[†] as few sites exceed the British threshold a qualifying level of 100 has been chosen to select sites for presentation in this report

Dunlin
Calidris alpina

GB max: 367,792 Jan
NI max: 12,257 Jan

International threshold: 13,300
Great Britain winter threshold: 5,600
Great Britain passage threshold: 2,000
All-Ireland threshold: 1,250

	S	M	L
GB change:	o	o	o
NI change:	-	o	o

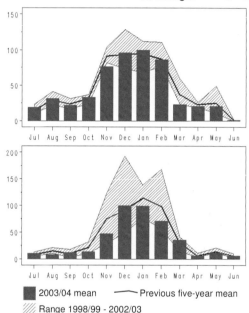

Annual Index
Trend

2003/04 mean
Previous five-year mean
Range 1998/99 - 2002/03

Figure 47.a, Annual indices & trend for Dunlin for GB (above) & NI (below).

Figure 47.b, Monthly indices for Dunlin for GB (above) & NI (below).

Three races of Dunlin regularly occur in the UK. The main wintering population is of the nominate race, whose breeding range extends from Scandinavia northwards and eastwards. During passage birds from the *arctica* and *schinzii* races, which breed in Greenland and Iceland, the latter also in Britain, supplement the numbers around UK estuaries.

Both Britain and Northern Ireland witnessed a major peak in Dunlin numbers in 1996/97, since which time numbers have fallen and have remained less variable. 2003/04 saw the British index reach its lowest value since 1987/88, signifying a gentle decline in numbers. During the same period the Northern Irish trend appears to be steadier, with a current value similar to previous years.

Dunlin numbers are highest between November and February and typically the 2003/04 counted maxima for both Britain and Northern Ireland were recorded during January. Monthly indices in Northern Ireland were below average throughout the year, even during the January peak count. In contrast, the corresponding monthly index for Great Britain was above average, emulating the proposed shift in wintering distribution for this species (Austin and Rehfisch 2005).

Of the 27 sites holding nationally or internationally important numbers of wintering Dunlin, only the Dee and Ribble Estuaries and Carlingford Lough witnessed a rise in their five-year means. Seven of the ten top sites with complete counts held peaks that were lower than in the previous winter. Such declines were particularly noticeable at the Severn Estuary and the Mersey Estuary, the latter holding over 30% fewer Dunlin in 2003/04 than in the previous winter, representing nearly 1.5 times the international threshold.

Especially high totals for the Dee Estuary, which almost doubled on the previous year, resulted in the highest total at any site during 2003/04. An increase of similar magnitude was witnessed at both the Ribble Estuary and Burry Inlet, the latter representing the site's highest total since 1996/97.

	99/00	00/01	01/02	02/03	03/04	Mon	Mean
Sites of international importance in the UK							
Mersey Estuary	42,120	60,330	45,756	58,463	40,170	Jan	49,368
Thames Estuary	(29,019)	44,907	48,104	53,755	(25,998)	Jan	48,922
The Wash	41,503	35,080	31,069	42,794	31,624	Feb	36,414
Dee Estuary (England/Wales)	21,627	41,656	34,448 [11]	21,266	41,679	Dec	32,135
Severn Estuary	(20,700)	(17,417)	20,401	25,734	23,801	Jan	23,312
Morecambe Bay	28,411	27,645	18,947	18,214	18,847	Jan	22,413
Humber Estuary	21,561	18,502	24,378	24,168	19,182 [11]	Dec	21,558
Langstone Harbour	24,090	23,790	17,500	17,320	24,286	Nov	21,397
Blackwater Estuary	16,792	(37,550)	15,004	18,806	13,958	Jan	20,422
Ribble Estuary	18,040	(36,473)	11,141	11,423	24,445	Jan	20,304
Chichester Harbour	(16,680)	16,773	17,947 [11]	15,661	12,552	Dec	15,923
Solway Estuary	14,746 [11]	(15,093)	(12,861)	(12,850)	(17,564)	Jan	15,801
Stour Estuary	15,168	15,822	16,469 [11]	12,863 [11]	9,268	Jan	13,918
Sites of national importance in Great Britain							
Forth Estuary	11,405	11,900	13,296	12,143	7,840 [11]	Feb	11,317
Swale Estuary	8,587	(7,795)	11,280	14,761	5,034	Jan	9,916
Dengie Flats	10,800	9,700	15,720	7,350	2,700	Feb	9,254
Lindisfarne	(8,148)	5,777	9,085	(9,991)	(9,503)	Jan	8,501
Medway Estuary	(8,591)	(5,118)	5,872	6,901	8,086	Dec	7,363
Colne Estuary	8,950	9,100	6,823	(350)	4,411	Jan	7,321
Burry Inlet	(9,271)	5,401	6,654	4,955	10,150	Jan	7,286
Duddon Estuary	10,000 [13]	(4,258)	5,415	3,942	7,680 [11]	Nov	6,759
Poole Harbour	6,693	4,852	(6,929)	(6,323)	(5,463)	Jan	6,199
Hamford Water	3,967	5,625	10,686 [11]	3,064	(3,476)	Dec	5,836
Sites of all-Ireland importance in Northern Ireland							
Strangford Lough	8,186 [11]	2,733 [11]	3,352	4,408 [11]	4,967 [11]	Feb	4,729
Lough Foyle	3,560	5,800	2,804	4,209	4,212	Jan	4,117
Carlingford Lough	1,861	(1,390)	(2,090)	(2,872)	(2,339)	Jan	2,291
Belfast Lough	1,242 [11]	1,366 [11]	1,278	1,193	1,461 [11]	Feb	1,308
Sites no longer meeting table qualifying levels in winter 2003/2004							
Outer Ards Shoreline	1,023	1,312		960	(993)	Jan	1,098
Dundrum Bay	(352)	(1,243)	(1,080)	(733)	(886)	Feb	(1,243)

Sites attaining international passage threshold in the UK in 2003				
The Wash	34,529	Aug	Humber Estuary	17,431	Apr
Ribble Estuary	22,370	Apr			

Sites attaining national passage threshold in Great Britain in 2003				
Alt Estuary	10,643	Aug	Dee Estuary (England/Wales)	3,467	Aug
Severn Estuary	9,317	Oct	Stour Estuary	2,960	Oct
Mersey Estuary	6,725	Jul	Morecambe Bay	2,864	Oct
Swale Estuary	6,346	Oct	Tees Estuary	2,849	Aug
Thames Estuary	5,909	Oct	Hamford Water	2,820	Oct
Medway Estuary	4,698	Oct	Dengie Flats	2,500	Aug
Solway Estuary	4,617	Oct	Breydon Water / Berney Marshes	2,359	Apr
Blackwater Estuary	4,038	Oct	North Norfolk Coast	2,066	Aug
Lindisfarne	3,613	Oct			

Broad-billed Sandpiper
Limicola falcinellus

Vagrant
Native Range: NE Europe, Asia, E&S Africa and Australia

GB max: 1 Oct
NI max: 0

One was recorded at the Humber Estuary (Stone Creek to Patrington) in October.

Buff-breasted Sandpiper
Tryngites subruficollis

Vagrant
Native Range: NE Siberia and America

GB max: 1   Oct
NI max: 0

One was recorded at Llyn Y Tarw in October.

Ruff
Philomachus pugnax

International threshold: ?
Great Britain threshold: 7*[†]
All-Ireland threshold: +[†]

GB max: 859   Aug
NI max: 9   Sep

*50 is normally used as a minimum threshold

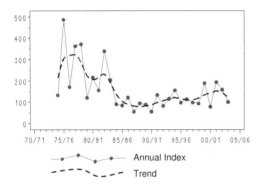

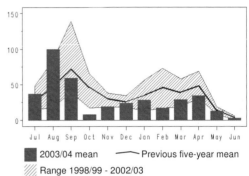

■ 2003/04 mean	— Previous five-year mean
▨ Range 1998/99 - 2002/03	

Figure 48.a, Annual indices & trend for Ruff for GB.

Figure 48.b, Monthly indices for Ruff for GB.

Although Ruff breed in relatively small numbers across parts of Europe, the majority of the population breeds across Siberia. Outside the breeding season, birds winter from northwest Europe to Africa with males outnumbering females in the north of this range. Autumn sees the strongest passage in the UK as birds migrate through much of western Europe.

For a scarce species that typically occurs in peak numbers during September, it is important to remember that changes recorded by the WeBS indices refer to the wintering population. Wintering numbers in Great Britain, which are currently approximately half

of the autumn peak, have fallen by 50% in the past two years, although the longer term trend appears more stable. The Ouse Washes remains the top site for this species holding nearly twice as many birds as any other in the UK, despite a 7% decline in the five-year mean.

The peak count in Northern Ireland was of seven individuals at Lough Foyle during September whilst wintering birds were even more scarce. With a peak of two birds recorded in February, Belfast Lough was the only site at which Ruff were counted during this period.

	99/00	00/01	01/02	02/03	03/04	Mon	Mean
Sites of national importance in Great Britain							
Ouse Washes	288	189	334	359	232 [13]	Nov	280
WWT Martin Mere	140	116	190	151	86	Jan	137
North Norfolk Coast	138 [12]	103	66	105	155	Nov	113
Lower Derwent Ings	111						111
Nene Washes	50	38	30	275	128	Feb	104
Breydon Water / Berney Marshes	144	52 [13]	155	55	43	Mar	90
Middle Yare Marshes	70	(33)	(37)	82	(17)	Feb	76
Swale Estuary	43	29	46	95	41	Dec	51
Ribble Estuary	41	63	5	76	21	Mar	41
Blackwater Estuary	41	10	49	82	19	Jan	40
Barleycroft Gravel Pit (Earith)	0	126		0	21	Jan	37

	99/00	00/01	01/02	02/03	03/04	Mon	Mean
Thames Estuary	25	(7)	34	35	43	Nov	34
Arun Valley	7	28	29	22	52	Feb	28
Dungeness Gravel Pits	21	55	0	42	7	Feb	25
Holland Marshes	45	23	41	6	12	Mar	25
Somerset Levels	2	15	(15)	29	33	Feb	20
Stodmarsh & Collards Lagoon	(37)	25	15	11	7	Feb	19
Abberton Reservoir	37	0	0	2	51	Nov	18
Sandbach Flashes	13	8		26	11	Nov	15
Cresswell Pond		15	(32)	1	12	Jan	15
Hamford Water	7	12	6 [11]	26	20	Feb	14
Humber Estuary	(18)	4	20 [13]	25	5 [11]	Jan	14
Confidential SE England Site	15	9	32	0	7	Dec	13
Hardley Flood		0		33	7	Nov	13
Rutland Water	36	9	8	4	10	Nov	13
Fen Drayton Gravel Pits	0	46	0	0	7	Dec	11
Solway Estuary	10 [11]	(0)	(0)	(1)	(3)	Dec	10
Fairfield SSSI	11	12	9	12	0		9
Tees Estuary	4	10	6	8	9	Mar	7
East Chevington Pools		1	14	(0)	7	Dec	7
Eyebrook Reservoir		25	2	0	0		7
Dee Estuary (England/Wales)	2	8	12	5	10	Jan	7
Hagnaby Lock Fen	0	0	6	19	9	Jan	7
Severn Estuary	1	1 [11]	3	21	(0)		7 ▲
Minsmere		8	8	5	6	Feb	7
Druridge Pool		0	21	0	8	Mar	7
Sites no longer meeting table qualifying levels in winter 2003/2004							
Adur Estuary				9 [11]	2 [11]	Feb	6
The Wash	0	3	14	(3)	0		4
Other sites attaining table qualifying levels in winter 2003/2004 in Great Britain							
Cresswell to Chevington Burn	0	0	0	6	11	Dec	3
Bothal Pond		0	0	7	9	Nov	4

Sites with more than 50 birds during passage periods in Great Britain in 2003

North Norfolk Coast	243	Oct	The Wash	71	Aug
Ouse Washes	137	Sep	Swale Estuary	54	Sep
Humber Estuary	110	Aug	WWT Martin Mere	54	Aug
Breydon Water / Berney Marshes	100	Jul	Rutland Water	52	Aug

[†] as no All-Ireland threshold has been set, a qualifying level of seven has been chosen to select sites for presentation in this report

---

Jack Snipe
Lymnocryptes minimus

International threshold:	?
Great Britain threshold:	?[†]
All-Ireland threshold:	250[†]

GB max: 122 Nov
NI max: 1 Dec

The UK lies on the northern edge of the wintering range for Jack Snipe, which has a disjunct distribution though parts of Western Europe and adjacent to Saharan Africa. The bird's secretive nature, preference for open marshy habitats and sparse distribution all contribute to the difficulties in monitoring this species through WeBS. The difficulties in detecting Jack Snipe are reflected in the totals at key sites, which show a high level of annual variation.

Of the 22 sites averaging over five birds only one (Waulkmill Glen and Littleton Reservoirs) held more than its five-year mean during 2003/04. The highest single count was of 16 birds in February at Doxey Marshes SSSI. Summed maxima for Great Britain were the lowest since 1999/2000 and since 2000/01 for Northern Ireland.

	99/00	00/01	01/02	02/03	03/04	Mon	Mean
Sites with mean peak counts of 5 or more birds in Great Britain[†]							
Chat Moss (Greater Manchester)			68 [26]				68
Doxey Marshes SSSI	18	6	64	(30)	16	Feb	27
Dornoch Firth			25 [11]				25
Chichester Harbour	23 [13]	31 [13]	16	39	7	Nov	23
Dee Estuary (England/Wales)	1	9	22 [11]	13	(9)	Nov	11

	99/00	00/01	01/02	02/03	03/04	Mon	Mean
Inner Moray and Inverness Firth	3	(3)	19	13	8	Dec	11
Fiddlers Ferry Pwr Stn Lagoons	6	4	32	6	0		10
Severn Estuary	15	12	9	7 [13]	5	Jan	10
Kemerton Lake					9	Feb	9
Waulkmill Glen / Littleton Resrs	3	15	6	10	12	Jan	9
Humber Estuary	2	(4)	5	13	(5) [11]	Nov	7
Lower Derwent Ings	7						7
Somerset Levels	(7)	(5)	(5)	(4)	(1)	Jan	(7)
Upton Warren LNR	9	12	5	6	3	Nov	7
Meadow Lane Gravel Pits St Ives	12	2	8	7	2	Feb	6
Mersey Estuary	12 [11]	5	6	5	3	Dec	6
North Cave Gravel Pits	4	3	15	4	3	Dec	6
Stour Estuary	3	6	12	2	6 [11]	Dec	6
Ardrossan-West Kilbride	3	(2)	6	8	2	Jan	5
Morecambe Bay	1	(2)	10	5	3	Jan	5
North Norfolk Coast	1	1	14 [11]	2	(1)	Nov	5
Shipton On Cherwell Quarry	7	5	3	6	2	Nov	5

[†] as few sites exceed the All-Ireland threshold and no British threshold has been set, a qualifying level of 5 has been chosen to select sites for presentation in this report

Snipe
Gallinago gallinago

International threshold: 20,000**
Great Britain threshold: ?[†]
All-Ireland threshold: ?[†]

GB max: 6,109 Nov
NI max: 433 Dec

Although Snipe breed across much of Britain and Ireland, wintering numbers are supplemented by birds from Iceland, northwest Europe, Scandinavia and western Russia. Found in a range of habitats both inland and coastal, Snipe are often difficult to detect due to their secretive habits.

British totals were the lowest since 1996/97 and over 30% lower than the all time maximum of 2001/02. Conversely, the Northern Irish maximum was the highest on record, surpassing the previous highest by some 18%. Twelve sites supported mean peaks greater than 200, although at only four of these did 2003/04 peaks exceeded their recent means. The Somerset Levels remained the top site for Snipe, where the decline in the site's five-year mean is likely to be a consequence of incomplete coverage during recent years. 2003/04 peak counts at Melby, Loch Saintear, Southampton Water, Strangford Lough and Upper Lough Erne all surpassed the national reporting threshold.

	99/00	00/01	01/02	02/03	03/04	Mon	Mean
Sites with mean peak counts of 200 or more birds in Great Britain[†]							
Somerset Levels	(1,578)	(1,817)	(854)	(963)	(308)	Nov	(1,817)
Lower Derwent Ings	621						621
Ouse Washes	218	58	1,685 [13]	126	233	Mar	464
Severn Estuary	396	(301)	(217)	(240)	(519)	Jan	458
North Norfolk Coast	188	207	1,169 [11]	92	121	Mar	355
Maer Lake	490	280	510	0	403	Dec	337
Doxey Marshes SSSI	65	149	544	(239)	390	Feb	287
Middle Yare Marshes	(57)	(217)	(545)	257	124	Feb	286
Cleddau Estuary	(154)	215	189	283	311	Jan	250
Arun Valley	185	335	166	242	134	Nov	212
Marston Sewage Treatment Wks	205						205
Sites with mean peak counts of 50 or more birds in Northern Ireland[†]							
Loughs Neagh and Beg	52	(33)	(15)	(129)	151	Nov	111
Belfast Lough	22	65	61	48	86 [11]	Dec	56
Larne Lough	93	60	57	16	52	Dec	56
Ballysaggart Lough				51	53	Nov	52

[†] as no British or All-Ireland thresholds have been set qualifying levels of 200 and 50 have been chosen to select sites, in Great Britain and Northern Ireland respectivley, for presentation in this report

Woodcock
Scolopax rusticola

International threshold: 20,000**
Great Britain threshold: ?
All-Ireland threshold: ?

GB max: 34 Jan
NI max: 1 Sep

WeBS is not a suitable survey for monitoring this non-wetland species, and relatively few are recorded. The peak in January was of only 46 birds, compared to a wintering population of at least several hundred thousand birds.

Woodcocks were noted at 52 sites this year, with counts in excess of four birds from only three sites: six at both Longueville Marsh and River Cam (Kingfishers Bridge) and five at Hamford Water, all in January.

Black-tailed Godwit
Limosa limosa

International threshold: 350
Great Britain threshold: 150
All-Ireland threshold: 90

	S	M	L
GB change:	+	++	++
NI change:	o	++	++

GB max: 28,731 Oct
NI max: 834 Oct

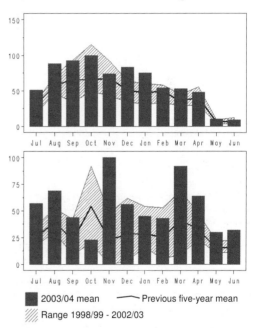

Annual Index
Trend

2003/04 mean   Previous five-year mean
Range 1998/99 - 2002/03

Figure 49.a, Annual indices & trend for Black-tailed Godwit for GB (above) & NI (below).

Figure 49.b, Monthly indices for Black-tailed Godwit for GB (above) & NI (below).

The majority of non-breeding Black-tailed Godwits recorded in Great Britain and Northern Ireland are of Icelandic origin (*islandica*). However, a small proportion of passage birds are of the nominate race, occurring mainly in the east and south of England, where small numbers also breed.

In line with recent breeding estimates of the Icelandic population the numbers of wintering Black-tailed Godwits continued to increase in Great Britain, and despite early indications in the mid to late 1990s that numbers of this

species were stabilising this has not been supported by subsequent data. The species has shown a less consistent increase in Northern Ireland; however, index values have risen consecutively for the past three years and the current value represents the highest ever reported. Peak counts were recorded during autumn passage (August to October) in Great Britain and during November in Northern Ireland.

Wintering numbers were stable in Great Britain before showing a slight decline in

February. This decline coincided with the peak counts at several inland sites, including the Ouse Washes and the River Avon, as birds disperse to inland feeding areas in late winter and early spring. Conversely, I-WeBS totals reveal peak numbers in the Republic of Ireland during January and February were almost double the numbers of preceding months. Pre-breeding movements through Ireland are highlighted with peaks during March and April in Northern Ireland.

Numbers on the Colne, Beaulieu and Orwell Estuaries declined such that these sites currently hold just nationally important numbers. Whilst the east and south coasts remain important for this species, recent increases at several sites away from these areas have continued. These include 10 and 20 percent increases in the five-year means for the Wash and the Dee Estuaries respectively.

	99/00	00/01	01/02	02/03	03/04	Mon	Mean
Sites of international importance in the UK							
The Wash	1,844	3,555	9,163	2,773	3,031	Dec	4,073
Dee Estuary (England/Wales)	2,543	2,366	4,624 [11]	3,955	4,493	Nov	3,596
Ouse Washes	2,130	268	3,273	3,468	3,137 [13]	Mar	2,455
Stour Estuary	1,862	2,846 [11]	2,593	1,927	1,607	Jan	2,167
Blackwater Estuary	(697)	(2,094)	(926)	(2,939)	1,232	Feb	2,088
Poole Harbour	2,051	1,134	(2,115)	(2,691)	(2,133)	Jan	2,025
Ribble Estuary	2,596	3,271	1,733	975	1,385	Jan	1,992
Thames Estuary	1,065	2,306	1,967	1,584	1,380	Jan	1,660
Swale Estuary	1,495	2,153	1,580 [11]	1,045	1,511	Mar	1,557
Breydon Water / Berney Marshes	883	1,376	1,607	1,142	1,277	Nov	1,257
R. Avon: R'gwood - Christchurch	0	2,630 [13]	3	3,002	170	Feb	1,161
Humber Estuary	1,685	545	921	1,311	914 [11]	Feb	1,075
Exe Estuary	1,113	880	737	890	(1,079)	Jan	940
Mersey Estuary	976	810	313	1,002	740	Feb	768
Medway Estuary	(389)	(0)	(662)	(199)	(154)	Dec	(662)
Southampton Water	522	1,265	(358)	196	(434)	Nov	661
Chichester Harbour	(511)	136	552	715	1,050	Nov	613
Hamford Water	371	601	366 [11]	490	414	Dec	448
Belfast Lough	401 [11]	383 [11]	492	545	367 [11]	Dec	438
Pagham Harbour	182	248	252	826	541	Mar	410
North West Solent	(231)	323	452	(261)	373	Mar	383 ▲
Sites of national importance in Great Britain							
Colne Estuary	(135)	450	344	(190)	253	Jan	349 ▼
Beaulieu Estuary	233	495	725	147	116	Jan	343 ▼
Langstone Harbour	(304)	(97)	442	314	245 [11]	Dec	334
Newtown Estuary	218 [11]	(86)	231	510	(173)	Mar	320
North Norfolk Coast	98	108	233	477	631	Mar	309
Orwell Estuary	395 [11]	73 [11]	260 [11]	407 [11]	389 [11]	Nov	305 ▼
Alde Complex	308	30	113	355	600	Feb	281
Crouch-Roach Estuary	252	(272)	(260)	(162)	(261)	Feb	261
Blyth Estuary (Suffolk)		271	244				258
Morecambe Bay	82	219	(117)	(143)	(403)	Nov	235
Deben Estuary	209	114	260	304	258	Jan	229
Meadow Lane Gravel Pits St Ives	0	800	0	(3)	0		200
Eden Estuary	182	170	221 [11]	206	220	Mar	200
Forth Estuary	93	55	232	243	291	Nov	183
Portsmouth Harbour	211	(70)	(84)	246 [11]	78	Nov	178
Fen Drayton Gravel Pits	0	780	1	0	0		156
Sites of all-Ireland importance in Northern Ireland							
Strangford Lough	259 [11]	83	153	189 [11]	267	Mar	190
Other sites attaining table qualifying levels in winter 2003/2004 in Great Britain							
Abberton Reservoir	0	0	0	0	392	Nov	78
Carmarthen Bay	(1)	2	8	(29)	331	Jan	114
Burry Inlet	99	7	30	60	222	Mar	84
Severn Estuary	35	5	141	193	200	Nov	115
Nene Washes	64	281	39	51	185	Mar	124 ▼
Christchurch Harbour	24	1	18	7	174	Dec	45
Other sites attaining table qualifying levels in winter 2003/2004 in Northern Ireland							
Lough Foyle	2	0	0	32	161	Nov	39

Sites attaining international passage threshold in the UK in 2003

The Wash	7,610	Oct	Swale Estuary	880	Aug
Dee Estuary (England/Wales)	3,652	Oct	Orwell Estuary	768	Sep
Mersey Estuary	2,407	Aug	Belfast Lough	706	Oct
Humber Estuary	2,108	Oct	Exe Estuary	581	Sep
Thames Estuary	1,804	Sep	Forth Estuary	478	Oct
Ribble Estuary	1,754	Aug	Deben Estuary	466	Sep
Stour Estuary	1,717	Sep	Langstone Harbour	457	Oct
Breydon Water / Berney Marshes	1,630	Aug	North Norfolk Coast	451	Sep
Blackwater Estuary	1,496	Apr	Severn Estuary	415	Aug
Poole Harbour	1,463	Oct	Medway Estuary	398	Sep
Chichester Harbour	955	Oct			

Sites attaining national passage threshold in Great Britain in 2003

Alde Complex	337	Oct	Eden Estuary	220	Apr
Southampton Water	299	Oct	Portsmouth Harbour	211	Oct
Burry Inlet	262	Oct	Solway Estuary	200	Sep
Morecambe Bay	227	Apr	Crouch-Roach Estuary	197	Apr
Colne Estuary	223	Sep	North West Solent	158	Oct

Sites attaining national passage threshold in Northern Ireland in 2003

Dundrum Bay	90	Sep

Bar-tailed Godwit
Limosa lapponica

International threshold:	1,200
Great Britain threshold:	620
All-Ireland threshold:	175

				S	M	L
GB max:	45,923	Feb				
NI max:	2,815	Dec	GB change:	o	o	o
			NI change:	o	o	o

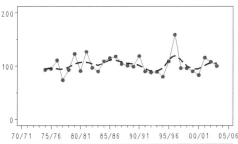

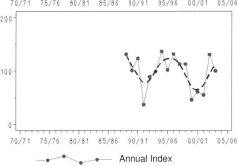

Annual Index

- - - - - Trend

Figure 50.a, Annual indices & trend for Bar-tailed Godwit for GB (above) & NI (below).

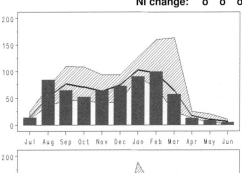

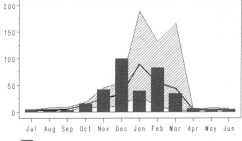

2003/04 mean — Previous five-year mean

Range 1998/99 - 2002/03

Figure 50.b, Monthly indices for Bar-tailed Godwit for GB (above) & NI (below).

The Bar-tailed Godwit is a true long-haul migrant. Whilst birds from the nominate race winter in Britain and Ireland and their breeding range extends from northeast Europe to western Siberia, many passage birds are of the *taymyrensis* race, which undertake a journey from their breeding areas in central Siberia to winter along the west coast of Africa.

Following a remarkable peak in 1996/97, the British index returned to former levels and despite falling 5% for the second year running remains within the typical range of fluctuation for this species. Wintering numbers in the UK are influenced by weather conditions in the Wadden Sea resulting in a high level of annual variation; however, the overall long-term trend shown by WeBS indices is one of stability.

In line with the monthly maxima, British indices rose steadily from October onwards to peak slightly above average in February.

During autumn passage, numbers in August were noteworthy, with the monthly index exceeding the previous five-year maximum; the August count at the Wash was the highest autumn total here to date, and the fourth highest site total ever recorded by WeBS anywhere.

Sixteen sites held mean peaks surpassing the international threshold during 2003/04, all of which were north of a line between the Thames and Dee Estuaries. Numbers at The Wash, Ribble and Alt Estuaries were below average while the Thames Estuary, Morecambe Bay and the Humber Estuary peaked above their five-year means. High numbers during February at Hamford Water means that this site creeps back into the list of nationally important sites for the first year since the revision of threshold levels. The high levels of annual variation were clearly demonstrated by Strangford Lough and Lough Foyle, numbers at which doubled and fell by three-quarters compared with the previous year, respectively.

	99/00	00/01	01/02	02/03	03/04	Mon	Mean
Sites of international importance in the UK							
The Wash	13,062	17,223	23,751	18,374	16,280	Jan	17,738
Ribble Estuary	4,346	(4,118)	20,950	3,111	11,301	Mar	9,927
Alt Estuary	8,001	6,146	12,098	7,103	6,503	Nov	7,970
Thames Estuary	2,584	(3,019)	(6,460)	3,751	8,989	Feb	5,446
Lindisfarne	(3,993)	4,066	5,237	(3,000)	(4,078)	Jan	4,652
Morecambe Bay	5,374	1,685	(938)	5,718	4,424	Nov	4,300
Humber Estuary	3,433	2,065	3,669	2,688	4,291 [11]	Jan	3,229
Dee Estuary (England/Wales)	232	990	12,163 [11]	127	1,209	Dec	2,944
Dengie Flats	900	1,388	4,970	3,112	1,550	Feb	2,384
Cromarty Firth	1,852 [11]	2,193	1,044	2,212	3,439	Dec	2,148
Solway Estuary	(931)	(1,434)	(2,106)	1,761	1,572	Jan	1,813
North Norfolk Coast	1,842	1,676	1,678 [11]	1,555	1,271	Jan	1,604
Strangford Lough	1,360	1,543	1,949 [11]	1,079	2,019	Feb	1,590
Forth Estuary	1,703	(1,542)	964	1,793	1,750 [11]	Feb	1,553
Lough Foyle	678	208	1,328	4,108	1,019	Dec	1,468
Tay Estuary	(1,250)	1,400	1,944	1,351	910	Feb	1,401
Sites of national importance in Great Britain							
Inner Moray and Inverness Firth	1,015	1,510	995	997	830	Jan	1,069
Dornoch Firth	837	406	1,136 [11]	1,561	1,068	Feb	1,002
Chichester Harbour	(462)	925	910	872	(910)	Jan	904
South Ford	1,052	1,042		549	950	Dec	898
Hamford Water	506	334	1,002	485	803	Feb	626 ▲
Other sites attaining table qualifying levels in winter 2003/2004 in Great Britain							
Blackwater Estuary	(223)	(128)	(95)	187	780	Feb	484
Eden Estuary	331	339	(400)	480	770	Dec	480

Sites attaining international passage threshold in the UK in 2003

The Wash	21,086	Aug	Thames Estuary	2,334	Oct
North Norfolk Coast	7,429	Sep	Forth Estuary	1,585	Sep
Alt Estuary	6,411	Aug	Lindisfarne	1,390	Sep
Tay Estuary	2,664	Sep	Solway Estuary	1,313	Sep

Sites attaining national passage threshold in Great Britain in 2003

Ribble Estuary	857	Oct	Cromarty Firth	783	Oct

Sites attaining national passage threshold in Northern Ireland in 2003

Lough Foyle	232	Oct	Strangford Lough	179	Oct

Bar-tailed Godwit (Al Downie)

Whimbrel
Numenius phaeopus

International threshold:	6,100	
Great Britain threshold:	+[†]	
All-Ireland threshold:	+[†]	

GB max: 784   Apr
NI max: 23   May

Whimbrel occurring in the UK are of the nominate race. This population migrates through Europe between their breeding grounds in Iceland, Scandinavia and western Siberia and their main wintering areas in West Africa.

As usual national peaks were recorded during spring and early autumn, particularly from April to September. Spring totals were higher than during autumn passage, which takes place over a longer period. The lower count in June coincided with the main breeding period.

The spring peak was more pronounced in Northern Ireland with April and May witnessing far more birds than were seen in the early autumn. Whimbrel are uncommon during winter and in 2003/04 were recorded at only 19 sites across the UK. The majority of these records were of single birds, although seven birds were present at the Tamar Estuary in March.

Sites with more than 50 birds during passage periods in Great Britain in 2003[†]

Severn Estuary	204	Apr	Breydon Water / Berney Marshes	55	May
Exe Estuary	134	Jul	North Norfolk Coast	55	Aug
The Wash	72	Jul	Morecambe Bay	54	Aug
Tamar Complex	64	Apr	Humber Estuary	53	Jul

[†] as no British or All-Ireland thresholds have been set a qualifying level of 50 has been chosen to select sites for presentation in this report

---

Curlew
Numenius arquata

International threshold:	4,200	
Great Britain threshold:	1,500	
All-Ireland threshold:	875	

GB max: 82,153   Jan
NI max: 5,697   Jan

	S	M	L
GB change:	o	o	+
NI change:	o	o	o

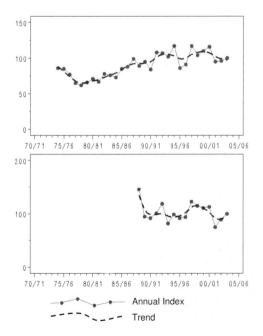

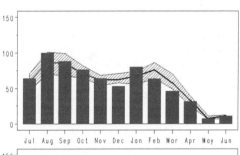

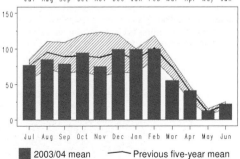

●— Annual Index
---- Trend

■ 2003/04 mean   —— Previous five-year mean
▨ Range 1998/99 - 2002/03

Figure 51.a, Annual indices & trend for Curlew for GB (above) & NI (below).

Figure 51.b, Monthly indices for Curlew for GB (above) & NI (below).

The distinctive sight and sound of the Curlew is characteristic of many coastal areas across Europe. Favouring estuaries and areas of fine sediment, Curlew can also be found in smaller numbers along open shores and inland marshes. Breeding occurs across much of the UK although the majority are found north of a line between the Severn and Humber Estuaries. The UK wintering population is a combination of birds that breed locally and those from Scandinavia.

Despite a fall in the annual indices of both Britain and Northern Ireland during 2001/02 subsequent data have indicated that numbers of this species continue to remain broadly stable. National indices rose slightly on the previous year in both Britain and Northern Ireland. Nevertheless summed maxima remained similar to previous years.

Monthly indices revealed a similar pattern to usual in Britain with peaks in August and again in January. With the exception of December, February and March indices were above average. Northern Ireland saw November counts below expected, however, the remaining months between October and February were comparable to the five-year mean.

Numbers recorded at key sites have generally remained stable during recent years and 2003/04 was no exception. However, an increase in the numbers at Chichester Harbour saw a peak count 10% higher than the five-year mean. Conversely, peak counts for the Outer Ards fell for the second year running, being 72% below the five-year mean.

	99/00	00/01	01/02	02/03	03/04	Mon	Mean
Sites of international importance in the UK							
Morecambe Bay	16,586	13,756	9,522	10,868	(10,866)	Mar	12,683
Solway Estuary	7,230	(4,497)	(4,311)	(3,701)	(4,531)	Jan	7,230
The Wash	5,056	4,058	4,339	4,757	4,036	Jan	4,449
Sites of national importance in Great Britain							
Dee Estuary (England/Wales)	3,373	4,583	4,305 [11]	3,270	4,978	Jan	4,102
Humber Estuary	3,532	4,044	4,277	3,941	3,530 [11]	Jan	3,865
Thames Estuary	(2,151)	(3,160)	(2,354)	3,763	(2,407)	Feb	3,763
Severn Estuary	(2,190)	(1,695)	(2,164)	3,615 [11]	2,528	Jan	3,072
Forth Estuary	2,777	2,524	(3,638)	3,229	2,891	Jan	3,012
Duddon Estuary	2,576	2,516	2,041	2,280	2,756	Nov	2,434
Lavan Sands	(1,836)	2,240	2,381	1,922 [11]	1,433	Dec	1,994
Inner Moray and Inverness Firth	2,456	1,698	1,473	1,961	1,809	Jan	1,879
North Norfolk Coast	1,863	1,686	2,302 [11]	1,430	1,539	Jan	1,764
Ribble Estuary	2,631	(1,709)	990	1,553	(1,857)	Jan	1,758
Mersey Estuary	1,507	1,976	1,562	1,270	1,804	Nov	1,624
Lindisfarne	(1,483)	1,636	1,822 [11]	1,338 [11]	(1,072)	Jan	1,599
Poole Harbour	1,712	1,484	1,577	1,605	1,427	Jan	1,561
Inner Firth of Clyde	1,497	(1,604)	(1,294)	(1,455)	(1,485)	Jan	1,551
Chichester Harbour	(1,389)	1,501	1,511	1,414	1,670	Jan	1,524 ▲
Sites of all-Ireland importance in Northern Ireland							
Lough Foyle	2,129	2,682	1,358	1,956	2,127	Feb	2,050
Strangford Lough	1,723 [11]	2,305	1,676	1,200	1,342 [11]	Jan	1,649
Outer Ards Shoreline	2,113	1,270		357	282	Jan	1,006
Sites no longer meeting table qualifying levels in winter 2003/2004							
Blackwater Estuary	(1,842)	(1,502)	(1,115)	(1,210)	969	Feb	1,328

Sites attaining international passage threshold in the UK in 2003					
The Wash	15,336	Aug	Dee Estuary (England/Wales)	5,727	Oct
Morecambe Bay	11,196	Sep			

Sites attaining national passage threshold in Great Britain in 2003					
Forth Estuary	3,941	Sep	Thames Estuary	1,974	Oct
Solway Estuary	3,913	Oct	Burry Inlet	1,755	Aug
Severn Estuary	2,898	Sep	Inner Firth of Clyde	1,739	Aug
Humber Estuary	2,517	Oct	Loch Leven	1,703	Oct
Mersey Estuary	2,480	Sep	Chichester Harbour	1,680	Jul
North Norfolk Coast	2,350	Aug	Cromarty Firth	1,595	Oct
Duddon Estuary	2,257	Sep	Swale Estuary	1,593	Oct
Lavan Sands	2,118	Aug			

Sites attaining national passage threshold in Northern Ireland in 2003					
Strangford Lough	1,788	Sep	Lough Foyle	1,250	Aug

Spotted Redshank
Tringa erythropus

International threshold: 1,000
Great Britain threshold: +[†]
All-Ireland threshold: +[†]

GB max: 172 Aug
NI max: 1 Dec

Spotted Redshanks breed from Scandinavia across much of sub-arctic Russia. The majority of this population winters in equatorial Africa but some birds remain in smaller numbers throughout Western Europe. The highest numbers of this species occur in the UK during passage periods, at which time they favour muddy shores, lagoons and lakes.

Summed totals for Britain exceeded 100 birds between July and October, with an August peak of 172. Wintering birds, between November and March, were recorded at 44 sites, four more than in the previous winter. Only four sites held double figures during the winter, the highest being 22 during February at the Camel Estuary. The only records from Northern Ireland were of single birds at Lough Foyle during December and January.

	99/00	00/01	01/02	02/03	03/04	Mon	Mean
Sites with mean peak counts of 10 or more birds in winter 2003/2004 in Great Britain[†]							
Tamar Complex	(36)	(7)	15	8 [11]	(3)	Nov	20
Burry Inlet	3	6	56	6	6	Nov	15
Thames Estuary	(7)	0	10	(26)	(1)	Feb	11
Severn Estuary	3	(19)	15	6 [11]	6	Jan	10
Other sites attaining table qualifying levels in winter 2003/2004 in Great Britain							
Beaulieu Estuary	7	5	5	6	12	Nov	7
Camel Estuary	(0)	0	(0)	0	22	Feb	7
North Norfolk Coast	3	11	6	6	11	Nov	7
Abberton Reservoir	0	0	0	0	20	Nov	4

Sites with more than 10 birds during passage periods in Great Britain in 2003

Minsmere	58	Jul	Breydon Water / Berney Marshes	17	Apr
The Wash	36	Jul	Dee Estuary (England/Wales)	13	Apr
North Norfolk Coast	35	Oct	Burry Inlet	10	Oct
Humber Estuary	27	Aug	Rutland Water	10	Sep

[†] *as no British or All-Ireland thresholds have been set a qualifying level of 10 has been chosen to select sites for presentation in this report*

Redshank
Tringa totanus

International threshold: 1,300
Great Britain threshold: 1,200
All-Ireland threshold: 245

GB max: 92,382 Oct
NI max: 9,527 Oct

	S	M	L
GB change:	o	o	+
NI change:	o	o	o

Redshank are widespread throughout the UK and although predominantly coastal in distribution outside the breeding season, many birds are present on inland marshes throughout the year. Wintering Redshank are found around coasts on a variety of substrates and are thought to consist of local breeders as well as individuals from the Icelandic and near European populations.

Britain saw a slight increase in Redshank numbers during 2003/04, although well within the margin of recent variation for this species. British numbers have remained broadly stable over the past 15 years. Northern Ireland has seen a less stable trend with numbers at their lowest for over five years following the all time peak of 1999/2000.

With the exception of October, which surpassed the previous five-year maximum, Northern Ireland saw monthly indices similar to average. British numbers were above the mean between August and October and, with the exception of January, below the mean thereafter.

Twenty-six sites held internationally important numbers during passage whilst an additional 11 surpassed this during winter. In line with the stable national trends, numbers at individual sites holding important numbers also saw little change, although Lough Foyle joined the list of sites supporting internationally important numbers whereas Lavan Sands dropped to nationally important.

The Humber Estuary held its highest total for several years being over 40% higher than the five-year mean; however, this did refer to counts made by the slightly different methodology of the WeBS Low Tide Counts.

Counts at the Cromarty Firth also surpassed its mean peak while the Inner Firth of Clyde, Alde Complex and Ythan Estuary all held peak numbers well below average.

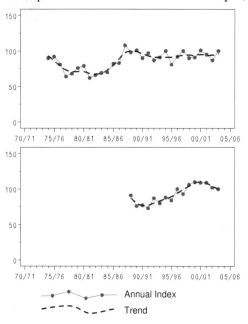

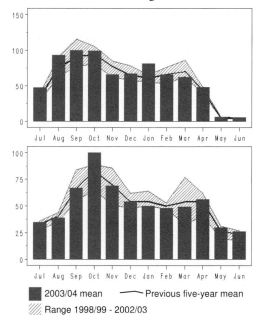

Figure 52.a, Annual indices & trend for Redshank for GB (above) & NI (below).

Figure 52.b, Monthly indices for Redshank for GB (above) & NI (below).

	99/00	00/01	01/02	02/03	03/04	Mon	Mean
Sites of international importance in the UK							
Morecambe Bay	7,262	8,604	6,274	6,650	6,715	Feb	7,101
Dee Estuary (England/Wales)	4,792	5,893	8,579 [11]	5,847	5,736	Dec	6,169
Humber Estuary	5,357	4,990	4,526	4,787	8,229 [11]	Nov	5,578
Mersey Estuary	4,476	6,045	4,690	4,143	6,050	Jan	5,081
Thames Estuary	(2,997)	(4,168)	4,479	(3,603)	(4,149)	Jan	4,479
Forth Estuary	3,742	4,040	4,204	4,194	4,576	Nov	4,151
The Wash	2,722	3,286	4,501	3,619	3,410	Jan	3,508
Blackwater Estuary	2,541	(4,199)	(3,539)	2,849	(1,818)	Feb	3,282
Strangford Lough	2,827	2,729	3,273 [11]	2,879 [11]	3,146 [11]	Nov	2,971
Ribble Estuary	2,622	(1,734)	1,877	3,882	(1,911)	Jan	2,794
Solway Estuary	(4,135)	(3,023)	1,668 [11]	(2,528)	(2,154)	Jan	2,702
Inner Moray and Inverness Firth	2,360	2,862	2,714	2,942	2,317	Jan	2,639
Severn Estuary	(1,254)	(1,528)	2,616	2,439 [11]	(1,865)	Nov	2,528
Inner Firth of Clyde	2,956 [11]	(2,324)	(2,433)	(1,589)	1,974	Dec	2,465
Duddon Estuary	2,367	2,816	1,596	1,849	2,508	Mar	2,227
Deben Estuary	1,996	2,881	1,999	2,017	1,869	Feb	2,152
Stour Estuary	2,511 [11]	2,038 [11]	2,261 [11]	1,769 [11]	2,010 [11]	Nov	2,118
Chichester Harbour	(1,342)	1,702	2,422	1,829	2,450	Jan	2,101
Alde Complex	(2,783)	2,742	2,071 [11]	1,456	1,430	Jan	2,096
Hamford Water	1,796	1,473	2,575 [11]	2,334	1,892	Feb	2,014
Orwell Estuary	2,197 [11]	1,637 [11]	2,279 [11]	1,825 [11]	1,939 [11]	Dec	1,975
North Norfolk Coast	1,473	1,412	3,915 [11]	1,299	1,401	Nov	1,900
Montrose Basin	1,800	1,509	2,511	1,830	1,803	Mar	1,891
Medway Estuary	(1,829)	(858)	(1,537)	(972)	(814)	Dec	(1,829)
Belfast Lough	2,108 [11]	1,677	2,261	1,540	1,452	Dec	1,808
Cromarty Firth	1,842 [11]	1,157	1,849	1,604	2,551	Dec	1,801
Colne Estuary	1,823	1,342	1,871	(97)	(868)	Feb	1,679
Swale Estuary	1,359	1,569	2,481	959	(1,352)	Dec	1,592
Tees Estuary	1,282	1,441	1,332	1,398	1,926	Nov	1,476
Breydon Water / Berney Marshes	1,474 [11]	1,456 [11]	1,207	1,497 [11]	1,630 [11]	Feb	1,453
Blyth Estuary (Suffolk)		1,265	1,481				1,373
Lough Foyle	844	1,974	1,104	1,606	1,198	Nov	1,345 ▲
Outer Ards Shoreline	1,308	1,428		1,351	1,228	Jan	1,329

144

	99/00	00/01	01/02	02/03	03/04	Mon	Mean
Sites of national importance in Great Britain							
Lavan Sands	(1,124)	1,270	1,126	1,525 [11]	1,248	Dec	1,292 ▼
Lindisfarne	684	975	1,825	(1,371)	1,503	Dec	1,272
Alt Estuary	1,627	1,470	1,090	931	945	Jan	1,213
Sites of all-Ireland importance in Northern Ireland							
Carlingford Lough	1,334	1,325	1,525	1,211	1,027	Nov	1,284
Dundrum Bay	801	1,051	(696)	(530)	(942)	Nov	931
Larne Lough	427	379	363	427	356	Dec	390
Bann Estuary	260	422	260	324	240	Jan	301
Sites no longer meeting table qualifying levels in winter 2003/2004							
Ythan Estuary	2,990	318	985	670	621	Nov	1,117

Sites attaining international passage threshold in the UK in 2003

Dee Estuary (England/Wales)	11,014	Sep	North Norfolk Coast	1,983	Aug
The Wash	9,339	Aug	Tay Estuary	1,979	Sep
Humber Estuary	8,362	Oct	Blackwater Estuary	1,931	Oct
Morecambe Bay	6,067	Sep	Chichester Harbour	1,871	Sep
Forth Estuary	5,462	Sep	Lindisfarne	1,789	Oct
Mersey Estuary	5,250	Oct	Severn Estuary	1,741	Oct
Strangford Lough	5,244	Oct	Deben Estuary	1,633	Oct
Solway Estuary	2,891	Oct	Inner Moray and Inverness Firth	1,624	Oct
Ribble Estuary	2,752	Oct	Duddon Estuary	1,600	Sep
Montrose Basin	2,649	Aug	Belfast Lough	1,493	Oct
Thames Estuary	2,570	Oct	Breydon Water / Berney Marshes	1,414	Oct
Tees Estuary	2,455	Oct	Stour Estuary	1,378	Oct
Cromarty Firth	1,996	Oct	Inner Firth of Clyde	1,319	Oct

Sites attaining national passage threshold in Great Britain in 2003

Hamford Water	1,299	Sep	Medway Estuary	1,221	Oct
Alde Complex	1,296	Oct	Swale Estuary	1,211	Oct

Sites attaining national passage threshold in Northern Ireland in 2003

Lough Foyle	826	Oct	Dundrum Bay	691	Aug
Carlingford Lough	812	Sep	Bann Estuary	324	Apr
Outer Ards Shoreline	784	Oct			

Greenshank
Tringa nebularia

International threshold:	3,100
Great Britain threshold:	6*
All-Ireland threshold:	9*

GB max:	1,909	Sep
NI max:	165	Sep

*50 is normally used as a minimum threshold

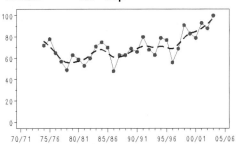

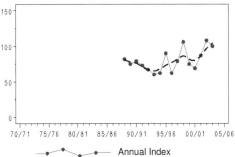

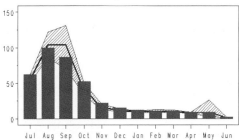

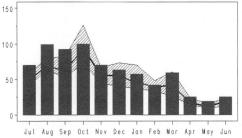

—•— Annual Index

---- Trend

■ 2003/04 mean   ⌒ Previous five-year mean

▨ Range 1998/99 - 2002/03

Figure 53.a, Annual indices & trend for Greenshank for GB (above) & NI (below).

Figure 53.b, Monthly indices for Greenshank for GB (above) & NI (below).

Restricted to northwest Scotland, UK breeding Greenshank are thought to make up the majority of our wintering population. Spring and autumn passage periods see a huge increase in numbers as birds from southern Europe and West Africa migrate between these wintering areas and their breeding areas across Scandinavia and western Siberia.

In Britain there are now indications that over-wintering Greenshank are starting to increase with this winter's peak of 391 in November the highest yet recorded. Despite a lower total than in the previous winter the species has shown a similar increase in Northern Ireland. Typically peak numbers

were recorded during autumn passage, with both national maxima peaking in September. Most passage birds have departed by November with a steady figure remaining throughout the winter. Northern Ireland counts were higher than the five-year mean in all months with July, August and September all reaching their highest value during this time.

Four of the five key sites within Northern Ireland held wintering numbers in excess of their five-year means. On the whole, winter site totals in Britain were unexceptional, although Southampton Water and Morecambe Bay held counts well above average.

	99/00	00/01	01/02	02/03	03/04	Mon	Mean
Sites of national importance in Great Britain							
Chichester Harbour	(19)	43	44	35 [13]	42	Nov	41
Tamar Complex	(25)	29	30	31 [11]	26	Dec	29
Kingsbridge Estuary	29	14	26	41	(36)	Nov	29
Fal Complex	(23)	26	26	27	32	Feb	28
Cleddau Estuary	(15)	27	34	28	20	Jan	27
Queens Valley Reservoir		17	20	19			19
Grouville Marsh	13	15	11	31	25	Dec	19
Taw-Torridge Estuary	16	19	14	16	19	Dec	17
Exe Estuary	13	14	14	18	14	Nov	15
Blackwater Estuary	2	(17)	(12)	27 [11]	12	Jan	15
Camel Estuary	(2)	9	(6)	(17)	17	Nov	14
Southampton Water	7 [11]	8	15	13	19	Nov	12
Foryd Bay	10	9	8	10	16	Nov	11
Inner Firth of Clyde	8	13	(12)	14	10	Nov	11
North West Solent	(10)	8	11	(5)	11	Nov	10
Solway Estuary	8	11	(11)	(8)	(6)	Jan	10
Jersey Shore	7	7	(13)				9
Yealm Estuary	7	6	7	15	8	Dec	9
Morecambe Bay	6	(5)	7	6	15	Nov	9 ▲
Burry Inlet	(28)	2	4	4	6	Nov	9
Poole Harbour	10	4	6	11	(6)	Feb	8
Thames Estuary	(3)	(3)	8	(3)	(5)	Jan	8
Lavan Sands	(4)	5	7	9	9	Nov	8
Tyninghame Estuary	7	8	7	11	9	Dec	8
Loch nan Capull (South Uist)					8	Dec	8 ▲
Helford Estuary	(14)	5	6	4	5	Jan	7
The Strand Colonsay	(7)						(7) ▲
Broadford Bay			(8)	(7)	6	Nov	7
Dee Estuary (England/Wales)	3	8	6	3	9	Jan	6
Hunterston Lagoon			3		9	Jan	6
Brading Harbour	5	7	5	6	8	Jan	6
Medway Estuary	7	3	8	(1)	5	Jan	6 ▲
North Norfolk Coast	3	7	9	3	(3)	Nov	6 ▲
Rough Firth	5	9	7	2	6	Jan	6 ▲
Ceann a Bhaign			4	8			6
The Wash	3	0	3	18	7	Nov	6
Sites of all-Ireland importance in Northern Ireland							
Strangford Lough	48	41	56	72	61	Dec	56
Lough Foyle	30	16	20	22	27	Nov	23
Carlingford Lough	14	13	18	14	16	Feb	15
Dundrum Bay	12	11	18	15	15	Nov	14
Larne Lough	8	9	(15)	15	11	Dec	12
Other sites attaining table qualifying levels in winter 2003/2004 in Great Britain							
Eden Estuary	2	3	(0)	6	9	Nov	5

The Wash	336	Jul	Dee Estuary (England & Wales)	76	Sep
Chichester Harbour	179	Sep	Exe Estuary	72	Sep
Blackwater Estuary	169	Sep	Burry Inlet	69	Oct
North Norfolk Coast	131	Aug	Stour Estuary	68	Aug
Strangford Lough	82	Sep	Dundrum Bay	58	Aug
Thames Estuary	78	Sep	Tamar Complex	57	Sep
			Swale Estuary	56	Oct

Lesser Yellowlegs
Tringa flavipes

Vagrant
Native Range: N & S America

GB max: 2   Oct
NI max: 0

Singles were at Hauxley Haven in May, at Cors Caron and Cowpen Marsh (Tees Estuary) in October, and an overwintering bird at the Hayle Estuary recorded monthly from November to March.

Green Sandpiper
Tringa ochropus

International threshold: 14,500
Great Britain threshold: ?[†]
All-Ireland threshold: ?[†]

GB max: 463   Aug
NI max: 0

Green Sandpipers peaked on WeBS sites during August at 468 birds and just over a hundred birds remained through most of the winter (although the true numbers in the UK would have been much higher as this species has a more dispersed distribution than many other waders). Eight sites held peaks greater than 15 birds; unsurprisingly these were all during July and August. Wintering birds, between November and February, were recorded on 140 sites, 12 of which held peaks of five or more. Most wintering birds were recorded in the southern half of Britain with the Somerset Levels being the only site to reach double figures during this period.

Sites with 15 or more birds during passage periods in Great Britain in 2003[†]

Humber Estuary	32	Aug	Swale Estuary	16	Oct
Tophill Low Reservoirs	30	Jul	Colne Estuary	15	Jul
Thames Estuary	27	Aug	Dungeness Gravel Pits	15	Aug
Upton Warren LNR	20	Jul	Rutland Water	15	Aug
Southampton Water	17	Aug			

[†] *as no British or All-Ireland thresholds have been set a qualifying level of 15 has been chosen to select sites for presentation in this report*

Wood Sandpiper
Tringa glareola

International threshold: 10,400[†]

GB max: 18   Jul
NI max: 0

Although a small breeding population of Wood Sandpiper exists in Scotland the western limit of the European breeding range essentially extends through Denmark and Norway. European breeders are most commonly seen in the UK during passage, although the bulk of the population migrate on a more easterly route, explaining why national peaks have never exceeded double figures.

During 2003 the spring peak was in May as usual, with nearly all records from inland sites. Autumn appearances were more evenly spread across sites with peaks of four at Lindisfarne and Tophill Low Reservoirs in July and Breydon Water / Berney Marshes in August. As usual there were no wintering records.

Sites with three or more birds during passage periods in Great Britain in 2003[†]

Breydon Water / Berney Marshes	4	Aug	Dungeness Gravel Pits	3	Sep
Lindisfarne	4	Jul	Thames Estuary	3	Aug
Tophill Low Reservoirs	4	Jul			

[†] *as no British or All-Ireland thresholds have been set a qualifying level of three has been chosen to select sites for presentation in this report*

Common Sandpiper
Actitis hypoleucos

International threshold: 17,000
Great Britain threshold: ?[†]
All-Ireland threshold: ?[†]

GB max: 945 Jul
NI max: 5 Jul

Common Sandpipers breed along upland streams and still waters through much of Britain and Ireland, predominantly in the north and west. Post-breeding migration to West Africa begins in July with birds returning in April, during which times they are seen widely in a variety of wetland habitats, although rarely in large numbers. Reflecting such movements, peak numbers were recorded in Britain and Northern Ireland during August and July respectively. An increasing number of birds overwinter in the UK, mainly in the southern half of Britain, and during 2003/04 wintering birds were present at 48 sites between November and March. The summed totals for these sites remained above 20 birds throughout this period, the highest single site count being ten during November at the Medina Estuary.

Sites with 40 or more birds during passage periods in Great Britain in 2003[†]

North Norfolk Coast	59	Aug	Rye Harbour and Pett Level	55	Jul
Abberton Reservoir	55	Aug	Morecambe Bay	52	Jul

[†] as no British or All-Ireland thresholds have been set a qualifying level of 40 has been chosen to select sites for presentation in this report

---

Turnstone
Arenaria interpres

International threshold: 1,000
Great Britain threshold: 500
All-Ireland threshold: 225

GB max: 11,110 Dec
NI max: 1,962 Jan

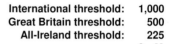

	S	M	L
GB change:	o	-	o
NI change:	o	o	-

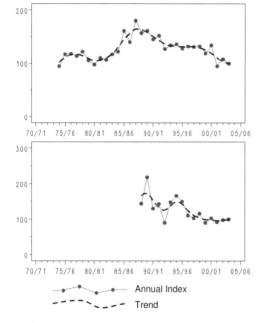

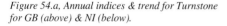

- ● - Annual Index
- - - - Trend

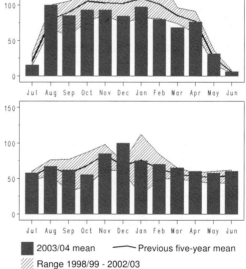

■ 2003/04 mean ⌒ Previous five-year mean
▨ Range 1998/99 - 2002/03

Figure 54.a, Annual indices & trend for Turnstone for GB (above) & NI (below).

Figure 54.b, Monthly indices for Turnstone for GB (above) & NI (below).

Turnstone are widespread around the British coastline with birds from two separate breeding populations occurring in the UK. The majority of wintering birds breed in Greenland and Eastern Canada whilst birds from the Scandinavian and Siberian population, which winter in western Africa, reach peak numbers during passage. According to current population estimates for the UK, about 20% of Turnstone are currently recorded on WeBS sites, showing the dispersed nature of this species along non-estuarine coasts.

WeBS sites in Britain have witnessed a steady decline in Turnstone numbers over the past 15 years and, with the exception of 2001/02, numbers in 2003/04 were at their lowest levels in 30 years. Northern Ireland also experienced its all time low in 2001/02 since which time, however, numbers have risen and are currently their highest for five years. Britain experienced below average indices in all months except August, whereas Northern Irish numbers peaked during December and with the exception of October were above average.

The most noticeable change in the table of British Turnstone numbers has been at the Mersey Estuary where numbers are down in single figures, having only three years earlier been the second most important UK site for this species. This is entirely due to the inclusion of Low Tide Counts from the mouth of the Mersey in the past, where large numbers occur, compared to the standard Core Counts, which do not cover the same area. Consequently numbers at this site have fallen by 70% on the previous five-year mean. Additionally, continuing low counts from Morecambe Bay means that the five-year peak mean for the site has fallen below the international importance threshold. Five-year means at the Northern Irish key sites remained unchanged.

	99/00	00/01	01/02	02/03	03/04	Mon	Mean
Sites of international importance in the UK							
Outer Ards Shoreline	1,102	879		1,086	1,081	Jan	1,037
Sites of national importance in Great Britain							
Thanet Coast	892	827	964	694	1,192	Dec	914
Morecambe Bay	1,181	1,175	825	588	766	Dec	907 ▼
Forth Estuary	762	989	610	940	699	Nov	800
Thames Estuary	(512)	632	(879)	(425)	(418)	Jan	756
Stour Estuary	716	708	614	(640)	537	Nov	644
Humber Estuary	785	659	499	529	723 [11]	Dec	639
Dee Estuary (England/Wales)	453	791	(405)	726	415	Nov	596
North Norfolk Coast	416	461	744	833	473	Jan	585
The Wash	(641)	515	(270)	579	354	Feb	522
Sites of all-Ireland importance in Northern Ireland							
Belfast Lough	399	(524)	432	401	485	Jan	448
Strangford Lough	301	248	227	206	225	Dec	241
Sites no longer meeting table qualifying levels in winter 2003/2004							
Mersey Estuary	703 [11]	(0)	17	7	8	Jan	184
Sites attaining international passage threshold in the UK in 2003							
Morecambe Bay	1,150	Apr	The Wash			1,044	Aug
Sites attaining national passage threshold in Great Britain in 2003							
North Norfolk Coast	727	Aug	Thanet Coast			600	Oct
Forth Estuary	711	Oct					
Sites attaining national passage threshold in Northern Ireland in 2003							
Outer Ards Shoreline	570	Oct	Carlingford Lough			230	Oct
Belfast Lough	481	Oct					

Red-necked Phalarope
Phalaropus lobatus

Scarce

GB max: 2 Sep
NI max: 0

Two were at Rutland Water in September.

Grey Phalarope
Phalaropus fulicarius

Scarce

GB max: 4 Oct
NI max: 0

Two were along the Amble to Chevington Burn stretch of the Northumberland Coast in October, with singles the same month at the Kent Estuary (Arnside to Sampool) in Morecambe Bay and the Thames Estuary (Leigh Marsh and Two Tree Island). Another single bird was at Belvide Reservoir in December.

Mediterranean Gull
Larus melanocephalus

International threshold: 8,400[†]

GB max: 90 Aug
NI max: 3 Jan

Three decades ago, Mediterranean Gull was a scarce visitor the UK and was just starting to be noted as a regular, albeit rare, breeding species. The increase in the northwest European population has been evident through the expansion of birds throughout Britain from the traditional southeast stronghold. During 2003/04 Mediterranean Gulls were recorded at 69 sites, compared to just 34 ten years ago. Surprisingly, the British maximum was somewhat lower than in the previous two years. However, as with all gull species the

optional inclusion of this group during WeBS counts should always be taken into account. The Solent remains the most important area for this species with Brading Harbour staying as the top site. Three birds at Belfast Lough and two at Lough Foyle represent the highest numbers of Mediterranean Gulls ever recorded by WeBS counts in Northern Ireland. Mediterranean Gulls were reported from a total of 60 sites during the Winter Gull Roost Survey in winter 2003/04 (BTO data).

	99/00	00/01	01/02	02/03	03/04	Mon	Mean
Sites with mean peak counts of 5 or more birds in Great Britain[†]							
Brading Harbour	51	35	28	126	57	Aug	59
Newtown Estuary	49	2	65	80	(15)	Mar	49
Chichester Harbour	(5)	36 [13]	4 [13]	(16)	(1)	Oct	20
Tamar Complex	27	28	14	30	0		20
Ryde Pier to Puckpool Point	15	16	8	45	9	Mar	19
Thames Estuary	(7)	13	13	20	27	Sep	18
Swansea Bay	6	11	20	16	19	Jul	14
Camel Estuary	4	(3)	(1)	8	25	Oct	12
North Norfolk Coast	10	(4)	(6)	(13)	(1)	Jul	12
Pagham Harbour	(0)	1	0	16			6
Ribble Estuary	0	(0)	9	7	8	Mar	6
Burry Inlet	(3)	3	(0)	7	(1)	Oct	5
Foreland	10	8	3	1	4	Dec	5
Llanon and Llansantffraid			6	3			5

[†] as no British or All-Ireland thresholds have been set a qualifying level of 5 has been chosen to select sites for presentation in this report

Little Gull
Larus minutus

International threshold: 840
Great Britain threshold: ?[†]
All-Ireland threshold: ?[†]

GB max: 450 Mar
NI max: 1 Mar

Little Gulls are principally recorded during passage periods with most winter records coming from coastal sites; the Winter Gull Roost Survey only recorded Little Gulls at six sites in winter 2003/04 (BTO data). High counts at the Alt Estuary during 2003/04 influenced the British maximum, which varies greatly with coverage. Roost counts at Hornsea Mere regularly record high numbers of Little

Gulls, though the peak count here in 2003/04 was deemed incomplete. Large numbers (up to 1,004) were also recorded passing offshore at Ness House Thorpeness, although these counts are not tabulated as they refer to birds moving through the site. Site peaks were most commonly recorded during autumn passage; peaks in spring were only recorded at two sites, both on the northwest coast.

	99/00	00/01	01/02	02/03	03/04	Mon	Mean
Sites of international importance in the UK							
Hornsea Mere	46	163	3,150 [12]	1,350 [12]	(940) [13]	Aug	1,177
Sites with mean peak counts of 5 or more birds in Great Britain[†]							
Alt Estuary	67	2	80	218	430	Mar	159
Monikie Reservoirs	155	0		60	0		54
Eden Estuary		44	(1)				44
Tay Estuary	(1)	(0)	(22)	50	36	Jul	43

	99/00	00/01	01/02	02/03	03/04	Mon	Mean
North Norfolk Coast	41	(17)	70	9	38	Sep	40
Minsmere		1	2	(15)	73	Aug	25
Tophill Low Reservoirs	2	2	0	10	110 [13]	Aug	25
Forth Estuary	1	1	22	41	20	Oct	17
Benacre Broad	15	30		0			15
East Chevington Pools			4	29	3	Jul	12
Humber Estuary	(1)	(10)	(0)	(2)	(12)	Sep	(12)
Morecambe Bay	5	3	31	1	9	Mar	10
Lindisfarne	2	(0)	0	(0)	26	Oct	9
Dengie Flats					8	Sep	8
St Andrews Bay			8				8
Dungeness Gravel Pits			(7)	(0)			(7)
Staines Reservoirs	10	1	0	18	0		6
Loch Fleet Complex	2	4	4	5	8	Dec	5
Walthamstow Reservoirs	0	22	1	0	0		5

[†] as no British or All-Ireland thresholds have been set a qualifying level of 5 has been chosen to select sites for presentation in this report

Black-headed Gull
Larus ridibundus

International threshold: 20,000
Great Britain threshold: 19,000[†]
All-Ireland threshold: ?[†]

GB max: 223,715 Jan
NI max: 16,178 Jan

Black-headed Gulls are the most numerous gull species recorded by WeBS, national maxima regularly surpassing 200,000 birds. As with the rest of the gulls their inclusion in WeBS counts is optional so the number of sites at which they have been counted limits these totals. Nevertheless, WeBS totals do indicate the widespread distribution of this common species, the top two sites showing that it frequents both coastal and inland sites. Many of the counts presented here have been obtained from the Winter Gull Roost Survey, which will provide a new population estimate for the species after 2005/06. Thus, more sites than usual have been identified as holding over

10,000 birds. The highest ever count at the Thames Estuary warrants its position as the top site during 2003/04. Two other sites qualified as internationally important and one further site as nationally important. Peak numbers recorded by WeBS occur in winter and, although only representing a small proportion of the national population, have been relatively stable over recent winters. Results from the Winter Gull Roost Survey counts show that winter numbers have declined over the last decade (Burton *et al.* 2005) and this is reflective of the recent trend in its breeding population (Seabird 2000: Mitchell *et al.* 2004).

	99/00	00/01	01/02	02/03	03/04	Mon	Mean
Sites of international importance in the UK							
Thames Estuary	(18,250)	(35,410)	(22,911)	30,275	43,601 [44]	Jan	36,938
Chew Valley Lake					29,800 [44]	Jan	29,800 ▲
The Wash	31,403	(9,008)	(16,136)	(15,999)	17,582 [44]	Jan	24,493
Sites of national importance in Great Britain							
Lower Derwent Ings					19,900 [44]	Jan	19,900 ▲
Sites with mean peak counts of 10,000 or more birds in Great Britain[†]							
Queen Mary Reservoir					16,836 [44]	Jan	16,836
Ribble Estuary	(12,450)	(6,793)	24,460	(821)	7,419 [44]	Jan	15,940 ▼
Tophill Low Reservoirs	18,000	12,500	25,000	11,900	8,900	Nov	15,260
Church Wilne Reservoir					15,000 [44]	Jan	15,000
Morecambe Bay	17,670	(17,610)	7,795	(17,772)	12,574	Aug	14,684
Grafham Water					14,470 [44]	Jan	14,470
Humber Estuary	6,960	(3,264)	(2,217)	(363)	21,450 [44]	Jan	14,205
Poole Harbour	10,629	(10,162)	(7,386)	(12,461)	17,707 [44]	Feb	14,168
Forth Estuary	(3,818)	(16,521)	(2,343)	(2,195)	11,554 [44]	Jan	14,038
Bewl Water	400	800	33,000 [12]	200	31,000 [44]	Dec	13,080
Portsmouth Harbour	(15,509)	(14,247)	4,881	15,311 [11]	12,153	Dec	12,420
Southfield Reservoir					12,000 [44]	Jan	12,000
Eyebrook Reservoir					11,300 [44]	Jan	11,300
Severn Estuary	(3,236)	(4,478)	(5,725)	9,209 [11]	13,139 [44]	Jan	11,174

	99/00	00/01	01/02	02/03	03/04	Mon	Mean
Pitsford Reservoir	10,000	10,000 [12]	10,000 [12]	12,000 [12]	10,000 [44]	Sep	10,400
Theale Gravel Pits	(106)		(262)	(235)	10,000 [44]	Oct	10,000
Sites with mean peak counts of 1,000 or more birds in Northern Ireland[†]							
Belfast Lough	4,028 [11]	7,496 [11]	8,986 [13]	5,503 [11]	7,095 [11]	Dec	6,622
Outer Ards Shoreline	8,040	3,290		4,945	5,113	Jan	5,347
Strangford Lough	2,767 [11]	3,588	3,503 [11]	3,518 [11]	3,388	Feb	3,353
Loughs Neagh and Beg			2,637	(4,036)	1,593	Mar	2,755
Lough Foyle	3,019	1,214	1,627	2,780	1,300 [44]	Jan	1,988
Larne Lough	2,639	942	2,060	733	831	Mar	1,441

[†] as few sites exceed the British threshold and no All-Ireland threshold has been set qualifying levels of 10,000 and 1,000 have been chosen to select sites, in Great Britain and Northern Ireland respectivley, for presentation in this report

Ring-billed Gull
Larus delawarensis

Vagrant
Native Range: N America

GB max: 4 Jan
NI max: 1 Nov

Single Ring-billed Gulls were noted at seven sites this year; Cromarty Firth, Hetton Lyons Park, Lough Foyle, Par Sands Pool, Portsmouth Harbour, Swansea Bay and Taw-Torridge Estuary. Many of these records appear to involve the return of birds from previous winters and these figures are unexceptional compared to the previous few years. The only Ring-billed Gull that was recorded by the 2003/04 Winter Gull Roost Survey was at Swansea Bay (BTO data).

Common Gull
Larus canus

International threshold: 17,000
Great Britain threshold: 9,000[†]
All-Ireland threshold: ?[†]

GB max: 64,678 Jan
NI max: 6,012 Aug

Whilst in the summer Common Gulls are a more regular sight for WeBS counters in the northern half of Britain and Northern Ireland, the species is widespread during winter and in 2003/04 was recorded on almost 900 sites. Many of the site totals include counts from the Winter Gull Roost Survey and this can explain the higher than usual totals at the Humber and Blyth Estuaries, West Water Reservoir, Chew Valley Lake, Loch of Skene and Rutland Water, as well as the inclusion in the table below of several sites at which gulls have not been recorded by WeBS counts. Six sites qualify as internationally important and three others as nationally important. Exceptional numbers have been reported roosting at Bewl Water since 2001/02, making this perhaps the most important current site in the country for the species (see WeBS News no. 18). As for all of the gulls five-year means are highly dependent of the coverage and survey methods used to ascertain site peaks, therefore any comparison with qualifying level thresholds must be done with this in mind. Unusually for Northern Ireland the summed maximum occurred during early autumn, typically the peaks in both Great Britain and Northern Ireland are recorded between November and February. Winter Gull Roost Survey counts indicate that numbers of wintering Common Gulls rose during the latter half of the last century, though there has been no clear trend over the last decade (Burton *et al.* 2005).

	99/00	00/01	01/02	02/03	03/04	Mon	Mean	
Sites of international importance in the UK								
Humber Estuary	(546)	(502)	(366)	(2,077)	29,000 [44]	Jan	29,000	▲
Tophill Low Reservoirs	42,000	24,500	33,000	23,100	16,530	Nov	27,826	
Bewl Water	450	50	63,000 [12]	50	75,000 [44]	Feb	27,710	▲
Derwent Reservoir	33,000 [12]	41,000 [12]	6,500	11,800 [12]	(6,500) [12]	Oct	23,075	
Hallington Reservoir	32,000 [12]	19,000 [12]	4	24,000 [12]	25,000 [12]	Dec	20,001	
Haweswater Reservoir	11,000 [12]	26,480 [12]	16,566 [12]	13,674 [12]	27,986 [13]	Mar	19,141	
Sites of national importance in Great Britain								
Eyebrook Reservoir					16,100 [44]	Jan	16,100	▲
Ullswater	(0)	(0)	(0)		11,470 [13]	Jan	11,470	▲
West Water Reservoir	(5,400)				10,050 [44]	Jan	10,050	▲

	99/00	00/01	01/02	02/03	03/04	Mon	Mean
Sites with mean peak counts of 3,000 or more birds in Great Britain[†]							
Rye Harbour and Pett Level					8,600 [44]	Jan	8,600
Solway Estuary	(2,671)	(2,247)	(1,398)	7,193	9,564 [44]	Sep	8,379
Colt Crag Reservoir	1,140 [12]	16,000 [12]		8,200 [12]	4,700 [44]	Jan	7,510
Blyth Estuary (Suffolk)		2,750	(1,337)		12,000 [44]	Jan	7,375
Ribble Estuary	(591)	(3,077)	8,653	(146)	6,036	Feb	7,345
Forth Estuary	(1,450)	(2,197)	(1,658)	(1,356)	6,321 [44]	Jan	6,321
Chew Valley Lake	1	2	(0)		18,200 [44]	Jan	6,068
Moray Firth		4,494 [1]	5,961 [1]	5,037 [1]	5,208 [1]	Nov	5,175
Southwold Sole Bay					5,000 [44]	Jan	5,000
Dee Estuary (England/Wales)	(3,466)	(572)	(1,519)	4,182	5,311	Jul	4,747
Eccup Reservoir	4,000	3,500	9,000	5,000	579 [44]	Jan	4,416
Tees Estuary	3,617	3,258	8,130	2,804	4,025	Dec	4,367
Durham Coast	4,120	(62)	(0)	(8)	(2)	Feb	4,120
Loch of Skene	586	1,390	570	433	17,284 [44]	Jan	4,053
Portmore Loch				(23)	3,900 [44]	Jan	3,900
Morecambe Bay	3,397	4,860	3,632	3,194	4,358	Dec	3,888
The Wash	(4,324)	3,681	(1,784)	2,482	4,912 [44]	Jan	3,850
North Norfolk Coast	5,271	460	(1,420)	(1,283)	5,600 [44]	Jan	3,777
Lower Derwent Ings					3,720 [44]	Jan	3,720
Lindisfarne	(170)	(630)	(2,920)	(370)	(3,644)	Jan	(3,644)
Thames Estuary	(3,870)	6,848	3,135	2,041	2,319 [44]	Jan	3,643
Pitsford Reservoir	6,000	2,000 [12]	3,000 [12]	4,000 [12]	3,000 [44]	Jan	3,600
Hule Moss	1,640 [13]	1,600 [13]	2,200 [13]	6,300 [13]	5,600 [13]	Oct	3,468
Rutland Water	500	4,000	50 [12]	100	12,080 [44]	Jan	3,346
Burry Inlet	(1,600)	5,085	1,513	2,315	4,239	Aug	3,288
Hamilton Low & Strathclyde Park					3,200 [44]	Jan	3,200
Alt Estuary	4,800	3,850	(1,235)	(810)	942 [44]	Jan	3,197
Sites with mean peak counts of 1,000 or more birds in Northern Ireland[†]							
Lough Foyle	3,759	6,095	3,300	4,606	(5,930)	Aug	4,738
Belfast Lough	533 [11]	1,416	2,103 [11]	2,718	2,644 [11]	Feb	1,883
Larne Lough	2,506	761	1,941	338	514	Feb	1,212
Outer Ards Shoreline	490	706		772	2,543	Jan	1,128

[†] as few sites exceed the British threshold and no All-Ireland threshold has been set qualifying levels of 3,000 and 1,000 have been chosen to select sites, in Great Britain and Northern Ireland respectivley, for presentation in this report

Lesser Black-backed Gull
Larus fuscus

International threshold:	5,300
Great Britain threshold:	500
All-Ireland threshold:	?[†]

GB max:	40,307	Aug
NI max:	1,545	Sep

The UK provides a stronghold for the *graellsii* race of Lesser Black-backed Gull, which occurs throughout much of Western Europe from Portugal in the south to Iceland and Greenland in the north. Birds of the *intermedius* race, predominantly from around southern Scandinavia, also occur in the UK on passage and in winter.

Peak numbers occur in late summer, though winter numbers have risen dramatically in recent decades (Burton *et al.* 2005) and the species now winters much further north than previously with many more records now from Northern Ireland and Scotland. The Northern Ireland maximum has continued to rise over the past few years, much of this being dependent on autumn numbers at Lough Neagh. As with the rest of the gulls their

inclusion in WeBS counts is optional so the number of sites at which they have been counted limits national maxima. Over one thousand sites contributed to the British total. Totals at several sites have been derived from Winter Gull Roost Survey Counts, this explaining the sharp rise in five-year means at Theale Gravel Pits, Chew Valley Lake, Queen Mary Reservoir, Cotswold Water Park (West), Roadford Reservoir, Chelmarsh, Belvide, Bartley and Hurleston Reservoirs, Dee Estuary, Burghfield Gravel Pits, Swithland Reservoir and Inner Firth of Clyde. Morecambe Bay remained the top UK site during 2003/04 with counts from the South Walney Island colony numbering around 30,000 in July and August. Five sites qualify as internationally important and 34 as nationally important, though it should be noted that the latter threshold is calculated from a winter population estimate and many sites qualify due to their autumn numbers. The Winter Gull Roost Survey will provide a new population estimate for the species after 2005/06.

	99/00	00/01	01/02	02/03	03/04	Mon	Mean	
Sites of international importance in the UK								
Morecambe Bay	41,945	40,590	31,620	36,461	31,479	Aug	36,419	
Theale Gravel Pits	(1)		(0)	(3)	20,000[44]	Sep	20,000	▲
Chew Valley Lake	(0)	(0)	(0)		7,015[44]	Jan	7,015	
Queen Mary Reservoir					6,656[44]	Jan	6,656	▲
Cotswold Water Park (West)	(570)	(203)	(687)	(25)	5,800[44]	Nov	5,800	▲
Sites of national importance in Great Britain								
Llys-y-fran Reservoir	12,000[12]	11,000[12]	6	2,000	90	Oct	5,019	▼
R. Avon: F'bridge - Ringwood	2,508	960	3,478	2,309	6,550[44]	Sep	3,161	
Alde Complex	5,661	(36)	767[11]	4,474	388[44]	Jan	2,823	▼
Severn Estuary	2,798	669	945	(3,072)	6,051[44]	Jan	2,707	
Rutland Water	1,500	600	2,000[12]	5,000	2,500	Sep	2,320	
Great Pool Westwood Park	2,000	2,000	1,350	2,000	3,800[44]	Jan	2,230	
Roadford Reservoir			52	70	6,031[44]	Oct	2,051	▲
Chelmarsh Reservoir		(300)	500	(34)	3,500[44]	Jan	2,000	▲
Alt Estuary	769	1,122	1,619	4,341	(945)	Sep	1,963	
Hule Moss	810[13]	3,300[13]	3,090[13]	2,100[13]	250[13]	Sep	1,910	
Wellington Gravel Pits	(2,500)	(2,400)		(1,400)	750	Oct	1,763	
Lower Windrush Valley GPs	(1,339)	2,424	3,166	871	484	Dec	1,736	
Thames Estuary	(405)	1,783	1,560	1,507	1,898[44]	Jan	1,687	
Longnewton Reservoir	1,800	340	970	2,680	1,890	Sep	1,536	
Belvide Reservoir	0				3,000[44]	Jan	1,500	▲
The Wash	1,993	1,139	(582)	855	898	Jul	1,221	
Bartley Reservoir					1,200[44]	Feb	1,200	▲
Llangorse Lake	1,060	1,050	1,170[13]	1,110[12]	1,140[13]	Sep	1,106	
Rodbourne Sewage Works	(1,100)						(1,100)	
Pitsford Reservoir	700	1,000[12]	550[12]	1,000[12]	2,000[13]	Aug	1,050	
Hayle Estuary	1,750	852	(340)	130	940	Feb	918	
Portworthy Mica Dam	465	750	(2,000)	419	700	Oct	867	
Cleddau Estuary	(1,246)	625	825	659	723	Mar	816	
Audenshaw Reservoirs	800[13]						800	
Hurleston Reservoir			65	700	1,500[44]	Oct	755	▲
NE Glamorgan Moorland Pools		732					732	
Colliford Reservoir	3,040	52	140	144	92	Mar	694	
Poole Harbour	888	565	(237)	285	997	Sep	684	
Solway Estuary	(725)	(195)	(243)	(673)	581[44]	Sep	660	
Dee Estuary (England/Wales)	(56)	(130)	(170)	(342)	648[44]	Jan	648	▲
Burghfield Gravel Pits					618[44]	Jan	618	▲
Crowdy Reservoir	1,000	1,000	60	850	34	Dec	589	
Middle Tame Valley Gravel Pits	(711)	425	(170)	(384)	(80)	Dec	568	
Frampton Pools	40	120	1,500	(250)			553	
Blyth Estuary (Suffolk)		886	(93)		200[44]	Jan	543	
Swithland Reservoir	(0)	2	2	36	2,050[44]	Nov	523	▲
Inner Firth of Clyde	378	393	(557)	544	705	Aug	515	▲
Nosterfield Gravel Pits	(566)	70	94	1,560	218	Jul	502	
Hollowell Reservoir					500[44]	Jan	500	
Farne Islands	(0)	500					500	
Sites no longer meeting table qualifying levels in WeBS-Year 2003/2004								
R. Nith: Keltonbank to Nunholm	(465)	(455)	(272)	(400)	(130)	Sep	(465)	
Chasewater					10[44]	Jan	10	
Sites with mean peak counts of 500 or more birds in Northern Ireland[†]								
Loughs Neagh and Beg			228	(1,218)	1,115	Sep	854	
Other sites attaining table qualifying levels in WeBS-Year 2003/2004 in Great Britain								
Camel Estuary	(160)	(128)	452	117	769	Feb	446	
Kennington Park	0	26	1	1	600	Dec	126	
Newport Pagnell Gravel Pits	1	1	2	0	530	Oct	107	

[†] *as no All-Ireland threshold has been set a qualifying level of 500 has been chosen to select sites for presentation in this report*

Herring Gull
Larus argentatus

International threshold: 13,000
Great Britain threshold: 4,500[†]
All-Ireland threshold: ?[†]

GB max: 52,874 Jan
NI max: 9,064 Feb

Following the fall in the number of Herring Gulls recorded by WeBS between 2000/01 and 2001/02 British maxima have remained within the 50,000s. Much of this change has been attributed to the decline in the numbers at Morecambe Bay, which are currently half of those three years ago. Despite this Morecambe Bay remains the only site to currently hold numbers exceeding the international qualifying threshold. In Britain nine sites surpassed the national qualifying threshold, three more than in 2002/03. Of these, totals at four sites, Queen Mary Reservoir, Forth Estuary, Rye Harbour and Pett Level and Hasting to Bexhill, appearing in the list for the first time in recent years, were obtained from Winter Gull Roost Survey counts. Numbers at the Alt Estuary have fallen below the national qualifying level for the first time since 1998/99. Conversely, roost counts at the nearby Ribble Estuary

revealed higher numbers than all but one previous WeBS count. Unfortunately these different survey methods as well as the optional recording of gulls during WeBS counts prevent any definite interactions between these two sites being identified. Peak numbers recorded by WeBS occur in winter and, though only representing a proportion of the national population, indicate a decline over recent winters. Winter Gull Roost Survey counts indicate that numbers have declined since a peak in the 1970s (Burton *et al.* 2005) and this is reflective of the trend in the species breeding population (Seabird 2000: Mitchell *et al.* 2004). Although there has been a decline in the WeBS British maxima, the 2003/04 maximum for Northern Ireland is similar to previous years. Most of the Northern Irish total refers to numbers at Belfast Lough.

	99/00	00/01	01/02	02/03	03/04	Mon	Mean	
Sites of international importance in the UK								
Morecambe Bay	20,553	20,530	12,170	14,373	10,551	Aug	15,635	
Sites of national importance in Great Britain								
Ribble Estuary	(7,287)	(9,032)	9,767	(209)	14,859 [44]	Jan	12,313	
The Wash	(5,589)	10,003	(7,603)	(7,640)	10,703 [44]	Jan	10,353	
Inner Moray and Inverness Firth	401	650		27,956 [11]	(2,341)	Jan	9,669	
Moray Firth		10,429 [1]	9,564 [1]	10,335 [1]	6,468 [1]	Nov	9,199	
Queen Mary Reservoir					8,279 [44]	Jan	8,279	▲
Forth Estuary	(3,605)	(3,828)	(1,868)	(1,925)	7,376 [44]	Jan	7,376	▲
North Norfolk Coast	15,291	3,895	5,062	3,964	2,500 [44]	Jan	6,142	
Rye Harbour and Pett Level					5,850 [44]	Jan	5,850	▲
Hastings to Bexhill					5,700 [44]	Jan	5,700	▲
Sites with mean peak counts of 2,500 or more birds in Great Britain[†]								
Alt Estuary	6,800	3,967	1,440	3,153	3,825 [44]	Jan	3,837	▼
Dee Estuary (England/Wales)	(1,412)	(2,000)	(778)	3,602	4,052 [44]	Jan	3,827	
Thames Estuary	(3,317)	(4,180)	2,867	(3,330)	(4,349)	Dec	3,609	
Alde Complex	7,186	(1,196)	2,061 [11]	2,087	2,372 [44]	Jan	3,427	
Chew Valley Lake					3,400 [44]	Jan	3,400	
Roughrigg Reservoir	152	133	47	1,121	15,144 [44]	Jan	3,319	
Troon Meikle Craigs					3,174 [44]	Jan	3,174	
Point of Ayre Gravel Pit			699	7,000	1,431	Aug	3,043	
Broadwater Lake - S. Harefield					3,000 [44]	Jan	3,000	
Solway Estuary	(2,962)	(2,165)	(2,719)	3,281	2,189 [44]	Nov	2,811	
Caldey Island					2,800 [44]	Jan	2,800	
Burry Inlet	2,693	4,428	2,106	2,834	1,904	Jul	2,793	
Guernsey Shore	(1,850)	(3,525)	1,972	2,127	(1,790)	Oct	2,541	
Sites with mean peak counts of 1,000 or more birds in Northern Ireland[†]								
Belfast Lough	3,637	6,749	9,157	7,046	7,536 [11]	Feb	6,825	
Outer Ards Shoreline	3,003	898		1,001	(1,351)	Jan	1,634	

[†] as few sites exceed the British threshold and no All-Ireland threshold has been set qualifying levels of 2,500 and 1,000 have been chosen to select sites, in Great Britain and Northern Ireland respectivley, for presentation in this report

Yellow-legged Gull / Caspian Gull
Larus michahellis / Larus (argentatus) cachinnans

International threshold: 7,000

GB max: 100 Aug
NI max: 0

Shortly before going to press, a recent taxonomic review by the British Ornithologists' Union promoted the ('Western') Yellow-legged Gull to specific rank, after many years of classification as a subspecies of Herring Gull (Sangster et al. 2005). However, the status of 'Caspian Gull' remains unresolved and it is still officially considered a race of Herring Gull.

Yellow-legged Gulls were recorded at 39 sites during 2003/04, six less than the previous year and there was a corresponding decrease in numbers. However, it is difficult to draw conclusions from this, as the recording of gulls during WeBS counts is optional and thus numbers are dependent on coverage. On the whole, numbers have increased in recent years, though in part this will be due to increased observer awareness. Peak numbers at Southampton Water, Thames Estuary, Poole Harbour, Portworthy Mica Dam, Great Pool Westwood Park and River Avon (Fordingbridge to Ringwood) have exceeded five birds at least twice since 2000/01. In line with recent years, the majority of birds that

were identified to race (115) were 'Western Yellow-legged Gulls' (*michahellis*), while only seven were 'Caspian Gulls' (*cachinnans*). Double figure counts of Western Yellow-legged Gull were at Kingsbridge Estuary (August), Thames Estuary (September and October) and Castlemartin Corse (March). Most records of Caspian Gull were of single birds; however, counts of two were recorded at the Thames Estuary in December and Pegwell Bay in February.

Yellow-legged Gulls were recorded at 45 sites during the Winter Gull Roost Survey in 2003/04, Caspian Gulls (*cachinnans*) being recorded as present at four of these.

Sites with five or more birds in 2003/04

Southampton Water	57	Aug		Castlemartin Corse	12	Mar
Thames Estuary	47	Sep		Great Pool Westwood Park	8	Dec
Poole Harbour	21	Sep		Wraysbury Reservoir	8	Aug
Kingsbridge Estuary	16	Aug		R. Avon: F'bridge - R'wood	7	Nov
Portworthy Mica Dam	15	Aug				

Iceland Gull
Larus glaucoides

International threshold: 2,000

GB max: 2 Feb
NI max: 4 Mar

With records from only seven sites during 2003/04 the number of Iceland Gulls recorded during WeBS was the lowest for several years. Four at Belfast Lough in March were noteworthy, whilst more typical singles were recorded at the Forth Estuary, Heritage Park

Loch, Island of Papa Westray, Joe's Pond, Loch Fleet and Widewall Bay. Counts of one or two Iceland Gulls were reported from 10 sites during the Winter Gull Roost Survey in winter 2003/04 (BTO data).

Glaucous Gull
Larus hyperboreus

International threshold: 10,000

GB max: 8 Jan
NI max: 2 Jan

In line with recent figures, Glaucous Gulls were noted at 17 sites during 2003/04. As usual most records referred to single birds although two were present at Belfast Lough, Lough Foyle and Burra Firth (Unst). Despite numbers at these regular sites being lower than

recent in years, nationally a clear peak of 11 was witnessed in January. A total of 10 sites held counts of one or two Glaucous Gulls during the Winter Gull Roost Survey in winter 2003/04 (BTO data).

Great Black-backed Gull
Larus marinus

International threshold: 4,700
Great Britain threshold: 400
All-Ireland threshold: ?[†]

GB max: 12,948 Oct
NI max: 775 Jan

2003/04 witnessed an increase in the five-year mean of Great Black-backed Gulls at a number of sites, mainly due to the inclusion of Winter Gull Roost Survey counts. In total 26 sites surpassed the threshold for national importance in Great Britain, ten more than in 2002/03. Again this includes several sites at which gulls are not normally recorded during standard WeBS counts. Both the British and Northern Irish maxima were broadly similar to the previous two years, though it should be noted that these totals only represent a fraction of the total wintering population. October

WeBS counts from the Wash revealed the highest ever total for the site, whereas the 2003/04 count at Tophill Low Reservoirs was well below average for the site. The majority of key sites are coastal areas, although several larger inland reservoirs and gravel pit complexes, notably in eastern England, have also proved important for roosting birds. Winter Gull Roost Survey counts suggest that there has been a slight decline in numbers over the last decade, following a large increase in the second half of the last century (Burton *et al.* 2005).

	99/00	00/01	01/02	02/03	03/04	Mon	Mean	
Sites of national importance in Great Britain								
The Wash	3,025	1,303	4,515	1,959	4,628	Oct	3,086	
Humber Estuary	(363)	(313)	(83)	(113)	2,200 [44]	Jan	2,200	▲
Tophill Low Reservoirs	2,200	1,880	900	3,030	223 [44]	Jan	1,647	
Hoveringham and Bleasby GPs					1,600 [44]	Jan	1,600	▲
Don Mouth to Ythan Mouth	(511)	(1,225)	(67)	(55)	(200)	Sep	(1,225)	
Thames Estuary	(505)	1,530	(412)	1,236 [11]	857 [44]	Jan	1,208	
Lynemouth Ash Lagoons					1,074	Sep	1,074	▲
Tees Estuary	463	1,558	(1,038)	701	1,523	Nov	1,061	
Grafham Water					1,050 [44]	Jan	1,050	▲
Lower Derwent Ings					1,041 [44]	Jan	1,041	▲
Dungeness Gravel Pits			(0)		1,000 [44]	Jan	1,000	▲
Coquet Island					980 [44]	Jan	980	▲
Ogston Reservoir					900 [44]	Jan	900	▲
Pegwell Bay	364	1,050	1,000	1,305 [11]	305	Jan	805	
Moray Firth		651 [1]	884 [1]	1,001 [1]	674 [1]	Nov	803	
Hanningfield Reservoir	(0)	(0)	(0)	1,098 [44]	437 [44]	Jan	768	
North Norfolk Coast	548	567	748	617	1,051	Oct	706	
Loch of Strathbeg	134	1,280 [13]	(129)	569	(606)	Dec	661	
Inner Moray and Inverness Firth	(99)	330		1,432 [11]	70	Jan	611	
Hastings to Bexhill					520 [44]	Jan	520	▲
Eyebrook Reservoir					500 [44]	Jan	500	▲
Portsmouth Harbour	872	1,028	54	304	186	Feb	489	
Morecambe Bay	451	(716)	331	353	(322)	Aug	463	
Guernsey Shore	(176)	(273)	(205)	353	560	Feb	457	▲
Forth Estuary	(183)	575	(108)	(211)	286 [11]	Nov	431	
Southfield Reservoir					408 [44]	Jan	408	▲
Romney Sands					400 [44]	Jan	400	
Sites no longer meeting table qualifying levels in WeBS-Year 2003/2004								
Fleet and Wey	312	213	576	87	200 [44]	Jan	278	
Chasewater					20 [44]	Jan	20	
Cresswell to Chevington Burn	612	190	49	45			224	

[†] *as no All-Ireland threshold has been set a qualifying level of 500 has been chosen to select sites for presentation in this report*

Kittiwake
Rissa tridactyla

International threshold: 20,000
Great Britain threshold: ?[†]
All-Ireland threshold: ?[†]

GB max: 5,948 Aug
NI max: 15 Sep

The Kittiwake is an exclusively coastal species, which is reflected in the list of sites at which 200 or more birds were recorded during 2003/04. The British maximum was higher than the previous two years while the Northern Irish total refers to a single count from Outer Larne Lough. The change in totals of this species will be reliant on coverage of the 'gulls' group, however, low totals from Nigg Bay and Girdleness compared to 1999/2000 have influenced the totals for Dee Estuary (Scotland). As they are predominantly maritime, Kittiwakes were recorded only a few sites by the Winter Gull Roost Survey, with a maximum count of 1,000 birds at Dungeness in January 2004 (BTO data).

	99/00	00/01	01/02	02/03	03/04	Mon	Mean
Sites with mean peak counts of 200 or more birds in Great Britain[†]							
Lunan Bay			0	400	3,400	Aug	1,267
Arran	3,000	225	1,700	185	290	Dec	1,080
Dee Estuary (Scotland)	3,220	774	36	162	248	Aug	888
Tweed Estuary	1,500		340	470	860	Aug	793
Loch of Strathbeg	37	200	0	940	1,370	Sep	509
Camas Shallachain			500				500
Farne Islands		0	920				460
Tees Estuary	401	153	20	30	1,492	Jul	419
Loch a` Phuill (Tiree)		36		1,128	28	Jul	397
Durham Coast	(386)	(3)	(0)	(0)	(0)		(386)
Forth Estuary	226	(254)	(274)	(453)	(426)	Oct	327
Tay Estuary	4	8	266	1,100	133	Aug	302
Don Mouth to Ythan Mouth	200	595	(18)	0	153	Aug	237
Beadnell to Seahouses	430	(104)	0	160	350	Jul	235
Solway Estuary	71	120	(574)	(300)	40	Mar	221
Broadford Bay			(0)	200	(20)	Aug	200

[†] as no British or All-Ireland thresholds have been set a qualifying level of 200 has been chosen to select sites for presentation in this report

Sandwich Tern
Sterna sandvicensis

International threshold: 1,700
Great Britain threshold: ?[†]
All-Ireland threshold: ?[†]

GB max: 10,674 Jul
NI max: 361 Apr

The Sandwich Tern has a widespread breeding population and occurs throughout much of coastal Europe. Britain and Ireland supports an estimated tenth of the world's breeding population, the majority of these at the Farne Islands, the Norfolk coast, northeast Scotland and Strangford Lough. In the winter, UK birds occur along the west coast of Africa and are known to continue down to South Africa.

In Britain, peak numbers were recorded during July and were similar to 2002. Unusually the Northern Irish peak was during spring as opposed to autumn and was lower than in recent years. However, the often incomplete coverage of important sites during the summer months, such as at Strangford Lough, prevents comparison of national maxima between years.

The Forth Estuary and North Norfolk Coast remain the only two sites, of those counted, to hold internationally important numbers. Numbers recorded at these two and other key sites remain highly variable, as shown by a 167% rise on the Tees Estuary and an 85% decline at Ythan Estuary compared to the previous year.

	1999	2000	2001	2002	2003	Mon	Mean
Sites of international importance in the UK							
North Norfolk Coast	(1,574)	(5,015)	(3,365)	(4,600)	4,170	Jun	4,595
Forth Estuary	(3,868)	3,424	(994)	(2,317)	(2,802)	Aug	3,646
Sites with mean peak counts of 200 or more birds in Great Britain[†]							
Humber Estuary	(154)	1,329	(124)	(396)	(303)	Sep	1,329

	1999	2000	2001	2002	2003	Mon	Mean
Cemlyn Bay and Lagoon			0		2,455	Jul	1,228
Tees Estuary	1,238	897	35	974	2,601	Aug	1,149
Dee Estuary (England/Wales)	629	(672)	(11)	1,632	716	Jul	992
Duddon Estuary	1,204	994	(0)	704	955	Jul	964
Solway Estuary	(59)	(78)	(235)	(206)	(548)	Aug	(548)
Pegwell Bay	432	320	660	360	(930)	Jul	540
Ythan Estuary				930	150	Sep	540
Lindisfarne	(350)	(260)	(100)		(4)	Jun	(350)
The Wash	(420)	310	512	150	223	Sep	323
Filey Bay	320						320
Tay Estuary	300	132	(167)	461	310	Aug	301
Morecambe Bay	(23)	110	(0)	220	531	Apr	287
Blyth Estuary (Northumberland)	600 [13]	202 [13]	237 [13]	22	24	Jul	217
Sites with mean peak counts of 200 or more birds in Northern Ireland[†]							
Dundrum Bay	234	166	296	722	264	Jul	336
Belfast Lough	239	195	409	357	136	Sep	267

[†] as no British or All-Ireland thresholds have been set a qualifying level of 200 has been chosen to select sites for presentation in this report

Roseate Tern
Sterna dougallii

Scarce

GB max:	36	Aug
NI max:	0	

Single birds were recorded at the Forth Estuary in June and September and the Hayle Estuary in July, but the largest gathering by far, and the largest ever count recorded by WeBS, was of 36 at St Mary's Island in August, doubtless deriving from the important breeding colony on nearby Coquet Island.

Common Tern
Sterna hirundo

International threshold:	1,900
Great Britain threshold:	?[†]
All-Ireland threshold:	?[†]

GB max:	6,265	Aug
NI max:	38	Jul

Common Terns breed at a variety of coastal and inland sites and despite benefiting from man-made gravel pits and the provision of nesting rafts all of the key sites during 2003/04 were coastal. The British maximum was the highest since 2000/01 and typically was recorded during August. However, as with all terns this is often dependent on the amount of coverage given to these groups. This is even more so for Northern Ireland at which birds were only reported from Dundrum Bay. Most autumn records refer to passage birds and during recent years counts at the Tees and Tay Estuaries have shown the variable nature of totals using the WeBS methodology.

	1999	2000	2001	2002	2003	Mon	Mean
Sites of international importance in the UK							
Humber Estuary	(21)	2,165	(6)	(291)	(280)	Aug	2,165
Sites with mean peak counts of 200 or more birds in Great Britain[†]							
Alt Estuary	1,156	1,292	129	868	1,664	Aug	1,022
Tees Estuary	1,038	876	5	696	1,678	Aug	859
North Norfolk Coast	599	(611)	(213)	(321)	419	Jun	543
Forth Estuary	(200)	356	(40)	(691)	(193)	Aug	524
Dee Estuary (England/Wales)	(348)	(246)	(3)	422	(384)	May	422
Chichester Harbour	(59)	209	500 [13]	(167)	(314)	Aug	355
Langstone Harbour				(15)	302	Aug	302
The Wash	370	(262)	(435)	(102)	122	Sep	297
Thames Estuary	(229)	(284)	(190)	(143)	(143)	Aug	(284)
Tay Estuary	600	40	6	700	23	Aug	274
Ythan Estuary				18	415	Jul	217

[†] as no British or All-Ieland thresholds have been set a qualifying level of 200 has been chosen to select sites for presentation in this report

Arctic Tern
Sterna paradisaea

International threshold: ?
Great Britain threshold: ?[†]
All-Ireland threshold: ?[†]

GB max: 2,245 Jul
NI max: 0

Arctic Terns breed throughout northern Europe, chiefly Iceland, around the North and Baltic Sea coasts, Scandinavia and into Siberia. Breeding colonies in the UK are essentially northern, the largest being in Orkney and Shetland. Arctic Terns were recorded at a total of 52 sites during 2003/04; unsurprisingly the majority of these were around the coasts of Scotland. The British maximum was similar to the previous year, although occurred a month earlier. Most counts refer to passage birds and are therefore unlikely to represent peak numbers at each site, as peaks at this time can be short-lived. Furthermore, the optional recording of terns during WeBS counts means that any changes in peaks should be treated with caution.

	1999	2000	2001	2002	2003	Mon	Mean
Sites with mean peak counts of 50 or more birds in Great Britain[†]							
Ythan Estuary				106	860	Jul	483
Forth Estuary	94	76	2	1,214	197	Jul	317
Eden Estuary	361	220	(53)	125	320	Jul	257
Tay Estuary	150	80	32	660	290	Jul	242
Farne Islands	0		(600)	(0)			200
Morecambe Bay	80	(103)		94	(178)	Apr	114
Loch a` Phuill (Tiree)		0		190	150	Jun	113
St Andrews Bay	283	170	44	29	0		105
Loch of Clumlie		250	150	0	0		100
Braewick Loch		45	70	170	50	Jul	84
The Houb (Whalsay)		100	0	120	82	Jul	76
Loch of Brow		200	100	0	0		75
Loch of Tankerness	(4)	75					75
Cambois to Newbiggin		0	5	246	0		63
Loch of Beith		5		150 [13]	31	Jul	62
Loch Indaal	30	61		51	76	Jun	55
Lunda Wick		190	0	6	2	Aug	50

[†] *as no British or All-Ireland thresholds have been set a qualifying level of 50 has been chosen to select sites for presentation in this report*

Arctic Tern (Mark Collier)

Little Tern
Sterna albifrons

International threshold: 340
Great Britain threshold: ?[†]
All-Ireland threshold: ?[†]

GB max: 914   Jul
NI max: 0

The British maximum was the highest for four years and as usual occurred during July. Almost half of this total was recorded on the North Norfolk Coast where many birds nest. In fact nearly all of the key sites are along the south and east coasts, which is the main focus of the UK breeding population. Little Terns do however, reach the north of Scotland and this is illustrated by three birds during July at Loch a` Phuill (Tiree) and two in April at Loch Paible (North Uist). East coast counts were even higher with up to 25 on the Eden Estuary during July. In total Little Terns were recorded at 28 sites, 13 fewer than in 2002/03. However, as with all the terns their inclusion in WeBS is optional for individual counters and, furthermore, they are present during the summer when many sites are not counted.

	1999	2000	2001	2002	2003	Mon	Mean
Sites of international importance in the UK							
North Norfolk Coast	(300)	(241)	(265)	(280)	(405)	Jul	(405) ▲
Sites with mean peak counts of 50 or more birds in Great Britain[†]							
Thames Estuary	297	161	(1)	(99)	(28)	Aug	229
Dee Estuary (England/Wales)	200	111	(0)	242	(256)	Jun	202
Blackwater Estuary	(120)	(101)	(50)	(3)	(20)	Aug	(120)
The Wash	148	(56)	(103)	(36)	68	Jul	108
Langstone Harbour				(140)	50	Jul	95
Fleet and Wey	154	125	0	59	58	Jun	79
Chichester Harbour	0	15	200 [13]	42	28	Aug	57
Swale Estuary	63	40	(8)	51	(57)	Jul	53
Stour Estuary	106	11	29	73	36	Aug	51

[†] *as no British or All-Ireland thresholds have been set a qualifying level of 50 has been chosen to select sites for presentation in this report*

Black Tern
Chlidonias niger

International threshold: 4,000
Great Britain threshold: ?
All-Ireland threshold: ?

GB max: 66   Sep
NI max: 0

With the exception of a single bird at Hanningfield Reservoir in August all of the Black Terns recorded during 2003/04 were seen during September. Most birds were recorded in the southern half of Britain although single birds were at the Alt and Forth Estuaries. For the first time in recent years all records of five or more birds refer to inland sites, indeed only three of the 16 sites at which birds were seen were coastal.

Sites with 5 or more birds in 2003/04

Great Pool Westwood Park	13	Sep	Tring Reservoirs	8	Sep
Willington Gravel Pits	13	Sep	Rutland Water	6	Sep
Foremark Reservoir	9	Sep			

White-winged Black Tern
Chlidonias leucopterus

Vagrant
Native Range: E Europe, S Asia and Africa

GB max: 1   Jun
NI max: 0

One long-staying bird was recorded at East Chevington Pools in both June and July, with another on the River Lune in Morecambe Bay in August.

Kingfisher
Alcedo atthis

International threshold: 2,000
Great Britain threshold: ?[†]
All-Ireland threshold: ?[†]

GB max: 482 Sep
NI max: 2 Nov

Despite its vivid colouration the Kingfisher is inevitably not well monitored by WeBS. With a wide distribution throughout much of Britain and Ireland and commonly inhabiting even the smallest of waterways, a substantial proportion of this population falls outside WeBS sites. Essentially a resident species in the UK, Kingfishers will however disperse in response to cold weather, during which time their presence increases at coastal sites.

Although WeBS methodology is not proficient in monitoring changes in the Kingfisher population, numbers at the top few sites are generally consistent year to year. The

Somerset Levels remains the principal site for Kingfisher, in spite of its lowest count for six years. A record 33 sites currently hold on average five or more birds, ten more than during the previous year. This is analogous with the rise in the British maximum, which is the highest since 1993.

Nationally, numbers peaked in Britain during September, after which time the totals gradually fell and had halved by February. Kingfishers were much more scarce in Northern Ireland with peaks of only two being recorded during November, December and March.

	99/00	00/01	01/02	02/03	03/04	Mon	Mean
Sites with mean peak counts of 5 or more birds in Great Britain[†]							
Somerset Levels	14	(10)	16	13	12	Nov	14
Wraysbury Gravel Pits	14	8	14	19	12	Sep	13
Colne Valley Gravel Pits	(9)	(11)	(3)	(4)	(4)	Jul	(11)
Middle Tame Valley Gravel Pits	(11)	(8)	(3)	(5)	(4)	Jul	(11)
Lee Valley Gravel Pits	8	(6)	12	(4)	10	Oct	10
Ditchford Gravel Pits	8	8	7		13	Oct	9
Eversley Cross and Yateley GPs	4	6	11	8	9	Jul	8
Pitsford Reservoir	4	5	11	9	11	Aug	8
Old Moor	6	8	4	(8)	7	Sep	7
Poole Harbour	11	4	(3)	6	(5)	Sep	7
Stour Estuary	6	4	6	(11)	6	Nov	7
R. Avon: Salisbury-Fordingbridge	(5)	(3)	(3)	(4)	(6)	Sep	(6)
Colwick Country Park	6						6
Deben Estuary	3	7	5	10	(7)	Sep	6
North Norfolk Coast	(11)	3	11 [4]	7	(6)	Oct	6
River Irwell	(6)	(2)	(1)	(2)	(2)	Nov	(6)
Southampton Water	(7) [11]	8	5	5	6	Oct	6
Thames Estuary	(3)	(6)	3	9	(7)	Dec	6
Arun Valley	3	6	(4)	(6)	4	Feb	5
Bewl Water	3	2	6	6	6	Oct	5
Chichester Gravel Pits	5	5	3	4	7	Oct	5
Exe Estuary	5	4	3	7	4	Dec	5
Gr Wst Canal: Basin - Greenway				3	6	Oct	5
Hoveringham and Bleasby GPs	5	(2)	(1)				5
Meadow Lane Gravel Pits St Ives	4	5	2	6	7	Oct	5
Middle Yare Marshes	(1)	(2)	7	4	4	Oct	5
Morecambe Bay	(2)	5	(2)	(4)	(4)	Sep	5
Ogston Reservoir					5	Sep	5
Ouse Washes	5	3 [13]	6	8 [13]	5	Oct	5
River Wye – Putson	(6)	5	(3)	4			5
Taw-Torridge Estuary	(3)	(3)	4	5	(5)	Nov	5
Thorpe Water Park	3	9	6	3	2	Dec	5
Walthamstow Reservoirs	4	5	(5)	6	6	Sep	5

[†] as no British or All-Ireland thresholds have been set a qualifying level of 5 has been chosen to select sites for presentation in this report

PRINCIPAL SITES

Table 6 below lists the principal sites for non-breeding waterbirds in the UK as monitored by WeBS. All sites supporting more than 10,000 waterbirds are listed, as are all sites supporting internationally important numbers of one or more waterbird species. Naturalised species (*e.g.* Canada Goose and Ruddy Duck) and non-native species presumed to have escaped from captive collections have been excluded from the totals, as have gulls and terns since the recording of these species is optional (see *Analysis*). Table 7 lists other sites holding internationally important numbers of waterbirds, which are not routinely monitored by standard WeBS surveys but rather by the Icelandic Goose Census and aerial surveys.

A total of 217 sites are listed in tables 6 and 7. Of these 201 supported one or more species in internationally important numbers and 87 held a five-year mean peak of 10,000 or more birds. Typically there are few changes to the top twenty sites listed in the principal sites table, with the order of the top ten rarely changing. The Wash remains as the key waterbird site with regard to numbers, holding similar numbers in 2003/04 as during the preceding five years. Despite numbers on the Ribble Estuary exceeding those of Morecambe Bay in three of the past five years, the Morecambe Bay average remains, albeit slightly, the higher of the two. One notable change is the loss of the Thames Estuary from the top five, which has slipped below the North Norfolk Coast and the Humber Estuary.

Total numbers on the Thames have remained relatively variable and the low five-year average up to 2003/04 was influenced by the lower values in the first and last years. The only other notable change among the top ten sites is the inclusion of the Somerset Levels, which has taken place of Loughs Neagh and Beg. Declines in the numbers of diving ducks identified at Loughs Neagh and Beg have contributed to the fall in total numbers; this is evident in that Scaup are no longer present at the site in internationally important numbers.

Five-year averages of sites holding 100,000 or more waterbirds were relatively similar compared to the previous year, with 69 of the 87 sites undergoing changes of less than 10%. Twelve sites witnessed an increase and 6 sites a decrease of 10% or more. The greatest increase was experienced at Loch of Lintrathen (32%), which can be explained by a high count of Pink-footed Geese during the National Grey Goose Census. Four other sites, Pegwell Bay, Loch Spynie, North Norfolk Coast and Carmarthen Bay each rose by over 20%, although the latter was due to the inclusion now of non-WeBS Common Scoter counts in the calculations (see *Analysis*). The greatest decrease was seen at Walland Marsh (-26%), numbers at which remained below 6,000 for the second year running. Both the Beaulieu and Ythan Estuaries (both 16% declines) held numbers around half that of in the previous year.

Table 6. Total number of waterbirds at principal sites in the UK, 1999/2000 to 2003/04 (includes data from all available sources) and species occurring in internationally important numbers at each. (Species codes for those listed are provided in Table 8.)

Site	99/00	00/01	01/02	02/03	03/04	Average	Int.Imp.species
The Wash	375,732	291,297	332,606	343,448	331,997	335,016	PG DB SU PT OC RP GP GV L. KN SS DN BW BA CU RK
Morecambe Bay	232,816	246,832	211,269	250,705	248,856	238,096	PG SU PT OC L. KN DN BA CU RK TT
Ribble Estuary	236,361	220,052	210,290	255,005	249,831	234,308	WS PG SU WN T. PT OC RP GV KN SS DN BW BA RK
North Norfolk Coast	222,755	182,543	185,040	212,403	283,089	217,166	PG DB WN T. PT RP KN SS BW BA RK
Humber Estuary	172,392	163,042	159,798	174,841	217,696	177,554	PG SU T. RP GP GV L. KN SS DN BW BA RK
Thames Estuary	128,050	182,093	170,052	189,416	155,068	164,936	DB SU GA T. SV OC AV RP GV KN DN BW BA CU RK
Dee Estuary (England/Wales)	92,234	135,105	195,671	126,998	171,819	144,365	SU T. PT OC KN DN BW BA CU RK
Solway Estuary	152,698	145,342	118,366	146,108	142,631	141,029	WS PG YS SU PT OC RP KN DN BA CU RK
Mersey Estuary	110,835	109,864	102,652	108,755	97,773	105,976	SU T. DN BW RK
Somerset Levels	78,705	114,208	115,043	102,572	85,154	99,136	MS WN GA T. PT SV L.

Site	99/00	00/01	01/02	02/03	03/04	Average	Int.Imp.species
Forth Estuary	75,904	95,572	88,189	109,386	91,353	92,081	SZ PG SU KN BA RK
Blackwater Estuary	84,495	122,125	66,468	81,684	63,700	83,694	DB GP GV DN BW RK
Swale Estuary	76,925	81,209	88,476	84,065	75,247	81,184	WN T. PT SV RP BW RK
Strangford Lough	70,896	66,164	80,345	79,352	88,429	77,037	MS QN SU GP KN BA RK
Loughs Neagh and Beg	97,261	100,883	63,314	52,151	58,934	74,509	CA MS WS PO TU GN
Ouse Washes	95,779	48,603	76,169	66,410	85,548	74,502	MS BS WS WN GA PT SV PO BW
Breydon Wtr/Berney Mshs	67,253	70,925	78,366	64,758	75,713	71,403	PG WN SV AV GP BW RK
Alt Estuary	54,745	58,649	90,064	63,498	64,974	66,386	GV KN SS BA
Severn Estuary	69,286	62,730	60,678	68,615	63,525	64,967	SU T. PT DN RK
Inner Moray/Inverness Firth	47,952	56,285	59,604	60,380	79,942	60,833	SZ PG JI QS RK
Loch of Strathbeg	37,425	52,014	68,133	49,350	79,109	57,206	WS PG YS
Lindisfarne	40,556	59,694	63,460	64,138	55,059	56,581	PG YS QS BA RK
Stour Estuary	56,038	59,566	59,771	50,215	48,621	54,842	PT GV KN DN BW RK
Chichester Harbour	47,324	47,390	51,505	44,805	43,588	46,922	DB DN BW RK
Burry Inlet	52,634	39,097	41,416	43,823	51,885	45,771	PT OC
Montrose Basin	41,123	49,598	63,742	37,019	35,450	45,386	PG RK
Langstone Harbour	43,938	42,696	33,743	37,449	43,718	40,309	DB DN BW
Dengie Flats	33,356	48,666	55,922	37,657	22,606	39,641	GV KN BA
Hamford Water	32,693	42,661	44,220	40,128	37,986	39,538	DB T. RP GV BW RK
Cromarty Firth	48,063	39,150	36,643	26,278	41,275	38,282	PG JI BA RK
Dornoch Firth	32,026	38,002	40,638	39,105	37,815	37,517	JI
Carmarthen Bay	35,071	34,174	31,356	36,917	47,067	36,917	CX GP
Loch Leven	30,870	31,868	38,128	39,588	37,335	35,558	MS PG T. SV
Lough Foyle	36,766	37,191	29,446	34,151	37,111	34,933	WS QN BA RK
WWT Martin Mere	37,706	22,189	37,284	38,839	30,751	33,354	WS PG T.
Medway Estuary	51,126	23,452	29,829	27,281	25,909	31,519	PT BW RK
Nene Washes	28,412	32,180	19,345	53,390	20,911	30,848	BS PT
West Water Reservoir	28,438	26,500	23,276	40,000	34,210	30,485	PG
Lower Derwent Ings	29,107	.	.	.	.	29,107	T.
Duddon Estuary	34,590	23,558	25,065	22,185	32,330	27,546	PT RK
Alde Complex	28,983	26,526	29,354	29,628	22,910	27,480	AV RK
Abberton Reservoir	33,788	25,923	20,581	20,677	31,276	26,449	SV PO
Poole Harbour	23,969	24,469	24,628	25,949	24,853	24,774	AV BW
Colne Estuary	35,404	36,316	25,738	4,184	19,224	24,173	DB BW RK
Tees Estuary	20,550	22,800	21,925	25,156	29,882	24,063	RK
Rutland Water	24,085	19,193	22,128	26,187	28,198	23,958	MS GA SV
Inner Firth of Clyde	23,429	23,692	22,904	23,201	23,631	23,371	RK
Orwell Estuary	23,507	20,046	21,529	24,840	25,247	23,034	BW RK
Tay Estuary	17,319	24,631	27,501	20,611	21,596	22,332	PG JI BA RK
Crouch-Roach Estuary	25,155	24,729	21,023	21,378	18,116	22,080	DB
Exe Estuary	20,936	21,159	24,724	20,581	22,716	22,023	BW
Pegwell Bay	11,324	17,375	21,296	28,464	25,320	20,756	
Belfast Lough	21,675	21,038	18,837	18,785	19,435	19,954	BW RK
Lavan Sands	18,493	19,059	17,282	21,777	21,060	19,534	
Carsebreck / Rhynd Lochs	20,205	23,454	19,941	15,252	16,530	19,076	PG
Cleddau Estuary	18,996	15,544	18,574	17,756	20,474	18,269	
Southampton Water	20,859	21,491	16,869	16,683	15,414	18,263	BW
Deben Estuary	18,122	18,868	16,969	17,081	17,813	17,771	RK
Blyth Estuary (Suffolk)	.	18,871	13,712	.	.	16,292	BW RK
Wigtown Bay	15,643	9,583	18,028	14,473	21,606	15,867	PG YS
Fleet and Wey	12,504	14,125	19,649	14,549	16,237	15,413	MS
Loch of Skene	9,064	25,163	17,136	11,004	13,696	15,213	PG JI
WWT Caerlaverock	22,332	7,951	11,814	19,416	14,144	15,131	WS YS
Pagham Harbour	16,077	16,051	14,301	13,220	14,563	14,842	DB BW
Eden Estuary	12,665	15,440	15,069	15,124	15,149	14,689	
Loch Spynie	5,670	15,999	15,467	19,524	15,748	14,482	PG JI
Walland Marsh	28,978	9,712	21,015	5,110	5,904	14,144	
Arun Valley	14,307	17,397	10,716	15,688	11,843	13,990	
Hule Moss	20,436	15,245	9,729	7,109	15,860	13,676	PG
Taw-Torridge Estuary	19,259	12,235	14,180	11,838	10,289	13,560	
Dungeness Gravel Pits	14,957	14,744	11,069	13,877	11,636	13,257	
Mersehead RSPB	8,810	14,503	13,464	15,666	11,083	12,705	YS
Loch of Harray	11,710	17,057	9,129	10,010	12,330	12,047	MS JI
Rye Harbour / Pett Level	10,929	9,854	11,209	10,512	16,620	11,825	
North West Solent	10,728	10,847	12,287	10,069	15,119	11,810	BW
Old Moor	8,641	13,281	12,091	12,455	11,862	11,666	
Beaulieu Estuary	12,284	16,975	11,769	11,140	5,989	11,631	BW
Dyfi Estuary	14,584	10,882	9,415	11,510	11,517	11,582	
Cotswold Water Park (W)	12,181	11,542	10,029	9,174	12,476	11,080	
Loch of Lintrathen	14,616	4,537	10,476	9,241	16,419	11,058	PG

Site	99/00	00/01	01/02	02/03	03/04	Average	Int.Imp.species
R. Avon: R'gwood/C'church	6,981	13,777	5,033	24,593	4,766	11,030	PT BW
Thanet Coast	11,234	9,955	9,639	16,144	7,966	10,988	
Middle Yare Marshes	9,400	10,572	13,804	10,681	9,739	10,839	
Portsmouth Harbour	8,196	6,036	8,190	15,004	16,420	10,769	
Outer Ards Shoreline	14,720	11,647	210	12,694	12,750	10,404	QN RK TT
Stodmarsh & Collards Lgn	14,245	10,982	10,224	7,741	8,224	10,283	
Ythan Estuary	18,290	2,147	13,567	10,753	6,359	10,223	RK
Carlingford Lough	10,029	8,431	9,593	10,601	10,282	9,787	QN
Cameron Reservoir	4,531	6,455	18,250	4,495	11,227	8,992	PG
Lee Valley Gravel Pits	8,722	8,122	9,587	9,313	8,983	8,945	GA
Chew Valley Lake	7,106	8,187	8,773	8,368	10,106	8,508	SV
R. Nith: Keltonbnk/Nunholm	10,212	7,883	7,487	6,667	10,006	8,451	PG YS
Upper Lough Erne	8,279	7,800	7,717	8,777	9,239	8,362	MS WS
R. Clyde: Carstairs/Thankertn	7,795	8,045	14,501	4,683	6,623	8,329	WS PG
Loch Fleet Complex	5,324	8,987	11,677	8,275	6,493	8,151	JI
Dundrum Bay	7,036	10,011	9,251	6,859	6,941	8,020	QN
R. Avon: F'bridge -R'wood	5,834	7,414	7,420	10,022	6,781	7,494	GA
Hornsea Mere	7,205	6,040	5,737	8,934	7,348	7,053	MS
Loch of Stenness	5,095	5,553	9,131	7,098	5,637	6,503	JI
Loch of Boardhouse	5,899	5,620	5,096	5,257	7,111	5,797	JI
Milldam & Balfour Mains Pls	5,851	3,759	5,036	7,753	6,219	5,724	JI
Horsey Mere	5,019	3,620	5,000	4,000	8,465	5,221	PG
Lochs Davan and Kinord	10,779	5,327	5,568	3,124	1,296	5,219	JI
Orchardton/Auchencairn Bays	2,894	3,107	.	5,563	8,143	4,927	PG YS
Wraysbury Gravel Pits	5,617	4,256	4,969	6,262	3,352	4,891	GA
Larne Lough	4,450	4,675	4,461	5,043	5,299	4,786	QN
R. Eden: Warcop/Little Salkeld	.	4,760	.	.	.	4,760	JI
Holburn Moss	2,453	6,066	1,774	6,373	6,875	4,708	PG
Heigham Holmes	6,268	.	2,500	.	.	4,384	PG
Slains Lochs	15,574	2,091	2,832	360	432	4,258	PG
Gladhouse Reservoir	6,720	1,610	4,316	1,342	5,879	3,973	PG
Kilconquhar Loch	2,908	3,777	3,287	3,937	5,874	3,957	JI
Loch Ken	3,568	3,905	2,887	4,216	3,964	3,708	NW JI
Lake of Menteith	2,861	5,327	730	4,958	4,639	3,703	PG
Tweed Estuary	2,712	3,924	3,805	3,519	4,009	3,594	MS
Dee Flood Meadows	2,393	4,129	4,603	3,887	2,859	3,574	PT
Threipmuir & Harlaw Res	5,749	2,048	865	3,878	4,916	3,491	JI
Loch Eye	3,182	2,205	5,211	1,926	4,476	3,400	JI
Loch Scarmclate	4,535	2,469	2,025	2,870	3,095	2,999	JI
Loch of Wester	1,765	1,129	5,476	.	.	2,790	JI
Loch Bee (South Uist)	2,606	3,945	1,416	3,047	2,593	2,721	JH
Lower Teviot Valley	1,255	4,828	1,134	2,781	.	2,500	JI
Loch a' Phuill (Tiree)	1,810	1,548	.	2,643	2,846	2,212	JH
Loch of Tankerness	5,130	5,679	4	1	1	2,163	JI
Killough Harbour	.	.	2,380	2,732	1,159	2,090	QN
Balranald RSPB (North Uist)	313	1,341	3,485	2,816	2,114	2,014	JH
Lower Lough Erne	2	.	.	2,931	2,485	1,806	MS
Avon Valley: Salisbury - F'bridge	1,253	2,496	1,202	1,212	1,950	1,623	MS
Melbost Sands, Broad Bay & Tong Saltings (Lewis)	1,133	1,542	1,727	.	.	1,467	JH
Tarbat Ness	3,002	1	.	866	795	1,166	PG
Loch Bhasapoll (Tiree)	1,713	1,085	.	777	983	1,140	JH
R. Earn / Lawhill Oxbows	.	2,649	1,281	161	223	1,079	JI
Loch Riaghain (Tiree)	885	916	.	646	515	741	JH
Loch Mor Baleshare	135	792	686	788	979	676	JH
Loch An Eilein (Tiree)	1,031	345	.	570	422	592	JH
Moine Mhor & Add Estuary	363	297	368	586	1,073	537	JH
Loch Ashie	.	481	.	.	.	481	SZ
Broad Water Canal	.	456	287	503	484	433	MS
Branahuie Saltings	.	.	324	.	.	324	JH
Loch Broom	66	367	.	.	.	217	JH
Loch Urrahag	73	203	27	.	.	101	JH

Table 7. Other sites in the UK holding internationally important numbers of waterbirds in 2003/04, which are not routinely monitored by standard WeBS surveys. (Species codes for those listed are provided in Table 8.)

Site	Int.Imp.species	Site	Int.Imp.species
Aberlady Bay Roost	PG	North Uist	JH YN
Beauly Firth Roost	JI	Baleshare & Carinish (Grimsay)	JH
Benbecula	JH	Balmartin To Vallay	JH
Berney Marshes	PG	Balranald, Clettraval and Tigharry	JH
Bute	JI	Benbecula Islands	JH
Caerlaverock WWT	WS	Berneray	JH YN
Caithness Lochs	JI	Clachan Na Luib to Bayhead	JH
Clachan and Whitehouse	JH	Malaclate To Grenitote	JH
Dupplin Lochs	PG	Oronsay	JH
Fala Flow	PG	Paible	JH
Findhorn Bay Roost	PG JI	Trumisgarry, Clachan & Newton	JH
Hule Moss (West)	PG	Orkney	JI YN
Island of Islay	NW YN	Deer & Shapinsay Sounds	ND
Islands South Of Barra	YN	South Walls (Hoy)	YN
Isle of Coll	NW JH YN	Pilling to Cockerham	PG
Isle of Colonsay	JH	Read's Island Flats	PG
Keills Peninsula and Isle of Danna	NW	Rhunahaorine	NW
Liverpool Bay	CX	Skinflats Roost	PG
Loch Eye and Cromarty Firth	PG JI	Sound of Barra (Barra)	YN
Loch Garten	JI	Sound of Gigha	ND
Loch Mullion	PG	Sound of Harris	YN
Loch Tullybelton	PG	South Uist	JH YN
Machrihanish	NW JH	Askernish To Smerclate	JH
Martin Mere and Ribble Estuary	WS PG	Bornish To Askernish	JH
Meikle Loch (Slains)	PG	Drimore To Howmore	JH
Moray Firth	SZ	Howbeg To Bornish	JH
Munlochy Bay Roost	JI	Lochdar, Gerinish To Drimore	JH
Myroe: Balleyhenry / Carrowmuddle	WS	Southwest Lancashire	PG
Nigg Bay	PG	Stranraer Lochs	NW
North Norfolk Coast & The Wash	PG	Strathearn (West)	PG JI
Holbeach St Matthew Roost	PG	Tay-Isla Valley	PG JI
Holkham Bay Roost	PG	Tayinloan	JH
Scolt Head Roost	PG	Tiree	NW JH YN
Snettisham Roost	PG	Tomme (Concrete Lane/Main Road)	WS
Wells-next-the-Sea	PG	Udale Bay	PG
Thornham Roost	PG	Whiteness to Skelda Ness	SZ
North Sutherland	YN	Wyre Estuary	PG
		Wyre Estuary: Arm Hill	PG
		Ythan Estuary and Slains Lochs	PG

Table 8. Species codes for species listed in tables 6 and 7.

AV	Avocet	OC	Oystercatcher
BA	Bar-tailed Godwit	PG	Pink-footed Goose
BS	Bewick's Swan	PO	Pochard
BW	Black-tailed Godwit	PT	Pintail
CA	Cormorant	QN	Light-bellied Brent Goose (Nearctic population)
CU	Curlew	QS	Light-bellied Brent Goose (Svalbard population)
CX	Common Scoter	RK	Redshank
DB	Dark-bellied Brent Goose	RP	Ringed Plover
DN	Dunlin	SS	Sanderling
GA	Gadwall	SU	Shelduck
GN	Goldeneye	SV	Shoveler
GP	Golden Plover	SZ	Slavonian Grebe
GV	Grey Plover	T.	Teal
JH	Greylag Goose (Northwest Scotland population)	TT	Turnstone
JI	Greylag Goose (Icelandic population)	TU	Tufted Duck
KN	Knot	WN	Wigeon
L.	Lapwing	WS	Whooper Swan
MS	Mute Swan	YN	Barnacle Goose (Nearctic population)
ND	Great Northern Diver	YS	Barnacle Goose (Svalbard population)
NW	Greenland White-fronted Goose		

WeBS Low Tide Counts

AIMS

Estuarine sites in the UK provide the most important habitat for non-breeding waterbirds, acting as wintering grounds for many migrants but also as stopover feeding locations for other waterbirds passing along the East Atlantic Flyway. Core Counts on estuaries tend to quantify birds present at high tide roosts. Although important, knowledge of roost sites provides only part of the picture, and does not elucidate the use that waterbirds make of a site for feeding.

The WeBS Low Tide Counts scheme has flourished since its inception in the winter of 1992/93, with most of the major estuaries covered at least once. The scheme aims principally to monitor, assess and regularly update information on the relative importance of inter-tidal feeding areas of UK estuaries for wintering waterbirds and thus to complement the information gathered by WeBS Core Counts.

The data gathered contribute greatly to the conservation of waterbirds by providing supporting information for the establishment and management of UK Ramsar sites and Special Protection Areas (SPAs) (for further details see *Site importance* under *ANALYSIS & PRESENTATION*), other site designations and whole estuary conservation plans. In addition, WeBS Low Tide Counts enhance our knowledge of the low water distribution of waterbirds and provide data that highlight regional variations in habitat use, whilst also informing protection of the important foraging areas identified. WeBS Low Tide Counts provide valuable information needed to gauge the potential effects on waterbirds of a variety of human activities which affect the extent or value of inter-tidal habitats, such as proposals for dock developments, recreational activities, tidal power barrages, marinas and housing schemes. Designing mitigation or compensation for such activities can be assisted using data collected under the scheme. Furthermore, the effects on bird distributions of climate change and sea level rise can be assessed.

METHODS

The scheme provides information on the numbers of waterbirds feeding on subdivisions of the inter-tidal habitat within estuaries. Given the extra work that Low Tide Counts entail, often by the same counters that carry out the Core Counts, WeBS aims to cover most individual estuaries about once every six years, although on some sites more frequent counts are made. Coordinated counts of waterbirds are made by volunteers each month between November and February on pre-established subdivisions of the inter-tidal habitat in the period two hours either side of low tide.

DATA PRESENTATION

Tabulated statistics

Table 9 presents three statistics for 18 of the more numerous waterbird species present on 13 estuaries covered during the 2003/04 winter: the peak number of a species over the whole site counted in any one month (with checks for count synchronicity made from assessing proximity of count dates and consultation with Local Organisers); an estimate of the mean number present over the winter for the whole site (obtained by summing the mean counts of each species for each count section) and the mean density over the site (in birds per hectare), which is the mean number divided by the total area surveyed (in hectares). The area value used for these calculations is the sum of the inter-tidal and non-tidal components of each count section but omits the sub-tidal areas (*i.e.* those parts of the count section which are under water on a mean low tide).

Dot density maps

WeBS Low Tide Count data are presented as dot density maps, with subdivision of count sections into basic habitat elements. The reason for such a subdivision is to ensure species are plotted on appropriate habitat areas and to improve the accuracy of density estimates. Each section for which a count has been made is divided into a maximum of three different habitat components:

Inter-tidal: Areas that lie between mean high water and mean low water.

Sub-tidal: Areas that lie below mean low water. In more 'open-coast'-type situations, a sub-tidal zone reaching 500 m out from the inter-tidal sections has been created arbitrarily, to indicate the approximate extent of visibility offshore from land-based counts.

Non-tidal: Areas that lie above mean high water (usually saltmarsh although some grazing marshes are also covered).

The mean count for the sector is then divided amongst a varying number of the different components, dependent on the usual habitat preferences of the species involved. For example, Dunlin dots are plotted exclusively on inter-tidal sections whereas Wigeon dots are spread across inter-tidal, sub-tidal and non-tidal areas (in proportion to the relative areas of these three components).

Currently, throughout all WeBS Low Tide Count analyses, mean low tide and mean high tide are taken from the most recent Ordnance Survey 1:25000 maps (in Scotland, the lines on the OS maps are mean low water springs and mean high water springs instead). It is recognised, unfortunately, that these maps represent the current real shape of the mudflats, water channels and saltmarshes to varying degrees of accuracy. However, in the interests of uniformity across the UK, the Ordnance Survey outlines are adhered to throughout the analyses. (© Crown copyright. All rights reserved. JNCC. License number 100017955.2005.)

The maps display the average number of birds in each count section as dots spread randomly across habitat components of count sections, thus providing an indication of both numbers and density. **It is important to note that individual dots do not represent the precise position of individual birds; dots have been assigned to habitat components proportionally and are then randomly placed within those areas. No information about the distribution of birds at a finer scale than the count sector level should be inferred from the dot density maps.**

For all maps in the present report, one dot is equivalent to one bird. The size of individual dots has no relevance other than for clarity.

Additionally, any count sections that were not covered are marked with an asterisk. It is hoped that dot density distributions and habitat components will lead to an easier and fuller appreciation of low tide estuarine waterbird distribution. Where maps appear in colour (Internet version only), the following conventions apply: blue = water; yellow = inter-tidal habitat (*e.g.* mudflat, sandflat); green = non-tidal habitat (*e.g.* saltmarsh, reedbed); grey = not covered. More detailed information concerning analysis and presentation of WeBS Low Tide Counts can be obtained from Alex Banks, the National Organiser (WeBS Low Tide Counts), or from the publication *Estuarine Waterbirds at Low Tide* (Musgrove *et al.* 2003).

ESTUARY ACCOUNTS

The main estuaries counted at low tide in the winter of 2003/04 are discussed. WeBS Low Tide Counts were carried out on 15 different sites, with site accounts for 13 of these. Other counts in the winter of 2003/04 were made on the Duddon Estuary (partial count) and Morecambe Bay (partial, mid-tide count). These sites are not included in site accounts, but data can be obtained from the WeBS Low Tide Count National Organiser upon request.

For the main site accounts, data were collected during the period November to February. Assessment of national and international importance is based on five-year peak mean counts from the main species accounts in this volume of *Wildfowl and Wader Counts*. Figure 55. shows the location of the sites discussed, and a site description is presented for each estuary. Distribution maps are presented for selected species, which are those of international or national importance where possible.

ACKNOWLEDGEMENTS

We are very grateful to the following people and organisations that contributed to the Low Tide Count scheme in the winter of 2003/04. Apologies to anyone omitted accidentally from the list.

C.R. Allan, K. Anderson, Bobby Anderson, Christopher Baines, Rufus Becca, Harry Bell, Alan Bell, Stuart Benn, Stewart Bonar, Ian Bray, Rhys Bullman, Simon Burton, Clare

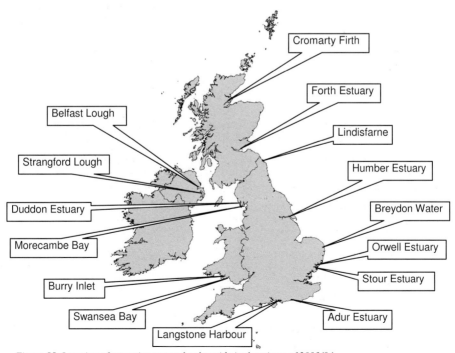

Figure 55. Location of estuaries counted at low tide in the winter of 2003/04.

Table 9. Peak and mean counts, and mean density (birds per hectare) of 18 waterbird species present on 13 estuaries covered by the 2003/04 WeBS Low Tide Counts. "+" indicates non-zero densities of <0.01 birds per hectare.

Species	Adur Estuary Peak No.	Mean No.	Mean Dns.	Belfast Lough Peak No.	Mean No.	Mean Dns.	Breydon Water Peak No.	Mean No.	Mean Dns.
Brent Goose	0	0	0	44	18	0.04	0	0	0
Shelduck	1	0	+	494	240	0.5	128	90	0.22
Wigeon	4	1	0.01	222	151	0.32	6,150	2,710	6.74
Teal	41	23	0.31	667	472	0.99	200	122	0.3
Mallard	7	6	0.08	284	249	0.52	308	205	0.51
Pintail	0	0	0	0	0	0	271	107	0.27
Oystercatcher	5	4	0.05	4,248	3,489	7.33	34	21	0.05
Ringed Plover	56	31	0.42	234	159	0.33	20	11	0.03
Golden Plover	0	0	0	14	5	0.01	8,850	3,831	9.53
Grey Plover	17	15	0.2	2	1	+	5	4	0.01
Lapwing	296	218	2.95	1,371	865	1.82	13,429	5,535	13.77
Knot	1	0	+	2	1	+	212	83	0.21
Dunlin	115	88	1.19	1,461	929	1.95	3,953	2,940	7.31
Black-tailed Godwit	0	0	0	367	291	0.61	763	636	1.58
Bar-tailed Godwit	0	0	0	97	54	0.11	0	0	0
Curlew	0	0	0	390	320	0.67	836	548	1.36
Redshank	53	44	0.59	1,407	1,254	2.63	1,630	1,380	3.43
Turnstone	54	25	0.34	301	256	0.54	14	5	0.01

Species	Burry Inlet Peak No.	Mean No.	Mean Dns.	Cromarty Firth Peak No.	Mean No.	Mean Dns.	Firth of Forth Peak No.	Mean No.	Mean Dns.
Brent Goose	609	456	0.08	3	1	+	0	0	0
Shelduck	426	373	0.07	688	374	0.12	876	799	0.12
Wigeon	1,155	978	0.18	16,494	7,092	2.23	3,110	2,616	0.38
Teal	240	116	0.02	809	573	0.18	1,916	1,105	0.16
Mallard	64	43	0.01	992	706	0.22	756	651	0.09
Pintail	556	348	0.06	540	136	0.04	2	1	+
Oystercatcher	13,831	11,416	2.08	2,561	2,383	0.75	5,944	5,916	0.86
Ringed Plover	37	37	0.01	65	36	0.01	303	231	0.03
Golden Plover	2,530	1,065	0.19	1,508	443	0.14	6,940	2,707	0.39
Grey Plover	193	164	0.03	0	0	0	354	323	0.05
Lapwing	1,685	850	0.15	1,907	1,084	0.34	3,330	1,959	0.29
Knot	1,120	581	0.11	4,900	2,218	0.7	6,907	4,327	0.63
Dunlin	5,486	4,785	0.87	4,338	1,923	0.6	7,840	6,378	0.93
Black-tailed Godwit	7	3	+	0	0	0	151	91	0.01
Bar-tailed Godwit	55	19	+	2,361	987	0.31	1,750	1,355	0.2
Curlew	533	423	0.08	1,230	912	0.29	2,493	1,649	0.24
Redshank	339	339	0.06	2,096	1,941	0.61	3,830	3,660	0.53
Turnstone	3	2	+	21	10	+	547	495	0.07

Species	Humber Estuary Peak No.	Mean No.	Mean Dns.	Langstone Harbour Peak No.	Mean No.	Mean Dns.	Lindisfarne Peak No.	Mean No.	Mean Dns.
Brent Goose	2,118	1,637	0.13	5,804	4,704	2.96	2,930	2,930	1.13
Shelduck	6,426	4,971	0.38	971	593	0.37	1,323	1,323	0.51
Wigeon	4,734	4,640	0.36	1,189	806	0.51	2,339	2,339	0.9
Teal	3,589	2,322	0.18	283	255	0.16	680	680	0.26
Mallard	2,330	2,016	0.16	118	108	0.07	264	264	0.1
Pintail	168	78	0.01	93	66	0.04	99	99	0.04
Oystercatcher	3,305	2,883	0.22	1,331	1,177	0.74	418	418	0.16
Ringed Plover	418	354	0.03	201	157	0.1	40	40	0.02
Golden Plover	47,706	36,145	2.78	0	0	0	3,822	3,822	1.48
Grey Plover	2,285	1,346	0.1	634	493	0.31	330	330	0.13
Lapwing	36,609	22,942	1.77	1,129	593	0.37	1,461	1,461	0.56
Knot	50,557	39,495	3.04	1,213	822	0.52	441	441	0.17
Dunlin	19,182	18,567	1.43	9,393	9,155	5.76	1,366	1,366	0.53
Black-tailed Godwit	914	567	0.04	245	167	0.11	0	0	0
Bar-tailed Godwit	4,291	2,663	0.2	416	286	0.18	160	160	0.06
Curlew	3,530	3,161	0.24	708	496	0.31	612	612	0.24
Redshank	8,229	6,689	0.51	697	505	0.32	797	797	0.31
Turnstone	723	461	0.04	226	140	0.09	54	54	0.02

Table 9. continued

Species	Orwell Estuary			Stour Estuary			Strangford Lough		
	Peak No.	Mean No.	Mean Dns.	Peak No.	Mean No.	Mean Dns.	Peak No.	Mean No.	Mean Dns.
Brent Goose	1,396	930	0.74	1,730	1,150	0.7	13,502	6,508	1.6
Shelduck	700	524	0.42	1,569	1,376	0.84	3,725	2,633	0.65
Wigeon	2,334	1,842	1.47	2,994	2,585	1.58	3,097	2,183	0.54
Teal	720	511	0.41	1,460	875	0.53	940	727	0.18
Mallard	561	510	0.41	563	434	0.26	492	339	0.08
Pintail	325	233	0.19	300	254	0.15	354	279	0.07
Oystercatcher	1,732	1,602	1.28	1,248	1,155	0.7	6,273	5,531	1.36
Ringed Plover	291	190	0.15	143	114	0.07	277	196	0.05
Golden Plover	451	226	0.18	7,083	3,028	1.85	15,988	6,306	1.55
Grey Plover	333	270	0.22	2,130	1,497	0.91	95	58	0.01
Lapwing	2,121	1,375	1.1	3,669	2,410	1.47	8,884	4,729	1.16
Knot	2,485	1,861	1.49	6,564	4,946	3.02	3,832	2,381	0.58
Dunlin	4,499	3,670	2.94	13,927	9,648	5.89	4,967	2,761	0.68
Black-tailed Godwit	389	267	0.21	1,571	1,014	0.62	208	158	0.04
Bar-tailed Godwit	12	3	+	103	91	0.06	1,122	468	0.11
Curlew	714	666	0.53	1,118	890	0.54	1,342	1,159	0.28
Redshank	1,939	1,721	1.38	2,010	1,700	1.04	3,146	2,792	0.69
Turnstone	198	161	0.13	417	321	0.2	115	104	0.03

Species	Swansea Bay		
	Peak No.	Mean No.	Mean Dns.
Brent Goose	0	0	0
Shelduck	1	0	+
Wigeon	0	0	0
Teal	0	0	0
Mallard	0	0	0
Pintail	0	0	0
Oystercatcher	2,857	1,757	1.44
Ringed Plover	70	51	0.04
Golden Plover	0	0	0
Grey Plover	17	9	0.01
Lapwing	0	0	0
Knot	0	0	0
Dunlin	1,093	646	0.53
Black-tailed Godwit	0	0	0
Bar-tailed Godwit	7	5	+
Curlew	59	44	0.04
Redshank	24	14	0.01
Turnstone	23	8	0.01

ADUR ESTUARY

Internationally important: None
Nationally important: None

Site description

The Adur Estuary is a small and narrow embanked estuary, roughly in the middle of the conurbation from Brighton to Littlehampton that stretches along the south coast of England. The estuary is sheltered, flowing into a natural harbour at its mouth, and is bordered by human developments on the south slopes of the South Downs, including the town of Shoreham-by-Sea along the south and west banks, and Shoreham Airport to the east. The estuary is designated as an SSSI, and includes some small areas of saltmarsh, and intertidal mudflats are exposed at low tide. The area is intensively farmed and agricultural land drainage has removed much of the tidal plain and created extensive lowland wet grasslands. The main leisure activities of the estuary are water-based, with sailing, power boating and in particular jet-skiing; some shooting occurs in the upper estuary. A commercial mussel fishery is in the mouth of the estuary, and some bait digging occurs. Shoreham has a large port, for which plans to extend handling facilities and onshore oil-holding tanks exist. A number of manufacturing industries and boat-building yards are also based in Shoreham.

Bird distribution

Few grebes were seen on the Adur in the winter of 2003/04, with only single Little and Great Crested Grebes recorded. Cormorants were similarly scarce, but Little Egrets were counted in small (<3) numbers in each of the count months. Grey Heron, Mute Swan and Shelduck were all recorded in single figures over the winter.

Teal were confined to the area downstream from the Norfolk Bridge, and it is on this section of river that the majority of saltmarsh is found. This area is therefore likely to provide the most suitable habitat for Teal to dabble in the muddy shallows for seeds and other plant material. The peak count of Teal was 41 in January, with a winter average of 23 birds. Other ducks recorded occasionally were Wigeon and Mallard, whilst one Red-breasted Merganser was also seen in February.

The Adur does not support notably high densities of any waterbird species, although the intertidal flats are used at low water by the nationally more abundant waders. No more than four Oystercatchers were seen. Most Ringed Plovers were recorded between the A27 bridge and the railway bridge on the middle reaches of the estuary (Figure 56). Numbers reached 56 in January but dropped to just six the following month. It is possible that weather may have affected counts of this species, as the estuary is sheltered and could harbour more birds during cold spells. There are exposed mudflats for foraging birds in the middle of the Adur, although densities of Ringed Plover were lower on the sector furthest down river, where intertidal habitat also exists. In contrast, Lapwing were recorded in higher densities on this sector, and were also found further upriver. A notable feature of Lapwing distribution on the Adur is that many were recorded in the fields to the west of the river, which comprise Shoreham Airport (Figure 56). These birds were roosting at this location, utilising the expanse of flat grassland in preference to the estuary itself. The peak count on this sector reached 202 in January. Dunlin were spread more evenly throughout the upper and lower parts of the estuary. Numbers of Dunlin varied throughout the winter, with over 100 counted in the first two months, dropping to 52 in January and recovering to 83 in February. Like Ringed Plover and Lapwing, Dunlin were not observed on the middle section between the railway bridge and the Norfolk Bridge. A few Redshank were counted on this sector, however, and the species was thinly spread across the intertidal areas of the river. Counts were no greater than the 53 recorded in January. Turnstone was the only species recorded in noteworthy densities on the middle sector of the river, peaking at 52 birds in January, and was more densely distributed here than elsewhere on the river. The habitat between the railway bridge and the Norfolk Bridge tends to be sand or shingle, and is thus more suitable for Turnstone than for the other species of wader that favour muddier substrates. Other occasional records were made of Knot, Ruff and Snipe.

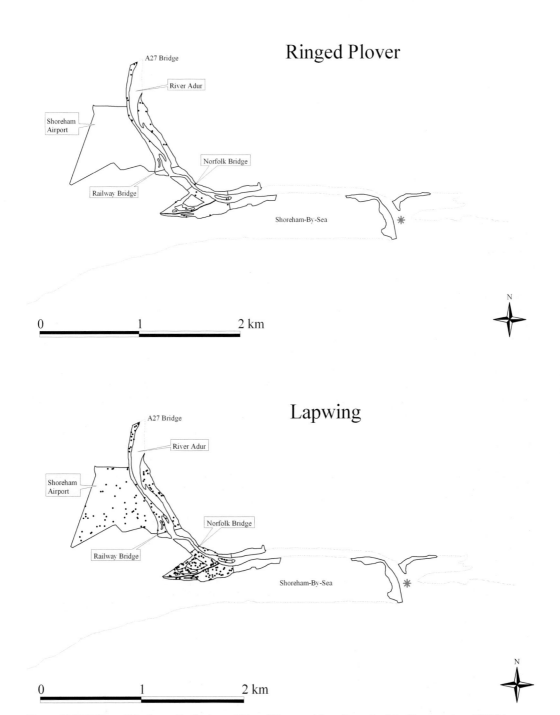

Figure 56. WeBS Low Tide Count distributions of Ringed Plover and Lapwing at the Adur Estuary, winter 2003/04.

BELFAST LOUGH

Internationally important:	Black-tailed Godwit, Redshank
Nationally important:	Great Crested Grebe, Shelduck, Scaup, Eider, Goldeneye,
(All-Ireland importance)	Red-breasted Merganser, Oystercatcher, Ringed Plover, Dunlin, Turnstone

Site description

Belfast Lough is a large sea lough in the northeast of Ireland, with the city of Belfast at its head. The area surveyed comprised the coast from Carrickfergus on the north shore around to the eastern end of Bangor on the south shore. Much of the site is afforded SPA and Ramsar status, with a further proposed SPA over open water. The outer parts of the lough's shore are generally rocky with some sandy bays, although more extensive areas of intertidal mud are found toward Belfast. Industrial land claim has reduced the area of the mudflats over the last 150 years, and Belfast has become the main port in Northern Ireland for heavy cargo. More recently, all of the area, including the important Belfast Harbour Pools, has been given a degree of protection. Extensive areas of the lough support commercial shellfisheries. There are problems of refuse disposal, pollution and general disturbance, but notably bait diggers on the north shore can pose potentially high levels of disturbance.

Bird distribution

Great Crested Grebe counts peaked at 856 in November, a figure greater than the 2002/03 count, but well below that in 2001/02. Their distribution was concentrated between Whitehouse Lagoon and Carrickfergus, and 81 birds were noted on Whitehouse Lagoon, where Low Tide Counts do not seem to have recorded the species previously. Birds on the southern coastline were generally distributed north of the RSPB Belfast Lough reserve, as far as Bangor. Cormorants were also concentrated just north of the reserve, with smaller numbers at Swineley Point and a few along the northern shore. Shags, however, were at Green Island in the north and between Grey Point and Swineley Point in the south. Grey Herons were reported, but a maximum of 29 was the lowest for five years. Mute Swans were at Victoria Park as in previous years, whilst this site and the RSPB reserve held most of the Greylag Geese (largely presumed to be re-established birds). Light-bellied Brent

Geese peaked at 44 in February; this is around the mean total for the last five winters. Shelduck were again confined to the extreme southwestern end of the lough, close to Belfast itself, with 494 in February exceeding the peak Core Count. The three common diver species, and Little Grebe, were also recorded.

Wigeon and Teal were to be found mainly on the RSPB reserve with lesser numbers off Holywood and near Belfast. Counts of both species exceeded Core Count figures with 222 Wigeon and 667 Teal. Mallard were found on Victoria Park, Whitehouse Lagoon and the RSPB reserve, the latter site also favoured by Shoveler. The small numbers of Tufted Duck and Pochard were confined to Victoria Park. Scaup numbers were higher than in any previous year with 669 in February being greater than Core Count figures. The main concentrations were to the west of Belfast docks, between Whitehouse Lagoon and Green Island, and between Holywood and Grey Point (Figure 57). Eider numbers peaked at 1,054 and were more numerous than previous years along the southern coastline. Just under 30 Long-tailed Duck were off Carrickfergus in February, whilst the count of 95 Common Scoter in November was greater than Core Count numbers. Two Velvet Scoter also accompanied them. Goldeneye and Red-breasted Merganser were widely distributed. Goosander, Water Rail, Moorhen and Coot were also noted in small numbers.

Oystercatcher and Redshank were the most widely distributed species in the lough, with highest concentrations of both in the southwestern corner; Figure 57. shows the distribution of Redshank. Ringed Plover peak counts exceeded Core Count numbers with 234 present in November, and these occurred in five widely distributed areas: Victoria Park, Whitehouse Lagoon, Bangor shore, Holywood and off Carrickfergus. Lapwing favoured the various pools in the southwestern end of the lough, with some birds using Bangor shore. Dunlin numbers peaked at 1,461 in February with most birds favouring the southwestern corner along with Whitehouse Lagoon and

Victoria Park. Numbers of Snipe were well above the peak Core Count with 86 recorded in December, mainly off Holywood and on the RSPB reserve. Black-tailed Godwits outnumbered Bar-tailed Godwits by three to one over the winter, the flats off Whitehouse Lagoon being the preferred habitat for both species. Numbers of both Curlew and Turnstone were much lower than Core Counts, although both species were widely distributed over the lough. Numbers of Knot continued to decline with the 2003/04 count the lowest for five years. Golden Plover, Grey Plover, Purple Sandpiper, Ruff and Greenshank were also noted in small numbers.

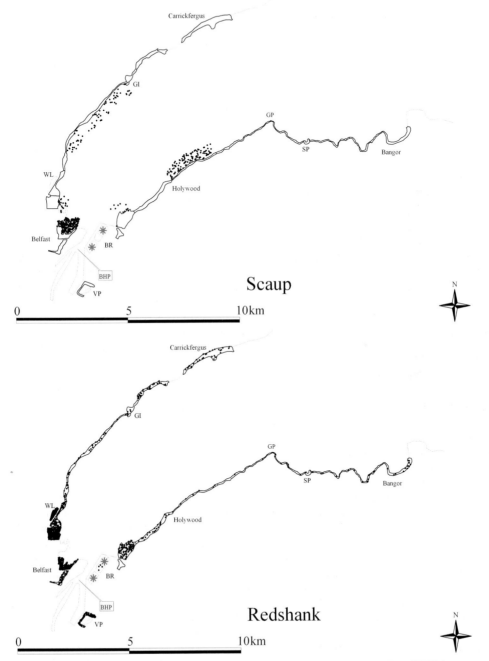

Figure 57. WeBS Low Tide Count distributions of Scaup and Redshank at Belfast Lough, winter 2003/04. (BHP=Belfast Harbour Pools, BR=RSPB Belfast Lough Reserve, GI=Green Island, GP=Grey Point, SP=Swinely Point, VP=Victoria Park, WL=Whitehouse Lake).

BREYDON WATER

Internationally important: Pink-footed Goose, Wigeon, Shoveler, Golden Plover, Black-tailed Godwit, Redshank

Nationally important: Bewick's Swan, European White-fronted Goose, Teal, Pintail, Avocet, Ruff

Site description

Breydon Water is a bar-built estuary separated from the North Sea by the spit of land on which Great Yarmouth sits. The estuary forms the lower reaches of the Yare and Waveney rivers, which drain much of central East Anglia. The rivers are tidal for many miles inland but only the estuary area from the confluence of the rivers is considered here. At high tide, Breydon Water forms a large lake but as the tide recedes, the only water that remains forms a narrow channel, well marked by buoys for the numerous leisure cruisers. There are small areas of saltmarsh, principally at the eastern end. To the north of the estuary stretches the huge expanse of the Halvergate Levels, Breydon Marshes and Berney Marshes. These form an extensive area of grazing marsh that has been subject to varying degrees of drainage in recent years. The main high tide roosts occur at the RSPB reserve at Berney Marshes (only accessible by boat, train or a very long walk) and in the eastern saltmarsh. The main conservation issues in the area involve boating, shooting and grazing marsh management. The river channel leading out through Great Yarmouth to the sea is highly industrialized.

Bird distribution

Shelduck were confined mainly to the eastern half of the estuary, with a scattering of records in the west and at Burgh Flats in the south. Greylag Geese favoured the southern end of the estuary with all sightings at Burgh Flats. Three Little Egrets were seen in December, along with five Mute Swans. Grey Heron and Pink-footed Goose were also recorded.

Wigeon numbered 6,150 in January, but this had dropped by a third a month later. The birds favoured most of the mudflats to the north of the Yare, with the exception of the easternmost section. Some birds also fed on the Burgh Flats at the southern end (Figure 58). Teal and Pintail were concentrated in the eastern half of the estuary with the majority of these north of the Yare. Teal numbers reached a peak in January, whilst the highest numbers of Pintail were in February. Mallard and Shoveler were more evenly distributed over the whole estuary, with Mallard occurring in denser patches at the Yarmouth end. Mallard numbers were similar to Core Counts; however, the count of 50 Shoveler was much lower than the Core Count of 322, suggesting many Shovelers make use of Berney Marshes.

Black-tailed Godwits favoured the mudflats in the southeast corner, the Burgh Flats and the area north of the river adjacent to Acle Marshes, with numbers again over the threshold for international importance. Avocet is another species that is wintering in increasing numbers - the peak count of 230 individuals in February a record Low Tide Count - with birds recorded on Burgh Flats and the flats north of the Yare adjacent to the Lockgates windmill at Acle Marshes (Figure 58). Ringed Plover numbers reached a maximum of 20 in February, and could in future increase in line with peak Core Counts that have been slowly increasing in the last five years, though high tide counts of this species are boosted by displacement by the tide (and human disturbance) from the beaches at Great Yarmouth. Lapwings were widely distributed within the estuary, both north and south of the river. The greatest numbers occurred at Burgh Flats with a peak of 13,429 in December. The peak Core Count for Lapwing in 2003/04 was greater at 15,890, but this is a decline of almost 25% since 1999/2000. Golden Plover numbers fluctuated over the winter, with birds distributed mostly in the eastern half of the estuary. Counts varied due to the species using non-tidal marshes and fields. Knot were widely distributed, favouring the flats in the eastern half of the estuary mainly north of the river. Curlew and Redshank occurred across the whole estuary, both north and south of the river, with Curlew peaking at 836 in January. Redshank density was greatest south of the river, at the eastern end of the estuary, and 1,630 recorded in February was higher than the Core Count figures. Greatest concentrations of Dunlin were found on the intertidal flats in the eastern half of the estuary and at Burgh Flats, but they were completely absent from other areas. Peak Turnstone numbers of 14 in February were modest but above Core Count figures. Oystercatcher, Grey Plover and Spotted Redshank were also recorded sporadically.

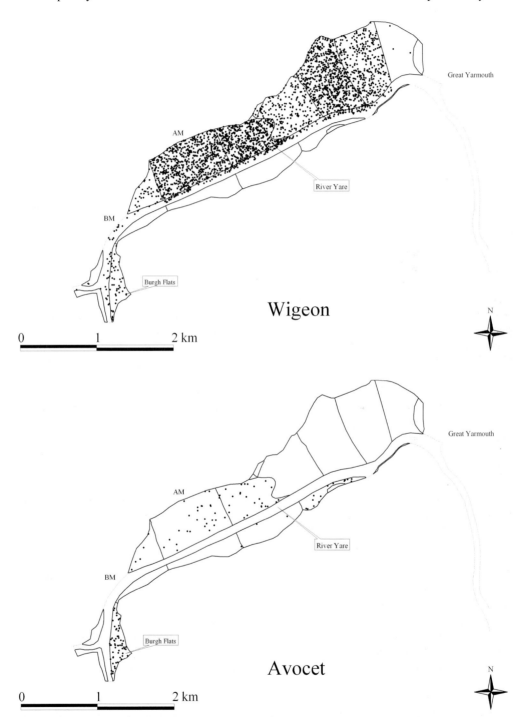

Figure 58. WeBS Low Tide Count distributions of Wigeon and Avocet at Breydon Water, winter 2003/04 (AM=Acle Marshes, BM=Berney Marshes).

BURRY INLET

Internationally important: Pintail, Oystercatcher
Nationally important: Dark-bellied Brent Goose, Shelduck, Shoveler, Knot, Dunlin

Site description

The Burry Inlet is a large estuarine complex, lying between the Gower Peninsula and the town of Llanelli in South Wales, and forms the estuary of the river Loughor. Its status as a Ramsar Site and an SPA is based on the birds supported by the large intertidal sand and mudflats and the extensive areas of saltmarsh mainly on the southern shore of the estuary. There are also substantial sand dune systems around the mouth of the estuary. Shellfishing is licensed at the site, with non-mechanical cockling in operation, and significant mussel production in the sub-tidal areas. Bait-digging activities occur. Sheep and cattle grazing are widespread in areas of saltmarsh. Tourism and recreational pressures are light, with walking, angling and birdwatching the principal pursuits. Whiteford NNR and the WWT National Wetland Centre at Llanelli provide notable refuges.

Bird distribution

Cormorants were mainly recorded in the outer reaches of the estuary, on both sides of the main river channel, whilst Great Crested Grebes were present in small numbers in the outer parts of the estuary. Low Tide Counts of Grey Heron reached 20 in January, the species being found in all areas. Little Egrets continued to increase at this site, as they have in many other areas of the UK. A peak count of 27 in January was much higher than the Core Count of 16, and was also higher than the five-year peak mean. These birds were recorded on the upper estuary, north of the Loughor Bridge and on the northern flats between Llanelli Docks and Burry Port. Both Dark-bellied Brent Geese and Shelduck were present on the estuary in nationally important numbers, but Low Tide Counts do not reflect this well. Brent Geese reached a maximum of 609 in February and were spread widely over the Llanrhidian Sands, south of the river channel and up to Burry Port. Shelduck, however, were distributed more centrally within the estuary, south of the main channel over Llanrhidian Sands and as far east as the WWT reserve.

The Burry Inlet is an important site for wildfowl, especially Pintail and Shoveler. Both species had their highest concentrations in the central estuary, south of the river on the Llanrhidian Sands (Pintail distribution is shown in Figure 59). It should be noted that one sector with traditionally high densities of these species could not be surveyed in 2003/04. Wigeon and Mallard used the tidal flats and saltmarsh north of Llanrhidian, eastwards to the Loughor Bridge, and smaller numbers were also recorded on the upper estuary. Teal were distributed in two areas of saltmarsh, to the west of Crofty and just south of the Loughor Bridge. Small numbers of five other wildfowl species (Scaup, Eider, Goldeneye, Red-breasted Merganser and Goosander) were recorded, mainly in the river channel between the WWT Llanelli reserve and Burry Port.

Oystercatchers are of particular note on the Burry Inlet, currently ranked the sixth most important site in the UK for the species. Low Tide Counts reached a peak in February with 13,831 birds. Most areas of tidal flats held aggregations of birds, as indicated in Figure 59. Three species, Grey Plover, Knot and Bar-tailed Godwit, were distributed in the area between Pen-clawdd on the south bank and Burry Port, the godwits mainly to the south of Penclacwydd on the north bank. Ringed Plover numbers peaked at 37 in January with birds found mainly between the WWT reserve and Llanelli Docks. The latter site also held the highest density of Redshank, although the whole estuary was utilised. Numbers of Golden Plover exceeded the Core Count figures for the last five years, peaking at 2,530 in February, with all of these on Llanrhidian Marsh. This sector was also the favoured location of Lapwing, with lesser numbers occurring on the upper estuary north of Loughor Bridge. Curlew were recorded in all areas and were widespread over the whole inlet. Dunlin numbers peaked at 5,486 in January and were recorded mostly on the central section of intertidal mudflat and to the north of Llanelli Docks, with the highest densities just to the south of Penclacwydd.

Pintail

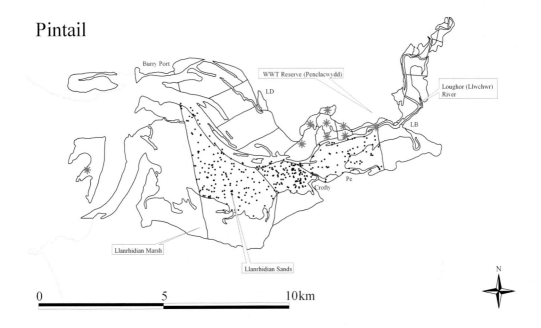

Oystercatcher

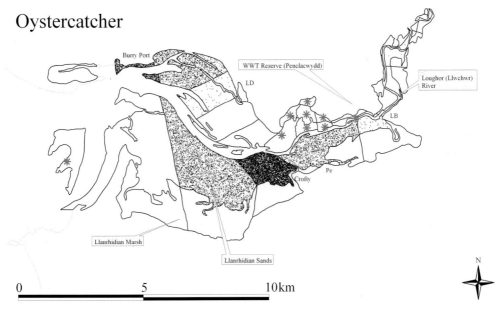

Figure 59. WeBS Low Tide Count distributions of Pintail and Oystercatcher at the Burry Inlet, winter 2003/04 (LB=Loughor Bridge, LD=Llanelli Docks, Pe=Pen-clawydd).

CROMARTY FIRTH

Internationally important: Pink-footed Goose, Bar-tailed Godwit, Redshank
Nationally important: Wigeon, Scaup, Knot

Site description

The Cromarty Firth is a long, sheltered estuary on the east coast of the Scottish Highlands, and is a Ramsar Site and SPA. Its narrow mouth encloses the remainder of the river, and the area has the largest expanse of intertidal flats in the Moray basin, fringed by well-developed saltmarsh around inflows. Some lengths of shore are rockier, with finer sediment in the bays, such as Nigg Bay, near the river mouth. These expanses of mudflat support notable eelgrass (*Zostera*) beds. A lagoon behind the shingle spit at Alness retains water at low tide. The estuary as a whole is dominated by industrial activity, including an oil terminal and a disused oil rig yard at Nigg, and a large metal industry complex at Invergordon. The sheltered shores provide prime agricultural land with cereal and improved grassland predominant. Grazing, both on these grasslands and on the areas of saltmarsh, is intensive and has led to some sand dune systems being converted to 'improved' grassland. Leisure activities exist but are not intensive, and include water sports and beach recreation around Cromarty, Dingwall and Alness. The RSPB has reserves on the estuary, at Nigg Bay and Udale Bay. Mussel cultivation and small-scale bait digging occur at Cromarty Bay.

Bird distribution

Slavonian Grebes peaked at 27 in November, almost all off Udale Bay. Cormorant and Shag were present in small numbers mainly in the outer half of the estuary. Grey Herons were widely distributed over the whole estuary. Mute Swans peaked at 93 in January, mostly in Udale and Nigg bays, and 11 Whooper Swans were recorded in November. Nearly 1,100 Greylag and over 900 Pink-footed Geese were reported over the winter, although the firth is principally of importance as an overnight roost for these species. The Greylag Geese were widely distributed with the highest density in the inner section, whilst the Pink-footed Geese occurred both on the inner estuary, and at Nigg Bay, particularly the eastern side. Shelduck numbers reached a record Low Tide Count of

688 in January. The flats of the inner estuary, Alness and Nigg Bay held the highest numbers. Red-throated Diver, Little Grebe and Canada, Barnacle and Brent Geese were recorded in small numbers.

Wigeon numbers varied greatly over the winter with record numbers of 16,494 in November dropping to just 1,410 by February. The greatest concentrations were in western Nigg Bay and Udale Bay, although birds were widespread in the inner estuary (Figure 60). Teal were absent completely from Nigg Bay, otherwise being widespread over the whole estuary, as were Mallard. Pintail peaked at 540 birds in January, exceeding Core Counts from the last five winters, with most of the birds found on the eastern half of Nigg Bay. This pattern is to be expected, as the species uses the bay as a foraging site, with birds moving to Bayfield Loch at high tide. Shoveler occurred only off Dalmore distillery, possibly benefiting from any discharge into the river. Scaup numbers totalled 58 in November, with the maximum Core Count only 13 in January. This appears to be a substantial reduction in numbers when compared to previous years. It should be noted that numbers have increased simultaneously on Inverness (Beauly) Firth, so it is likely that local movement explains this decline (Dave Butterfield *pers. comm.*). Most of the Scaup, Eider, Long-tailed Duck and Goldeneye were found in the outer Udale Bay area. The latter species was also found alongside Red-breasted Merganser along the length of the estuary, predominantly in the main channel. A single Tufted Duck was recorded in December.

Low Tide Counts of Redshank exceeded the international importance threshold in all months, but peaked at 2,096 in January. This species is widely distributed throughout the whole estuary, utilizing all of the bays and much of the shoreline (Figure 60). Oystercatchers were found mainly in Nigg and Udale Bays with smaller numbers elsewhere. Knot and Bar-tailed Godwit were present in nationally important numbers in the estuary, the greatest densities occurring at Nigg Bay, with Knot also occurring at Udale Bay. Curlew were found throughout the Cromarty Firth, whereas Golden Plover were confined to the eastern flats in Nigg Bay. Lapwing were widespread with Dingwall, Alness, Dalmore and the eastern side of Nigg Bay all used. Alness and Nigg Bays were also favoured by Dunlin, although lesser numbers were found in the inner estuary and Udale Bay. Ringed Plover were widely distributed, but at low abundance. Snipe and Turnstone were also recorded.

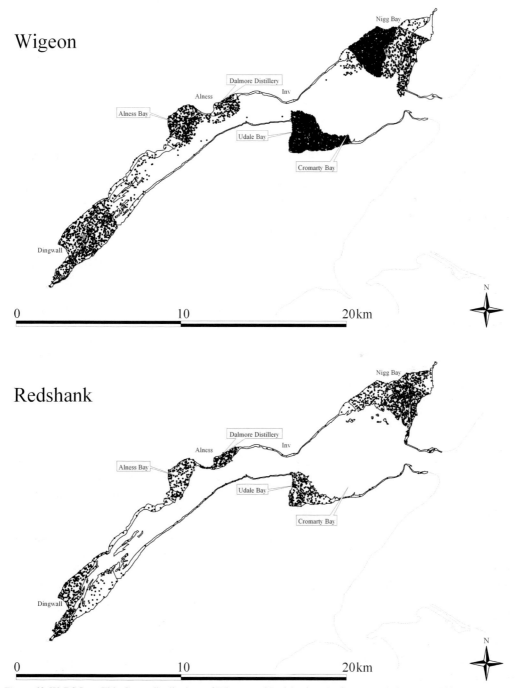

Figure 60. WeBS Low Tide Count distributions of Wigeon and Redshank at the Cromarty Firth, winter 2003/04 (Inv=Invergordon).

FIRTH OF FORTH

Internationally important: Slavonian Grebe, Pink-footed Goose, Shelduck, Knot, Bar-tailed Godwit, Redshank

Nationally important: Red-throated Diver, Great Crested Grebe, Cormorant, Whooper Swan, Greylag Goose, Teal, Scaup, Eider, Long-tailed Duck, Common Scoter, Velvet Scoter, Goldeneye, Red-breasted Merganser, Oystercatcher, Ringed Plover, Golden Plover, Sanderling, Dunlin, Black-tailed Godwit, Curlew, Turnstone

Site description

The Forth is the largest estuary on the east coast of Scotland, extending seawards from Alloa out to Fife Ness and Dunbar. Edinburgh represents the largest city on the Forth, with other towns such as Alloa, Grangemouth and Kirkcaldy also present. The inner estuary has extensive intertidal mudflats with saltmarsh between Alloa and Grangemouth. The inner estuary banks are heavily urbanised and there has been severe industrial pollution in the past. The outer estuary eastwards of the Forth Bridge widens into a series of exposed bays. Here the intertidal flats are predominantly sandy and the shoreline varied, with rocky outcrops, sand-and-shingle flats, and mussel beds. Further eastwards are Aberlady and Gullane Bays, an extensive area of mudflat, saltmarsh and sand dune. Much of the estuary is designated as a Ramsar site and SPA. Aberlady Bay is a Local Nature Reserve, and the RSPB own two further reserves. Almost all types of possible human-related activities and disturbance occur, including onshore and offshore leisure, heavy industry, an offshore oil terminal and an oilrig repair site. Shooting, bait collecting and shell fishing are also disturbance factors.

Bird distribution

All eight common diver and grebe species were recorded. Most Great Crested Grebes were in Largo Bay and off Musselburgh, with Largo Bay also the favoured area for Red-necked, Black-necked and Slavonian Grebes. Cormorants were widely distributed over the firth, the only area without any sightings being the southern shore between Grangemouth and the Forth bridges. Shags were present in similar numbers to Cormorant, but were concentrated mainly at Auldhane and on Drum Sands. Grey Herons were thinly distributed throughout the firth with the most on the inner estuary. Mute Swans gathered at Musselburgh and at Cramond on the southern shore, whilst Whooper Swans were at Hedderwick Sands throughout. Pink-footed Geese were recorded in two areas, a small flock at Grangemouth and

more abundantly at Aberlady Bay. A flock of Greylag Geese were at Torry Bay in January. The Shelduck peak occurred in November, with birds widespread including Tyninghame, Aberlady Bay, Inverkeithing Harbour, Dalgety Bay and Grangemouth, where the largest flock was seen in November, perhaps including some birds finishing their moult.

Wigeon numbers fluctuated over the winter with a peak in November. Concentrations were widespread with Tyne Mouth (near Tyninghame), Auldhane, Gosford and Aberlady Bays, Torry Bay, Grangemouth and Alloa supporting the largest flocks. Teal favoured upstream areas, especially Ironmill Bay, Grangemouth, and east of the Kincardine Bridge up to Alloa. Mallard were widespread, with the largest flock of 285 birds at Scoughall Rocks near Tyninghame. Numbers of Eider increased as the winter progressed, peaking at 3,611 in February. Birds were fairly evenly distributed along both coasts in the outer estuary (Figure 61). Long-tailed Ducks were limited to two areas, Largo Bay and Musselburgh. Common Scoter were low in numbers but widespread, with most at Largo and Gullane Bays and off Methil. Velvet Scoter numbers increased over the winter to 418 in February, and showed a preference for Musselburgh and Largo Bay, being joined by two Surf Scoters in February at the latter site. Goldeneye and Red-breasted Merganser were generally dispersed along both coastlines, upriver as far as Alloa, although the largest concentrations occurred at Musselburgh and Largo Bay respectively. Small numbers of Goosander were found, with most noted around Leith. Pintail, Shoveler, Tufted Duck, Scaup, Ruddy Duck and Moorhen were also noted.

Oystercatchers were widespread, particularly east of the bridges, the greatest concentrations at Tyne Mouth, Aberlady Bay, Musselburgh and on Drum Sands. Ringed Plovers were widespread on the southern shore, although Largo Bay held the highest density of birds. Golden Plover numbers peaked in November but dropped to just 229 in

February, most birds on the flats near Grangemouth, and in Aberlady and Gosford Bays. Grey Plover numbers remained fairly constant, most birds occurring at Leith and Largo Bay. Lapwing numbers were the highest for three winters, although far below the Low Tide Count in 1992/93. However, the favoured areas remained the same as previously. Knot were distributed around much of the estuary, favouring areas where mudflats were extensive, such as at Kinneil. Since 1992/93 the peak low tide Sanderling count has more than doubled, most found at Kircaldy and Largo Bay. Purple Sandpipers were mainly on the outer sectors of the estuary. Dunlin increased over the winter, mostly found in the south shore bays. Black-tailed Godwits have increased since the 1992/93 Low Tide Count with most around Grangemouth. Bar-tailed Godwit (Figure 61) and Curlew had similar distribution patterns, with the greatest densities occurring at Tynemouth, Aberlady Bay, Gosford Bay, Musselburgh, Drum Sands and Grangemouth. Redshank numbers remained fairly constant throughout, with over 3,000 counted in each month and an almost uninterrupted distribution around the whole coastline. Turnstone showed a fairly even distribution along both shores east of the bridges. Ruff, Jack Snipe, Snipe and Greenshank were also recorded.

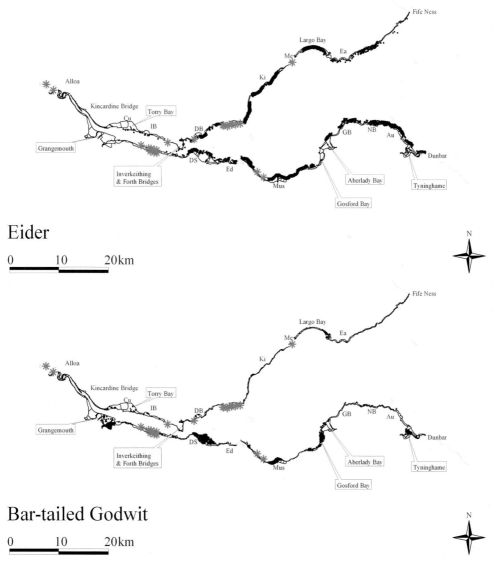

Eider

0   10   20km

Bar-tailed Godwit

0   10   20km

Figure 61. WeBS Low Tide Count distributions of Eider and Bar-tailed Godwit at the Firth of Forth, winter 2003/04 (Au=Auldhane, DB=Dalgety Bay, DS=Drum Sands, Ea=Earlsferry, Ed=Edinburgh, GB= Gullane Bay, IB=Ironmill Bay, Ki=Kirkcaldy, Me=Methil, Mus=Musselburgh, NB= North Berwick).

HUMBER ESTUARY

Internationally important: Pink-footed Goose, Shelduck, Golden Plover, Lapwing, Knot, Dunlin, Black-tailed Godwit, Bar-tailed Godwit, Redshank

Nationally important: Dark-bellied Brent Goose, Teal, Shoveler, Goldeneye, Oystercatcher, Avocet, Ringed Plover, Grey Plover, Sanderling, Ruff, Turnstone, Curlew

Site description

The Humber Estuary is one of the largest estuaries in the UK, stretching for approximately 70 km from Goole to Spurn Point, and is protected as an SPA and Ramsar site. It forms the confluence of the rivers Ouse and Trent, which collectively drain a large part of central and northern England. The estuary encompasses a great diversity of habitats, including non-tidal islands, saltmarsh, grazing marsh, intertidal mud and sand flats, reed bed, shingle bar and dunes. A managed realignment scheme is underway at Paull Holme Strays, with more schemes planned. A third of the estuary is exposed at low tide, with the second highest tidal range in Britain (7.2 m). The Humber is markedly industrialised in places, and the five main ports (including Kingston-Upon-Hull and Grimsby) handle an estimated 80 m tonnes of cargo each year. Arable farming is particularly well established around the estuary. Use of the Humber is therefore extensive and varied, with activity including substantial industrial operations, large-scale fisheries, agriculture, tourism and other recreational pursuits such as wildfowling, sailing, walking and birdwatching.

Bird distribution

Cormorants and Grey Herons were widespread in small numbers, with the only large gatherings adjacent to Read's Island. The jetty at New Holland held the majority of Mute Swans, the birds feeding on spilt grain from docking operations. The largest flock of 4,000 Pink-footed Geese was found at Read's Island in November, with 800 more at Whitton Ness. Canada, (presumed re-established) Barnacle and Greylag Geese were mostly found on the inner estuary. Dark-bellied Brent Geese were present in nationally important numbers and were concentrated on a section of the southern shore between Humberston and Mablethorpe. The highest density was typically at Grainthorpe Haven, with lesser numbers in Spurn Bight. Two Light-bellied Brents were amongst them in February. Shelduck occurred throughout the estuary with major concentrations at Pyewipe, Little Humber, Whitton Ness and Broomfleet.

Wigeon were distributed over the whole estuary, but the greatest densities were found in the Blacktoft / Broomfleet area and at Read's Island. Gadwall were found only in noteworthy numbers at Blacktoft Sands, where 44 were counted in December. Low Tide Counts of Teal peaked in January with Blacktoft, Broomfleet, Read's Island and Saltfleet all harbouring high concentrations of this widespread species. Mallards were present in all areas of the estuary, extending well upriver into both rivers Trent and Ouse (Figure 62). Pintails were found only in three areas, at Spurn Bight, Goxhill Haven and at Read's Island. North Killingholme Pits were the favoured haunt of Shoveler in December, this same site also hosting a single Smew in February. Small numbers of both Pochard and Tufted Duck were found at Goxhill Haven in January, though both of these species are recorded in far greater numbers on Core Counts. A low tide count of 54 Goldeneye in January at the New Holland jetty was a notable record compared to recent winters. Three Goosanders were present in the Trent near Keadby for most of the winter. Other species noted included Red-throated Diver, Little and Great Crested Grebes, Bittern, Little Egret, Bewick's Swan, Whooper Swan, Bean Goose, Moorhen and Coot.

Oystercatcher favoured the outer estuary on both shores with Spurn Bight, Grainthorpe Haven and the flats off Cleethorpes having the highest densities. Bar-tailed Godwits also favoured the outer areas, and peaked in January. The highest densities occurred at Cleethorpes, Pyewipe, Stone Creek, and Spurn Bight. Sanderlings were on the south shore from Grimsby southwards, with smaller numbers at Spurn, Stone Creek and Goxhill Haven. Grey Plover numbers were high this winter, the majority counted between Paull and Spurn. Snipe were found mostly at Blacktoft and at Saltfleet. Numbers of Turnstone reported were higher than those recorded on Core Counts with a peak of 723 in December, the highest densities found between Goxhill and New Holland. Ringed Plover favoured the traditionally preferred Pyewipe area, although they were found widely in smaller numbers. Curlews were typically evenly distributed throughout the estuary. Dunlins occurred in large numbers on the outer estuary; although Salt End to Spurn held the highest densities, they were also common further upstream as far as Broomfleet. The pattern for Black-tailed Godwit remained the same as in previous years, with most foraging at low water in the Pyewipe area. Lapwing continued to increase, with high numbers of birds in the whole estuary. Numbers peaked at 36,609 in December though only 2,800 were noted in February. The largest numbers of Knot for over five years were observed in November, with over 50,000 present in the outer estuary, mainly between Paull and Spurn on the north shore and Grimsby to Saltfleet on the south shore. Golden Plovers were also present in record numbers over the entire estuary (Figure 62) with 47,700 recorded in December. This site held more Golden Plovers than any other in the UK in the winter of 2003/04. Small numbers of scarcer waders were also recorded, counters recording diverse species such as Avocet, Ruff, Jack Snipe, Whimbrel, Spotted Redshank and Green and Common Sandpipers.

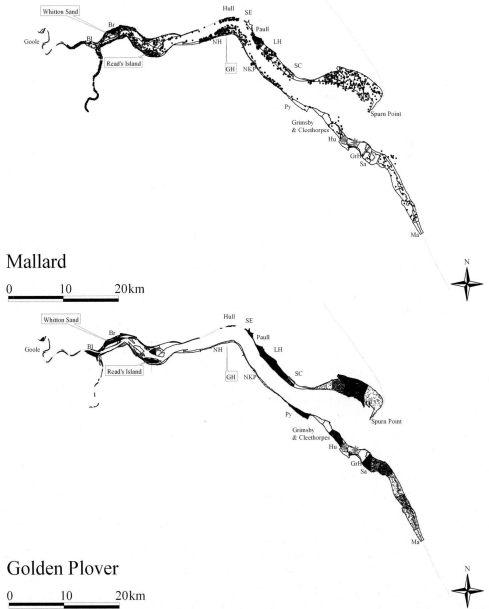

Mallard

0   10   20km

Golden Plover

0   10   20km

Figure 62. WeBS Low Tide Count distributions of Mallard and Golden Plover at the Humber Estuary, winter 2003/04 (Bl=Blacktoft, Br=Broomfleet, GH=Goxhill Haven, GrH=Grainthorpe Haven, Hu=Humberston, LH= Little Humber, Ma=Mablethorpe, NH= New Holland, NKP=North Killingholme Pits, Py=Pyewipe, Sa=Saltfleet, SC=Stone Creek, SE=Salt End).

LANGSTONE HARBOUR

Internationally important: Dark-bellied Brent Goose, Dunlin
Nationally important: Red-breasted Merganser, Ringed Plover, Grey Plover, Black-tailed Godwit

Site description

Langstone Harbour lies between Portsmouth and Chichester Harbours on the south coast. At high tide, the estuary resembles a land-locked lake but at low tide, this basin of saltmarsh and intertidal flats is predominately muddy, becoming sandier towards the harbour mouth. The intertidal mudflats have areas of eelgrass (*Zostera*) that are amongst the most extensive in Britain. Four islands lie within the harbour and around these is the largest and most diverse area of saltmarsh. A large proportion of the vegetation is dominated by cordgrass *Spartina,* although there is evidence that this is suffering dieback. On the northern shore of the harbour lies Farlington Marshes Local Nature Reserve (LNR), a peninsula of enclosed grassland and marsh. Other conservation measures exist in the form of Ramsar and SPA designations, a LNR at Kench and an RSPB reserve. The whole area is surrounded by urban development, although most of the land immediately adjacent to the shore is relatively open. Leisure pursuits are numerous; power-boating and water-skiing take place, whilst sailing is widespread throughout the estuary. Walking and birdwatching constitute the main land-based recreation. Netting for fish, shellfishing, bait-digging and wildfowling also occur. In the long-term, predicted sea-level rise is likely to be a key issue, due to the potential loss of the undisturbed low islands that act as important roost sites.

Bird distribution

Little Grebes were found only in the north of the harbour, whilst Great Crested Grebes were far more widespread. Black-necked Grebes peaked at four, all in the main channel in the northeast of the harbour. Cormorants and Grey Herons were found throughout the harbour, the latter favouring the southern end. Little Egrets peaked at 73 in November and were found in all areas of the harbour, typical of their ubiquity around the Solent. Canada Geese were only on Farlington Marshes whilst small numbers of Mute Swan were widely distributed. Numbers of Dark-bellied Brent

Geese reached 5,804 in February. This figure represented the highest Low Tide Count in recent years, and was higher than any peak Core Count since the 1999/2000 winter. The birds were widespread over the harbour, with the highest densities in the north at Farlington, Chalkdock Lake and near the outfall from Brockhampton Sewage Works (Figure 63). One Light-bellied Brent Goose was found amongst them. Shelduck peaked in February; the northern half of the harbour was favoured slightly with higher densities at Farlington and off Brockhampton Sewage Works.

Wigeon numbers fluctuated over the winter but peaked in February, most birds using Farlington Marshes and Chalkdock Lake in the north. Gadwall, Teal and Shoveler were found exclusively at Farlington. Mallard and Pintail had a slightly more widespread distribution with the majority at Farlington and on the flats to the east. Goldeneye and Red-breasted Merganser were found in all the channels throughout the harbour. Moorhen and Coot were restricted to Farlington Marshes and Milton Pools. Small numbers of Tufted Duck, Eider and a single Water Rail were also noted.

Oystercatcher numbers were fairly evenly distributed over the harbour, although higher densities were found in the Chalkdock Lake area. Ringed Plover and Grey Plover were widespread over the harbour with the highest densities found around Chalkdock Lake. The largest aggregations of Lapwing were at Farlington Marshes and the tidal flats to the west, with very few noted on other areas. Knot were clustered off Portsea Island in the west, and in the south east corner. Dunlin were the most abundant species present in the harbour, and were present in all areas (Figure 63). The harbour is an internationally important site for this species, however the 9,393 birds recorded on the Low Tide Count in February is far lower than the maximum Core Count of 24,286 for the same period, suggesting that the birds recorded at roost are feeding elsewhere, possibly in Portsmouth and Chichester Harbours. Another species present in nationally important numbers is Black-tailed

Godwit, with birds widespread around the outer flats. Bar-tailed Godwit favoured the southern half of the harbour. Curlew and Redshank were widespread over the whole area with slightly higher densities near Brockhampton Sewage Works in the north.

Turnstone peaked at 226 in February mostly at Chalkdock Lake and the flats to the east. The following species of wader were also found in small numbers: Avocet, Sanderling, Little Stint, Snipe, Greenshank and Common Sandpiper.

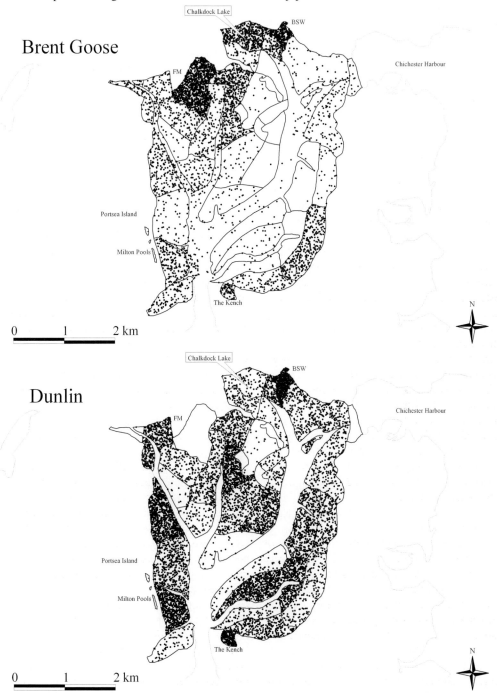

Figure 63. WeBS Low Tide Count distributions of Dark-bellied Brent Goose and Dunlin at Langstone Harbour, winter 2003/04 (BSW=Brockhampton Sewage Works, FM=Farlington Marshes).

LINDISFARNE

Internationally important: Pink-footed Goose, Barnacle Goose, Light-bellied Brent Goose, Bar-tailed Godwit

Nationally important: Whooper Swan, Shelduck, Wigeon, Eider, Golden Plover, Grey Plover, Knot, Dunlin, Curlew, Redshank

Site description

Lindisfarne forms one of the largest intertidal areas in northeast England. This site, as one of only two barrier beach systems within the UK, has an unusual structure. The majority of the site is sandy, although there are increasing amounts of silt in parts of Budle Bay and Fenham Flats. Several freshwater creeks traverse the flats at low tide. Saltmarsh exists between Goswick and Fenham, especially around the causeway to Holy Island, and along the southwestern shore of Budle Bay. Extensive sand dunes occur on several parts of the site, with dune slacks, dune heath and dune pasture also represented. The eastern shoreline of Holy Island is mainly rocky, with a few patches of shingle. There is a small harbour on Holy Island but no other industry is present. Recreational activities are generally water-based and occur mainly in Budle Bay, though beach recreation is widespread over the entire area, as are walking and birdwatching. Some grazing and hand-gathering of mussels occurs, as does wildfowling, but this is strictly licensed. Wildlife conservation is in force, with the area protected by SPA and Ramsar status, and in 1997 a waterbird refuge was set up on the southern Fenham Flats.

Bird distribution

It should be noted that only a single count was made during the winter, in November 2003, as part of the ongoing Northumberland Atlas project (hence the 1 km grid squares used as count sections).

Cormorant and Shag occurred in similar numbers to one another, on or adjacent to Holy Island. Small numbers of Mute Swan were found on Holy Island and in Budle Bay, whilst a flock of seven Barnacle Geese associated with the Pink-footed Geese on Fenham Flats. Greylag Goose numbers reached 307 (a record Low Tide Count), the majority of which were on Ross Black Sands. Lindisfarne, the only regular British wintering site for the Svalbard population of Light-bellied Brent Goose, supported 2,930 birds in November, distributed over the flats from Beal Point to Ross Point and across to Holy Island (Figure 64). Some of the densest concentrations occurred on parts of Fenham Flats, whilst Budle Bay was avoided completely. Shelduck favoured Fenham Flats and the western end of Budle Bay, these areas being amongst the least sandy and offering the best feeding habitat. Other species recorded included Red-throated Diver, Great Crested and Slavonian Grebes and Grey Heron.

Budle Bay held the densest flocks of Wigeon, although the refuge area at the southern end of Fenham Flats also supported some. The latter site was also favoured by a flock of 99 Pintail. Teal were concentrated north of Beal Point and in Budle Bay, with a wider distribution in the southeast part of Fenham Flats and Holy Island. Mallard were distributed across the area with the only major gathering in the south east of Budle Bay. The lough on Holy Island had the only Shoveler, Moorhen and Coot recorded. Eider numbers off the north and south ends of Holy Island were somewhat lower than Core Count peaks, possibly as birds moved offshore with the tide. Just over 100 Common Scoters were recorded, the lowest Low Tide Count for five years, with most birds occurring at Ross Point. Goldeneye, Red-breasted Merganser and Goosander were noted in small numbers.

Oystercatchers were widely distributed, the greatest concentrations being on the northern and southern shorelines of Holy Island. Holy Island also had the highest numbers of Ringed Plover. Golden Plover flocks favoured Fenham Flats and Budle Bay as well as Holy Island. Grey Plover were distributed over the Fenham Flats mainly in the refuge area, with a few recorded around Holy Island and in Budle Bay. Concentrations of Lapwing were in Budle Bay and off Goswick, and birds were widespread across Fenham Flats and Holy Island. Knot favoured Budle Bay, and Dunlin tended to feed at Fenham Flats. The majority of the few Sanderling recorded were at Emmanuel Head to the north of Holy Island. Bar-tailed Godwit had a wide distribution across most areas, but with concentrations in Budle Bay and the north shore of Holy Island. Curlew showed a generally similar distribution to the former species, but in greater numbers, with large gatherings across Holy Island and at Goswick and Ross Black Sands (Figure 64). Redshank was the most widely distributed of all those species noted; the highest density was in the southern part of Budle Bay. Small numbers of Turnstone were found around the shores of Holy Island, whilst two Jack Snipe and three Snipe were also recorded in November.

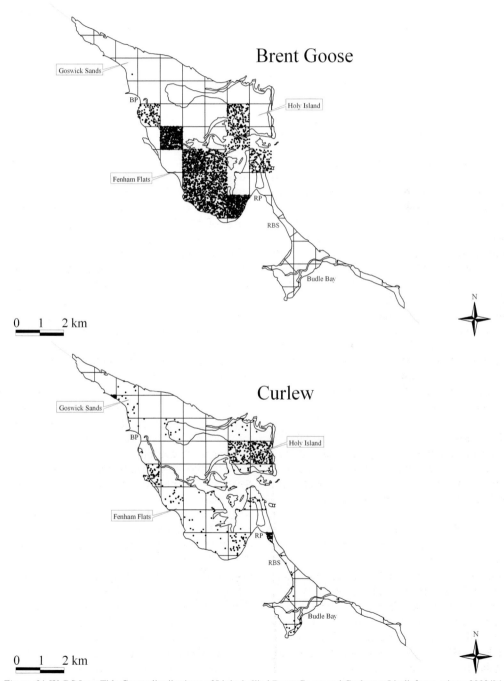

Figure 64. WeBS Low Tide Count distributions of Light-bellied Brent Goose and Curlew at Lindisfarne, winter 2003/04 (BP=Beal Point, RBS=Ross Black Sands, RP=Ross Point).

ORWELL ESTUARY

Internationally important: Redshank
Nationally important: Dark-bellied Brent Goose, Gadwall, Pintail, Grey Plover, Black-tailed Godwit

Site description

The Orwell Estuary extends from Ipswich to the Port of Felixstowe where it meets the Stour Estuary. Much of the intertidal substrate is fairly muddy, although it becomes sandier towards the mouth. In mitigation for the latest port development, both the north and south shores of the lower reaches of the estuary have had soft silts placed behind stiff clay bunds within the intertidal areas, changing the substrate once again. Long stretches of farmland and wet meadow are situated along the mid-estuary, the latter providing roost sites for waterbirds. In the past, the main conservation issues concerned dock and marina developments. Dockland expansion at Felixstowe, since around 1964, has claimed all of the lower reaches of the Orwell's northern shore. Trimley Marshes Nature Reserve was established in 1989 as compensation for the loss of intertidal habitat to dockland development, and is managed by the Suffolk Wildlife Trust. The reserve now provides a roost and safe refuge site for several thousand waterbirds during the winter period, as well as breeding sites for terns and other species (although it has not replaced the lost intertidal feeding areas). Other problems confronting the Orwell are pollution and disturbance from sailing and other leisure activities.

Bird distribution

Little Grebes were present at Trimley Marshes and in the upper part of the Orwell. Contrastingly, Great Crested Grebes were widespread although numbers were lower than in recent years. Cormorant, Little Egret and Grey Heron were all present in higher numbers at low tide than in previous years, with the 39 Grey Herons in February being a four-year high. The two heron species were generally around the mouth and at Trimley Marshes. Mute Swans were to be found on the upper part of the Orwell, particularly in the vicinity of Ipswich. Large numbers of Greylag and Canada Geese were recorded, mostly from Loompit Lake and Trimley Marshes. Dark-bellied Brent Geese were typically concentrated around the southern end of the estuary, particularly Trimley Marshes and Jill's Hole. A single Black Brant was noted in February (the fourth consecutive winter at this site). Five Barnacle Geese of unknown origin were also present in February. Shelduck were distributed over the whole estuary with a peak of 700 in February. Their numbers have remained at this level for three years so the previous decline seems to have levelled off.

Wigeon numbers were down on the last few years. As is customary, they were widely distributed with Jill's Hole and Trimley Marshes the most favoured sites. Gadwall were found mainly at Loompit Lake, peaking at 376 in November then declining as the winter progressed. Mallard and Shoveler numbers were the highest Low Tide Counts for three years with most birds concentrated on Loompit Lake and Trimley Marshes. Most Pintail were encountered on Trimley Marshes and between the Orwell Bridge and Nacton (Figure 65). Trimley Marshes was also the site favoured by Teal and Ruddy Duck. Goldeneye and the few Red-breasted Mergansers recorded were found throughout the estuary on the river channel. Pochard and Tufted Duck numbers were the lowest for three years, but as usual favoured the marshes at Trimley and Loompit Lake. Mandarin was recorded for the first time on a Low Tide Count at this site in February. Water Rail, Moorhen and Coot were also recorded in their highest numbers.

Oystercatcher numbers remained high through the winter and in line with recent years most were between Mulberry Middle and Nacton on the north shore and off Redgate Hard on the south shore. Ringed Plovers were distributed throughout in higher than usual numbers, whilst the flock of Golden Plover was on the flats off Stratton Hall. Dunlin and Grey Plover were encountered throughout the whole estuary, with most occurring on both shores between Nacton and the Orwell Bridge. Lapwings were found mainly on Redgate Hard and off Stratton Hall, in their highest numbers for five years. In contrast, Curlew, although evenly distributed, were present in the lowest numbers for five years. Most Black-tailed Godwit occurred just south of the Orwell Bridge at Black Ooze flats and off Redgate Hard (Figure 65). Numbers of Knot were higher than last winter, mainly foraging on the inner estuary, between Mulberry Middle and

Nacton. Redshank favoured the same areas as the previous species, although they were generally more widely distributed throughout the estuary. Smaller numbers of Turnstone occurred than in 2002/03 although they were still found throughout the area. Small numbers of Avocet, Snipe, Bar-tailed Godwit and a single Spotted Redshank were recorded. Sanderlings were not noted in any month this winter.

The Orwell Estuary is counted by Suffolk Wildlife Trust under contract to Harwich Haven Authority. These data are generously made available to The Wetland Bird Survey.

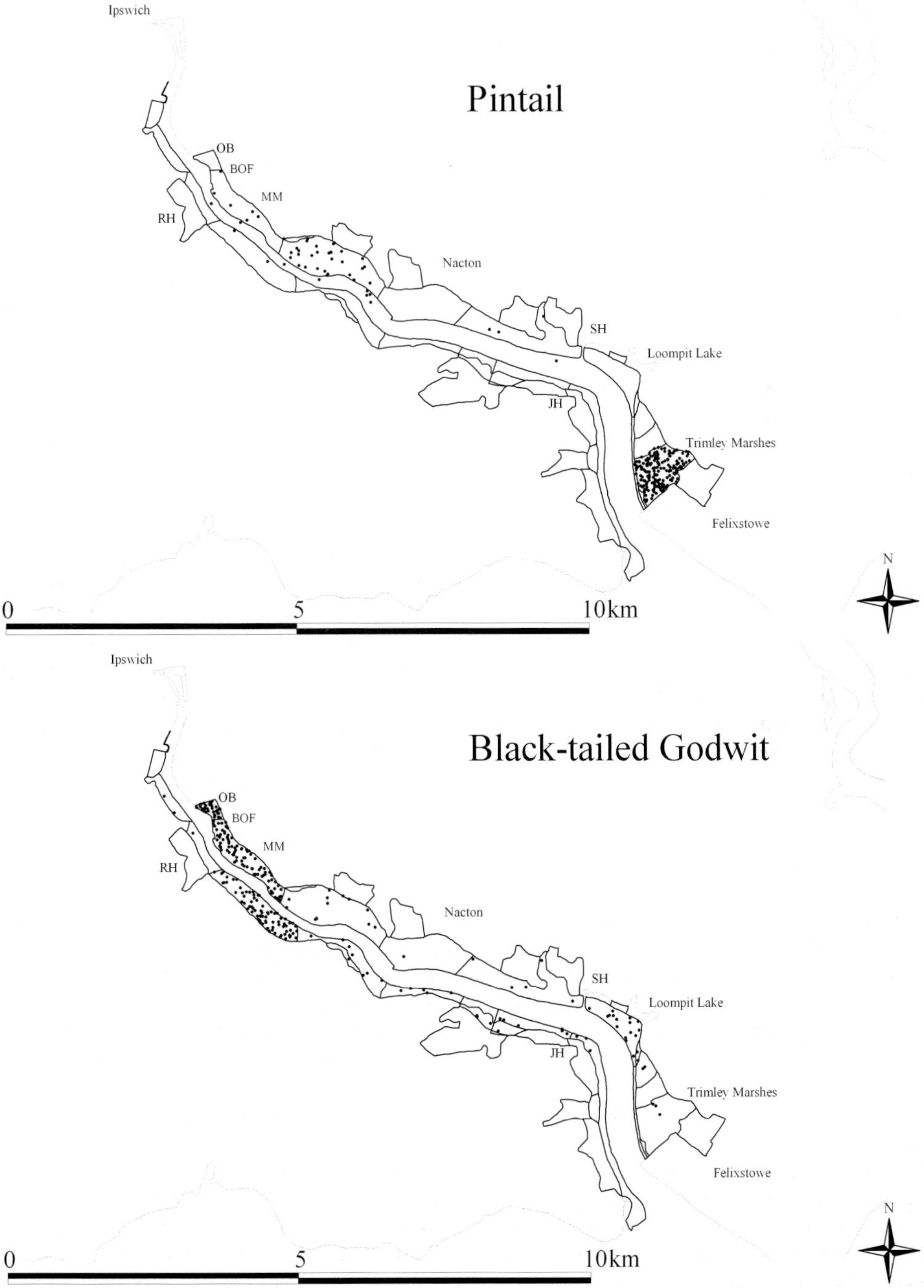

Figure 65. WeBS Low Tide Count distributions of Pintail and Black-tailed Godwit at the Orwell Estuary, winter 2003/04 (BOF=Black Ooze Flats, JH=Jill's Hole, Mulberry Middle, OB=Orwell Bridge, RH=Redgate Hard, SH=Stratton Hall).

STOUR ESTUARY

Internationally important: Pintail, Grey Plover, Knot, Dunlin, Black-tailed Godwit, Redshank

Nationally important: Great Crested Grebe, Dark-bellied Brent Goose, Shelduck, Goldeneye, Golden Plover, Turnstone

Site description

The Stour is a long and straight estuary, which forms the eastern end of the border between Suffolk and Essex. The estuary's mouth converges with that of the Orwell as the two rivers enter the North Sea. The outer estuary is sandy and substrates become progressively muddier further upstream. There are five shallow bays; Seafield, Holbrook and Erwarton along the north shore and Copperas and Jacques on the south side. Over much of its length, the estuary is bordered by sharply rising land or cliffs, leaving little room for saltmarsh development, which occurs mainly as a fringe with a substantial proportion of *Spartina*. The rising land and cliffs are covered by ancient coastal woodland with agricultural land behind. Since much of this land is private, there is very little disturbance to most of the estuary. Nature conservation in the area includes the Stour Estuary SSSI and the estuary is part of the Stour and Orwell Estuaries Ramsar site and SPA. Major parts of both Copperas and Erwarton Bays are owned or leased by RSPB and substantial adjacent woodlands are owned by Woodland Trust and Essex Wildlife Trust. Some sailing and shooting occurs. A governmental decision is soon expected regarding proposed port development at Bathside Bay.

Bird distribution

Great Crested Grebes were well distributed along the main channel, and numbers of this species and Little Grebe were high for recent years. Additionally, nine Slavonian Grebes formed a site record. Cormorant and Grey Heron were widely distributed, whilst the increase in Little Egret numbers was reflected with a peak of 38 in November. Mute Swans were concentrated mainly off Manningtree and Mistley, and at Harwich near the mouth of the estuary. Canada Geese preferred the west of Copperas Bay. Dark-bellied Brent Geese were widely distributed throughout the estuary, with concentrations off Mistley and at Stutton Mill, and on the eastern side of Holbrook Bay.

Shelducks were located over the whole estuary (Figure 66), but tended to favour the western end; numbers were down on the previous winter. Small numbers of Great Northern Diver, Red-necked Grebe, White-fronted Geese, Barnacle Geese and a single Bar-headed Goose were also recorded.

Wigeon were widely distributed throughout the estuary with concentrations at Stutton Mill, and in Jacques and Erwarton Bays but none around Bathside Bay. Teal numbers were up by a third on 2002/03 with most in Copperas Bay in the east and on the flats off Mistley in the west. Mallards were found over the whole estuary, but mainly south of the river channel in Copperas Bay. Most Pintails were found off Mistley and in Copperas Bay, although the peak was less than half that of the previous winter. Goldeneye reached 233 in December, most of which were in the river channel off Mistley. Red-breasted Mergansers, like Goldeneye, favoured the river channel, but were not concentrated in any specific area. The count of 45 Goosander in February in Jacques Bay was a record for the site. Occasional Mandarin, Gadwall, Shoveler, Eider, Common Scoter, Smew, Water Rail and Moorhen were also noted.

Oystercatchers were found throughout much of the estuary with the greatest concentrations present in Jacques and Holbrook Bays and off Stutton Mill, whilst Ringed Plover preferred Bathside Bay. Over 7,000 Golden Plovers were present in December with all the bays except Holbrook and Bathside being used by large numbers. Grey Plovers were distributed over the whole estuary, the highest densities observed in Holbrook Bay. Lapwing and Knot both favoured the inner half of the estuary. The low tide count of nearly 14,000 Dunlin in December exceeded the international importance threshold, and was well in excess of the peak Core Count for the winter, suggesting movements of feeding birds into the site. The only area not used by large numbers of Dunlin was the eastern side of

Copperas Bay. Black-tailed Godwit numbers peaked in November; the densest concentrations as usual were towards the western end of the estuary (Figure 66). Bar-tailed Godwit favoured the central part of the estuary, in Holbrook and Copperas Bays with small numbers elsewhere. Both Redshank and Curlew were widespread over the whole estuary and were present in all of the bays, though both were less dense towards the east of the estuary. Turnstones were present in nationally important numbers on the Core Counts, numbers were somewhat lower at low tide, most birds occurring in Holbrook, Copperas and Erwarton bays. Other species of wader recorded included Avocet, Sanderling, Curlew Sandpiper, Ruff, Jack Snipe, Snipe, Spotted Redshank and Greenshank.

The Stour Estuary is counted by Suffolk Wildlife Trust under contract to Harwich Haven Authority. These data are generously made available to The Wetland Bird Survey.

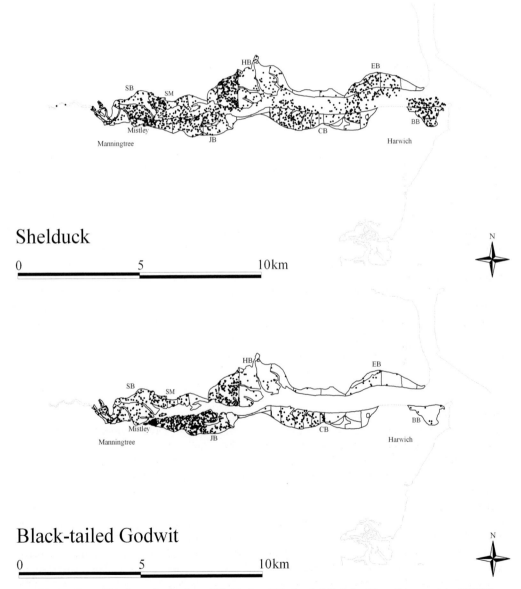

Figure 66. WeBS Low Tide Count distributions of Shelduck and Black-tailed Godwit at Stour Estuary, winter 2003/04. (BB=Bathside Bay, CB=Copperas Bay, EB=Erwarton Bay, HB=Holbrook Bay, JB=Jacques Bay, SB=Seafield Bay, SM=Stutton Mill).

STRANGFORD LOUGH

Internationally important: Mute Swan, Light-bellied Brent Goose, Shelduck, Golden Plover, Knot, Bar-tailed Godwit, Redshank

Nationally important:
(All-Ireland importance) Great Crested Grebe, Whooper Swan, Wigeon, Teal, Mallard, Pintail, Shoveler, Eider, Goldeneye, Red-breasted Merganser, Coot, Oystercatcher, Ringed Plover, Grey Plover, Lapwing, Dunlin, Black-tailed Godwit, Curlew, Greenshank, Turnstone

Site description

Strangford Lough is a large shallow sea lough on the east coast of Northern Ireland, protected as a SPA, a Marine Nature Reserve, and a Ramsar Site. The site includes the Narrows, a deep rocky channel to the Irish Sea. The main body of the lough is sheltered to the east by the Ards Peninsula, and is fed by various rivers and tributaries. Downpatrick and Newtownards are the largest human habitations nearby. Within the lough there are numerous rocky outcrops and small islands. The north of the lough in particular holds extensive intertidal mud and sand flats and there are countless other bays and inlets, and large expanses of open water, providing a wide diversity of habitat. Since 2001, mobile gear fishing has been banned in Strangford Lough to allow populations of the Horse Mussel *Modiolus modiolus* to recover. Static fishing and catching of crustaceans still occurs. There is some recreational activity within the lough, including sailing. Despite the enormity of Strangford Lough, dedicated counters are able to count along the majority of its shoreline, and do so at low tide annually - an impressive achievement.

Bird distribution

Both Little and Great Crested Grebes were found around the mouth of the Narrows and in the southwest corner near Castle Island; additional concentrations of Great Crested were found off the Comber River, whilst Little Grebe was more frequent in Ardmillan Bay at low tide. Most Cormorants were distributed within the Strangford Narrows, with other aggregations further north into the lough. Shag were also present in the Narrows, with further birds along the southeastern shore and around the western islands. A single Little Egret again appeared at Strangford Lough. Grey Herons were patchily distributed around the shallows of the lough.

The greatest concentration of Mute Swans was found in Ardmillan Bay. Canada Geese were confined largely to the areas off the western islands, whilst re-established Greylags were most densely distributed west of Chapel Island. Light-bellied Brent Geese peaked at 13,502 in November, a high count in line with record numbers recorded by the dedicated census this autumn. Numbers dwindled throughout the winter as birds moved away from this key arrival site to winter more widely around the Irish coast. Within Strangford Lough, the species is fairly abundant throughout but especially on the northern intertidal flats.

Shelduck numbers also declined through the winter; the species was distributed across most of the flats within the lough, although once more the very north was most heavily exploited. Pockets of dense Wigeon distribution around the lough were notable at Castleward Bay, south of Gores Island, between the Comber River and Mahee Island, and near Greyabbey. Gadwall were confined largely to Castleward Bay. Teal distribution was patchy, with some flocks in the Narrows, and others in bays and shallows around the lough, especially near Mahee Island and the Comber River outflow. Mallard densities were highest in the traditionally favoured locations of Castleward Bay and the area around Danes Point. Pintails were restricted to Ardmillan Bay, the north near Ballyreagh, and the areas around Greyabbey. Shovelers were similarly restricted, the majority of birds recorded around the mouth of the Comber River. Eider and Goldeneye were concentrated along the northwest shore, around Mahee Island and at the Yellow Rocks area in the east. Red-breasted Mergansers were concentrated at Castleward Bay and Ballymorran Bay, with scattered groups elsewhere including from Danes Point to Gores Island in the southwest corner (Figure 67).

Oystercatchers were ubiquitous, with dense concentrations in the north of the lough and along the mid-shore. Ringed Plovers typically favoured Ringcreevy and the Narrows. The majority of Golden Plovers were present in dense flocks on the extensive intertidal zone in the far north of the lough, as well as flats near Ballymorran Bay, Chapel Island, Yellow Rocks and the Narrows. The much scarcer Grey Plovers were around the Greyabbey islands and near the Comber mouth. Lapwings were ubiquitous around the lough. Knot distribution was similar to that seen recently, most birds being concentrated on the flats between Paddy's Point and Ballyreagh, although numbers were relatively low this year. Dunlin occurred on most intertidal habitat within the lough (Figure 67), with notable exceptions at Ardmillan Bay and along the south shore. Black-tailed Godwits were found mostly at the mouth of the Comber, with a few in Ballymorran Bay. The more abundant Bar-tailed Godwit was found in greatest concentrations at Castle Espie and Butterlump Stone. Curlew and Redshank were evenly spread around the lough. Greenshank were found in isolated patches, notably Ardmillan Bay and out to Mahee Island. Turnstones were recorded on the rocky shores of the Narrows, and also on sectors of intertidal habitat in the north of the lough. Additional species seen throughout the winter in small numbers included Black-necked Grebe, Great Northern Diver, Whooper Swan, Pochard, Scaup, Snipe, Jack Snipe, Purple Sandpiper and Common Sandpiper.

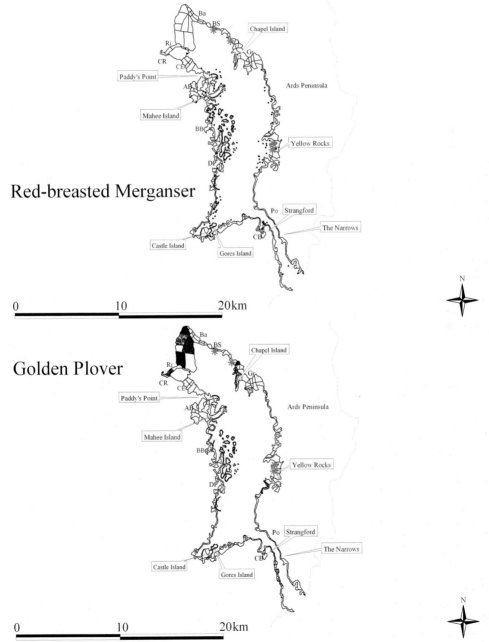

Figure 67. WeBS Low Tide Count distributions of Red-breasted Merganser and Golden Plover at Strangford Lough, winter 2003/04 (AB=Ardmillan Bay, Ba=Ballyreagh, BB=Ballymorran Bay, BS=Butterlump Stone, CB=Castleward Bay, CE=Castle Espie, CR=Comber River, DP=Danes Point, Gr=Greyabbey, Po=Portaferry, Ri=Ringcreevy).

SWANSEA BAY

Internationally important: None
Nationally important: Oystercatcher, Sanderling

Site description

Swansea Bay was a new site for WeBS Low Tide Counts, encompassing the intertidal habitat between The Mumbles and Baglan Bay, incorporating the Tawe and Nedd (Neath) estuaries, with additional sections in the east at Margam Sands. The site is surrounded on all sides by urban developments, principally Swansea and Port Talbot. Swansea Bay and the Tawe have undergone industrialisation and dock construction, leading to a loss of intertidal habitat. The largest portion of flats lies within the bay itself and is a mixture of mud and sand, becoming sand and shingle towards the Mumbles. Behind the flats between Black Pill and Brynmill is a narrow band of sand dunes dominated by dune grassland. The Nedd Estuary is a narrow channel flanked on both sides by mudflats that become sandier towards the mouth; saltmarsh is concentrated at Neath and Crymlyn Burrows. The sand dunes at Crymlyn are the remnants of the once extensive system that fringed the whole bay. Recreational pressures are widespread and varied, including sailing, bathing, walking, windsurfing, water- and jet-skiing. Domestic landfill, an oil refinery and an underground oil pipeline are potentially of conservation concern, and spillages from the pipeline have occurred. However, SSSIs are designated at Crymlyn and Swansea Bay.

Bird distribution

Oystercatcher is one of the key species at Swansea Bay. This winter the peak low tide count was in November and totalled 2,857 birds. Counts for the site also exceeded 2,000 in December, but declined to just over 1,000 in February. Low Tide peak counts were slightly in excess of Core Counts, and it may be that areas that are not surveyed as roost sites, such as that around Swansea Docks, may support some birds that later feed within the bay. The majority of Oystercatchers were concentrated in the west of the bay around The Mumbles, exploiting the expansive intertidal flats (Figure 68). An additional concentration was recorded in the area adjacent to the Guildhall, with further aggregations at the mouth of the

Nedd and a few individuals at Margam Sands.

Ringed Plovers were evenly distributed at three locations around the bay - The Mumbles, the mouth of the Nedd and off Margam Burrows. Sanderling numbers built up from only seven birds in November to a peak of 135, which was recorded in both December and February. The site holds nationally important numbers of Sanderling, with a peak Core Count of 200 in November of the same winter. At low tide, the majority of Sanderlings were feeding in sectors relatively near to the mouths of the rivers Tawe and Nedd, as well as further round the bay at Margam Sands (Figure 68). The sectors near the Nedd outflow are bordered by industrial development and docks, and it is possible that the intertidal areas are relatively undisturbed by recreation, profiting foraging Sanderling. Dunlin favoured some of the same sectors as Sanderling near the mouth of the Nedd, but by far the greatest concentrations were found in the far west at The Mumbles. Dunlin numbers were greatest in November and February, peaks recorded at 870 and 1,093 respectively. This suggests that Swansea Bay may serve as a feeding site during times of Dunlin movement, supported by lower counts of 455 and 161 in December and January. Alternatively there may be local movements between Swansea Bay and other sites in the Bristol Channel. Curlews were thinly distributed around the bay, with denser concentrations in the muddy lower reaches of the Nedd, north of Baglan Bay. The small numbers of Redshank and Turnstone observed, however, were restricted to The Mumbles. Counts of both species peaked in November. Additional sporadic and small counts of Bar-tailed Godwit and Grey Plover were recorded throughout the winter.

Gulls were prevalent at Swansea Bay, with Black-headed Gull in particular found in relatively high concentrations on all sectors counted. Numbers peaked at 3,647 in December, a substantial count. Also notable was the peak count of Herring Gull, which reached over 2,800 in December, and the peak count of 718 Common Gulls in the same month. Lesser and Great Black-backed Gulls were also present, but the real reward for diligent gull counting came in the shape of two sightings of Mediterranean Gull and one Ring-billed Gull.

Waterbirds other than waders and gulls were relatively scarce during Low Tide Counts at Swansea Bay, with low numbers of Great Crested Grebes, Cormorants, Grey Herons and Shelduck noted around the site.

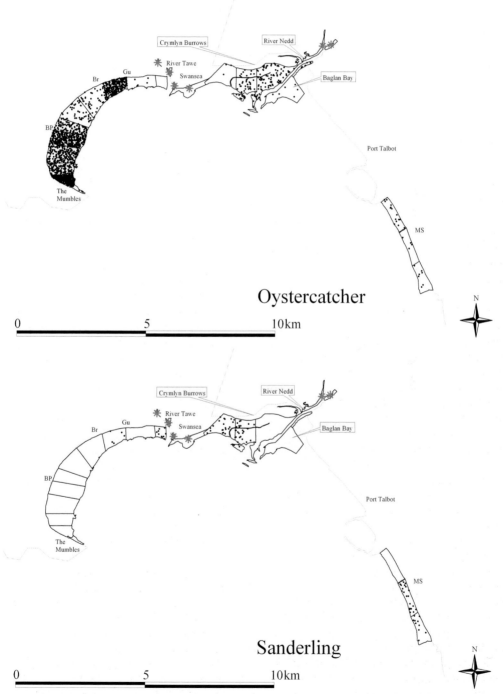

Figure 68. WeBS Low Tide Count distributions of Oystercatcher and Sanderling in Swansea Bay, winter 2003/04 (BP=Black Pill, Br=Brynmill, Gu=Guildhall, MS=Margam Sands).

References

Austin, G.E. & Rehfisch, M.M. 2005. Shifting nonbreeding distributions of migratory fauna in relation to climatic change. *Global Change Biology* 11: 31-38.

Banks, A.N., Bolt, D., Bullock, I., Haycock, B., Musgrove, A., Newson, S., Fairney, N., Sanderson, W., Schofield, R., Smith, L., Taylor, R. & Whitehead, S. 2005. *Ground and aerial monitoring protocols for in shore Special Protection Areas*. Countryside Council for Wales Marine Monitoring Report No: 11, 89pp.

Baylis, S.M., Austin, G.E., Musgrove, A.J. & Rehfisch, M.M. 2005. *Estimating Great Cormorant Phalacrocorax carbo Population Change as an Aid to Management*. BTO Research Report No. 406.

Bibby, C.J., Burgess, N.D., Hill, D.A. & Mustoe, S. 2000. *Bird Census Techniques. Second Edition*. Academic Press, London.

BOURC. 1999. British Ornithologists' Union Records Committee: 25th Report (October 1998). *Ibis* 141: 175-180.

Brazil, M. 2003. *The Whooper Swan*. T & AD Poyser, London.

Buckland, S.T., Anderson, D., Burnham, K., Laake, J., Borchers, D. & Thomas, L. 2001. *Introduction to distance sampling: estimating abundance of biological populations*. Oxford University Press, Oxford.

Buckland, S.T., Anderson, D.R., Burnham, K.P., Laake, J.L., Borchers, D.L. & Thomas, L. (editors). 2004. *Advanced Distance Sampling*. Oxford University Press.

Burton, N.H.K., Musgrove, A.J., Rehfisch, M.M., Sutcliffe, A. & Waters, R.J. 2003. Numbers of wintering gulls in the United Kingdom, Channel Islands and Isle of Man: a review of the 1993 and previous Winter Gull Roost Surveys. *British Birds* 96: 376-401.

Burton, N.H.K., Banks, A.N., Calladine, J.R., Austin, G.E., Armitage, M.J.S. and Holloway, S.J. 2005. *Indexing winter gull populations in England, Wales, Scotland and Northern Ireland: an analysis of data from the 1953 to 2004 Winter Gull Roost Surveys*. BTO Research Report 380, Thetford.

Cranswick, P.A., Kirby, J.S., Salmon, D.G., Atkinson-Willes, G.L., Pollitt, M.S. & Owen, M. 1997. A history of wildfowl counts by The Wildfowl & Wetlands Trust. *Wildfowl* 47: 217-230.

Crowe, O. 2005. *Ireland's Wetlands and their Waterbirds: Status and Distribution*. BirdWatch Ireland, Newcastle, Co. Wicklow.

Danielsen, F., Skov, H. & Durnick, J. 1993. Estimates of the wintering population of Red-throated Diver *Gavia stellata* and Black-throated Diver *Gavia arctica* in northwest Europe. *Proceedings of the 7th Nordic Congress of Ornithology, 1990*. pp18-24.

Dean, B.J., Webb, A., McSorley, C.A., Schofield, R.A. & Reid, J.A. 2004. *Surveillance of wintering seaducks, divers and grebes in UK inshore areas: Aerial surveys and shore-based counts 2003/04*. JNCC report 357.

Forshaw, W.D. 1998. *Report on wild geese and swans in Lancashire, 1997/98*. Unpubl. report, 9pp.

Fox, A.D. & Francis, I. 2004. *Report of the 2003/2004 national census of Greenland White-fronted Geese in Britain*. Greenland White-fronted Goose Study, Kalø.

Gilbert, G., Gibbons, D.W. & Evans, J. 1998. *Bird Monitoring Methods*. RSPB, Sandy.

Griffin, L.R. & Mackley, E.R. 2004. *WWT Svalbard Barnacle Goose Project Report 2003-04*. WWT Internal report, Slimbridge.

Hastie, T. & Tibshirani, R. 1990. *Generalized Additive Models*. Chapman & Hall, London.

Heubeck, M. & Mellor, M. 2005. *SOTEAG ornithological monitoring programme: 2004 summary report*. SOTEAG, Aberdeen.

Holmes, J.S., Marchant, J., Bucknell, N., Stroud, D.A. & Parkin, D.T. 1998. The British List: new categories and their relevance to conservation. *British Birds*, 92: 2-11.

Holmes, J.S. & Stroud, D.A. 1995. Naturalised birds: feral, exotic, introduced or alien? *British Birds*, 92: 2-11.

Hötker, H. & West, R. 2005. Population size, population development and habitat use by Avocets in Western Europe at the end of the 20th century. *Wader Study Group Bulletin.* 107: 57-65.

Jackson, S.F., Austin, G.E. & Armitage, M.J.S. (in press). Surveying waterbirds away from major waterbodies: implications for waterbird population estimates in Britain. *Bird Study.*

Kershaw, M. & Cranswick, P.A. 2003. Numbers of wintering waterbirds in Great Britain, 1994/1995-1998/1999: I. Wildfowl and selected waterbirds. *Biological Conservation* 111: 91-104.

Kirby, J.S., Salmon, D.G., Atkinson-Willes, G.L. & Cranswick, P.A. 1995. Index numbers for waterbird populations, III. Long-term trends in the abundance of wintering wildfowl in Great Britain, 1966/67 to 1991/92. *Journal of Applied Ecology* 32: 536-551.

Maclean, I.M.D., Austin, G.E., Mellan, H.J. and Girling, T. 2005. *WeBS Alerts 2003/2004: Changes in numbers of wintering waterbirds in the United Kingdom, its Constituent Countries, Special Protection Areas (SPAs) and Sites of Special Scientific Interest (SSSIs).* BTO Research Report No. 416 to the WeBS partnership. BTO, Thetford. Available: http://blx1.bto.org/webs/alerts/index.htm.

Mitchell, P.I., Newton, S.F., Ratcliffe, N. & Dunn, T.E. 2004. *Seabird Populations of Britain and Ireland Results of the Seabird 2000*. T & AD Poyser, London.

Musgrove, A.J. 2002. The non-breeding status of the Little Egret in Britain. *British Birds* 95: 62-80.

Musgrove, A.J., Langstone, R.H.W., Baker, H. & Ward, R.M. 2003. *Estuarine Waterbirds at Low Tide: the WeBS Low Tide Counts 1992/93 to 1998/99.* WSG/BTO/WWT/RSPB/JNCC, Thetford.

Ogilvie, M. 2004. Rare breeding birds in the United Kingdom in 2002. *British Birds*, 97: 492-536.

Prŷs-Jones, R.P., Underhill, L.G. & Waters, R.J. 1994. Index numbers for waterbird populations. II Coastal wintering waders in the United Kingdom, 1970/71-1990/91. *Journal of Applied Ecology* 31: 481-492.

Ramsar Convention Bureau. 1988. *Convention on Wetlands of International Importance especially as Waterfowl Habitat.* Proceedings of the third meeting of the Conference of the Contracting Parties, Regina, Canada, 1987. Ramsar, Switzerland.

Rees, E.C., White, G.T. & Bruce, J.H. 2000. *Whooper Swans wintering in the Black Cart Floodplain: winter 1999-2000.* WWT Wetland Advisory Service report to Scottish Enterprise.

Rehfisch, M.M, Austin, G.E., Armitage, M.J.S., Atkinson, P.W., Holloway, S.J., Musgrove, A.J. & Pollitt, M.S. 2003. Numbers of wintering waterbirds in Great Britain and the Isle of Man (1994/1995-1998/1999): II. Coastal waders (Charadrii). *Biological Conservation* 112: 329-341.

Rehfisch, M.M, Austin, G.E., Holloway, S.J., Allan, J.R. & O'Connell, M. 2004. An approach the assessment of change in the number of Canada Geese *Branta canadensis* and Greylag Geese *Anser anser* in southern Britain. *Bird Study* 49: 50-59.

Rogers, N.J., & the Rarities Committee. 2004. Report on rare birds in Great Britain in 2003. *British Birds* 2004, 558-625

Rose, P.M. & Scott, D.A. 1997. *Waterfowl Population Estimates - Second Edition.* Wetlands International Publ. 44, Wageningen, The Netherlands.

Rose, P.M. & Stroud, D.A. 1994. Estimating international waterfowl populations: current activity and future directions. *Wader Study Group Bulletin* 73: 19-26.

Rowell, H.E. & Hearn, R.D. 2005. *The 2003 Icelandic-breeding Goose Census.* The Wildfowl & Wetlands Trust / Joint Nature Conservation Committee, Slimbridge.

Rowell, H.E., Ward, R.M., Hall, C. & Cranswick, P.A. 2004. *The Naturalised Goose Survey 2000.* The Wildfowl & Wetlands Trust, Slimbridge.

Rowell, H.E. & Robinson, J.A. 2004. *Feeding areas for Dark-bellied Brent Geese Branta bernicla bernicla around Special Protection Areas (SPAs) in the UK.* The Wildfowl & Wetlands Trust, Slimbridge.

Sangster, G., Collinson, J.M., Helbig, A.J., Knox, A.G. & Parkin, D.T. 2005. Taxonomic recommendations for British Birds: third report. *Ibis* 147: 821-826.

Scott, D.A. & Rose, P.M. 1996. *Atlas of Anatidae populations in Africa and western Eurasia.* Wetlands International Publication No. 41. Wetlands International, Wageningen, The Netherlands, 336 pp.

Simpson, J. & Maciver, A. 2004. *Population and distribution of Bean Geese in the Slamannan area 2003/2004.* Report to Bean Goose Action Group.

Stenning, J. 1998. *Moray Firth monitoring: winter 1997-98.* RSPB report to Talisman Energy, 4pp.

Swann, B., Brockway, I.K., Frederiksen, M., Hearn, R.D., Mitchell, C. and Sigfusson, A. 2005 Within-winter movements and site fidelity of Icelandic Greylag Geese *Anser anser. Bird Study*, 52, 25-36.

Underhill, L.G. 1989. *Indices for waterbird populations.* BTO Research Report 52.

Underhill, L.G. & Prŷs-Jones, R. 1994. Index numbers for waterbird populations. I. Review and methodology. *Journal of Applied Ecology*, 31: 463-480.

van Roomen, M, van Winden, E., Koffijberg, K., Boele, A., Hustings, F., Kleefstra, R., Schoppers, J., van Turnhout, C., SOVON Ganzen- en Zwanenwerkgroep & Soldaat, L. 2004. *Watervogels in Nederland in 2002/2003.* Sovon-monitoringrapport 2004/02, RIZA-rapport BM04/09, SOVON Vogelonderzoek Nederland, Beek-Ubbergen.

Vinicombe, K., Marchant, J. & Know, A. 1993. Review of status and categorization of feral birds on the British List. *British Birds*, 75: 1-11.

Voisin, C., Godin, J. and Fleury, A. 2005. Status and behaviour of Little Egrets wintering in western France. *British Birds*, 98: 468-475.

Waltho, C.M. 2004. *Firth of Clyde Eider News: No 5. August 2004.* Private report

Way, L.S., Grice, P., MacKay, A., Galbraith, C.A., Stroud, D.A. & Pienkowski, M.W. 1993. *Ireland's internationally important bird sites: a review of sites for the EC Special Protection Area network.* JNCC, Peterborough, 231 pp.

Wetlands International. 2002. *Waterbird Population Estimates - Third Edition. Wetlands International Global Series No. 12,* Wageningen, the Netherlands.

Woolmer, A., Smith, L. & Hayward, P.J. *Carmarthen Bay Infauna/Scoter Project: Final report March 2001.* University of Wales, Swansea report to CCW, Contract No FC 73-02-123. 43 pp.

Worden, J., Mitchell, C.R., Merne, O.J. & Cranswick, P.A. 2004. *Greenland Barnacle Geese Branta leucopsis in Britain and Ireland: results of the international census, March 2003.* The Wildfowl & Wetlands Trust, Slimbridge.

Glossary

The terms listed below are generally restricted to those that have been adopted specifically for use within WeBS or more widely for monitoring.

Autumn For waders, autumn comprises July to October inclusive. Due to differences in seasonality between species, a strict definition of autumn is not used for wildfowl.

British Trust for Ornithology (BTO) The BTO is a well-respected organisation, combining the skills of professional scientists and volunteer birdwatchers to carry out research on birds in all habitats and throughout the year. Data collected by the various surveys form the basis of extensive and unique databases, which enable the BTO to objectively advise conservation bodies, government agencies, planners and scientists on a diverse range of issues involving birds.

Complex site A *WeBS site* that consists of two or more *sectors*.

Core Counts The fundamental WeBS counts that monitor all types of wetlands throughout the UK once per month on priority dates. Used to determine population estimates and trends and identify important sites.

Local Organiser Person responsible for coordinating counters and counts at a local level, normally a county or large estuary, and the usual point of contact with the *WeBS office*.

Incomplete counts When presenting counts of an individual species, a large proportion of the number of birds was suspected to have been missed, *e.g.* due to part coverage of the site or poor counting conditions, or when presenting the total number of birds of all species on the site, a significant proportion of the total number was missed.

I-WeBS An independent but complementary scheme operating in the Republic of Ireland to monitor non-breeding waterbirds, organised by the IWC BirdWatch Ireland, the National Parks and Wildlife Service (Ireland) and The Wildfowl & Wetlands Trust.

Joint Nature Conservation Committee (JNCC) JNCC is the statutory body constituted by the Environmental Protection Act 1990 to be responsible for research and advice on nature conservation at both UK and international levels. The committee is established by English Nature, Scottish Natural Heritage and the Countryside Council for Wales, together with independent members and representatives from the Countryside Commission and Northern Ireland, and is supported by specialist staff.

Low Tide Counts (LTC) WeBS counts made at low tide to assess the relative importance of different parts of individual estuaries as feeding areas for intertidal waterbirds.

Royal Society for the Protection of Birds (RSPB) The RSPB is the charity that takes action for wild birds and the environment in the UK. The RSPB is the national BirdLife partner in the UK.

Spring For waders, spring comprises April to June inclusive. Due to differences in seasonality between species, a strict definition of spring is not used for wildfowl.

Waterbirds WeBS follows the definition adopted by Wetlands International. This includes a large number of families, those occurring regularly in the UK being divers, grebes, cormorants, herons, storks, ibises and spoonbills, wildfowl, cranes, rails, waders and gulls and terns.

Waterfowl Used as a collective term in this publication to refer to all *waterbirds* excluding gulls, terns and Kingfisher.

WeBS count unit The area/boundary within which a count is made. The generic term for *sites*, *sub-sites* and *sectors*.

WeBS Office Main administrative centre for the day-to-day running of WeBS and main point of contact for information or data pertaining to WeBS (see *Contacts* section).

WeBS sector The unit of division of large *sites* into areas that can be counted by one person in a reasonable time period. They are often demarcated by geographic features to facilitate recognition of the boundary by counters. The finest level at which data are recorded.

WeBS site A biologically meaningful area that represents a discrete area used by waterbirds such that birds regularly move within but only occasionally between sites. The highest level at which count data are stored.

WeBS sub-site A grouping of *sectors* within a *site* to facilitate coordination. In most cases, sub-sites also relate to biologically meaningful units for describing waterbird distribution.

Wildfowl & Wetlands Trust (WWT) Founded by Sir Peter Scott in 1946, WWT is the largest wildlife conservation charity specialising in wetlands and the wildlife they support in the UK. It has pioneered the bringing together of people and wildlife for the benefit of both and seeks to raise awareness of the value of wetlands, the threats they face and the actions needed to save them. To this end, WWT has eight centres throughout the UK and is dedicated to saving wetlands for wildlife and people.

Winter For waders, winter comprises November to March inclusive. Due to differences in seasonality between species, a strict definition of winter is not used for wildfowl.

1% criterion The Ramsar Convention has established site selection criteria. Criterion 6 states that ". . . a wetland should be considered internationally important if it regularly supports 1% of the individuals in a population of one species or subspecies of waterbird".

1% threshold This logically derives from the *1% criterion* and relates to the number of birds that are used as the nominal 1% of the population for the purposes of site selection. Thus, an international population of 75,215 Shelduck has a derived 1% threshold (adopting rounding conventions) of 750.

Appendices

APPENDIX 1. INTERNATIONAL AND NATIONAL IMPORTANCE

Any site recognised as being of international ornithological importance is considered for classification as a Special Protection Area (SPA) under the EC Directive on the Conservation of Wild Birds (EC/79/409), whilst a site recognised as an internationally important wetland qualifies for designation as a Ramsar site under the Convention on Wetlands of International Importance especially as Waterfowl Habitat. Criteria for assessing the international importance of wetlands have been agreed by the Contracting Parties to the Ramsar Convention on Wetlands of International Importance (Ramsar Convention Bureau 1988). Under criterion 6, a wetland is considered internationally important if it regularly holds at least 1% of the individuals in a population of one species or subspecies of waterbird, while criterion 5 states that any site regularly supporting 20,000 or more waterbirds also qualifies. Britain and Ireland's wildfowl belong, in most cases, to the northwest European population and the waders to the east Atlantic flyway population (Wetlands International 2002)

A wetland in Britain is considered nationally important if it regularly holds 1% or more of the estimated British population of one species or subspecies of waterbird, and in Northern Ireland important in an all-Ireland context if it holds 1% or more of the estimated all-Ireland population.

The 1% thresholds for British, all-Ireland and international waterbird populations, where known, are listed in Table A1. Thus, any site regularly supporting at least this number of birds potentially qualifies for designation under national legislation, or the EC Birds Directive or Ramsar Convention. The international population for each species and subspecies is also specified in the table. However, it should be noted that, where 1% of the national population is less than 50 birds, 50 is normally used as a minimum qualifying threshold for the designation of sites of national or international importance.

It was agreed at the meeting of the Ramsar Convention in Brisbane that population estimates will be reviewed by Wetlands International every three years and 1% thresholds revised every nine years (Rose & Stroud 1994; Ramsar Resolution VI.4). 1% thresholds have not been derived for introduced species since protected sites would not be identified for these birds.

Sources of qualifying levels represent the most up-to-date figures following recent reviews: for wildfowl in Britain see Kershaw & Cranswick (2003); for waders in Britain see Rehfisch et al. (2003); for gulls in Britain see Burton et al. (2003); for all-Ireland importance for divers see Danielsen et al. (1993) and for other waterbirds see Whilde (in prep.) cited in Way et al. (1993). International criteria follow Wetlands International (2002).

It should be noted that for some populations, where the British total is the international total, the precise figure given for the estimates may differ because of different rounding conventions applied in the relevant publications.

Table A1. 1% thresholds for national and international importance

	Great Britain	all-Ireland	International	Subspecies/Population
Red-throated Diver	49	*10	10,000	NW Europe (non-br)
Black-throated Diver	*7	*1	10,000	*arctica*
Great Northern Diver	*30	?	50	NW Europe (non-br)
Little Grebe	78	?	3,400	*ruficollis*
Great Crested Grebe	159	*30	4,800	*cristatus*
Red-necked Grebe	*2	?	1,000	*grisegena*, NW Europe (non-br)
Slavonian Grebe	*7	?	35	*auritus*, NW Europe (large billed)
Black-necked Grebe	*1	?	2,800	*nigricollis*, Europe, N Africa
Cormorant	230	?	1,200	*carbo*, NW Europe
Shag	?	?	2,400	*aristotelis*
Little Egret	?	?	1,300	*garzetta*, W Europe, NW Africa
Grey Heron	?	?	2,700	*cinerea*, W Europe, NW Africa (br)

	Great Britain	all-Ireland	International	Subspecies/Population
Mute Swan: *British*	375	n/a	380	Britain
Irish	n/a	100	100	Ireland
Bewick's Swan	81	*25	290	*bewickii*, NW Europe (non-br)
Whooper Swan	57	100	210	Iceland (br)
Bean Goose: *Taiga*	*4	+	1,000	*fabalis*
Pink-footed Goose	2,400	+	2,400	Greenland, Iceland (br)
European White-fronted Goose	58	+	10,000	*albifrons*, Baltic-North Sea
Greenland White-fronted Goose	209	140	300	*flavirostris*
Greylag Goose: *Iceland*	819	*40	1,000	*anser*, Iceland (br)
Hebrides/N Scotland	90	n/a	90	*anser*, NW Scotland
Barnacle Goose: *Greenland*	450	75	540	E Greenland (br)
Svalbard	220	+	230	Svalbard (br)
Dark-bellied Brent Goose	981	+	2,200	*Bernicla,* W Siberia (br)
Light-bellied Brent Goose: *Canada*	+	200	200	*hrota*, Ireland (non-br)
Svalbard	*30	+	50	*hrota*, Svalbard, N Greenland (br)
Shelduck	782	70	3,000	NW Europe (br)
Wigeon	4,060	1,250	15,000	NW Europe (non-br)
Gadwall	171	+	600	*strepera*, NW Europe (br)
Teal	1,920	650	4,000	NW Europe (non-br)
Mallard	3,520	500	**20,000	*platyrhynchos*, NW Europe (non-br)
Pintail	279	60	600	NW Europe (non-br)
Garganey	+	+	**20,000	W Africa (non-br)
Shoveler	148	65	400	NW & C Europe (non-br)
Red-crested Pochard	+	+	500	C Europe & W Mediterranean
Pochard	595	400	3,500	NE & NW Europe (non-br)
Tufted Duck	901	400	12,000	NW Europe (non-br)
Scaup	76	*30	3,100	*marila*, W Europe (non-br)
Eider	730	*20	15,500	*mollissimma*, NW Europe[1]
Long-tailed Duck	160	+	**20,000	W Siberia, N Europe (br)
Common Scoter	500	*40	16,000	*nigra*
Velvet Scoter	*30	+	10,000	*fusca*, Baltic, W Europe (non-br)
Goldeneye	249	110	4,000	*clangula*, NW & Central Europe (non-br)
Smew	*4	+	400	NW & C Europe (non-br)
Red-breasted Merganser	98	*20	1,700	NW & C Europe (non-br)
Goosander	161	+	2,700	*merganser*, NW Europe[2]
Moorhen	7500	?	**20,000	*chloropus*, Europe, N Africa (br)
Coot	1,730	250	17,500	*atra*, NW Europe (non-br)
Oystercatcher	3,200	500	10,200	*ostralegus*, Europe, NW Africa
Avocet	*35	+	730	W Europe (br)
Ringed Plover: *winter*	330	125	730	*hiaticula*, Europe & N Africa (non-br)
passage	300			
Golden Plover	2,500	2,000	9,300	*altifrons*, Iceland & Faeroes, E Atlantic[3]
Grey Plover	530	*40	2,500	E Atlantic (non-br)
Lapwing	**20,000	2,500	**20,000	Europe (br)
Knot	2,800	375	4,500	*islandica*
Sanderling: *winter*	210	*35	1,200	E Atlantic, W & S Africa (non-br)
passage	300			
Purple Sandpiper	180	*10	750	*maritima*, E Atlantic
Dunlin: *winter*	5,600	1,250	13,300	*alpina,* W Europe (non-br)[4]
passage	2,000			
Ruff	*7	+	?	W Africa (non-br)
Jack Snipe	?	250	?	NE Europe (br)
Snipe	?	?	**20,000	*gallinago*, Europe (br)
Woodcock	?	?	**20,000	Europe (br)
Black-tailed Godwit	150	90	350	*islandica*
Bar-tailed Godwit	620	175	1,200	*lapponica*
Whimbrel	+	+	6,100	*islandicus*
Curlew	1,500	875	4,200	*arquata*
Spotted Redshank	+	+	1,000	Europe (br)
Redshank	1,200	245	1,300	*brittanica*[5]
Greenshank	*6	*9	3,100	Europe (br)
Green Sandpiper	?	?	14,500	Europe (br)
Common Sandpiper	?	?	17,000	N, W & C Europe (br)
Turnstone	500	225	1,000	*interpres*, NE Canada, Greenland (br)

Table A1. continued

	Great Britain	all-Ireland	International	Subspecies/Population
Little Gull	?	?	840	N, C & E Europe (br)
Black-headed Gull	19,000	?	**20,000	N & C Europe (br)
Common Gull	9,000	?	17,000	*canus*
Lesser Black-backed Gull	500	?	5,300	*graellsii*
Herring Gull	4,500	?	13,000	*argentatus*[6]
Great Black-backed Gull	400	?	4,700	NE Atlantic
Kittiwake	?	?	**20,000	*tridactyla*, E Atlantic (br)
Sandwich Tern	?	?	1,700	*sandvicensis*, W Europe (br)
Common Tern	?	?	1,900	*hirundo*, S, W Europe (br)
Little Tern	?	?	340	*albifrons*, W Europe (br)
Black Tern	?	?	4,000	*niger*

?	*Population size not accurately known.*
+	*Population too small for meaningful figure to be obtained.*
*	*Where 1% of the British or all-Ireland wintering population is less than 50 birds, 50 is normally used as a minimum qualifying level for national or all-Ireland importance respectively.*
**	*A site regularly holding more than 20,000 waterbirds qualifies as internationally important by virtue of absolute numbers.*

1   The degree of interchange of UK Eiders with birds on the continent is unclear, and although Wetlands International (2002) has recommended that birds in Britain and Ireland should be treated as a separate biogeographical population, a recent review of available data by DEFRA's SPA and Ramsar Scientific Working Group has found limited evidence to support this conclusion, and recommended that for site-selection purposes, British Eider continue to be considered as a component of the four groups of the Northwest European groups of the race *mollissima* with an international 1% threshold of 15,500. It is hoped that future genetic studies will help clarify the situation.

2   Although Wetlands International (2002) considers Goosanders breeding in Scotland, northern England and Wales to be a discrete population, a recent review of available data by DEFRA's SPA and Ramsar Scientific Working Group has found limited evidence to support this conclusion for the time being, and recommended that for site-selection purposes, British Goosanders continue to be considered as a component of the NW and C European population of Goosander, with an international 1% threshold of 2,700.

3   Three populations of Golden Plover listed by Wetlands International (2002) overlap in the UK in winter. Draft guidelines from Ramsar suggest that the largest of the three thresholds (*i.e.* that for *altifrons*, Iceland & Faeroes, E Atlantic) should be used for site-selection purposes.

4   Whilst several populations of Dunlin occur in the UK at different times of the year, most wintering birds are referable to the listed population.

5   Three populations of Redshank listed by Wetlands International (2002) overlap in the UK in winter: *totanus* E Atlantic (non-br), *robusta* and *brittanica*. Most *totanus* winter outside the UK but the other populations are known to occur widely. Draft guidelines from Ramsar suggest that the larger of the two thresholds (*i.e.* that for *brittanica*) should be used for site-selection purposes.

6   Two populations of Herring Gull overlap in the winter in the UK; *argentatus* and *argenteus*. Draft guidelines from Ramsar suggest that the larger of the two thresholds, *i.e.* that for *argentatus*, should be used for site-selection purposes.

APPENDIX 2.   LOCATIONS OF WeBS COUNT SITES MENTIONED IN THIS REPORT

Table A2 provides details of all WeBS sites that are mentioned in this report. Sites are listed alphabetically, with details of the Ordnance Survey 1-km square that the centre of the sites falls into and the region also provided. Principal Core Count sites, as listed in Table 6, are highlighted in **bold**. Numbers following Principal Core Count sites refer to the sites' location in Figure A1.

Note that this is not an exhaustive list of sites counted during 2003/04, simply those mentioned in this report.

Table A2. Details of sites mentioned in this report. Numbers following Principal Core Count sites refer to the sites' location in figure A1.

Site	1-km sq	Region	
Abberton Reservoir	**TL9717**	**Essex**	104
Abbey Pool (Tresco)	SV8914	Cornwall	
Aberlady Bay	NT4581	Lothians	
Adur Estuary	TQ2006	W Sussex	
Alde Complex	**TM4257**	**Suffolk**	99
Allestree Park Lakes	SK3440	Derbyshire	
Allington Gravel Pit	SU4717	Hampshire	
Alnmouth	NU2410	N'thumberland	
Alt Estuary	**SD2903**	**Merseyside**	83
Alton Water	TM1536	Suffolk	
Amble to Chevington Burn	NU2802	N'thumberland	
Ampton Water	TL8770	Suffolk	
Angler's Country Park	SE3716	W Yorkshire	
Anstruther Harbour	NO5603	Fife	
Ardivachar Point	NF7345	Western Isles	
Ardleigh Reservoir	TM0328	Essex	
Ardrossan	NS2045	Ayrshire & Arran	
Arran	NR9535	Ayrshire & Arran	
Arun Valley	**TQ0314**	**W Sussex**	138
Ashleworth Ham	SO8326	Glos	
Auchenharvie	NS2541	Ayrshire & Arran	
Auchlochan Pond	NS8037	Lanarkshire	
Audenshaw Reservoirs	SJ9196	Gtr Manchester	
Avon Estuary	SX6745	Devon	
Avon Valley: Salisbury to Fordingbridge	**SU1619**	**Wiltshire**	128
Axe Estuary	SY2590	Devon	
Ayr to North Troon	NS3427	Ayrshire & Arran	
Ballysaggart Lough	H7961	Tyrone	
Balnakeil Bay Durness	NC3869	Highland	
Balranald (RSPB Reserve)	**NF7169**	**Western Isles**	12
Bann Estuary	C7935	Londonderry	
Barcombe Mills Res	TQ4314	E Sussex	
Bardolf Water Meadows	SY7796	Dorset	
Barleycroft GP (Earith)	TL3672	Cambridgeshire	
Barn Elms Reservoirs	TQ2277	Gtr London	
Barons Folly	NT6426	Roxburgh	
Barrow Gurney Res	ST5367	Avon	
Barrow Upon Trent GP	SK3428	Derbyshire	
Bartley Reservoir	SP0081	W Midlands	
Barton Broad	TG3621	Norfolk	

Site	1-km sq	Region	
Baston & Langtoft GPs	TF1212	Lincolnshire	
Bay of Sandoyne to Holme Sound	HY4600	Orkney	
Bayfield Loch	NH8271	Highland	
Beadnell to Seahouses	NU2231	N'thumberland	
Beaulieu Estuary	**SZ4297**	**Hampshire**	132
Beauly Firth	NH5848	Highland	
Beddmanarch Bay & Alaw Estuary	SH2779	Anglesey	
Bedfont & Ashford GPs	TQ0872	Gtr London	
Belfast Lough	**J4083**	**Down**	63
Belhus Woods CP	TQ5782	Gtr London	
Belvide Reservoir	SJ8610	Staffordshire	
Benacre Broad	TM5383	Suffolk	
Benbecula	NF8152	Western Isles	
Besthorpe and Girton Gravel Pits and Fleet	SK8165	Notts	
Bewl Water	TQ6733	E Sussex	
Billing Sewage Works	SP8362	Northants	
Bittell Reservoirs	SP0275	Hereford & Worcs	
Black Cart Water (Gryfe-White Cart)	NS4767	Renfrew	
Blackwater Estuary	**TL9307**	**Essex**	106
Blagdon Lake	ST5159	Avon	
Blatherwyke Lake	SP9796	Northants	
Blenheim Park Lake	SP4316	Oxfordshire	
Blithfield Reservoir	SK0524	Staffordshire	
Blyth Estuary	**TM4675**	**Suffolk**	98
Bolton-on-Swale GPs	SE2498	N Yorkshire	
Bothal Pond	NZ2487	N'thumberland	
Bough Beech Reservoir	TQ4947	Kent	
Brading Harbour	SZ6388	Isle of Wight	
Bradley Pools	SK2245	Derbyshire	
Braewick Loch	HU2478	Shetland	
Bramshill Park Lake	SU7560	Hampshire	
Branahuie Saltings	**NB4631**	**Western Isles**	11
Brent Reservoir	TQ2287	Gtr London	
Bressay Sound	HU4741	Shetland	
Breydon Water & Berney Marshes	**TG4706**	**Norfolk**	97
Broad Water Canal	**J1462**	**Antrim**	69
Broadford Bay	NG6523	Skye	
Broadwater Lake	TQ0589	Hertfordshire	
Brown Moss	SJ5639	Shropshire	

Name	Grid Ref	County	Page
Buckden & Stirtloe Pits	TL2066	Cambridgeshire	
Burghfield Gravel Pits	SU6870	Berkshire	
Burra and Trondra	HU3633	Shetland	
Burra Firth (Unst)	HP6114	Shetland	
Burry Inlet	**SS5096**	**Dyfed**	119
Busbridge Lakes	SU9742	Surrey	
Bute	NS0761	D'barton/Argyll	
Buxton Pavilion Gardns	SK0573	Derbyshire	
Caistron Quarry	NU0001	N'thumberland	
Caithness Lochs	ND1859	Highland	
Caldey Island	SS1496	Dyfed	
Cambois to Newbiggin	NZ3084	N'thumberland	
Camel Estuary	SW9275	Cornwall	
Cameron Reservoir	**NO4711**	**Fife**	36
Cannop Ponds	SO6010	Glos	
Cardigan Bay	SN5293	Merioneth	
Carlingford Lough	**J1814**	**Down**	68
Carmarthen Bay	**SN2501**	**Dyfed**	120
Carsebreck & Rhynd Lochs	**NN8609**	**Perth & Kinross**	41
Carsington Water	SK2451	Derbyshire	
Cassington & Yarnton GPs	SP4710	Oxfordshire	
Castle Park Lochan	NS7894	Central	
Castlemartin Corse	SR9099	Dyfed	
Cemlyn Bay & Lagoon	SH3393	Anglesey	
Chasewater	SK0307	W Midlands	
Chat Moss	SJ7196	Gtr Manchester	
Cheddar Reservoir	ST4454	Somerset	
Chelmarsh Reservoir	SO7387	Shropshire	
Chetwynd Pool	SJ7420	Shropshire	
Chew Valley Lake	**ST5659**	**Avon**	123
Chichester Gravel Pits	SU8703	W Sussex	
Chichester Harbour	**SU7700**	**W Sussex**	136
Chilham & Chartham Gravel Pits	TR0954	Kent	
Christchurch Harbour	SZ1791	Dorset	
Church Wilne Reservoir	SK4632	Derbyshire	
Clachan & Whitehouse	NR7959	Argyll	
Clatto Reservoir	NO3607	Fife	
Cleddau Estuary	**SN0005**	**Dyfed**	121
Clifford Hill GPs	SP7859	Northants	
Cloddach Gravel Pit	NJ2059	Grampian	
Clumber Park Lake	SK6374	Notts	
Cochrage Loch	NO1549	Perth & Kinross	
Colliford Reservoir	SX1772	Cornwall	
Colne Estuary	**TM0614**	**Essex**	105
Colne Valley GPs	TQ0391	Hertfordshire	
Colney Gravel Pits	TG1708	Norfolk	
Colonsay/Oronsay	NR3793	Colonsay	
Colt Crag Reservoir	NY9478	N'thumberland	
Colwick Country Park	SK6039	Notts	
Colwyn Bay	SH9079	Clwyd	
Connaught Water	TQ4095	Essex	
Conwy Bay	SH7481	Caernarvon	
Coombe Country Park	SP3979	Warwickshire	
Coombe Hill Canal	SO8626	Glos	
Copped Hall Pond	TL4301	Essex	
Coquet Island	NU2804	N'thumberland	
Cors Caron (Cors Tregaron)	SN6863	Dyfed	
Cotswold Water Park (East)	SU1999	Glos	
Cotswold Water Park (West)	**SU0595**	**Glos**	117
Cowden Loch & Ponds	NN7820	Perth & Kinross	
Cranwich Gravel Pits	TL7795	Norfolk	
Cresswell Pond	NZ2894	N'thumberland	
Cresswell to Chevington Burn	NZ2895	N'thumberland	
Cromarty Firth	**NH7771**	**Highland**	23
Crouch-Roach Estuary	**TQ9895**	**Essex**	108
Crowdy Reservoir	SX1483	Cornwall	
Cuckmere Estuary	TV5197	E Sussex	
Cuttmill Ponds	SU9145	Surrey	
Dagenham Chase GP	TQ5186	Gtr London	
Dart Estuary	SX8456	Devon	
Darwell Reservoir	TQ7121	E Sussex	
Dean Heritage	SO6610	Glos	
Deben Estuary	**TM2942**	**Suffolk**	100
Dee Estuary	**SJ2675**	**Cheshire**	85
Dee Flood Meadows	**SJ4059**	**Cheshire**	86
Dee Mouth to Don Mouth	NJ9507	Grampian	
Dengie Flats	**TM0302**	**Essex**	107
Derwent Reservoir	NZ0251	Durham	
Derwent Water	NY2520	Cumbria	
Didlington Lakes	TL7796	Norfolk	
Dinton Pastures	SU7872	Berkshire	
Diss Mere	TM1179	Norfolk	
Ditchford Gravel Pits	SP9468	Northants	
Doddington Pool	SJ7146	Cheshire	
Don Mouth to Ythan Mouth	NJ9819	Grampian	
Dorchester Gravel Pits	SU5795	Oxfordshire	
Dornoch Firth	**NH7384**	**Highland**	21
Douglas Estate Ponds	NS8432	Lanarkshire	
Doxey Marshes SSSI	SJ9024	Staffordshire	
Drakelow Gravel Pit	SK2320	Derbyshire	
Draycote Water	SP4469	Warwickshire	
Drumgay Lough	H2448	Fermanagh	
Druridge Pool	NZ2796	N'thumberland	
Duddon Estuary	**SD2081**	**Cumbria**	75
Dundrum Bay	**J4235**	**Down**	67
Dungeness GPs	**TR0619**	**Kent**	141
Duns Dish	NO6460	Angus	
Dupplin Lochs	NO0320	Perth & Kinross	
Durham Coast	NZ4349	Durham	
Dyfi Estuary	**SN6394**	**Dyfed**	88
Dysynni Estuary	SH5702	Merioneth	
Earls Barton Gravel Pits	SP8863	Northants	
East Chevington Pools	NZ2799	N'thumberland	
East Unst	HP6506	Shetland	
Easting & Sand Wick	HP6202	Shetland	
Eccup Reservoir	SE3041	W Yorkshire	
Eden Estuary	**NO4719**	**Fife**	35
Ellesmere Lakes	SJ4133	Shropshire	

Location	Grid Ref	County	Page
Elstow Clay Pit	TL0445	Bedfordshire	
Entrance to Deer & Shapinsay Sounds	HY5612	Orkney	
Erme Estuary	SX6249	Devon	
Esthwaite Water	SD3596	Cumbria	
Etherow Country Park	SJ9791	Gtr Manchester	
Eversley Cross & Yateley Gravel Pits	SU8061	Hampshire	
Exe Estuary	**SX9883**	**Devon**	**125**
Eyebrook Reservoir	SP8595	Leicestershire	
Fairburn Ings	SE4627	N Yorkshire	
Fairfield SSSI	TQ9626	Kent	
Fal Complex	SW8541	Cornwall	
Fala Flow	NT4258	Lothians	
Farne Islands	NU2136	N'thumberland	
Fen Drayton Gravel Pits	TL3470	Cambridgeshire	
Fergus Loch	NS3918	Ayrshire & Arran	
Fiddlers Ferry Power Station Lagoons	SJ5585	Cheshire	
Filey Bay	TA1279	N Yorkshire	
Findhorn Bay	NJ0462	Grampian	
Firth of Clyde	NS2778	D'barton/Argyll	
Fleet and Wey	**SY6976**	**Dorset**	**126**
Fleet Pond	SU8255	Hampshire	
Fonthill Lake	ST9331	Wiltshire	
Foreland	SZ6587	Isle of Wight	
Foremark Reservoir	SK3224	Derbyshire	
Forest of Dean Ponds	SO6010	Glos	
Forfar Loch	NO4450	Angus	
Fort Henry Ponds & Exton Park Lake	SK9412	Leicestershire	
Forth Estuary	**NT2080**	**Lothians**	**38**
Forth Grangemouth to Kincardine Bridge	NS9284	Central	
Foryd Bay	SH4459	Caernarvon	
Fowey Estuary	SX1254	Cornwall	
Foxcote Reservoir	SP7136	Bucks	
Frampton Pools	SO7507	Glos	
Gadloch	NS6471	Lanarkshire	
Garths Loch Scatness	HU3809	Shetland	
Gatton Park	TQ2753	Surrey	
Gerrans Bay	SW8937	Cornwall	
Girvan to Turnberry	NS2003	Ayrshire & Arran	
Gladhouse Reservoir	**NT2953**	**Lothians**	**46**
Godmanchester GP	TL2571	Cambridgeshire	
Grafham Water	TL1568	Cambridgeshire	
Grand Western Canal: Basin to Greenway	SS9812	Devon	
Great Pool Westwood Park	SO8763	Hereford & Worcs	
Gresford Flash	SJ3453	Clwyd	
Grindon Lough	NY8067	N'thumberland	
Grouville Marsh	WV6949	Channel Islands	
Gruinard Bay	NG9590	Highland	
Guernsey Shore	WV2575	Channel Islands	
Hacosay, Bluemill & Colgrave Sounds	HU5595	Shetland	
Haddo House Lakes	NJ8734	Grampian	
Hagnaby Lock Fen	TF3459	Lincolnshire	
Hallington Reservoir	NY9776	N'thumberland	
Hamford Water	**TM2225**	**Essex**	**103**
Hamilton Low Parks and Strathclyde Park	NS7257	Lanarkshire	
Hampton & Kempton Reservoirs	TQ1269	Gtr London	
Hanningfield Reservoir	TQ7398	Essex	
Hardley Flood	TM3899	Norfolk	
Harewood Lake	SE3144	W Yorkshire	
Harrow Lodge Park	TQ5286	Gtr London	
Hastings to Bexhill	TQ7708	E Sussex	
Hauxley Haven	NU2802	N'thumberland	
Haweswater Reservoir	NY4713	Cumbria	
Hay-a-Park Gravel Pits	SE3658	N Yorkshire	
Hayle Estuary	SW5436	Cornwall	
Headley Mill Pond	SU8138	Hampshire	
Heigham Holmes	**TG4420**	**Norfolk**	**94**
Helford Estuary	SW7526	Cornwall	
Heritage Park Loch	NS6255	Lanarkshire	
Herne Bay	TR1768	Kent	
Hetton Lyons Park	NZ3647	Tyne & Wear	
Hickling Broad	TG4121	Norfolk	
Hilfield Park Reservoir	TQ1596	Hertfordshire	
Hill Ridware Lake	SK0717	Staffordshire	
Hillsborough Main Lake	J2458	Down	
Hirsel Lake	NT8240	Berwickshire	
Hogganfield Loch	NS6467	Lanarkshire	
Holbeach St Matthew	TF4334	Lincolnshire	
Holburn Moss	**NU0536**	**N'thumberland**	**51**
Holkham Bay	TF8845	Norfolk	
Holland Marshes	TQ8696	Essex	
Hollowell Reservoir	SP6872	Northants	
Holme Pierrepont GPs	SK6239	Notts	
Holy Loch - Toward Pnt	NS1672	D'barton/Argyll	
Hornsea Mere	**TA1947**	**Humberside**	**77**
Horsey Mere	**TG4422**	**Norfolk**	**95**
Houghton Green Pool	SJ6292	Cheshire	
Hoveringham and Bleasby Gravel Pits	SK7047	Notts	
Hoveton Great Broad	TG3116	Norfolk	
Hule Moss	**NT7149**	**Berwickshire**	**48**
Humber Estuary	**TA2020**	**Humberside**	**79**
Hunterston Lagoon	NS2054	Ayrshire & Arran	
Hunterston Sands	NS1852	Ayrshire & Arran	
Hurleston Reservoir	SJ6255	Cheshire	
Ingrebourne Valley	TQ5485	Gtr London	
Inner Firth of Clyde	**NS3576**	**D'bton/Argyll**	**44**
Inner Moray and Inverness Firth	**NH6752**	**Highland**	**24**
Island of Egilsay	HY4730	Orkney	
Island of Islay	NR3060	Islay	
Island of Papa Westray	HY4952	Orkney	
Islands South Of Barra	NF6393	Western Isles	
Isle of Coll	NM2055	Coll	
Isle of Colonsay	NR3896	Colonsay	
Isle of Cumbrae	NS1656	Ayrshire & Arran	
Isle of Lismore	NM8441	Lismore	
Jersey Shore	WV6249	Channel Islands	
Joe's Ponds	NZ3248	Tyne & Wear	

Keills Peninsula & Isle of Danna	NR7385 Argyll		
Kemerton Lake	SO9436 Hereford & Worcs		
Kenfig Pool	SS7981 Glamorgan		
Kennington Park	TQ5681 Essex		
Kentra Moss and Lower Loch Shiel (Moidart)	NM6668 Highland		
Kilconquhar Loch	**NO4801 Fife**	37	
Killimster Loch	ND3056 Highland		
Killington Reservoir	SD5991 Cumbria		
Killough Harbour	**J5437 Down**	66	
King George V Res	TQ3796 Gtr London		
King George VI Res	TQ0473 Surrey		
King's Bromley GPs	SK1116 Staffordshire		
King's Dyke, Whittlesey	TL2397 Cambridgeshire		
Kingsbridge Estuary	SX7441 Devon		
Kinnordy Loch	NO3654 Angus		
Kirkabister to Dury Voe	HU5159 Shetland		
Kirkabister to Wadbister Ness	HU4453 Shetland		
Kirkby-on-Bain GPs	TF2360 Lincolnshire		
Knight & Bessborough Reservoirs	TQ1268 Surrey		
Kyle of Durness	NC3765 Highland		
Lackford GPs	TL7971 Suffolk		
Lade Sands	TR0921 Kent		
Lake of Menteith	**NN5700 Central**	42	
Lakenheath Fen	TL7186 Suffolk		
Langstone Harbour	**SU6902 Hampshire**	135	
Langtoft Gravel Pits	TF1111 Lincolnshire		
Larne Lough	**D4200 Antrim**	62	
Lavan Sands	**SH6474 Caernarvon**	87	
Lee Valley Gravel Pits	**TL3807 Hertfordshire**	115	
Leighton Moss	SD4875 Lancashire		
Leybourne & New Hythe GPs	TQ6959 Kent		
Liden Lagoon	SU1983 Wiltshire		
Lindisfarne	**NU1041 N'thumberland**	53	
Linford Gravel Pits	SP8442 Bucks		
Linga Beach	HU5599 Shetland		
Little Loch Broom	NH0491 Highland		
Little Mollands Pits	TQ5982 Essex		
Little Paxton Gravel Pits	TL1963 Cambridgeshire		
Little Weighton Pond	SE9933 Humberside		
Livermere	TL8771 Suffolk		
Liverpool Bay	SD0313 Merseyside		
Liverpool Bay: Blackpool Ribble	SD2730 Merseyside		
Liverpool Bay: Formby	SD1909 Merseyside		
Liverpool Bay: Formby Burbo	SD2600 Merseyside		
Liverpool Bay: Ribble	SD2623 Merseyside		
Liverpool Bay: Shell Flat	SD1035 Merseyside		
Llangorse Lake	SO1326 Powys		
Llanon & Llansantffraid	SN5166 Dyfed		
Llyn Alaw	SH3986 Anglesey		
Llyn Traffwll	SH3276 Anglesey		
Llyn Y Tarw	SO0297 Powys		
Llynnau Y Fali	SH3076 Anglesey		
Llys-y-fran Reservoir	SN0324 Dyfed		
Loch a' Phuill	**NL9541 Tiree**	18	
Loch An Eilein	**NL9843 Tiree**	17	
Loch Ardnave	NR2872 Islay		
Loch Ashie	**NH6234 Highland**	25	
Loch Bee	**NF7743 Western Isles**	14	
Loch Bhasapoll	**NL9746 Tiree**	16	
Loch Broom	**NH0988 Highland**	8	
Loch Connell	NX0168 D & Galloway		
Loch Eriboll	NC4359 Highland		
Loch Ewe	NG8486 Highland		
Loch Eye	**NH8379 Highland**	22	
Loch Fleet Complex	**NH7896 Highland**	19	
Loch Fyne	NR9894 D'barton/Argyll		
Loch Gairloch	NG7674 Highland		
Loch Garten	NH9718 Highland		
Loch Gelly	NT2092 Fife		
Loch Gruinart Floods	NR2767 Islay		
Loch Indaal: Bruichladdich -Laggan	NR3261 Islay		
Loch Insh & Spey Marshes	NH8304 Highland		
Loch Ken	**NX7168 D & Galloway**	54	
Loch Kindar	NX9664 D & Galloway		
Loch Leven	**NO1401 Perth & Kinross**	39	
Loch Linnhe - Camas Shallachain	NM9862 Highland		
Loch Lomond	NS3599 D'barton/Argyll		
Loch Long & Loch Goil	NS2191 D'barton/Argyll		
Loch Mor Baleshare	**NF7662 Western Isles**	13	
Loch Moraig	NN9066 Perth & Kinross		
Loch Mullion	NN9833 Perth & Kinross		
Loch nan Capull	NF7516 Western Isles		
Loch of Beith	HU3789 Shetland		
Loch of Boardhouse	**HY2725 Orkney**	1	
Loch of Brow	HU3815 Shetland		
Loch of Clickimin	HU4641 Shetland		
Loch of Clumlie	HU4017 Shetland		
Loch of Harray	**HY2915 Orkney**	3	
Loch of Hillwell	HU3713 Shetland		
Loch of Lintrathen	**NO2754 Angus**	33	
Loch of Mey	ND2773 Highland		
Loch of Skene	**NJ7807 Grampian**	30	
Loch of Spiggie	HU3716 Shetland		
Loch of Stenness	**HY2812 Orkney**	4	
Loch of Strathbeg	**NK0758 Grampian**	27	
Loch of Swannay	HY3127 Orkney		
Loch of Tankerness	**HY5109 Orkney**	5	
Loch of Wester	**ND3259 Highland**	6	
Loch Oire	NJ2860 Grampian		
Loch Riaghain	**NM0347 Tiree**	15	
Loch Ryan	NX0565 D & Galloway		
Loch Scarmclate	**ND1859 Highland**	7	
Loch Spynie	**NJ2366 Grampian**	26	
Loch Tullybelton	NO0034 Perth & Kinross		
Loch Urrahag	**NB3148 Western Isles**	9	
Lochs Beg & Scridain	NM5027 Mull		
Lochs Davan & Kinord	**NO4499 Grampian**	31	

Site	Grid Ref	County	Page
Loe Pool	SW6424	Cornwall	
Longnewton Reservoir	NZ3616	Cleveland	
Longueville Marsh	WV6748	Channel Islands	
Looe Estuary	SX2553	Cornwall	
Lost & Golding Hill & Baldwins Hill Ponds	TQ4297	Essex	
Lough Foyle	**C6025**	**Londonderry**	61
Lough Money	J5345	Down	
Loughs Neagh & Beg	**J0575**	**Armagh**	70
Lower Derwent Ings	**SE6938**	**Humberside**	78
Lower Lough Erne	**H1060**	**Fermanagh**	71
Lower Teviot Valley	**NT6725**	**Roxburgh**	50
Lower Windrush Valley Gravel Pits	SP4004	Oxfordshire	
Lunan Bay	NO6950	Angus	
Lunda Wick	HP5704	Shetland	
Lunning & Lunna Holm	HU5070	Shetland	
Lynemouth Ash Lagoons	NZ3089	N'thumberland	
Lynford Gravel Pit	TL8194	Norfolk	
Machrihanish	NR6522	Argyll	
Maer Lake	SS2007	Cornwall	
Malltraeth RSPB	SH4471	Anglesey	
Marston Sewage Works	SK9042	Lincolnshire	
Martin Mere & Ribble Estuary	SD4015	Lancashire	
Martnaham Loch	NS3917	Ayrshire & Arran	
Meadow Lane Gravel Pits St Ives	TL3270	Cambridgeshire	
Medway Estuary	**TQ8471**	**Kent**	110
Melbost Sands &Tong Saltings & Broad Bay	**NB4534**	**Western Isles**	10
Mersehead RSPB Reserve	**NX9255**	**D & Galloway**	58
Mersey Estuary	**SJ4578**	**Cheshire**	84
Middle Pool	SJ6811	Shropshire	
Middle Tame Valley	SP2096	Warwickshire	
Middle Yare Marshes	**TG3504**	**Norfolk**	96
Milldam & Balfour Mains Pools	**HY4817**	**Orkney**	2
Minsmere	TM4666	Suffolk	
Moine Mhor & Add Est	**NR8293**	**Argyll**	43
Monikie Reservoirs	NO5038	Angus	
Montrose Basin	**NO6958**	**Angus**	32
Moray Coast	NJ2868	Grampian	
Moray Firth	NH8060	Highland	
Morecambe Bay	**SD4070**	**Lancashire**	76
Munlochy Bay	NH6752	Highland	
Nafferton Mere	TA0558	Humberside	
Nene Washes	**TF3300**	**Cambridgeshire**	90
Ness House Thorpeness Offshore	TM4761	Suffolk	
Netherfield Gravel Pits	SK6339	Notts	
Newbold Quarry & Pits	SK2019	Staffordshire	
Newport Pagnell GPs	SP8845	Bucks	
Newsham Park	SJ3791	Merseyside	
Newtown Estuary	SZ4291	Isle of Wight	
North Bay	NF7546	Western Isles	
North Bressay	HU5143	Shetland	
North Cave Wetlands	SE8833	Humberside	
North Fetlar	HU6592	Shetland	
North Norfolk Coast	**TF8546**	**Norfolk**	93
North Sutherland	NC5363	Highland	
North Uist	NF8070	Western Isles	
North Warren & Thorpeness Mere	TM4658	Suffolk	
North West Solent	**SZ3395**	**Hampshire**	131
Moorland Pools	SO0808	Glamorgan	
North-west Yell Sound	HU3886	Shetland	
Nosterfield Gravel Pits	SE2779	N Yorkshire	
Nunnery Lakes	TL8781	Norfolk	
Ogston Reservoir	SK3760	Derbyshire	
Old Moor	**SE4302**	**S Yorkshire**	80
Old Romney	TR0025	Kent	
Orchardton & Auchencairn Bays	**NX8151**	**D & Galloway**	59
Orkney	HY2915	Orkney	
Ormesby Reservoir	TG4515	Norfolk	
Orwell Estuary	**TM2238**	**Suffolk**	101
Osterley Park Lakes	TQ1478	Gtr London	
Otmoor	SP5614	Oxfordshire	
Ouse Washes	**TL5394**	**Cambridgeshire**	91
Outer Ards Shoreline	**J6660**	**Down**	64
Outwood	TQ3246	Surrey	
Pagham Harbour	**SZ8796**	**W Sussex**	137
Panshanger Estate	TL2812	Hertfordshire	
Papil Water Fetlar	HU6090	Shetland	
Par Sands Pools & St Andrews Road	SX0853	Cornwall	
Passfield Pond	SU8234	Hampshire	
Paultons Bird Park	SU3116	Hampshire	
Pegwell Bay	**TR3563**	**Kent**	113
Pitsford Reservoir	SP7669	Northants	
Plym Estuary	SX5055	Devon	
Point of Ayre Gravel Pit	NX4504	Isle of Man	
Pontllyfni - Aberdesach	SH4252	Caernarvon	
Poole Harbour	**SY9988**	**Dorset**	127
Portmore Loch	NT2550	Borders	
Portsmouth Harbour	**SU6204**	**Hampshire**	134
Portworthy Mica Dam	SX5660	Devon	
Potteric Carr	SE5900	S Yorkshire	
Pugneys CP Lakes	SE3218	W Yorkshire	
Queen Elizabeth II Res	TQ1167	Surrey	
Queen Mary Reservoir	TQ0769	Surrey	
Queen Mother Res	TQ0076	Berkshire	
Queens Valley Res	WV5652	Channel Islands	
Quendale Bay	HU3712	Shetland	
Quendale to Virkie	HU3709	Shetland	
R. Clyde: Carstairs to Thankerton	**NS9842**	**Lanarkshire**	49
Ramsbury Lake	SU2671	Wiltshire	
Ranworth and Cockshoot Broads	TG3515	Norfolk	
Ravensthorpe Res	SP6770	Northants	
Ravenstruther	NS9343	Lanarkshire	
Red Point to Port Henderson	NG7470	Highland	
Red Wharf	SH5582	Anglesey	
Redwell Fishery	SD5469	Lancashire	

The Wash	**TF5540 Lincolnshire**	**92**
Theale Gravel Pits	SU6570 Berkshire	
Thoresby Lake	SK6370 Notts	
Thornham	TF7344 Norfolk	
Thorpe Water Park	TQ0268 Surrey	
Thrapston Gravel Pits	SP9979 Northants	
Threave Estate	NX7362 D & Galloway	
Threipmuir & Harlaw Res & Bavelaw Marsh	**NT1764 Lothians**	**45**
Thurso Bay	ND1169 Highland	
Thwaite Flat & Roanhead Ponds	SD2174 Cumbria	
Tiree	NL9741 Tiree	
Tophill Low Reservoirs	TA0748 Humberside	
Torside Reservoir	SK0698 Derbyshire	
Traigh Luskentyre	NG0798 Western Isles	
Tring Reservoirs	SP9113 Hertfordshire	
Trinity Broads	TG4614 Norfolk	
Troon Meikle Craigs	NS3228 Ayrshire & Arran	
Tweed Estuary	**NT9853 N'thumberland**	**52**
Twyford Gravel Pits	SU7875 Berkshire	
Tyberton Pools	SO3839 Hereford & Worcs	
Tyninghame Estuary	NT6379 Lothians	
Tyttenhanger GPs	TL1804 Hertfordshire	
Ullswater	NY4420 Cumbria	
Upper Loch Torridon	NG8955 Highland	
Upper Lough Erne	**H3231 Fermanagh**	**72**
Upper Quoile River	J4745 Down	
Upper Rivington Res	SD6214 Lancashire	
Upper Tay	NN9557 Perth & Kinross	
Upton Warren	SO9367 Hereford & Worcs	
Uyea Sound	HP5900 Shetland	
Vasa Loch Shapinsay	HY4718 Orkney	
Walland Marsh	**TQ9824 Kent**	**140**
Walmore Common	SO7415 Glos	
Walthamstow Res	TQ3589 Gtr London	
Warkworth Lane Ponds	NZ2793 N'thumberland	
Water Sound	ND4795 Orkney	
Waulkmill Glen & Littleton Reservoirs	NS5257 Renfrew	
Wellington GPs	SO5047 Hereford & Worcs	
Wemyss Bay to Fairlie	NS2059 Ayrshire & Arran	
West Water Reservoir	**NT1252 Borders**	**47**
W Whalsay & Sounds	HU5264 Shetland	
West Yell	HU4485 Shetland	
Westfield Marshes	ND0664 Highland	
Weybread Pits	TM2481 Suffolk	
Whinney Loch	NT8967 Berwickshire	
Whiteness-Skelda Ness	HU3547 Shetland	
Whitlingham CP	TG2508 Norfolk	
Whitrig Bog	NT6235 Borders	
Widewall Bay	ND4292 Orkney	
Wigan Flashes	SD5803 Gtr Manchester	
Wigtown Bay	**NX4456 D & Galloway**	**60**
Wilderness Pond	SS8277 Glamorgan	
Wilkhaven to Rockfield	NH9384 Highland	
William Girling Res	TQ3694 Gtr London	
Willington	TL1050 Bedfordshire	
Winnal Mere	SU4930 Hampshire	
Wintersett & Cold Hiendley Reservoirs	SE3714 W Yorkshire	
Woburn Park Lakes	SP9632 Bedfordshire	
Woodford Ponds	TQ4092 Essex	
Woodhorn Flashes	NZ2988 N'thumberland	
Woolston Eyes	SJ6588 Cheshire	
Wraysbury Gravel Pits	**TQ0074 Berkshire**	**116**
Wraysbury Pond	TQ0073 Berkshire	
Wraysbury Reservoir	TQ0274 Surrey	
WWT Caerlaverock	**NY0565 D & Galloway**	**56**
WWT Martin Mere	**SD4015 Lancashire**	**82**
Wyver Lane Marsh	SK3449 Derbyshire	
Yar Estuary	SZ3588 Isle of Wight	
Yealm Estuary	SX5449 Devon	
Ythan Estuary	**NK0026 Grampian**	**29**

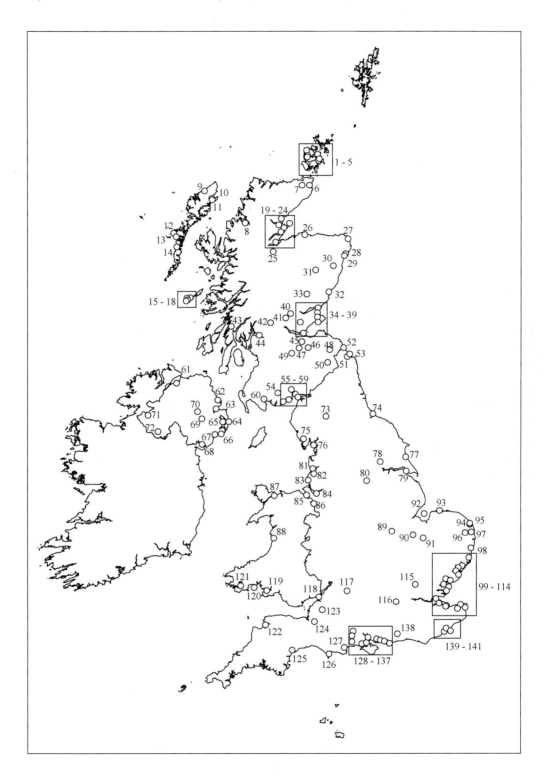